Employment Law in Practice

Employment Law in Practice

THE CITY
LAW SCHOOL
CITY, UNIVERSITY OF LONDON
—— EST 1894 ——

Authors

Nigel Duncan, Professor of Legal Education, The City Law School
Her Honour, Judge Jennifer Eady QC
Peter Hungerford-Welch, Barrister, Assistant Dean, The City Law School
Snigdha Nag, Barrister, Senior Lecturer, The City Law School
John Sprack, CPD Trainer, former Employment Judge and Reader, ICSL

Editor

Nigel Duncan, Professor of Legal Education, The City Law School

Series Editor

Julie Browne, Director of Bar Training, Associate Professor of Law,
The City Law School

OXFORD
UNIVERSITY PRESS

OXFORD
UNIVERSITY PRESS

Great Clarendon Street, Oxford, OX2 6DP,
United Kingdom

Oxford University Press is a department of the University of Oxford.
It furthers the University's objective of excellence in research, scholarship,
and education by publishing worldwide. Oxford is a registered trade mark of
Oxford University Press in the UK and in certain other countries

Tenth edition 2012
Eleventh edition 2014
Twelfth edition 2016

Impression: 2

Published in the United States of America by Oxford University Press
198 Madison Avenue, New York, NY 10016, United States of America

British Library Cataloguing in Publication Data
Data available

Library of Congress Control Number: 2015953379

ISBN 978-0-19-878773-0

Printed in Great Britain by
Ashford Colour Press Ltd, Gosport, Hampshire

FOREWORD

These manuals have been written by a combination of practitioners and members of staff of the City Law School (formerly the Inns of Court School of Law), and are designed primarily to support training on the Bar Professional Training Course (BPTC), wherever it is taught. They provide an extremely useful resource to assist in acquiring the skills and knowledge that practising barristers need. They are updated regularly and are supported by an Online Resource Centre, which can be used by readers to keep up to date throughout the academic year.

This series of manuals exemplifies the practical and professional approach that is central to the BPTC.

I congratulate the authors on the excellent standard of the manuals and I am grateful to Oxford University Press for their ongoing and enthusiastic support.

Peter Hungerford-Welch
Barrister
Assistant Dean (Professional Programmes)
The City Law School
City, University of London
2018

PREFACE

A person's employment is usually one of the most important things in his or her life. It gives not only a livelihood but an occupation, an identity and a sense of self-esteem. The law has changed to recognize this social reality.
(per Lord Hoffmann in Johnson v Unisys *[2003] 1 AC 518, at 539)*

This Manual is designed to provide you with a basic introduction to those areas of employment law which are most likely to be encountered by a barrister in the early years of practice. It has been written to support the Employment Law option on the Bar Professional Training Course (BPTC) taught at the City Law School, City, University of London. However, it also stands alone and is intended to be an effective guide for anyone with a general legal background who wishes to understand how to bring and defend cases in the employment tribunals.

If you are using this Manual as part of your studies on the BPTC you will need to note the references to specific required reading before attending certain classes. Some of the materials will be actively used in some classes. Others are designed as preparatory reading. You will find precedents and checklists, which should be useful in preparing for the Practical Training Exercises and subsequently in practice. The Manual will not provide you with all the answers to questions which will arise in classes and Practical Training Exercises, and you will therefore be expected to refer to the other sources identified. The chapter headings are generally self-explanatory. They are organised in the interests of logical coherence, but you will sometimes find the need to cross-refer. For example, questions of the fairness or otherwise of a dismissal may depend in part upon the provisions of the employee's contract of employment, or the terms which might be implied into it. In all areas you will need to keep in mind the remedies available and the procedures for seeking them.

Employment law continues to develop. Since the 12th edition there have been few legislative changes affecting employment tribunal practice. However, case law has developed apace, with fresh interpretations of the legislation, particularly in the discrimination field and in relation to remedies, with areas of conflicting authority resolved. The Supreme Court decision that employment tribunal fees were unlawful should make tribunal adjudication available to more claimants and has also clarified our understanding of indirect discrimination. The entire Manual and, in particular, the final chapter of practical precedents have been updated to reflect these and other current developments in practice.

These materials state the law as at 1 October 2017.

Nigel Duncan,
Professor of Legal Education, The City Law School

GUIDE TO USING THIS BOOK

The Bar Manuals series includes a range of tools and features to aid your learning. This guide will outline the approach to using this book, and help you to make the most out of each of the features within.

Practical-based approach
The authors have written a manual that is designed to help you to advise and represent clients in cases which might come before the employment tribunals. As such it is not a conventional textbook. Indeed, depending on whether you have studied employment law before, you may use it in different ways.

New to employment law?
In Chapter 3, you will find an explanation of the sources of employment law, which will help you to understand the substantive law. In Chapters 5–10 you will find an exposition of those substantive areas that arise regularly in employment tribunals. If you wish to develop your theoretical or contextual understanding of the law you may find conventional academic texts useful; examples are suggested in Chapter 2.

Studied employment law before?
The content of Chapters 5–10 will be familiar to you but you may find it useful for refreshing your memory.

All readers
The focus of the substantive Chapters 5–10 is on the issues which arise in practice and thus gives you a starting point for your legal research in practitioner texts and the primary sources (which are presented in Chapter 2). Chapter 4 explains in some detail the procedure to be used in preparing and presenting cases before the employment tribunal. This enables you to make practical use of your legal research. A particular feature of the manual is Chapter 11, which provides a series of precedents that show you how a variety of different actions might be pursued. This helps to explain the interaction between the substantive and procedural rules.

Features to aid your analysis
Flow charts feature in several chapters, which take you through the series of decisions required in order to decide whether liability can be established in any particular situation. These include cross-references to the paragraphs in the text which explain the issues concerned more fully.

Features to aid your practice
Chapter 11 contains a series of problem situations covering many of the causes of action which come before employment tribunals. In each case the required forms are presented and completed, and any formal requests to the tribunal or to the opponent are drafted. This provides concrete examples of the procedural steps presented in Chapter 4 and a series of precedents which will be helpful when you are preparing exercises for class or taking your own cases. A particular feature is the detailed commentary applied to each document, explaining the rationale for the way in which it has been drafted.

Online updates
Employment law is a field which changes rapidly. For further material and updates to selected manuals in this series please visit the online resources at www.oxfordtextbooks.co.uk/orc/barmanuals/.

OUTLINE CONTENTS

DETAILED CONTENTS

TABLE OF CASES

TABLE OF LEGISLATION

UK Secondary Legislation

Abbreviations

1.1 Abbreviations

The following abbreviations are used in this Manual:

ACAS	Advisory, Conciliation and Arbitration Service
AIA	Asylum and Immigration Act 1996
CA	Court of Appeal
CAB	Citizens Advice Bureau
CCR	County Court Rules
CFA 2014	Children and Families Act 2014
CJEU	Court of Justice of the European Union
CLSA	Courts and Legal Services Act 1990
CMD	case management decisions
COET	Central Office of the Employment Tribunals
CPR	Civil Procedure Rules 1998
CS	Court of Session
DDA 1995	Disability Discrimination Act 1995
DDA 2005	Disability Discrimination Act 2005
DDPs	dismissal and disciplinary procedures
DWP	Department for Work and Pensions
EA 1990	Employment Act 1990
EA 2002	Employment Act 2002
EA 2008	Employment Act 2008
EAA 1973	Employment Agencies Act 1973
EAT	Employment Appeal Tribunal
EAT Rules	Employment Appeal Tribunal Rules 1993 (SI 1993/2854)
EC	European Community
ECA 1972	European Communities Act 1972
ECHR	European Convention on Human Rights
ECJ	European Court of Justice
ECtHR	European Court of Human Rights
EE(A) Regs	Employment Equality (Age) Regulations 2006 (SI 2006/1031)
EE(RB) Regs	Employment Equality (Religion or Belief) Regulations 2003 (SI 2003/1660)
EE(SD) Regs	Employment Equality (Sex Discrimination) Regulations 2005 (SI 2005/2467)
EE(SO) Regs	Employment Equality (Sexual Orientation) Regulations 2003 (SI 2003/1661)

EHRC	Equality and Human Rights Commission
EPA 1970	Equal Pay Act 1970
EPCA 1978	Employment Protection (Consolidation) Act 1978
EqA 2010	Equality Act 2010
ERA 1996	Employment Rights Act 1996
ERA 1999	Employment Relations Act 1999
ERD	expected return date
ER(DR)A 1998	Employment Rights (Dispute Resolution) Act 1998
ERRA 2013	Enterprise and Regulatory Reform Act 2013
ETA 1996	Employment Tribunals Act 1996
ET(CRP) Regs	Employment Tribunals (Constitution and Rules of Procedure) Regulations 2013 (SI 2013/1237)
ETEJO	Employment Tribunals Extension of Jurisdiction (England and Wales) Order 1994 (SI 1994/1623)
ETO	economic, technical or organisational [reason, etc]
EWC	expected week of childbirth
FTE Regs	Fixed Term Employees (Prevention of Less Favourable Treatment) Regulations 2002 (SI 2002/2034)
FW Regs	Flexible Working Regulations 2002
GOQs	genuine occupational qualifications
GPs	grievance procedures
HASAWA 1974	Health and Safety at Work etc. Act 1974
HHJ	His/Her Honour Judge
HL	House of Lords
HRA 1998	Human Rights Act 1998
HSE	Health and Safety Executive
IA 1986	Insolvency Act 1986
ICR	Industrial Cases Reports
ILO	International Labour Organization
IRA 1971	Industrial Relations Act 1971
IRLB	*Industrial Relations Law Bulletin*
IRLR	Industrial Relations Law Reports
ITR	Industrial Tribunal Reports
KIR	Knight's Industrial Reports
LAG	Legal Action Group
MPL Regs	Maternity and Parental Leave Regulations 1999 (SI 1999/3312)
NDN	non-discrimination notice
NI	National Insurance
NMWA 1998	National Minimum Wage Act 1998
NMW Regs	National Minimum Wage Regulations 1999 (SI 1999/584)
PA 1977	Patents Act 1977
PAL Regs	Parental and Adoption Leave Regulations 2000 (SI 2002/2788)
PHA 1997	Protection from Harassment Act 1997
PIDA 1998	Public Interest Disclosure Act 1998
PSA 1993	Pensions Schemes Act 1993
PTW Regs	Part Time Workers (Prevention of Less Favourable Treatment) Regulations 2000 (SI 2000/1551)
ROA 1974	Rehabilitation of Offenders Act 1974
RPA 1965	Redundancy Payments Act 1965

RRA 1976	Race Relations Act 1976
SC	Supreme Court
SDA 1975	Sex Discrimination Act 1975
SDA 1986	Sex Discrimination Act 1986
SIA 1978	State Immunity Act 1978
SOSR	some other substantial reason
TCA 2002	Tax Credits Act 2002
TCEA 2007	Tribunals, Courts and Enforcement Act 2007
TFEU	Treaty on the Functioning of the European Union
THEA 1998	Teaching and Higher Education Act 1998
TUC	Trades Union Congress
TULRA 1974	Trade Union and Labour Relations Act 1974
TULR(C)A 1992	Trade Union and Labour Relations (Consolidation) Act 1992
TUPE 1981	Transfer of Undertakings (Protection of Employment) Regulations 1981 (SI 1981/1794)
TUPE 2006	Transfer of Undertakings (Protection of Employment) Regulations 2006 (SI 2006/246)
TURERA 1993	Trade Union Reform and Employment Rights Act 1993
UCTA 1977	Unfair Contract Terms Act 1977
WA 1986	Wages Act 1986
WT Regs	Working Time Regulations 1998
WTD	Working Time Directive (No 93/104)

Note: While some European provisions are technically the product of the European Economic Community, others of the European Community and yet others of the European Union, this text will use the common expression European Union (EU) except where specific reference is intended to be made to one of the other bodies.

2

Sources for further study and preparation of cases

2.1 This Manual

This Manual is designed to introduce you to the main concepts you need to understand in order to engage in employment tribunal practice; to draw your attention to the legislative provisions and the leading cases; and to explain distinctions particular to this field of practice. It does not provide you with all the materials you will need to prepare cases for the tribunal or to undertake the realistic cases you will meet on the Bar Professional Training Course. You will find it necessary, in addition, to undertake further legal research which will require the use of practitioner texts and primary sources. For this reason the Manual makes occasional reference to specific practitioner texts. Moreover, when referred to legislation or case law you should always read the statutes, regulations or judgments, rather than relying on what may be a fairly brief summary of their significance.

2.2 Primary sources

2.2.1 Statutory materials

You should be familiar with accessing statutory material through electronic and hard-copy sources, so that you are prepared for all circumstances.

2.2.1.1 Electronic sources

The commercial providers (Lawtel, Lexis Library and Westlaw) all provide statutes and statutory instruments online. Useful information is also available through government websites such as those of the National Archive (<http://www.legislation.gov.uk/>), where both existing and draft legislation is available, and the Department of Business, Energy and Industrial Strategy (<https://www.gov.uk/government/organisations/department-for-business-energy-and-industrial-strategy>) where consultation on legislative proposals is available. Another useful website which provides free relevant news and updating is <http://danielbarnett.co.uk>. For further guidance on electronic sources, see the *Opinion Writing and Case Preparation Manual*.

2.2.1.2 Paper sources

There are three current statute books on the market, presented in descending order of price. *Wallington* is authoritative, has the most detailed index, contains cross-references to *Harvey* and is to be found on the desks of employment judges. The other titles are more selective in the material presented and less thoroughly indexed, but should include most of the provisions you will need.

Wallington, P. (ed.), *Butterworths Employment Handbook*, 25th edn, London: Butterworths, 2017;

Kidner, R. (ed.), *Blackstone's Statutes on Employment Law 2017–18*, Oxford: Oxford University Press, 2017;

Lauterburg, D. (ed.), *Core Statutes on Employment Law, 2017–18*, Basingstoke: Palgrave Macmillan, 2017.

2.2.2   Law reports

Many employment cases are reported in the ordinary reports with which you are acquainted (for example, AC, QB, WLR, All ER). However, you should develop familiarity with the specialist series:

Industrial Cases Reports (ICR); and

Industrial Relations Law Reports (IRLR).

These both appear monthly and are generally quicker to report cases than the general series of law reports. IRLR is usually the quicker of the two, and each month's issue contains a brief comment on the cases reported in that issue ('Highlights') which is useful for keeping up to date. You will need to refer to both. Cases reported in any of the main or specialist series may easily be accessed through the main electronic services: Lawtel, Lexis Library and Westlaw. Some, particularly older, cases appear only in the general series or in other specialist law reports such as Knight's Industrial Reports (KIR) (now International Journal of Law and Management) or Industrial Tribunal Reports (ITR).

2.3   Practitioner works

You will need to make regular use of practitioner texts. The main online and loose-leaf text is:

Osman, C. and Smith, I. (eds.), *Harvey on Industrial Relations and Employment Law*, London: Butterworths, 2017, loose-leaf, or electronically on Lexis Library;

A competitor in one volume is: Mansfield, G. et al (eds.), *Blackstone's Employment Law Practice*, 9th edn, Oxford: Oxford University Press, 2017,

In addition, *Tolley's Employment Handbook*, 31st edn, produced by a number of solicitors and barristers, London: LexisNexis, 2017 is a useful one-volume practitioner text.

Harvey is regarded as the standard text by most practitioners in the employment tribunals and it is convenient in that the same text is available both online and in hard copy. A monthly Bulletin provides regular updating information.

In addition, the Legal Action Group publishes books that give practical guidance to those advising clients and representing in employment tribunals:

Cunningham, N. and Reed, M., *Employment Tribunal Claims: Tactics and Precedents*, 4th edn, London: LAG, 2013, and supported by an updating blog maintained by the authors (<http://etclaims.co.uk/>). Royalties on this book go to the Free Representation Unit;

Lewis, T., *Employment Law: An Adviser's Handbook*, 12th edn, London: LAG, 2017;

O'Dempsey, D., Casserley, C., Robertson, S. and Beale, A., *Discrimination in Employment*, London: LAG, 2013.

2.4   Texts

Particularly if you have not studied employment law before, you may find some of the general academic textbooks helpful, for example:

Smith, I. and Baker, A., *Smith & Wood's Employment Law*, 13th edn, Oxford: Oxford University Press, 2017;

Painter, R. and Holmes, A., *Cases and Materials on Employment Law*, 10th edn, Oxford: Oxford University Press, 2015;

and, in the discrimination field:

Sargeant, M., *Discrimination and the Law*, 2nd edn, Oxford: Routledge, 2017;

2.5   Periodicals

Helpful ideas may also be found from arguments presented in the specialist journals and the updating periodicals. Also, articles on employment law appear regularly in all the main general legal periodicals.

2.5.1   Specialist journals

The leading specialist journal is the *Industrial Law Journal*, containing articles, comment, case notes, reports and reviews. See also the *British Journal of Industrial Relations*.

2.5.2   Updating periodicals

IDS Brief (IDSB), available through Westlaw. See also the more substantial *IDS Handbooks* which aim to keep practitioners abreast of major areas within the field.

The monthly and weekly publications, *Legal Action* and *New Law Journal*, are invaluable for up to date information on recent cases, often before they have been reported, and articles surveying a particular topic, often from a highly practical perspective. They are a valuable addition to the more in-depth treatment in the academic legal journals.

In addition there are web-based updating services. You can subscribe without charge to Daniel Barnett's employment law mailing list at <http://danielbarnett.co.uk> which provides speedy notification of new cases (usually before they are officially reported) as well as legislative and other developments.

The sources of employment law

3.1 Introduction

The fundamental source of UK employment law is the common law, as the employment relationship is based on the common law of contract. However, the myth that a contract is a freely entered agreement between two equal bargaining partners is evidently invalid when it addresses the employment relationship. Most aspirant employees, particularly at times of high unemployment, have little option but to accept the terms offered to them by the employer. The fear of unemployment may also mean employees have little protection against employers' attempts to change contractual terms in ways which worsen conditions of employment. Trade unions had sought to use their collective power to establish some balance in the relationship and, where their organisation was effective, had often achieved this. However, the process of achieving agreement often involved industrial strife which was damaging to employers, employees and the national economy. Avoiding this strife was among the motives which led to the introduction of legislation which gave individual employees a series of rights. Thus a second major source is legislation of the UK Parliament, much of it consolidated into the Employment Rights Act 1996 (ERA 1996) and the Employment Tribunals Act 1996 (ETA 1996), as amended.

The third major source, since the UK's accession to the European Community in 1972, is a body of European law, which has had a particular impact in the employment field. Provisions of the Treaties, Council Directives and decisions of the Court of Justice of the European Union (CJEU) (which consists of the European Court of Justice (ECJ) and the General Court) all have a significant part to play. At the time of writing the continuing status of this body of law is uncertain, as the Government negotiates the terms of the UK's exit from the European Union. Also note that the implementation of the Human Rights Act 1998 (HRA 1998) has incorporated most provisions of the European Convention on Human Rights (ECHR) into UK domestic law.

Just as it is unwise to study the common law rules in a particular area without considering statutory provisions (which override them), or to consider statutory provisions without considering the judgments of the courts which interpret them, so it is unwise to consider the UK or European Union (EU) sources in isolation. The various EU sources are better treated as an integral part of UK domestic law than as a supervening foreign source. This point will be developed further later.

3.2 The common law

An understanding of the common law principles of contract is an essential underpinning to any understanding of employment law. The relationship between employer and employee is one of contract and fundamental contract principles arise regularly in the employment tribunals. Here are some examples.

The principles of offer and acceptance will help you to understand when an employment contract comes into existence (see *Sarker v South Tees Acute Hospitals NHS Trust* [1997] IRLR 328, at **5.7.2**) and the relationship between the contract itself and the written statement of terms required by ERA 1996, s 1 (see **5.2.3**). Together with concepts of consideration it will help you to understand the fact that a unilateral variation of the terms of the contract will be treated as a breach, entitling the employee to remedies in both the courts and the employment tribunal (see **5.7.2**). The concept of repudiatory breach will help you to understand the doctrine of constructive dismissal (see **6.4.1.3**) and the use of implied terms has enabled the courts and tribunals to put flesh on that doctrine (see **5.2.4**). The common law doctrine of frustration will help to explain the distinction between dismissals and other forms of termination (see **6.4.2**).

What is more, the legislation which has overlaid the basic contract principles has sometimes made use of those principles in achieving its objectives. The Equal Pay Act 1970 (now consolidated into the Equality Act 2010 (EqA 2010), Pt 5, Chapter 3), for example, uses the concept of statutory implied terms to import the 'sex equality clause' into every contract of employment.

A final point to make which emphasises the significance of basic contract principles is that since 1994 employment tribunals have had the jurisdiction to hear breach of contract claims in a variety of situations (see **5.7**), claims which are often combined with unfair dismissal claims in the tribunals.

Caution should nevertheless be exercised in assuming that common law principles necessarily apply. You may recall the 'postal rule' in contract. The Supreme Court has rejected this interpretation in deciding the effective date of termination. Here the relevant date is when the employee reads or has a reasonable opportunity of reading the letter of dismissal (*GISDA Cyf v Barratt* [2010] IRLR 1073, see **4.2.1**). Employment law is seen as a coherent code designed to protect employee rights. The court argues that 'the need to segregate intellectually common law principles relating to contract law, even in the field of employment, from statutorily conferred rights is fundamental'.

3.3 UK legislation

Most of the legislation which is applied in the employment tribunals has been brought into force since the early 1960s. In order to understand the way the legislative input to employment law has developed over the years it is necessary to consider the changing aims of the legislature and the influences upon it. The changes of government in 1970, 1974, 1979, 1997, 2010 and 2015 will be a self-evident cause of different ideologies being brought to bear on the content of employment law. However, it is important to recognise that other influences have had an impact on government, whatever its own attitude. For example, the International Labour Organization (ILO), established in 1919 and now an agency of the United Nations, has produced a number of Conventions to which the UK is a signatory. Although failure to comply with those Conventions is not a matter which is justiciable in the courts, their existence provides standards which governments are under pressure to adopt. This pressure can take the form of censure by the ILO—as happened when, in 1984, the Government sought to remove the right to belong to a trade union from civil servants employed at GCHQ (subjected to judicial review in *Council of Civil Service Unions v Minister for the Civil Service* [1985] AC 374)—and governments seek to avoid it. The other major external pressures arise from membership of the EU and incorporation of much of the ECHR by the HRA 1998. These will be discussed at **3.5** and **3.6**.

The legislation of the 1960s tended to be piecemeal in nature. Statutes such as the Contracts of Employment Act 1963 and the Redundancy Payments Act 1965 (RPA 1965) (subsequently consolidated) made specific provisions to meet clearly identified problems. The latter Act, for example, was introduced at a time of significant technological change which required major changes in the structure and skills required of the workforce. The RPA 1965 was designed to encourage people to accept redundancy situations and to use their payments to retrain for the new technological jobs. Whether the payments were really sufficient to achieve this must be a matter of question, but the Act may have reduced the likelihood of industrial disputes flowing from redundancy situations.

The legislation of the Labour Government of 1974–79 flowed not only from the desire to provide social and economic stability, but was the result of the 'social contract' between the Government and the Trades Union Congress (TUC). It not only provided a floor of statutory rights for employees, but provided assistance for trade unions in organising, seeking recognition and undertaking collective bargaining. The major planks of individual protection were centred around dismissal and discrimination on grounds of race or sex.

The Conservative Government elected in 1979 took the view that market forces should play a greater part in the employment field. The protection of the existing legislation was seen as an obstacle to that aim and deregulation as an effective way of improving economic performance. While the position of trade unions was radically worsened during this period, the extent of deregulation of the position of employees individually was limited. For example, instead of abolishing unfair dismissal provisions, the period of employment necessary before protection applied was extended in stages from six months to two years and the burden of proof in establishing that a dismissal was reasonable was lifted from employers. This was in part because the electorate were reluctant to see their rights as employees removed. Another major factor was the Government's obligations under the Treaty of Rome.

One example of this suffices to exemplify the importance of recognising the significance of ideology for the understanding of this legislation. The Acquired Rights Directive (77/187/EEC) required Member States to introduce laws protecting employees' rights when the business they work for is transferred from one owner to another. This was implemented by the Transfer of Undertakings (Protection of Employment) Regulations 1981 (SI 1981/1794) (TUPE 1981). The drafting of these regulations limited them to 'commercial' enterprises, a limit which did not appear within the Directive itself. This was to protect the Government's privatisation programme and the introduction of compulsory competitive tendering in the public sector, itself a major plank in the programme of deregulation. Decisions of the ECJ such as *Dr Sophie Redmond Stichting v Bartol* [1992] IRLR 366 have made it clear that this limitation is unacceptable and the regulations have had to be amended. This tension informed the development of the law during the 1980s and 1990s and needs to be understood in light of the way in which European law impacts on UK domestic legislation and case law.

The election of a Labour Government in 1997 produced legislation focused on both substantive employment law and tribunal procedure as well as the HRA 1998 which is beginning to have an impact on the work of employment tribunals. In particular, the ERA 1996 enables the introduction of measures in a number of areas. For example:

(a) *Unfair dismissal.* There has been a substantial increase in the ceiling for the compensatory award for unfair dismissal. Waiver clauses in fixed-term contracts preventing unfair dismissal claims are outlawed, as is the sacking of strikers during the first 12 weeks of a properly constituted strike. Thereafter the employer must take reasonable steps to end the strike for a dismissal to be fair.

(b) *Disciplinary hearings.* Employees are entitled to be accompanied by a trade union representative or fellow employee to hearings raising 'serious issues'. Tribunals may order employers who deny this right to pay up to two weeks' pay in compensation.

(c) *Family-friendly policies.* Improvements to maternity provisions have been introduced (see **Chapter 9**), plus new rights to up to three months' unpaid parental leave and reasonable time off to deal with a domestic incident. These rights have been extended to unconventional family relationships.

(d) *Marginal employees.* Part-time and fixed-term workers receive rights proportional to those of full-timers.

Subsequently, the Employment Act 2008, s 3 provided for an uplift to tribunal awards where employers fail to meet procedural standards.

The coalition Government taking power in 2010 implemented the Equality Act of that year, but (see **Chapter 8**) withheld implementation of certain provisions of which it disapproved. The Enterprise and Regulatory Reform Act 2013 introduces provisions stated to reduce the burden on businesses including a number which impact on employees' remedies. Thus the maximum compensatory award for unfair dismissal cases (a sum increased annually by order, was restricted to 52 weeks' gross pay (SI 2013/1949), a significant reduction given that the median wage at the time was below £25,000.

In 2013 employment tribunal fees were introduced by statutory instrument, requiring claimants to pay fees of up to £1,200. This produced an immediate significant drop in the number of claims and research showed that it had failed to achieve the stated goal of reducing unmeritorious claims. It was held to be void ab initio by the Supreme Court in *R (on the application of Unison) v Lord Chancellor* [2017] UKSC 51.

Generally, most new employment protection legislation covers 'workers' rather than the narrower category of 'employees' (see **5.1.1**).

3.4 European Union law

It was said at **3.1** that it is better to perceive the law of the EU as part of UK domestic law than as something superimposed from outside. It is true that, generally, rules of international law are binding in the UK only when they have been translated into domestic law by legislative provision. EU law, however, is different because of the European Communities Act 1972, s 2(1) (ECA 1972), which provides:

all such rights, powers, liabilities, obligations and restrictions from time to time created or arising by or under the Treaties, and all such remedies and procedures from time to time provided for by or under the Treaties, as in accordance with the Treaties are without further enactment to be given legal effect or used in the United Kingdom shall be recognised and available in law, and be enforced, allowed and followed accordingly . . .

Thus the Act provides prospectively for EU provisions to be treated as part of domestic law as and when they are introduced. It is important also to remember that EU law prevails over inconsistent domestic law, even to the extent that provisions in statutes may be declared invalid (*Factortame v Secretary of State for Transport* [1989] 2 All ER 692). The 1972 Act remains in force at the time of writing. However, in the White Paper 'Legislating for the United Kingdom's withdrawal from the European Union' (Cm 9446) the Government has indicated its intention to pass a European Union (Withdrawal) Bill. According to the White Paper this will:

- repeal the European Communities Act 1972;
- bring all EU laws onto the UK books; and
- create powers to make secondary legislation.

This means that the provisions introduced since 1972 in order to meet with the UK's obligations under the various EU treaties will continue to have effect. The power to make secondary legislation will make it possible for future governments to repeal, amend or augment these provisions. None of this can happen until after the process of withdrawing from the EU has been completed, in other words, not before March 2019 at the earliest. Thus, the EU provisions explained below will continue to have effect until the Withdrawal Bill becomes an Act of Parliament.

To explore this further we need to consider the different sources of EU law.

3.4.1   The Treaties—primary sources

These are the primary source of EU law. For our purposes the important Treaties are the EC Treaty (the Treaty of Rome) 1957; the Single European Act 1986; the Treaty on European Union (the Maastricht Treaty) 1992; the Treaty of Amsterdam 1997 and the Treaty of Lisbon 2007. The major provisions of the EC Treaty are now contained in the Treaty on the Functioning of the European Union (TFEU), a renaming of the Treaty of Rome carried out by the Lisbon Treaty and implemented on 1 December 2009.

3.4.1.1   Treaty on the Functioning of the European Union (EC Treaty (Treaty of Rome) 1957)

Title III of the Treaty of Rome which was adopted by the UK in 1972 is headed 'Social Policy' and committed the EU to harmonisation in a number of areas crucial to employment. Article 117 (now TFEU art 151) identified promotion of improved working conditions and an improved standard of living for workers. Article 118 (now TFEU art 153) gave the Commission the task of promoting close co-operation between Member States in a number of areas, including employment, labour law and working conditions and the right of association and collective bargaining. None of this establishes any substantive rules, but art 119 (now TFEU art 157) did so in the specific area of equal pay:

Each Member State shall . . . ensure and subsequently maintain the application of the principle that men and women should receive equal pay for equal work.

This is clear and specific enough as to the rights it establishes. It is crucial to note that the significance of the provision goes beyond the duty of the Member State to introduce appropriate legislation. In *Defrenne v SABENA (No 2)* [1976] ECR 455 the ECJ held that art 119 (now TFEU art 157) had direct effect in Member States. Thus any individual may bring a claim based on art 157 in a court or tribunal even if UK legislation is inconsistent with it.

The practical effect of this is that the Treaty is to all intents and purposes as binding as an Act of Parliament. Indeed, it carries more weight as it is to be preferred to the domestic Act if the two are inconsistent. An example of this can be found in *Macarthys Ltd v Smith* [1980] IRLR 209 (see **10.2.2**).

The terminology which is used to describe this is 'direct effect' (see *Van Gend en Loos* [1963] ECR 1). Two types of direct effect are recognised, both of which apply to Treaty provisions. 'Vertical' direct effect refers to the binding effect on Member States. 'Horizontal' direct effect refers to the effect on individual citizens (or other persons) within Member States. Treaty provisions have vertical direct effect because they are binding on Member States and also horizontal direct effect because they can be used by (and against) individuals in litigation in domestic courts and tribunals. The same is not true of Directives (see **3.4.2.1**).

3.4.1.2   Single European Act 1986

This amended the EC Treaty in ways significant for the development of employment law. The election of a Conservative administration in the UK had led to the vetoing of most proposals for new Directives in the employment field. The new Treaty introduced art 100A (later 95, now TFEU art 114), which provided for qualified majority voting in the Council of Ministers (the main legislative body of the EC) in respect of certain areas. 'The rights and interests of employed persons' were expressly excluded by para 2, but other relevant areas, such as health and safety were included, and given further support by the introduction of art 118A (later 138, now TFEU art 154). Article 118B (later 139, now TFEU art 155) addressed the improvement of collective relations at work.

3.4.1.3   Treaty on European Union (Maastricht) 1992

By this Treaty all the Member States except the UK committed themselves to harmonisation of their policies in a number of areas, including: health and safety, working conditions, equality at work between men and women, social security, protection of workers made redundant, conditions of employment for non-EU nationals, representation and defence of workers and employers. The UK's initial 'opt-out' from this 'social chapter' meant that developments taken under these provisions did not bind the UK. Note, however, that many of these areas could be developed by powers derived from the 1957 Treaty (for example, those in the Social Policy provisions mentioned at **3.4.1.1**), which would be binding on the UK. In addition, some employers operating internationally chose to implement provisions in the UK, although not legally obliged to do so, in order to maintain consistency across their various divisions. Since 1997 the UK has signed up to the social chapter, and legislation has been introduced in some of these areas.

3.4.1.4   Treaty of Amsterdam 1997

This Treaty recognises employment issues as key, introducing a new title on employment; it extends the object of sex equality beyond equal pay and empowers the Council to take action to combat discrimination on grounds of sex, racial or ethnic origin, religion or belief, disability, age or sexual orientation. This has resulted in the Framework Directive 2000/78 (see **Chapter 8**).

3.4.1.5   Treaty of Lisbon 2007

This Treaty expanded the powers of the European Union in certain areas and revised the earlier Treaties. Its work on the EC Treaty has been consolidated into the TFEU with effect from 1 December 2009.

3.4.2   Legislation—secondary sources

The Treaties enable the passing of a number of types of EU legislation, which are therefore best seen as secondary sources. This is not the place for a full discussion of all the different legislative powers of the EU. These are set out in TFEU art 288 (formerly art 249 EC Treaty) and include Regulations, Directives and decisions. For the purposes of employment law we need only consider Directives in detail. You should note, however, that Regulations are general rules which apply throughout the EU. They are directly applicable (both vertically and horizontally) and may be relied on by individuals in national courts without any need for enactment by Member States. Decisions are addressed to specified persons or Member States. They are also binding and require no further implementation. They operate mostly in the field of competition law.

3.4.2.1   Directives

The major EU legislative source for UK employment law is the series of Directives adopted since 1975. These include: the Framework Directive on Equal Treatment in Employment 2000/78; Acquired Rights Directive 2001/23; Working Time Directive 2003/88; Equal Treatment Directive 2006/54; and the Framework Directive on Parental Leave 2010/18.

These Directives act, in effect, as instructions to Member States to introduce into domestic law provisions to meet the standards of the Directive. An example can be seen in the Equal Pay Directive:

Article 2

Member States shall introduce into their national legal systems such measures as are necessary to enable all employees who consider themselves wronged by failure to apply the principle of equal pay to pursue their claims by judicial process. . .

It should be apparent from this that Directives have vertical direct effect. They bind Member States to make specific provisions in their domestic legislation. However, they do not have horizontal direct effect. Thus individual citizens of a Member State cannot have claims brought against them on the strength of a Directive until the legislature of their State has introduced the necessary domestic legislation. This was stated clearly by the ECJ in *Marshall v Southampton and South West Hampshire Area Health Authority (Teaching)* [1986] ECR 723, at p 749:

according to Article 189 of the EEC Treaty [now TFEU art. 288] the binding nature of a Directive, which constitutes the basis for the possibility of relying on the Directive before a national court, exists only in relation to each Member State to which it is addressed. It follows that a Directive may not of itself impose obligations on an individual and that a provision of a Directive must not be relied upon as against such a person.

The consequence of this, however, needs to be carefully noted. It does not mean that no action can be based on a Directive. It is simply that only the Member State which has failed to implement the Directive can be the defendant. This has the peculiar consequence that employees of emanations of the State may seek enforcement of rights provided for in Directives, but not implemented in national legislation, while employees of private companies may not. This also makes it necessary to state with precision which employers do constitute emanations of the State for these purposes.

This question was addressed by the ECJ in *Foster v British Gas plc* [1990] IRLR 354. The court held that an emanation of the State for these purposes could be defined as 'an organisation, whatever its legal form, which is subject to the authority or control of the State or which has been made responsible, pursuant to a measure adopted by the State, for providing a public service under the control of the State and has for that purpose special powers beyond those which result from the normal rules applicable between individuals'. The three elements of this test (subject to State control; responsibility for a public service; and having special powers) should be seen as disjunctive (*Kampelmann v Landschaftsverband Westfalen-Lippe* [1998] IRLR 333). It is not therefore necessary that all three be present. Applying this test in the House of Lords, Lord Templeman said that the 'commercial' nature of British Gas was irrelevant to this test, and that the 'control' element of the test should be given a purposive rather than a narrow construction. British Gas (before privatisation) therefore fell within the public sector. Such organisations probably remain emanations of the State after privatisation as it was held by the Divisional Court in *Griffin v South West Water Services Ltd* [1995] IRLR 15 that the test is not whether the body concerned is under the control of the State, but whether the service it provides is subject to State control. This broad definition would appear, in most cases, to include privatised industries which had formerly been in State ownership. However, the 'public service' element of the test must be established. In *Doughty v Rolls-Royce* [1992] IRLR 126 the applicant was unable to rely on the Equal Treatment Directive because Rolls-Royce did not provide services. Thus it was not an emanation of the State even though the State was the sole shareholder at the time of the complaint.

Foster and *Doughty* were both cases concerning commercial organisations in which the State had a stake. The test in *Foster* will not necessarily apply in other circumstances. Thus in *NUT v Governing Body of St Mary's Church of England (Aided) Junior School* [1997] IRLR 242 the Court of Appeal held that the tripartite test in *Foster* was not intended to be exclusive and found that a voluntary aided school was an emanation of the State even if the governors had no special powers (the third element of the *Foster* test). This should encourage a more inclusive approach to the concept of 'emanation of the State'.

This distinction produces the anomalous result that employees within the private sector may not rely on Directives, while those employed by an emanation of the State may (but see **3.4.3.2**). The proper route to avoid such an anomaly is, of course, the introduction of measures by the State to give effect to the Directive in question. However, the Grand Chamber of the ECJ has subsequently decided (*Kücükdeveci v Swedex GmbH & Co KG* [2010] IRLR 346) that the principle of equal treatment in employment is a general principle of EU law, as a result of which national courts are under a duty to disapply domestic legislation which is contrary to that principle. In this case German legislation on minimum notice periods ignored service under the age of 25. Thus, even if the Framework Directive 2000/78 is only vertically applicable, employees of private sector organisations may be able to enforce its principles.

A further stimulus to encourage Member States to implement Directives fully and promptly was the decision in *Francovich v Italian Republic* [1992] IRLR 84 in which the ECJ held that in certain circumstances an individual (for example, a private sector employee) denied a remedy because of the failure of the State to implement a Directive may seek a remedy in damages against the State. The scope of this was limited in *Brasserie du Pêcheur SA v Germany/Factortame (No 3)* [1996] IRLR 267. By contrast, in *Dillenkofer and others v Federal Republic of Germany* [1997] IRLR 60 the ECJ held that there was no need to show fault or negligence for a *Francovich* claim to succeed. This is a significant example of the extent to which EU principles may apply in situations where there has been no domestic legislation.

It is normal for a Directive to provide a date by which Member States must implement it. However, this does not entitle States to introduce legislation conflicting with the underlying principle during the intervening period. National courts must set aside any such provision even before the deadline for implementing the Directive has expired (*Mangold v Helm* [2006] IRLR 143).

In interpreting Directives it is important to remember that it is the Directive itself, not its preamble, which indicates what must be implemented by Member States. The recitals in the preamble are a useful guide to interpretation, but have no binding force (*Maruko v Versorgungsanstalt der deutschen Bühnen* [2008] IRLR 450).

3.4.2.2 Charter of Fundamental Rights of the European Union

This Charter, in effect since the Treaty of Lisbon, has been ruled by the Supreme Court to have direct effect (*RFU v Consolidated Information Services* [2012] UKSC 55). This has had an impact in the employment field in the case of *Benkharbouche v. Embassy of the Republic of Sudan* [2015] IRLR 301. Here, the respondent claimed state immunity but it was held by the Court of Appeal that the relevant provisions of the State Immunity Act 1978 should be disapplied as non-compliant with the provision in art 47 of the Charter of a right to an effective remedy and a fair trial.

3.4.3 Decisions of the ECJ and the General Court—tertiary sources

The Court of Justice of the European Union (CJEU) is comprised of the ECJ and the General Court (until 2009 the Court of First Instance). Their decisions apply and supplement the sources considered so far. As such they may be seen as a tertiary source. They use general principles of law to inform their task. These include: the principle of proportionality (don't use a sledgehammer to crack a nut); the principle of non-discrimination; the principle of legal certainty (encompassing the protection of legitimate expectation and non-retroactivity); and the right to be heard.

The CJEU holds a prime position in the hierarchy of courts. Its decisions are binding on all UK courts in respect of the interpretation of the legislation of the EC. UK courts and tribunals may put questions to it in respect of any matter involving the interpretation of EU legislation, past ECJ decisions or the interpretation of domestic legislation which is claimed to meet the requirements of the Treaties or of a Directive.

3.4.3.1 Member State responsibility

This pivotal role has led to major developments in the law. On a number of occasions the Government has been required to bring in amending legislation because of ECJ rulings that it is in breach of its Treaty obligations. Well-known examples of this include *EC Commission v UK* (Case 61/81) [1982] IRLR 333, resulting in the Equal Pay (Amendment) Regulations 1983 which introduced the concept of equal value claims (see **10.2.3.3**), *Marshall v Southampton and South West Hampshire Area Health Authority (Teaching) (No 2)* [1993] IRLR 425, resulting in the lifting of the artificial cap on discrimination compensation by the Sex Discrimination and Equal Pay (Remedies) Regulations 1993 and *R v Secretary of State for Employment, ex p Equal Opportunities Commission* [1995] AC 1, resulting in the removal of the weekly hours' criterion for unfair dismissal, etc claims. An interesting consequence of the second of these examples is the extension of the principle applying to EU provisions to other areas of domestic law, as the Government responded by introducing the Race Relations (Remedies) Act 1994 to apply the same principle to race discrimination claims even though there was no race discrimination provision to be found at that time in EU law.

3.4.3.2   Indirect effect

What is more, the ECJ's role has to some extent undermined the sharp distinction between vertical and horizontal direct applicability established by *Marshall* (*No 1*) in respect of Directives. This is sometimes known as the doctrine of indirect effect. In *Von Colson and Kamann v Land Nordrhein-Westfalen* [1984] ECR 1891 the ECJ identified the courts of Member States as having the responsibility of interpreting domestic legislation introduced in order to comply with a Directive 'in the light of the wording and the purpose of the Directive'.

The House of Lords initially took a restrictive approach to this principle. Thus in *Duke v GEC Reliance Ltd* [1988] AC 618 it was held that the fact that the Sex Discrimination Act 1975 pre-dated the Equal Treatment Directive 1976 and was not designed to give effect to the Directive, meant that it was not necessary to interpret it with a view to meeting the objectives of the Directive.

This view was overruled by the ECJ in *Marleasing SA v La Comercial Internacional de Alimentación SA* [1992] 1 CMLR 305, where the court held:

It follows that, in applying national law, where the provisions in question were adopted before or after the Directive, the national court called upon to interpret it is required to do so, as far as possible, in the light of the wording and purpose of the Directive in order to achieve the result pursued by the latter . . .

The UK courts' response may best be seen in the House of Lords decision in *Webb v EMO Air Cargo UK Ltd* [1993] IRLR 27. The principle that domestic legislation must be interpreted in accordance with the ECJ's interpretation of the relevant Directive was accepted, but with two caveats. The first flows from *Duke*:

. . . if that could be done without distorting the meaning of the domestic legislation;

the second from *Marleasing* itself:

. . . only if it is possible to do so. That means that the domestic law must be open to an interpretation consistent with the Directive whether or not it is also open to an interpretation inconsistent with it.

In effect this means that the UK courts must seek an interpretation of domestic legislation which accords with that of the relevant Directive, and choose such an interpretation if that is possible without distortion, even if an alternative interpretation may on the face of it be more natural to the wording. Clearly this leaves the possibility that the domestic legislation may be incapable of such an interpretation. If this is the case individuals will be unable to rely on the Directive (unless they are claiming against an employer who is an emanation of the State) until appropriate amending legislation is introduced. Where the Directive concerned is the Framework Directive 2000/78, a claim against a private sector employer may be available (*Kücükdeveci v Swedex GmbH & Co KG* [2010] IRLR 346). A *Francovich* claim (see **3.4.2.1**) may also sometimes be possible.

An example of a case which illustrates the significance of this is *Attridge Law v Coleman* [2007] IRLR 88. Here it was clear that the literal wording of the Disability Discrimination Act 1995 (DDA 1995) did not cover a claimant who suffered less favourable treatment because her disabled son required care. The wording of the Framework Directive, however, is 'on grounds of disability' and the tribunal referred the matter to the ECJ, which held in *Coleman v Attridge Law* [2008] IRLR 722 that such 'associative discrimination' was unlawful. The Equality Act 2010 contains provisions designed to address this problem (see **8.3.2.3**).

3.5 Human Rights Act 1998

Decisions since the implementation of HRA 1998 have tended to reflect the cautious approach of the ECJ. However, a number of provisions of the ECHR may have an impact on employment cases.

It has always been clear that public sector employers must abide by HRA 1998. In addition, the Court of Appeal (CA) has held that these principles may also affect private sector employers. In *X v Y* [2004] IRLR 625 dismissal of a charity worker for failing to disclose a caution for gross indecency in a public toilet was held not to be in breach of art 8, as the incident took place in a public place. However, the court pointed out the s 3 obligation on the tribunal to give effect to employment legislation in a way which is compatible with ECHR rights. Mummery LJ held that '[t]here would normally be no sensible grounds for treating public and private employees differently in respect of unfair dismissal'. He went on to provide guidance as to how tribunals should approach HRA 1998 points arising in unfair dismissal claims.

Employers should ensure that their disciplinary procedures comply with art 6 (right to a fair trial). Specific procedural safeguards, including the right to cross-examine, might be required where allegations are serious (*R (Bonhoeffer) v General Medical Council* [2012] IRLR 37). Monitoring staff emails and telephone conversations may infringe art 8 (right to respect for private and family life) which may also affect the law on dress codes at work (see **8.2.7**). Article 9 (freedom of thought, conscience and religion) goes further than the discrimination provisions in force at the time and may well go further than the EqA 2010, s 10 which only protects against discrimination on grounds of religion, religious belief or similar philosophical belief (see **8.2.7**). Article 14 (discrimination) which does not stand alone but may found a claim where a right protected by another Article is denied on discriminatory grounds, is more broadly drafted than other anti-discrimination provisions. Indications of the courts' approach to HRA 1998 cases may be seen in subsequent cases. In *McGowan v Scottish Water* [2005] IRLR 167, covert surveillance of the claimant's home was held to raise a strong presumption that art 8 had been breached. In the event, however, the principle of proportionality was applied to justify the actions as they were central to the employer's investigation of falsifying time sheets.

The difference between art 9 (relating to religion) and the related provisions of the Equality Act 2010 may be seen in *Mba v Mayor and Burgesses of the London Borough of Merton* [2014] IRLR 145. This concerned an employee's objection to Sunday working. The tribunal had rejected the claim on the grounds that this was not a 'core' Christian belief. The Court of Appeal rejected this analysis as it was not required to satisfy the right in art 9. However, they did find in favour of the respondent as the requirement to work on Sundays, in the circumstances, was justified. Intriguingly, the court pointed out that where an individual's belief was not a core belief it would tend to be easier for the employer to find someone else to perform the task, and thus more difficult to justify.

An important judgment of the European Court of Human Rights (ECtHR) in linked cases of indirect discrimination on grounds of religion or belief is *Eweida v United Kingdom* [2013] IRLR 231. This introduces a concept of balance where beliefs come into conflict. It is discussed further at **8.2.7**.

It may otherwise be regarded as rare for HRA 1998 to offer a remedy where the normal provisions do not. This may be seen in *Pay v Lancashire Probation Service* where the claimant, who worked with sex offenders, was dismissed for his involvement with a sado-masochism and bondage website. Having lost in the Employment Appeal Tribunal

(EAT) ([2004] IRLR 129) he also failed in the ECtHR (unreported) who confirmed that his dismissal did not contravene art 14 and did not constitute discrimination on grounds of sexual orientation.

Instances of declarations of incompatibility do occasionally arise in the employment field. In *R (Wright) v Secretary of State for Health* [2007] IRLR 507 the Administrative Court declared that the Care Standards Act 2000, which permits termination of care workers' employment without a hearing, is incompatible with both art 6 and art 8 of the ECHR.

The composition and practice of the tribunals and courts are also subject to the requirements of the Act. However, grounds of national security may override art 6 rights. In *Home Office v Tariq* [2011] IRLR 843 the Supreme Court held that it was not incompatible with either EU or ECHR provisions to exclude the claimant and his representative from part of tribunal proceedings on the grounds of national security. What is more, the usual requirement that the claimant be given the gist of the allegations against him so that he can instruct representatives so that they can be challenged did not apply, as his liberty was not at risk.

3.6 Principles of interpretation

The relationship between EU, ECHR and domestic legislation outlined at **3.5** is further complicated by the different approaches taken to legislative drafting and interpretation (and thus the role of the courts) in common law systems such as that in England and Wales and civil law systems such as those in Europe on which EU law is based. This is a complex subject and it will only be briefly sketched here.

3.6.1 Approach towards legislative drafting

The approach to statutory drafting in the UK has traditionally been to produce detailed provisions which attempt to cover all eventualities. The increasing tendency to pass framework-enabling statutes does not make a major change in this, as the detailed provisions are then brought into effect through statutory instruments and other regulations.

By contrast, EU legislation tends to establish broad principles. The detail is not incorporated into the primary legislation, but is left for the working out of national legislatures, national courts and the CJEU. This is partly because of the doctrine of subsidiarity, which requires decisions to be taken at as local a level as is appropriate. It also flows in part from the recognition of changing social and economic circumstances and the probability that interpretations will vary in the light of change. Lord Templeman, writing extra-judicially (in the foreword to Holland and Webb, *Learning Legal Rules* (Oxford University Press)) gave a clear example:

> The differences [in construing English and Community legislation] are substantial; arts 30 and 35 of the Treaty of Rome, prohibiting quantitative restrictions on imports and exports, enabled the European Court of Justice to establish a free trade regime which could only have been established by about four English statutes containing 500 sections and 15 Schedules and hundreds of statutory instruments.

For another example (although simplistic and not a fair comparison), compare the equal pay provisions: EqA 2010, Pt 5, Chapter 3 with TFEU art 157 (formerly art 141 of the EC Treaty).

3.6.2 Interpreting EU provisions

These differences in the approach to drafting have an inevitable consequence on the approach adopted by the courts to statutory interpretation in the two systems.

In the UK the predominant approach has been for the courts to see their role as limited to a literal interpretation of the statute. Law students will be familiar with the debate between the more purposive interpreters (exemplified by Lord Denning), who are willing to interpret creatively when they come across a lacuna in the law, and others who take a narrower view of their task, perceiving any such creative tendencies as usurping the legislative function. Nevertheless, both categories of judge would see themselves as staying within the strict wording of the Act as far as possible, and would consider the intention of Parliament, at the time of the passage of the Act in question.

By contrast, the ECJ clearly adopts a teleological or purposive approach to interpretation. The judges are required to consider the purpose and context of the text to be applied. Thus in *Defrenne* [1976] ECR 455, interpreting art 119 (now TFEU art 157), the court emphasised not only the social and economic purpose of art 119, but also its relationship to other provisions such as art 117 (now TFEU art 151). The judges in the ECJ see themselves as having the task of *developing* the law laid down in framework by the Treaty provision or Directive concerned. Indeed, one of the objections of many in the UK is that the ECJ has in fact developed the principles of the legislation far beyond what it had been thought to cover at the time of its introduction. There is, of course, scope for disagreement about the developments in the law introduced by the ECJ. However, their function in developing the law is clearly anticipated by the very approach to drafting. An example of how such developments can take place can be seen in the cases on gender reassignment and sexual orientation (see **8.1**).

The composition and structure of the ECJ is relevant to understanding how the court works. It must ensure consistency in interpretation across the 28 Member States. There are 28 judges from the different States, thus bringing the experience of 28 different legal systems to their deliberations. Their decision must be a collegiate one without dissenting judgments. In coming to their decision they have the assistance of an Opinion from one of the eight Advocates-General. In practice it is unusual for the ECJ to depart fundamentally from the Advocate-General's Opinion.

A similar approach can be seen in decisions of the European Court of Human Rights (ECtHR), where the Convention is seen as a 'living instrument' which needs to be interpreted in the light of changing conditions and expectations:

> the Convention is a living instrument which must be interpreted in the light of present-day conditions and . . . the increasingly high standard being required in the area of the protection of human rights and fundamental liberties correspondingly and inevitably requires greater firmness in assessing breaches of the fundamental values of democratic societies. (*Öcalan v Turkey* (App No 46221/99) (2005) 41 EHRR 45)

Given that the UK courts must also consider the wording and purpose of EU legislation and the ECHR in construing relevant domestic legislation, they must also accept some of these same tasks. This changed approach has not been easy for them to adopt, but the principle seems now to be accepted. In *Litster v Forth Dry Dock and Engineering Co* [1990] 1 AC 546 Lord Templeman said:

> the courts of the United Kingdom are under a duty to follow the practice of the European Court by giving a purposive construction to Directives and regulations issued with the purpose of complying with Directives.

It is true that the courts have not consistently taken this view. However, that it is the correct approach has been confirmed by the ECJ in *Coloroll Pension Trustees Ltd v Russell* [1994] ECR I-4389:

national courts are bound to provide the legal protection which individuals derive from the direct effect of provisions of the Treaty . . . They are therefore bound, particularly in the context of Article 119 [now 141], to the full extent of their discretion under national law, to interpret and apply the relevant domestic provisions in conformity with the requirements of Community law and, where this is not possible, to disapply any incompatible provisions.

This, although applying a Treaty provision, goes further to refer to EU law in general and clearly requires national courts not merely to adopt a thoroughgoing purposive approach, but to reject domestic provisions when they are incompatible with EU law.

The combination of these EU and ECHR principles can be seen to be influencing the approach taken by the judiciary in England and Wales. Lord Browne-Wilkinson, writing extra-judicially, suggested that judges, in interpreting legislation, 'seek to ensure that the meritorious triumph and the dirty dogs lick their wounds' (in B. Markesinis (ed.), *The Impact of the Human Rights Act on English Law*, Oxford: Oxford University Press 1998, 22). Arguments to persuade the judge that a particular outcome meets this goal will need to be framed on the basis of changing standards with an appeal to objectivity in assessing those standards. This perspective, however, is not uniform and practitioners will need to be familiar with conventional approaches to interpretation as well. The task has become no simpler, and it will become more complex after the forthcoming repeal of the European Communities Act 1972. Whether judges will revert to a more traditional approach to interpretation is currently an open question and will no doubt be the subject of argument by counsel.

3.7 Conclusion

The process of common law, domestic legislative and EU sources becoming thoroughly integrated was bound to take time and may now never be realised. However, the analysis presented here should indicate that none of the sources identified should be perceived in isolation and that all will continue to need to be considered if the legal context of employment problems is to be understood.

4

Employment tribunal procedure

Procedure in employment tribunals is governed by the Employment Tribunals (Constitution and Rules of Procedure) Regulations 2013 (SI 2013/1237) (ET(CRP) Regs 2013); the Employment Tribunal Rules of Procedure (referred to in this chapter as 'the Employment Tribunal Rules') are contained in Schedule 1.

Rule 2 of the Employment Tribunal Rules sets out an overriding objective, namely 'to deal with cases fairly and justly'. This includes, so far as practicable:

(a) ensuring that the parties are on an equal footing;

(b) dealing with the case in ways which are proportionate to the complexity or importance of the issues;

(c) avoiding unnecessary formality and seeking flexibility in the proceedings;

(d) avoiding delay, so far as compatible with proper consideration of the issues; and

(e) saving expense.

Rule 2 requires tribunals to give effect to the overriding objective when exercising their powers or interpreting the Rules, and requires the parties to 'assist the Tribunal to further the overriding objective and in particular shall co-operate generally with each other and with the Tribunal'.

Regulation 11 of the ET(CRP) Regs 2013 empowers the President of Employment Tribunals to issue Practice Directions about the procedure of employment tribunals. This is to ensure that tribunals adopt a consistent approach to procedural issues and to the interpretation of their powers under the Employment Tribunal Rules of Procedure. Practice Directions issued under this Regulation should be regarded as binding on tribunals.

The power to issue Practice Directions is supplemented by rule 7 of the Employment Tribunal Rules, which provides that the President may publish guidance as to matters of practice and as to how the powers conferred by the Rules may be exercised. Rule 7 states that tribunals 'must have regard to any such guidance, but they shall not be bound by it'.

4.1 Presenting a claim

Rule 8 of the Employment Tribunal Rules governs the procedure for starting a claim. Rule 8(1) provides that a claim 'shall be started by presenting a completed claim form (using a prescribed form)'. The prescribed form is known as an ET1. Rule 9 makes it clear that two or more claimants may make their claims on the same form 'if their claims are based on the same set of facts'.

4.1.1 Tribunal fees

The Employment Tribunals and the Employment Appeal Tribunal Fees Order 2013 (SI 2013/1893) prescribed fees for tribunal proceedings. One fee was payable by a claimant when a claim form was presented to an employment tribunal, and another when the claim was listed for a final hearing.

No fee was payable if the party was in receipt of a qualifying benefit (such as income support or income-based jobseeker's allowance), and provision was made for remission of some or all of the fees depending on the claimant's gross annual income. However, in *R (Unison) v Lord Chancellor* [2017] UKSC 51, the Supreme Court held that these fees (which were, in practice, unaffordable for many would-be claimants) effectively prevented access to justice, and were therefore unlawful.

4.1.2 Rejection of the claim

The claim will be rejected if it is not made on the prescribed form, or if it does not contain the name and address of each claimant and each respondent, or if it does not contain an 'early conciliation number' or confirmation that 'early conciliation' is not applicable (see r 10 of the Employment Tribunal Rules). A claim will also be rejected if it is not accompanied by the appropriate tribunal fee, or an application for remission of the fee (r 11).

Rule 12(2) provides that a claim (or part of a claim) will be rejected if an Employment Judge considers that it is 'one which the Tribunal has no jurisdiction to consider', or is 'in a form which cannot sensibly be responded to or is otherwise an abuse of the process', or if it does not contain an 'early conciliation number' or confirmation that 'early conciliation' is not applicable. A claim form which has been rejected will be returned to the claimant, together with a notice setting out the judge's reasons for rejecting the claim (or part of it). It is worth noting that the grounds upon which a claim may be rejected under r 12 are very narrow.

Under r 13(1), a claimant whose claim has been rejected (in whole or in part) may apply for reconsideration of the decision to reject the claim on the basis that the decision was wrong, or that the defect can be rectified. The application for reconsideration must be made in writing to the tribunal within 14 days of the date that the notice of rejection was sent (r 13(2)). If the claimant does not request a hearing (or if an Employment Judge decides, on considering the application, that the claim should be accepted in full), the application is determined without a hearing; otherwise the application is considered at a hearing attended only by the claimant (r 13(3)).

If the judge decides that the original rejection of the claim was correct, but that the defect has now been rectified, the claim 'shall be treated as presented on the date that the defect was rectified' (r 13(4)). This provision is rather ambiguous, but it is submitted that the best interpretation would be that the claim is deemed to have been presented on the date when the application for reconsideration was presented to the tribunal (under r 13(2)).

4.2 Time limit for bringing a claim

The time limits for bringing claims are governed by primary legislation rather than the Employment Tribunal Rules.

It should be noted that s 207B of the Employment Rights Act 1996 (inserted by the Enterprise and Regulatory Reform Act 2013) makes provision for extensions of time limits to facilitate conciliation before institution of proceedings. Under s 207B(2), Day A is the date when the prospective claimant complies with the duty under s 18A to contact ACAS before instituting proceedings; Day B is the date on which the claimant receives a certificate issued under s 18A(4) marking the end of the conciliation period. Section 207B(3) stipulates that, in working out when a time limit expires, the period beginning with the day after Day A and ending with Day B is not to be counted. For details of early conciliation, see **4.8**.

4.2.1 Unfair dismissal

The complaint must be presented to the Regional Office within three months of the effective date of termination or 'within such further period as the tribunal considers reasonable in a case where it is satisfied that it was not reasonably practicable for the complaint to be presented before the end of that period of three months' (ERA 1996, s 111(2)(b)). The 'effective date of termination' (EDT) is defined in ERA 1996, s 97(1): in summary, where a contract of employment is terminated by notice, the date on which the notice expires; otherwise, the date on which the termination takes effect (see **6.5**).

Where a dismissed employee exercises a right of internal appeal, there may be a question as to when the time period starts to run. In *Drage v Governors of Greenford High School* [2000] IRLR 314, the employee was dismissed and the decision to dismiss him was upheld following an internal appeal. The Court of Appeal held that the critical question, where there is contractual provision for an internal appeal, is whether during the period between the initial notification of dismissal and the outcome of the appeal the employee stands: (a) dismissed with the possibility of reinstatement (in which case, time starts to run from the date of the initial dismissal); or (b) suspended with the possibility of the proposed dismissal not being confirmed and the suspension thus being ended (in which case, time starts to run from the date when the appeal is rejected). That depends on the construction of the contract and on the circumstances of the dismissal. By contrast, in *Rabess v London Fire and Emergency Planning Authority* [2017] IRLR 147, the employee had been dismissed summarily for gross misconduct; following an internal appeal, the dismissal was changed to a dismissal with notice. The Court of Appeal held that the effective date of termination did not, in the circumstances of the case, change by reason of anything that occurred on the internal appeal, and so the three-month time limit ran from the date when the original summary dismissal took effect.

In *GISDA Cyf v Barratt* [2010] IRLR 1073, the Supreme Court had to decide what is the effective date of termination where an employer notifies an employee by letter that he or she has been summarily dismissed on grounds of a repudiatory breach of contract. The court held that the EDT in such a case is when the employee actually reads the letter of dismissal (or had a reasonable opportunity of reading it). The same approach was applied to a contractual in *Newcastle upon Tyne NHS Foundation Trust v Haywood* [2017] IRLR 629.

The first day of the three-month limitation period is the date of termination itself (*Hammond v Haigh Castle* [1973] IRLR 91; *Pruden v Cunard Ellerman Ltd* [1993] IRLR 317). In *Pruden* it was said that the correct method of determining the last day of the period is to take the day and date of the dismissal and to go forward three calendar months. So, if the date of termination is 14 January, time begins to run on 14 January and expires at midnight on 13 April. If there is no corresponding date in the month at the end of the period, the last day of the month is taken: so if the termination takes place on 31 August, the three-month period ends on 30 November. In *Wang v University of Keele* [2011] IRLR 542 (EAT), the claimant was sent an email on the afternoon or evening of 3 November giving three months' notice of termination. He presented his unfair dismissal claim on 2 May. It was held that the period of notice began on 4 November; the effective date of termination was therefore 3 February, and the statutory limitation period ended on 2 May. A claim is 'presented' when it is delivered to the tribunal (*Hammond v Haigh Castle & Co Ltd* [1973] IRLR 91; *House v Emerson Electric Industrial Controls* [1980] ICR 795). The form may be delivered at any time up to midnight on the last day of the limitation period; it does not have to be delivered during office hours, and it does not have to be put into the hands of a member of the tribunal staff (*Post Office v Moore* [1981] ICR 623). In *Tyne and Wear Autistic Society v Smith* [2005] IRLR 336 (EAT), it was held that an application submitted via the Internet is 'presented' to an employment tribunal when it is successfully submitted online to the Employment Tribunals Service website. Once successful submission has been achieved, the complaint will have been presented even if there are subsequent problems within the computer of the website host, or within the computer of the Employment Tribunal Office, or in communications between the two. Where the three-month time limit has expired, it is open to the claimant to argue that it was not 'reasonably practicable' to present the application in time. The burden of proving that it was not reasonably practicable rests on the claimant. This is a question of fact (*Palmer v Southend-on-Sea Borough Council* [1984] ICR 372).

Applications to extend time are dealt with at a preliminary hearing. In *Wall's Meat v Khan* [1978] IRLR 499 the Court of Appeal held that two questions have to be considered:

- Is the tribunal satisfied that it was not reasonably practicable for the complaint to be presented in time?

- Is the tribunal satisfied that the further period taken before lodging the complaint was a reasonable one?

The court went on to hold that the first question requires the claimant to show a 'just cause or excuse' for not presenting the claim in time or that they were prevented from doing so by some physical or mental impediment.

It must be emphasised that, once the claimant has satisfied the tribunal that it was not reasonably practicable to present the application within the time limit, the claimant then has to show that the application was presented within a reasonable time after the expiry of the time limit (*Westward Circuits Ltd v Read* [1973] ICR 301; *Taylorplan Services Ltd v Jackson* [1996] IRLR 184). In *Thompson v Northumberland County Council* (EAT, 14 September 2007, unreported), it was not disputed that it was not 'reasonably practicable' for the claimant to have presented her claim within the initial three-month period; the issue was whether the delay by the claimant from the end of that three-month period until the date when the claim was presented was 'reasonable'. Silber J said that, although the two tests are different, they both embrace the concept of reasonableness, although the 'reasonably practicable' test has the additional requirement of practicability. Matters of crucial importance in determining the reasonableness aspect (rather than the 'practicable' aspect) of the test of 'reasonably practicable' are likely to be of substantial importance in ascertaining if a claimant has, after the end of the three-month period, launched proceedings 'within such period as the tribunal considers reasonable'. Thus, an employment tribunal should investigate what the employee knew and what knowledge the employee should have had if he or she had acted reasonably in all the circumstances.

Because it is a question of fact whether or not presentation within the time limit was 'reasonably practicable', it is highly unlikely that the EAT will reverse the decision of an employment tribunal to extend, or not to extend, time. See, for example, *Birmingham Midshires Building Society v Horton* [1991] ICR 648 (EAT); *Chief Constable of Lincolnshire Police v Caston* [2009] EWCA Civ 1298, [2010] IRLR 327.

In older case law, the power to extend time was interpreted very restrictively. See, for example, *Dedman v British Building & Engineering Appliances Ltd* [1974] ICR 53 (CA) and *Wall's Meat Co Ltd v Khan* [1979] ICR 52 (CA). However, in *Marks & Spencer plc v Williams-Ryan* [2005] EWCA Civ 470, [2005] IRLR 562, the claimant had been advised by a Citizens Advice Bureau (CAB) that she should exhaust the employers' internal appeal procedure; the time limit had expired before she was told that her appeal had failed. Lord Phillips of Worth Matravers MR (at [20]) said that s 111(2) 'should be given a liberal interpretation in favour of the employee', and went on to say (at [21]) that:

> when deciding whether it was reasonably practicable for an employee to make a complaint to an employment tribunal, regard should be had to what, if anything, the employee knew about the right to complain to the employment tribunal and of the time limit for making such a complaint. Ignorance of either does not necessarily render it not reasonably practicable to bring a complaint in time. It is necessary to consider not merely what the employee knew, but what knowledge the employee should have had had he or she acted reasonably in all the circumstances.

His Lordship went on to say that, although *Dedman* establishes that, where an employee fails to meet the time limit because of a solicitor's negligence, the adviser's fault will defeat any attempt to argue that it was not reasonably practicable to make a timely complaint to an employment tribunal, there is no binding authority which extends that principle to a situation where advice is given by a CAB. The mere fact of seeking advice from the CAB cannot, as a matter of law, rule out the possibility of demonstrating that it was not reasonably practicable to make a timely application to an employment tribunal. It may well depend on who gave the advice and in what circumstances ([32]). In *Northamptonshire County Council v Entwhistle* [2010] IRLR 740, the EAT considered the approach to be taken where a claim is out of time because of the fault of a solicitor. Underhill J said (at [5]) that it is not 'reasonably practicable' for an employee to present a claim within the primary time limit if he or she was, reasonably, in ignorance of that time limit. However, so far as inaccurate legal advice is concerned, his Lordship distinguished between cases where the adviser's failure to give the correct advice is itself reasonable (for example, where the adviser was misled by the employer as to a material matter) and cases where the solicitor's error was negligent. Where a claimant has consulted skilled advisers, the question of reasonable practicability is to be judged by what the claimant could have done if given such advice as the advisers should reasonably have given. It follows that, where the advice was negligent, the solicitor did not give the claimant the advice that should have been given ([11]); in such a case, an extension of time will not be granted (and the claimant will be left to pursue a claim for negligence against the solicitor in order to obtain compensation).

In *Machine Tool Industry Research Association v Simpson* [1988] IRLR 212 (CA), the claimant sought an extension on the ground that information came to her attention after the expiry of the time limit calling into question the veracity of the employer's statement that the dismissal was due to redundancy. Purchas LJ said that 'fundamentally the exercise to be performed is a study of the subjective state of mind of the employee'. His Lordship went on to say that the expression 'reasonably practicable' imports meant that it must be reasonable for the claimant not to be aware, during the currency of the three-month limitation period, of the factual basis upon which a claim could be made to the tribunal; if that is established, it cannot be reasonably practicable to expect a claimant to bring a case based upon facts of which he or she is ignorant. Moreover, the claimant must establish that the knowledge gained has, in the circumstances, been gained reasonably, and that that knowledge is either crucial, fundamental or important to the change of belief from one in which the claimant does not believe that there are grounds for an application, to a belief which is reasonably and genuinely held, that there are grounds for making such an application.

Where the claimant seeks to rely on postal delays, the test is whether or not the claimant could reasonably have expected the claim form to arrive in time, given such factors as the date and place of posting. See *Burton v Field Sons & Co Ltd* [1977] ICR 106 (EAT) and *Beanstalk Shelving Ltd v Horn* [1980] ICR 273 (EAT).

In *Sealy v Consignia plc* [2002] 3 All ER 801, the employee wanted to bring a claim for unfair dismissal. He posted his claim form to the tribunal on Friday 6 October 2000. To be within the three-month time limit, the form should have arrived by Sunday 8 October 2000 but in fact it was not received until Tuesday 10 October. Brooke LJ said (at [31]) that if a claimant sends a claim form by post, it will be assumed, unless the contrary is proved, that the claim was presented at the time when the letter would have been delivered in the ordinary course of post. If the claim is sent by first-class post, it may be concluded that in the ordinary course of post it will be delivered on the second day after it was posted (excluding Sundays and public holidays). If the claim does not arrive at the time when it would be expected to in the ordinary course of post, a tribunal may conclude that it was not reasonably practicable for the claim to be presented within the prescribed period. If a form is date-stamped on a Monday by a tribunal office so as to be outside a three-month period which ends on the Saturday or Sunday, a tribunal may find as a fact that it was posted by first-class post not later than the Thursday and arrived on the Saturday, or alternatively to extend time as a matter of discretion if satisfied that the letter was posted by first-class post not later than the Thursday. In *Initial Electronic Security Systems Ltd v Avdic* [2005] IRLR 671 the claimant attempted to email her claim form to the employment tribunal at 4 pm on the day when the time limit was due to expire. The transmission was not received. Had the transmission been successful, her claim would have been presented in time. The EAT held that the employment tribunal had not erred in holding that it was not reasonably practicable for the claimant to present her unfair dismissal application in time, since she had attempted to email her claim form to the employment tribunal in time and had no reason to suspect or believe that the transmission had not been successful. Burton J held that the reasonable expectation of the sender of an email communication is that, in the absence of any indication to the contrary, it will be delivered and will arrive within a very short time after transmission, normally no more than 30 or 60 minutes.

In *Schultz v Esso Petroleum* [1999] 3 All ER 338, the Court of Appeal held that in assessing whether or not it was reasonably practicable to present the claim form within the three-month period in a case where a claimant was hoping to avoid litigation by pursuing alternative remedies, it is necessary, while looking at the period as a whole, to focus upon the closing stages rather than the early stages of the three months. It follows that a period of disabling illness should not be given similar weight, irrespective of when it occurred within the three months. The tribunal's approach should vary according to whether the period of illness fell in the earlier weeks or in the more critical later weeks leading up to the expiry of the three months. In the present case, the tribunal had not done that and so it had misdirected itself on the approach to be taken to the question of reasonable practicability.

In *Marley (UK) Ltd v Anderson* [1996] IRLR 163, the claimant presented his claim form out of time and then sought to amend it to add another ground. The Court of Appeal held that even though the first complaint was out of time, and there were no reasons for extending the time limit, the second ground should be considered separately. The fact that the claimant was precluded by lapse of time from pursuing one claim out of time therefore did not prevent him proceeding with the second complaint about the same dismissal on different grounds brought within a reasonable period of the discovery of those fresh grounds.

In *Gillick v BP Chemicals Ltd* [1993] IRLR 437, it was held by the EAT that where the claim form was lodged within the time limit, a new respondent may be added (as well as or instead of the original respondent) even if the time limit has since expired.

4.2.2 Redundancy

The claim must be presented to the employment tribunal within six months of the 'relevant date' (which is defined by ERA 1996, s 145, in the same way as the 'effective date of termination') unless it appears to the tribunal that it is 'just and equitable that the employee should receive a redundancy payment' having regard to the reason for the delay and all other relevant circumstances. However, the tribunal only has jurisdiction to extend time if the claimant presents the claim during the period of six months immediately following the first six-month period. See ERA 1996, s 164.

4.2.3 Discrimination claims

Claims relating to unlawful discrimination brought pursuant to the Equality Act 2010, s 120, cannot be brought after the end of the period of three months starting with the date of the act to which the complaint relates (s 123(1)(a)). Again, time may be extended where it is 'just and equitable' to do so (s 123(1)(b)). *Robertson v Bexley Community Centre* [2003] EWCA Civ 576, [2003] IRLR 434 involved an application to extend time for commencing a claim of racial discrimination. Auld LJ (at [33]) said that an employment tribunal has a very wide discretion in determining whether or not it is 'just and equitable' to extend time. The tribunal is entitled to consider anything that it thinks relevant. However, his Lordship emphasised (at [25]) that time limits are exercised strictly in employment cases. There is no presumption that the tribunal should hear a claim out of time; on the contrary, a tribunal cannot hear a complaint unless the claimant convinces it that it is just and equitable to extend time. The exercise of discretion is thus the exception rather than the rule. Accordingly, an appeal against a tribunal's refusal to consider an application out of time in the exercise of its discretion should only succeed where the EAT can identify an error of law or principle making the decision of the tribunal plainly wrong. In *Chohan v Derby Law Centre* [2004] IRLR 685, it was held by the EAT that, in a discrimination case, wrong advice by a legal adviser (giving a potential claim for negligence against the solicitor) should be regarded as a valid excuse for a late claim, since it would be 'just and equitable' to hear the case out of time.

In *Rathakrishnan v Pizza Express (Restaurants) Ltd* [2016] IRLR 278, the EAT held (at [14]) that the exercise of the wide discretion to extend time 'involves a multi-factorial approach. No single factor is determinative.' It follows that a failure to provide a good excuse for the delay in bringing the claim will not *inevitably* result in an extension of time being refused (although it will be a relevant factor).

4.2.4   Protection of wages

A complaint about an unlawful deduction of wages under Part II, ERA 1996 must be made within three months of the latest payment of wages from which the deduction has been made, unless it is not reasonably practicable to present the complaint within that time (s 23(2) and (4)). Thus the provision is identical to that which governs unfair dismissal complaints. See also the Employment Tribunals Extension of Jurisdiction (England and Wales) Order 1994 (SI 1994/1623) (ETEJO 1994), which deals with breach of contract cases brought under the Employment Tribunals Act 1996 (ETA 1996), ss 3 and 8.

4.3   Responding to the claim

Rule 15 provides that, unless the claim is rejected, the tribunal must send a copy of the claim form, together with a prescribed response form (known as an ET3), to each respondent. Rule 16(1) requires that the response must be on a prescribed form and must be presented to the tribunal office within 28 days of the date that the copy of the claim form was sent by the tribunal. A response form may include the response of more than one respondent if they are responding to a single claim and either they all resist the claim on the same grounds or they do not resist the claim (r 16(2)). A response form may include the response to more than one claim if the claims are based on the same set of facts and either the respondent resists all of the claims on the same grounds or the respondent does not resist the claims (r 16(3)).

Under r 17(1), the tribunal will reject a response if it is not made on a prescribed form or if it does not contain the respondent's full name and address or if it does not state whether the respondent wishes to resist any part of the claim. Rule 18(1) stipulates that a response that is received outside the prescribed time limit must be rejected unless an application for extension has already been made under rule 20 or the response includes or is accompanied by such an application (in which case the response shall not be rejected pending the outcome of the application).

Under r 19(1), a respondent whose response has been rejected may apply for reconsideration of the decision to reject it on the basis that the decision was wrong or that the defect can be rectified. The application for reconsideration must be in writing and must be presented to the tribunal within 14 days of the date that the notice of rejection was sent (r 19(2)). If the respondent does not request a hearing (or if the Employment Judge decides, on considering the application, that the response should be accepted in full), the judge will determine the application without a hearing. Otherwise the application is considered at a hearing attended only by the respondent.

4.3.1   Extensions of time for presenting response

Rule 20(1) enables the respondent to make an application for an extension of time for presenting the response. The application (which is sent to the tribunal and to the claimant) must set out the reason why the extension is sought and, unless the time limit has not yet expired, must be accompanied by a draft of the response which the respondent wishes to present, or an explanation of why that is not possible (r 20(1)). The claimant may oppose the application by giving written notice to that effect, explaining why the application is opposed, within 7 days of receipt of the application (r 20(2)). The application may be determined without a hearing (r 20(3)).

In *Kwiksave Stores v Swain* [1997] ICR 49, the EAT held that, when deciding whether or not to grant an extension of the period for responding to the claim, the tribunal must first consider the respondent's explanation for the failure to comply with the time limit. The longer the delay, the better the explanation has to be. If the tribunal takes the view that the employer has not put forward a reasonable explanation for the delay, the extension should be refused. If the tribunal decides that the employer has put forward a reasonable explanation, it must then balance the prejudice which the respondent would suffer if the extension were to be refused against the prejudice the claimant would suffer if the extension were to be granted. In order to balance the prejudice, the tribunal must take account of the merits of the respondent's case. It follows that the respondent must supply the tribunal with all the factual material necessary to explain the delay and with details of the matters on which the defence would be based.

4.4   Effect of non-presentation or rejection of response

Rule 21 of the Employment Tribunal Rules applies where the time limit for presenting a response has expired but no response has been presented, or where the response has been rejected and no application for reconsideration is outstanding, or where the respondent has stated that no part of the claim is contested. Under r 21(2), an Employment Judge has to decide whether, on the available material (including any further information which the parties are required by a judge to provide), a determination can properly be made of the claim, or part of it. To the extent that a determination can be made, the judge will issue a judgment accordingly. Otherwise, a hearing is fixed before a judge alone (r 21(2)). The respondent is entitled to notice of any hearings and decisions of the tribunal but, unless and until an extension of time is granted, is entitled to participate in any hearing only to the extent permitted by the judge (r 21(3)).

4.5   Initial consideration of the claim

Rule 26(1) of the Employment Tribunal Rules provides that, as soon as possible after the acceptance of the response, an Employment Judge should consider all the documents held by the tribunal in relation to the claim, to confirm whether there are arguable complaints and defences within the jurisdiction of the tribunal (and for that purpose the judge may order a party to provide further information). Unless the claim is dismissed, the judge should make a case management order (unless one has already been made). This may deal with the listing of a preliminary or final hearing, and may propose judicial mediation or other forms of dispute resolution.

4.5.1 Dismissal of claim (or part)

Rule 27(1) provides that, where the Employment Judge considers either that the tribunal has no jurisdiction to consider the claim (or part of it), or that the claim (or part of it) has no reasonable prospect of success, the tribunal must send a notice to the parties setting out the judge's view, and the reasons for it, and ordering that the claim (or the part in question) is to be dismissed on the date specified in the notice unless, before that date, the claimant has presented written representations to the tribunal explaining why the claim (or part) should not be dismissed. If no such representations are received, the claim is dismissed with effect from the specified date; no further order is required to effect the dismissal of the claim (r 27(2)). If representations are received within the specified time, they are considered by an Employment Judge, who will either permit the claim (or part) to proceed, or fix a hearing for the purpose of deciding whether the claim should be permitted to proceed. The respondent may, but is not required to, attend and participate in the hearing (r 27(3)). If any part of the claim is permitted to proceed, the judge will make a case management order (r 27(4)).

4.5.2 Dismissal of response (or part)

Under r 28(1), where an Employment Judge considers that the response to the claim (or part of it) has no reasonable prospect of success, the tribunal will send a notice to the parties setting out the judge's view, and the reasons for it, and ordering that the response (or the part in question) is to be dismissed on the date specified in the notice unless, before that date, the respondent has presented written representations to the tribunal explaining why the response (or part) should not be dismissed. If no such representations are received, the response is dismissed from the specified date without the need for a further order (r 28(2)). If representations are received within the specified time, they will be considered by an Employment Judge, who will either permit the response (or part) to stand, or fix a hearing for the purpose of deciding whether it should be permitted to do so. The claimant may, but need not, attend and participate in the hearing (r 28(3)). If any part of the response is permitted to stand, the judge will make a case management order (r 28(4)). Where the response is dismissed, the effect is as if no response had been presented in the first place (r 28(5)).

4.6 Case management orders

Rule 29 of the Employment Tribunal Rules empowers the tribunal, at any stage of the proceedings, and on its own initiative or on application by a party, to make a 'case management order'. The rule goes on to provide that a case management order 'may vary, suspend or set aside an earlier case management order where that is necessary in the interests of justice, and in particular where a party affected by the earlier order did not have a reasonable opportunity to make representations before it was made'.

Rule 30(1) enables a party to make an application for a particular case management order. The application may be made at a hearing or may be presented in writing to the tribunal. Where a party applies in writing, they must notify the other parties that any objections to the application should be sent to the tribunal as soon as possible (r 30(2)). The tribunal may deal with the application in writing or may order that it be dealt with at a preliminary or final hearing (r 30(3)).

The Employment Tribunal Rules go on to make provision for a number of specific orders related to case management.

4.6.1 Disclosure of documents and information

Rule 31 empowers the tribunal to order 'any person in Great Britain to disclose documents or information to a party (by providing copies or otherwise) or to allow a party to inspect such material as might be ordered by a county court'.

In *British Aerospace v Green* [1995] IRLR 433, the Court of Appeal said that disclosure should be ordered only where the claimant can demonstrate that the document(s) sought is/are relevant to an issue which has already been raised. In that case it was said that where the claimant alleges unfair dismissal in the context of redundancy, documents relating to retained employees will only be relevant in exceptional circumstances. However, in *FDR Ltd v Holloway* [1995] IRLR 400 (EAT), Mummery J adopted a less restrictive approach on the basis that such documents may be relevant to the issue of whether the selection criteria had been applied fairly. Thus, the essential test is one of relevance (*Ministry of Defence v Meredith* [1995] IRLR 539).

In *Birds Eye Walls Ltd v Harrison* [1985] ICR 278 (EAT), it was held that a party who chooses to make voluntary disclosure of any documents in his possession must not be unfairly selective in that disclosure. Waite J said (at p 288):

Once ... a party has disclosed certain documents (whether they appear to him to support his case or for any other reason) it becomes his duty not to withhold from disclosure any further documents in his possession or power (regardless of whether they support his case or not) if there is any risk that the effect of withholding them might be to convey to his opponent or to the tribunal a false or misleading impression as to the true nature, purport or effect of any disclosed document ...

Applications for disclosure and inspection can raise questions of confidentiality. The leading cases on this topic are *Science Research Council v Nasse* and *BL Cars Ltd v Vyas*, reported together at [1980] AC 1028. The House of Lords established that confidentiality alone is not a ground for withholding disclosure/inspection but confidentiality is a matter which the tribunal may take into account. On the other hand, the fact that a document is relevant does not automatically entitle the claimant to see that document, although relevance is an important factor to be taken into account. The House of Lords encouraged the use of pragmatic solutions, such as covering up names or substituting letters of the alphabet for names.

Although relevance does not automatically entitle a party to see confidential material, a party seeking disclosure or inspection must establish a 'prima facie prospect of relevance of the confidential material to an issue which arises in the litigation; put another way, whether it is reasonable to expect that there is any real likelihood of such relevance emerging from the examination' (*British Railways Board v Natarajan* [1979] ICR 326, at p 333, *per* Arnold J). See also *Canadian Imperial Bank of Commerce v Beck* [2009] EWCA Civ 619, at [22] (*per* Wall LJ).

Legal professional privilege may be raised as a reason for not producing certain documents. However, in *New Victoria Hospital v Ryan* [1993] IRLR 202, the EAT emphasised that legal professional privilege should be strictly confined to qualified legal advisers such as solicitors and counsel and does not extend to advice from personnel consultants.

Rule 10(5) provides that an order under r 10(2)(d) which requires a person other than a party to grant disclosure or inspection of material may be made 'only when the disclosure sought is necessary in order to dispose fairly of the claim or to save expense'.

4.6.2 Requirement to attend to give evidence

Under r 32, the tribunal may order any person in Great Britain to attend a hearing to give evidence, produce documents or produce information.

Under the ETA 1996, s 7(4), a fine not exceeding level 3 (currently £1,000) may be imposed following summary conviction for failure without reasonable excuse to comply with a witness order.

The criteria for making a witness order were considered by Sir John Donaldson in *Dada v Metal Box Co Ltd* [1974] ICR 559, at p 563. An order should be made only where the witness is likely to be able to give evidence which is relevant to an issue in dispute in the case (and so the party applying for an order should summarise the evidence which that witness is expected to give and show its relevance). Furthermore, the tribunal should be satisfied that it is necessary to issue a witness order; thus, a witness order should be made only where the witness would not attend if no order were made. An example of such a case would be where the claimant in an unfair dismissal case wishes to call as a witness someone who is still employed by the respondent. For instance, in *Eagle Star Insurance Co v Hayward* [1981] ICR 860, it transpired that another employee had received a final warning for misconduct which was very similar to the misconduct for which the claimant had been dismissed. The EAT upheld the granting of a witness order to secure the attendance of the relevant manager to give evidence regarding the circumstances of the allegations against the other employee. Such an order was necessary since the manager would not otherwise attend and it was relevant to the issue of the fairness of the claimant's dismissal to see whether the employer had been inconsistent in his treatment of the two employees.

In *Clapson v British Airways* [2001] IRLR 184, the EAT held that an employment tribunal has an unrestricted power, of its own motion, to call a witness and require that witness to give evidence to the tribunal, even where the witness is one of the parties. However, a tribunal should be very cautious before deciding to call a witness whom neither of the parties wishes to call, especially where the witness is one of the parties to the case. Ordinarily, where there is a disputed area of fact, or where allegations have been made to witnesses for one party which have not been supported by evidence from the other party, the tribunal should deal with the situation by simply drawing the inevitable adverse inference against the party who has not given evidence.

Where a witness order is obtained by a party, the tribunal must send a copy of that order to all parties (*Jones v Secretary of State for Business Innovation and Skills* (EAT, 29 June 2017)).

4.6.3 Addition, substitution and removal of parties; participation by other persons

Under r 34, the tribunal may (either on its own initiative, or on the application of a party or any other person wishing to become a party) add any person as a party, by way of substitution or otherwise, 'if it appears that there are issues between that person and any of the existing parties falling within the jurisdiction of the Tribunal which it is in the interests of justice to have determined in the proceedings'. The tribunal is also empowered to remove any party apparently wrongly included.

By virtue of r 35, the tribunal may permit any person to participate in proceedings, on such terms as it may specify, in respect of any matter in which that person has a legitimate interest.

4.6.4   Lead cases

Under r 36, where a tribunal considers that two or more claims give rise to 'common or related issues of fact or law', the tribunal (or the President) may make an order specifying one or more of those claims as a 'lead case' and staying the other claims. When the tribunal makes a decision in respect of the common or related issues it sends a copy of its decision to the parties in the related cases, and that decision is binding on those parties (r 36(2)) unless, within 28 days after the date on which the tribunal sent a copy of the decision to a party, that party applies in writing for an order that the decision does not apply to, and is not binding on the parties to, a particular related case (rule 36(3)). If a lead case is withdrawn before the tribunal makes a decision in respect of the common or related issues, the tribunal decides whether another claim should be specified as a lead case, and whether any order affecting the related cases should be set aside or varied (r 36(4)).

4.6.5   Striking out

Rule 37(1) provides that, at any stage of the proceedings (either on its own initiative or on the application of a party), a tribunal may strike out all or part of a claim or response on any of the following grounds:

(a) that it is scandalous or vexatious or has no reasonable prospect of success;

(b) that the manner in which the proceedings have been conducted by or on behalf of the claimant or the respondent (as the case may be) has been scandalous, unreasonable or vexatious;

(c) for non-compliance with any of these Rules or with an order of the tribunal;

(d) that it has not been actively pursued;

(e) that the tribunal considers that it is no longer possible to have a fair hearing in respect of the claim or response (or the part to be struck out).

However, by virtue of r 37(2), a claim or response cannot be struck out unless the party in question has been given a reasonable opportunity to make representations, either in writing or (if the party so requests) at a hearing.

Where a response is struck out, the effect is as if no response had been presented in the first place (r 37(3)).

4.6.5.1   Striking out where claim vexatious or has no reasonable prospect of success

In *Department of Education & Science v Taylor* [1992] IRLR 308 (QBD), Auld J ruled that the burden of proof lies on the party seeking to strike out the other party's case to show that it is a clear case for the exercise of the tribunal's discretionary power to do so.

In *Dolby v HM Prison Service* [2003] IRLR 694, the EAT said that an employment tribunal has four options where a case is regarded as one which has no reasonable prospect of success: it may strike out the application if it is convinced that that is the proper remedy in the particular case; it may order an amendment to be made to the claim; it may order a deposit to be paid (see **4.6.7**); or it may decide at the end of the case that the claim was misconceived and that the claimant should pay costs. The EAT said that the tribunal must adopt a two-stage approach: first, to decide whether the application is misconceived and, secondly, if so, to decide whether as a matter of discretion to order the application to be struck out, amended or, if there is an application, that a pre-hearing deposit should be ordered.

In *Ezsias v North Glamorgan NHS Trust* [2007] EWCA Civ 330, [2007] IRLR 603, Maurice Kay LJ (at [29]), said that it would 'only be in an exceptional case that an application to an employment tribunal will be struck out as having no reasonable prospect of success when the central facts are in dispute. An example might be where the facts sought to be established by the claimant were totally and inexplicably inconsistent with the undisputed contemporaneous documentation.' It is submitted that the strike out option will generally be appropriate only in cases where the Employment Judge or tribunal is satisfied that there is no need to consider the evidence, or where there is no conflict of evidence.

It is not an abuse of process for a claimant to bring (or continue) a claim for unfair dismissal even if the employer has offered to pay the maximum compensation which the tribunal could order (*Telephone Information Services v Wilkinson* [1991] IRLR 148; *NRG Victory Reinsurance Ltd v Alexander* [1992] ICR 675), since the claimant is entitled to seek a finding of unfair dismissal. It would seem to follow that it would be an abuse of process to pursue a claim for unfair dismissal if the employer has paid (or offered to pay) the maximum statutory compensation and has made an admission that the employee was unfairly dismissed.

The EAT gave further guidance on the criteria for dealing with strike out applications in *Balls v Downham Market High School & College* [2011] IRLR 217, where the claim had been struck out on the ground that it had no reasonable prospect of success. Lady Smith said (at [6]):

Where strike out is sought or contemplated on the ground that the claim has no reasonable prospects of success ... the tribunal must first consider whether, on a careful consideration of all the available material, it can properly conclude that the claim has no reasonable prospects of success. I stress the word 'no' because it shows that the test is not whether the claimant's claim is likely to fail nor is it a matter of asking whether it is possible that his claim will fail. Nor is it a test which can be satisfied by considering what is put forward by the respondent either in the ET3 or in submissions and deciding whether their written or oral assertions regarding disputed matters are likely to be established as facts. It is, in short, a high test. There must be no reasonable prospects.

In *Tayside Public Transport Company Ltd v Reilly* [2012] IRLR 755, a Scottish case, it was held (at [30]) that:

where the central facts are in dispute, a claim should be struck out only in the most exceptional circumstances ... There may be cases where it is instantly demonstrable that the central facts in the claim are untrue ... But in the normal case where there is a 'crucial core of disputed facts', it is an error of law for the Tribunal to pre-empt the determination of a full hearing by striking out.

Examples of cases where it might be appropriate to exercise the strike out power include:

- cases in which the facts have already been litigated and the claimant has no fresh or different evidence but insists on pursuing the case;
- cases where the facts are not in dispute, but the interpretation placed on those facts by one party is clearly wrong;
- cases in which a party's application is not itself sufficient to lead to a successful outcome for him, and the party has stated at the pre-hearing review that no further evidence or witnesses would be called.

4.6.5.2   Striking out for misconduct in the proceedings

Rule 37 also confers the power to strike out if a party conducts their case in a manner which is 'scandalous, unreasonable or vexatious'. The main use of this power is to dismiss the case of a party who behaves disruptively during the hearing. Before striking out, the tribunal must consider whether striking out is a proportionate response to the conduct complained of, and whether a fair trial is possible despite that conduct (*Ogunleye v Greater Manchester Probation Committee* (EAT, 2 September 2002, unreported)). In *Bolch v Chipman* [2004] IRLR 140 (EAT), Burton P (at [55]) said that there must be a conclusion by the tribunal that the proceedings have been conducted unreasonably by or on behalf of the party in question, and also that a fair trial is not possible (since, save in exceptional circumstances, a striking out order is not regarded simply as a punishment). If the tribunal concludes that a fair trial is not possible, there still remains the question of what remedy is appropriate and proportionate. For example, a tribunal might (exercising its case management powers) debar a respondent from taking any further part on the question of liability but permit him to take part on the question of compensation.

In *Blockbuster Entertainment Ltd v James* [2006] EWCA Civ 684, [2006] IRLR 630, Sedley LJ (at [5]) observed that the power to strike out a claim under r 18(7) is a draconic power, not to be exercised readily. 'It comes into being if … a party has been conducting its side of the proceedings unreasonably. The two cardinal conditions for its exercise are either that the unreasonable conduct has taken the form of deliberate and persistent disregard of required procedural steps, or that it has made a fair trial impossible.' If either of these conditions is fulfilled, 'it becomes necessary to consider whether, even so, striking out is a proportionate response'. His Lordship added (at [21]) that the tribunal has to consider 'whether there is a less drastic means to the end for which the strike-out power exists'. The answer has to take into account whether the tribunal is ready to try the claims or whether there is still time in which orderly preparation can be made. If a straightforward refusal to admit late material or applications will enable the hearing to go ahead, or if they can be accommodated without unfairness, it can only be in a wholly exceptional case that a history of unreasonable conduct which has not until that point caused the claim to be struck out will now justify its summary termination.

4.6.5.3   Striking out for non-compliance with the Rules or a tribunal order

In *Abegaze v Shrewsbury College of Arts & Technology* [2009] EWCA Civ 96, [2010] IRLR 238, the Court of Appeal said that, before making an order striking out a claim, the judge should consider a lesser measure, such as an 'unless' order first.

In *National Grid Co Ltd v Virdee* [1992] IRLR 555, the EAT held (in a case involving failure to comply with an order for disclosure of documents) that the claim form or response should be struck out only if, as a result of the failure to comply with the tribunal's order, a fair trial of the case is no longer possible.

In *Eclipse (UK) Ltd v Cornwall*, 26 March 1997, unreported, the EAT overturned the decision of a tribunal to strike out the response for failure to comply with an order for disclosure of documents. The EAT held that since the order for disclosure related to documents relevant to only two of the issues raised by the case, the employer should have been debarred from defending only those issues. Furthermore, the employer should have been given a final chance to comply with the order. A costs penalty may also be incurred. For example, in *Thomas v R C Frame Erectors Ltd*, The Times, 7 August 1991 (EAT), a third party had to be served with a witness order because he was in possession of documents which the respondent had been ordered to disclose to the claimant but the respondent refused to permit the third party to disclose them to the claimant. The increased costs caused by the need to seek an order against the third party should be borne by the respondent, said the EAT.

In *Harris v Academies Enterprise Trust* [2015] IRLR 208, Langstaff J noted (at [33]) that the Civil Procedure Rules require that cases must be dealt with 'justly and at proportionate cost' (r 1.1(1)), whereas the Employment Tribunal Rules require that cases must be dealt with 'fairly and justly'. It would therefore 'be a mistake to suggest that the CPR applied in the Tribunals in the same way as they apply in the civil courts'. His Lordship went on to say that tribunals should exercise their case management powers to ensure that the case is heard promptly, and that evidence is kept within reasonable bounds (including the exclusion of evidence that is of only marginal relevance), but that this falls short of a requirement that employment tribunals should take the same approach as the civil courts (set out in *Mitchell v News Group Newspapers Ltd* [2013] EWCA Civ 1537, [2014] 1 WLR 795 and subsequent case law). It follows that an Employment Judge 'is not required as a matter of law in the Employment Tribunal to deal with a claim as if the CPR applied when they do not' (at [39]).

4.6.5.4   Striking out where claim not actively pursued

This power is rarely invoked, as the timetable for the conduct of the proceedings is largely governed by the tribunal itself. In *Rolls Royce plc v Riddle* [2008] IRLR 873 (EAT), Lady Smith (at [19] and [20]) said that cases of failure to actively pursue a claim will fall into one of two categories: (a) where there has been 'intentional and contumelious' default by the claimant (the question then arises whether, given such conduct, it is just to allow the claimant to continue to have access to the tribunal for his claim); and (b) where there has been 'inordinate and inexcusable delay such as to give rise to a substantial risk that a fair trial would not be possible or there would be serious prejudice to the respondent' (the question then arises as to whether or not there can still be a fair trial and, if there is doubt about that, whether the claim should then be prevented from going any further).

4.6.6   Unless orders

Under r 38(1), an order made by a tribunal may specify that, if it is not complied with by the date specified, the claim or response (as the case may be, or part of the claim or response), shall be dismissed without further order. A party whose claim or response has been dismissed (in whole or in part) as a result of such an order may apply to the tribunal in writing, within 14 days of the date when notice of the decision was sent, to have the order set aside on the basis that it is in the interests of justice to do so. Unless the application includes a request for a hearing, the tribunal may determine it on the basis of written representations. In *Mace v Ponders End International Ltd* [2014] IRLR 697, the EAT emphasised the importance of ensuring that such orders identify with clarity what is required for compliance (bearing in mind, for example, that unrepresented parties may misunderstand legal terminology).

4.6.7   Deposit orders

Rule 39(1) provides that if the tribunal, at a preliminary hearing (under r 53) considers that any specific allegation or argument in a claim or response has 'little reasonable prospect of success', it may make an order requiring a party (known as 'the paying party') to pay a deposit not exceeding £1,000 as a condition of continuing to advance that allegation or argument. When deciding the amount of the deposit the tribunal must have regard to the paying party's ability to pay the deposit (r 39(2)). If the paying party fails to pay the deposit by the date specified, the specific allegation or argument to which the deposit order relates is struck out (r 39(4)).

Rule 39(5) stipulates that, if the tribunal at any stage following the making of a deposit order decides the specific allegation or argument against the paying party for 'substantially' the reasons given in the deposit order, the paying party is, unless the contrary is shown, to be treated as having acted unreasonably in pursuing that specific allegation or argument (for the purpose of r 76), the deposit is be paid to the other party or parties; otherwise the deposit is refunded. Where a costs or preparation time order is made against the paying party in favour of the party who received the deposit, the amount of the deposit counts towards the settlement of that order (r 39(6)).

In *Hemdan v Ishmail* [2017] IRLR 228, Simler J observed (at [10]) that 'the purpose of a deposit order is to identify at an early stage claims with little prospect of success and to discourage the pursuit of those claims by requiring a sum to be paid and by creating a risk of costs ultimately if the claim fails', adding (at [12]) that the test to be applied is 'less rigorous' than the test for striking out. Significantly, her Ladyship went on to say (at [15]) that, once a tribunal concludes that a claim or allegation has little reasonable prospect of success, 'the making of a deposit order is a matter of discretion and does not follow automatically'. The means of the paying party must be taken into account. Simler J (at [16]), said that, 'it is essential that when such an order is deemed appropriate it does not operate to restrict disproportionately the fair trial rights of the paying party or to impair access to justice'. It follows that an order to pay a deposit must 'be one that is capable of being complied with ... If a deposit order is set at a level at which the paying party cannot afford to pay it, the order will operate to impair access to justice' ([17]).

4.6.8   Additional case management orders that might be made

Rule 29 makes it clear that the powers identified in the case management section of the Rules 'do not restrict [the] general power' to make case management orders. Thus, a tribunal can make a case management order even if there is no specific power to make that particular order in the Employment Tribunal Rules. Examples of orders which a tribunal might make (based on powers contained in a previous version of the Employment Tribunal Rules) include those discussed in **4.6.8.1–4.6.8.3.**

4.6.8.1   Provision of additional information

A tribunal might order a party to provide further information about the case they are putting forward. In *Byrne v Financial Times* [1991] IRLR 417, the EAT set out some general principles applicable to the making of orders for further particulars: the other party should not be taken by surprise at the last minute; particulars should only be ordered when necessary in the interests of justice or to prevent an adjournment; the order should not be oppressive; particulars are for the purpose of identifying issues in the case and not for the purpose of producing evidence; complicated 'pleadings battles' should not be encouraged. It follows that the purpose of a request for further particulars must be to enable a party to elicit sufficient information about the allegations made by the other side, in order to know what case will have to be met at the hearing. So, for example, if the response alleges that the reason for dismissal was that the claimant was not performing their duties satisfactorily, the employer will have to provide details of the way in which the employee's performance fell short.

In *White v University of Manchester* [1976] ICR 419, the EAT warned against the refusal of requests for further particulars where the refusal would have the effect of forcing the affected party to seek an adjournment of the case, thus bringing about delay and increasing costs.

A request for particulars should not be used simply to find out what witnesses the other side will be calling. However, where the identity of a person is relevant to an issue in the case, particulars may be sought of that person's identity. If, for example, the claimant says that the dismissal was unfair because someone else was guilty of the same misconduct as that alleged against the claimant but was not dismissed, the employer is entitled to know the identity of the employee to whom the claimant is referring (for example, *P&O European Ferries (Dover) Ltd v Byrne* [1989] IRLR 254).

Further particulars of any loss claimed by the claimant will not usually be ordered until there has been a finding of unfair dismissal (see *Colonial Mutual Life Assurance v Clinch* [1981] ICR 752).

4.6.8.2 Postponements

Rule 30A makes provisions for postponement of hearings. A party seeking a postponement must apply to the tribunal 'as soon as possible after the need for a postponement becomes known' (r 30A(1)). For these purposes, postponement of a hearing includes any adjournment which causes the hearing to be held or continued on a later date (r 30A(4)).

Postponement may be appropriate, for example, if court proceedings are pending in respect of a matter closely connected with employment tribunal proceedings (for example, *JMCC Holdings Ltd v Conroy* [1990] ICR 179 (EAT)). Where the postponement is sought on the basis that proceedings are pending elsewhere, the correct approach is to ask in which forum the action is most conveniently and appropriately to be tried, bearing in mind all the surrounding circumstances, including the complexity of the issues, the amount involved, the technicality of the evidence and the appropriateness of the procedures (see, for example, *Bowater plc v Charlwood* [1991] IRLR 340 (EAT)).

In *Teinaz v Wandsworth LBC* [2002] EWCA Civ 1040, [2002] IRLR 721, Peter Gibson LJ (at [21]) said that:

A litigant whose presence is needed for the fair trial of a case, but who is unable to be present through no fault of his own, will usually have to be granted an adjournment, however inconvenient it may be to the tribunal or court and to the other parties. That litigant's right to a fair trial under article 6 of the European Convention on Human Rights demands nothing less. But the tribunal or court is entitled to be satisfied that the inability of the litigant to be present is genuine, and the onus is on the applicant for an adjournment to prove the need for such an adjournment.

His Lordship went on to say (at [22]) that, where there is some evidence that a litigant is unfit to attend but the tribunal has doubts about the genuineness or the sufficiency of that medical evidence, it has a discretion to direct that further evidence be called or that the legal representatives (if any) of the other party be permitted to obtain evidence from the doctor.

Under r 30A, where an application for a postponement is made less than seven days before the date on which the hearing is due to begin, or where a tribunal has ordered two or more postponements of a hearing in the same proceedings on the application of the same party and that party makes an application for a further postponement, a postponement (or, as the case may be, further postponement) may be permitted in only three circumstances: (a) all other parties consent to the postponement, and either it is practicable and appropriate for the purposes of giving the parties the opportunity to resolve their disputes by agreement, or else it is otherwise in accordance with the overriding objective; (b) the application was necessitated by an act or omission of another party or the tribunal itself; or (c) there are exceptional circumstances.

4.6.8.3   Amendment of claim or response

It is open to a tribunal to allow amendment of the ET1 or ET3. So, for example, a claim for a redundancy payment can be amended to include a claim for unfair dismissal, provided that the time limit for presenting an unfair dismissal claim has not expired. If the time limit for the presentation of the second claim has expired at the date of the application to amend, the application should be regarded as one to commence proceedings out of time.

Where the amendment is sought at a late stage (for example, during the hearing of an unfair dismissal claim the respondent asserts a different reason for dismissal to that originally given) the amendment should not be allowed unless 'it can genuinely be said that the amendment is no more than for the purpose of giving an appropriate label to a fully established set of facts' (*per* Phillips J in *Blue Star Ship Management v Williams* [1978] ICR 770, at p 776).

If the respondent wishes the tribunal to consider not only whether the dismissal was for one reason, for example, redundancy, but also to go on to consider (if they decide that the reason given was not the reason) whether it was for a different reason, for example, for 'some other substantial reason', both reasons must be pleaded. Where the respondent initially puts the case on one footing in the response and then, during the hearing, wants the tribunal to consider the case on an alternative footing, it will be necessary to amend the response. In such a case, both sides must be given a full opportunity to present evidence and argument on the issue which has been added (*Murphy v Epsom College* [1985] ICR 80; *Burkett v Pendletons (Sweets) Ltd* [1992] ICR 407).

In *Harvey v Port of Tilbury London Ltd* [1999] IRLR 693, the claimant lodged his claim form in February 1997, claiming that he had been unfairly dismissed in December 1996. He made no mention of the fact that he suffered from a back problem. In April 1997 he saw the employer's response which alleged that his back problem made him incapable of work. In September 1997 he sought to amend the claim form to include a claim under the Disability Discrimination Act 1995 (DDA 1995). The question was whether this additional claim was out of time and, if it was, whether it was 'just and equitable' to extend time. It was held that if the claimant had been seeking to add a complaint relating to his disability to the reasons as to why his dismissal had been unfair, that amendment would have been allowed. However, he was seeking relief under the DDA 1995, and that constituted a freestanding claim. Where the statutory three-month time limit has expired and it is not just and equitable to extend time, then a complaint presented as an amendment is totally barred in the same way that it would be if it had been presented as a new application. However, the fact that there are existing proceedings can be taken into consideration in deciding whether it is just and equitable to extend time. In the present case, the amendment would have added a wholly new cause of action for direct discrimination; and it was possible that a claim for direct discrimination could succeed where a claim for unfair dismissal would fail. The Employment Judge had properly balanced the injustice and hardship suffered by refusing the application with the injustice and hardship of granting it, and so had not erred in law in the exercise of his discretion.

The power to allow the amendment of a claim form or response will normally be exercised by an Employment Judge alone prior to the substantive hearing (unless, of course, the need for amendment arises in the course of the hearing).

In *Selkent Bus Co Ltd t/a Stagecoach Selkent v Moore* [1996] IRLR 661, the EAT held that the Employment Judge is not obliged to seek or consider written or oral representations before deciding whether or not to allow the amendment sought. However, the application must be decided in a judicial manner. Where the application is obviously hopeless, leave to amend can be refused without seeking or considering representations from the other party. Where the application is not obviously hopeless, it is open to the Employment Judge to seek representations from the other party and to make a decision on the question of amendment after hearing both sides. Where the Employment Judge takes the view that the proposed amendment is not sufficiently serious or controversial to justify seeking representations, he may allow the amendment without seeking representations; the other side can then seek to have the order rescinded or varied.

The EAT in *Selkent* went on to consider the approach to be taken to the application for leave to amend the claim form. The Employment Judge must balance the injustice and hardship of allowing the amendment against the injustice and hardship of refusing the amendment. Relevant factors include: is the amendment sought a minor one (for example, correcting a clerical error, or adding factual details to existing allegations, or adding or substituting a different 'label' for facts which have already been pleaded) or is it a substantial one, making entirely new factual allegations which change the basis of the existing claim? If the amendment sought adds a new cause of action, the tribunal must consider whether that new cause of action is out of time (and, if so, whether the time limit ought to be extended). The Rules do not lay down any time limits for the making of applications to amend; an application should not be refused solely because there has been delay in making it. However, the reason for the delay is a relevant consideration, especially where the application is made close to the hearing date and where the amendment seeks to add facts which were known to the claimant when the claim form was presented.

So, in *Selkent*, the application for leave to amend was refused. The amendment involved the pleading of a new cause of action (unfair dismissal for trade union reasons) and fresh primary facts would have to be established to support that cause of action. There was no explanation as to why those facts, of which the claimant must have been aware at the time of the application, were not pleaded in the claim form. Furthermore, no hardship was caused by the refusal of the application, since the claimant still had his original claim for unfair dismissal.

4.6.9 Non-compliance with the Rules or tribunal orders

Rule 6 provides that failure to comply with any provision of the Employment Tribunal Rules (except those relating to the requirement to present or respond to a claim) or with any order of the tribunal (except unless orders and deposit orders) 'does not of itself render void the proceedings or any step taken in the proceedings'. In the case of such non-compliance, the tribunal 'may take such action as it considers just, which may include all or any of the following':

(a) waiving or varying the requirement;

(b) striking out the claim or the response (in whole or in part);

(c) barring or restricting a party's participation in the proceedings;

(d) awarding costs.

4.7   Preliminary hearings

Rule 53 makes provision for preliminary hearings. Under r 53(1), at a preliminary hearing the tribunal may do one or more of the following:

(a) conduct a preliminary consideration of the claim with the parties and make a case management order (including an order relating to the conduct of the final hearing);

(b) determine any preliminary issue (defined in r 53(3) as any substantive issue which may determine liability, for example, an issue as to jurisdiction or as to whether an employee was dismissed);

(c) consider whether a claim or response, or any part, should be struck out;

(d) make a deposit order;

(e) explore the possibility of settlement or alternative dispute resolution (including judicial mediation).

Rule 53(2) makes it clear that there may be more than one preliminary hearing in any case.

A preliminary hearing may be directed by the tribunal on its own initiative following its initial consideration (under r 26) or at any time thereafter, or as the result of an application by a party. Where the hearing involves consideration of any preliminary issues, the parties should be given at least 14 days' notice of the hearing; otherwise, they must be given 'reasonable' notice (r 54).

Preliminary hearings are normally conducted by an Employment Judge sitting alone, However, where notice has been given that any preliminary issues are (or may be) decided at the hearing, a party may request that the hearing be conducted by a full tribunal, in which case an Employment Judge decides whether that would be desirable (r 55).

Preliminary hearings are conducted in private, except that where the hearing involves a determination of any preliminary issue or consideration of whether a claim or response should be struck out, in which case any part of the hearing relating to such a determination is usually held in public, and the tribunal may in such a case direct that the entire hearing should take place in public (r 56).

By virtue of r 48, a tribunal conducting a preliminary hearing may order that it be treated as a final hearing (or vice versa), if the tribunal is properly constituted for the purpose and if it is satisfied that neither party will be materially prejudiced by the change.

4.8   Conciliation

Section 18A of the ETA 1996 (as amended by the Enterprise and Regulatory Reform Act 2013) provides that, in the case of employment tribunal proceedings specified in s 18 (including, for example, unfair dismissal proceedings under s 111 of the Employment Rights Act 1996, claims in respect of redundancy payments under s 163 of the 1996 Act and discrimination claims under s 120 or s 127 of the Equality Act 2010), a prospective claimant must first have submitted the details of his or her claim to ACAS before presenting a claim to an employment tribunal. Under s 18A(3), an ACAS conciliation officer must, within a prescribed period, 'endeavour to promote a settlement between the persons who would be parties to the proceedings' (that is, a settlement that avoids proceedings being instituted: subs (6)). The prescribed period is one calendar month from the date when ACAS received the request to conciliate: r 6(1) of the Early Conciliation Rules of Procedure, in the schedule to the Employment Tribunals (Early Conciliation: Exemptions and Rules of Procedure) Regulations 2014 (SI 2014/254). Under r 6(2), the period for early conciliation may be extended by a conciliation officer, provided that the prospective claimant and prospective respondent consent to the extension and the conciliation officer considers that there is a reasonable prospect of achieving a settlement before the expiry of the extended period.

Section 18A(4) provides that, if during the prescribed period, the conciliation officer concludes that a settlement is not possible, or if the period expires without a settlement having been reached, the conciliation officer must issue a certificate to the prospective claimant. A claimant is not permitted to present a claim to an employment tribunal without such a certificate (s 18A(8)). However, the conciliation officer may continue to endeavour to promote a settlement after the expiry of the prescribed period (s 18A(5)). Section 18A(9) provides that, if the prospective claimant is no longer employed by the employer, the conciliation officer may attempt to promote either the claimant's reinstatement or re-engagement or, if the claimant does not wish to be reinstated or re-engaged, or it is not practicable to do so, seek to promote agreement between the parties as to a sum by way of compensation to be paid by the employer to the prospective claimant. Section 19A makes provision for the enforcements of compensation agreed in settlements reached in this way.

In *Science Warehouse Ltd v Mills* [2016] IRLR 96, the EAT held that, where a claimant seeks to amend an existing claim by adding a new claim, it is not necessary to undergo the ACAS early conciliation process again in respect of this new cause of action.

Section 18B places an additional duty on ACAS to promote settlement in certain cases in which the duty under s 18A does not apply.

If the conciliation officer manages to bring about a settlement, any further tribunal proceedings on that matter are barred under ERA 1996, s 203(2)(e).

In *Clarke v Redcar & Cleveland Borough Council* [2006] IRLR 324, the EAT accepted the following principles relating to settlement of tribunal cases with the assistance of a conciliation officer: (a) the ACAS officer has no responsibility to see that the terms of the settlement are fair on the employee; (b) the ACAS officer must never advise as to the merits of the case; (c) it is not for the tribunal to consider whether the officer correctly interpreted his duties; it is sufficient that the officer intended and purported to act under his statutory power; (d) if the ACAS officer were to act in bad faith or adopt unfair methods when promoting a settlement, the agreement might be set aside and might not operate as a bar to proceedings (*per* HHJ McMullen, QC, at [36]).

4.9   The hearing

By virtue of r 58 of the Employment Tribunal Rules, the tribunal must give the parties not less than 14 days' notice of the date of the final hearing (i.e. the hearing at which the tribunal determines the claim, or such parts as remain outstanding following the initial consideration (under r 26) or any preliminary hearing: r 57).

Rule 59 stipulates that (subject to the power conferred by r 50 and subject to an exception related to national security), the final hearing must be in public.

Rule 42 requires the tribunal to consider any written representations from a party, including a party who does not propose to attend the hearing, if they are delivered to the tribunal and to all other parties not less than 7 days before the hearing.

Rule 43 provides that, where a witness is called to give oral evidence, any witness statement of that person ordered by the tribunal is to stand as that witness's evidence in chief unless the tribunal orders otherwise. The rule goes on to stipulate that witnesses must be required to give their oral evidence on oath or affirmation. Rule 43 also empowers the tribunal, if it considers it in the interests of justice to do so, to exclude from the hearing any person who is to appear as a witness in the proceedings until such time as that person gives evidence.

By virtue of r 44, any witness statement which stands as evidence in chief is to be available for inspection during the course of the hearing by members of the public attending the hearing unless the tribunal decides that all or any part of the statement is not to be admitted as evidence, in which case the statement or that part is not be available for inspection.

Normally, where an order on witness statements is made, a tribunal will order that there should be simultaneous exchange of the witness statements of all the witnesses the parties intend to call and that no witness whose statement has not been exchanged can be called at the hearing without leave of the tribunal (see *Eurobell (Holdings) plc v Barker* [1998] ICR 299). However, in *Badii v Bournemouth University* (18 December 1996, unreported) the EAT said that there is nothing wrong with the tribunal ordering sequential (instead of simultaneous) exchange of witness statements if that would assist to clarify the issues in the case. This approach was followed in *Thomson v Panasonic Business Systems (Sales) Ltd* (EAT, 4 October 1999, unreported).

Where the tribunal allows a witness statement to stand as examination-in-chief, the witness will simply be cross-examined on the contents of that statement. This enables employment tribunals to adopt a procedure similar to that in the High Court and the County Court. Guidance on when witness statements should, and should not, be read out at a tribunal hearing was given by the EAT in *Mehta v Child Support Agency* [2011] IRLR 305. At [16], Underhill J said:

(1) We do not believe that it is a requirement of fairness in every case that the statements of every witness be read aloud in full, or indeed at all. In very many cases the process of reading aloud a document which the tribunal can more efficiently and more effectively read out of court achieves nothing of value and is contrary to the overriding objective inasmuch as it wastes the time of the tribunal and the parties ...

(2) On the other hand, there may in particular cases and circumstances be good reason for a witness statement, perhaps particularly of a claimant and even more particularly of an unrepresented claimant, being read aloud either in whole or in part ... Another legitimate consideration is that it can be unfair to a witness to be exposed to hostile cross-examination without some opportunity to settle themselves by answering some friendly or at least neutral questions. None of these considerations, we emphasise, necessarily means that any part of a witness statement must be read aloud: they are simply matters to be taken into account.

(3) We emphasise that it need not be all or nothing. It may make sense for only part of a statement to be read aloud or for a witness to be 'walked through' his or her statement by counsel, summarising parts and pausing for the key points to be read out and/or elucidated or amplified (eg to deal with queries raised at an earlier stage in the hearing). Sometimes where a lawyer-drafted witness statement covers a factual episode of particular importance, a tribunal

> may wish to hear the witness give the evidence of that episode in chief in his or her own
> words ...
>
> (4) Deciding what course to take in any particular case must be a matter for the tribunal in the exercise
> of its case management powers, whether exercised by an employment judge at a case management
> discussion or subsequently at the hearing ...

Rule 45 is an important provision because it enables the tribunal to control the way in which the parties conduct their cases. It provides:

> A Tribunal may impose limits on the time that a party may take in presenting evidence, questioning witnesses or making submissions, and may prevent the party from proceeding beyond any time so allotted.

Where proceedings are determined by a full tribunal, it will consist of a legally qualified Employment Judge (a barrister or solicitor of at least seven years' standing) together with two lay members. One of the lay members is drawn from a panel consisting of representatives of employers; the other is drawn from a panel representing employees (reg 9).

4.9.1   Employment Judge sitting alone

In those cases falling within the ETA 1996, s 4(3), the tribunal comprises a legally qualified Employment Judge sitting alone unless the Employment Judge takes the view that this would be inappropriate. In deciding that question, the Employment Judge has to have regard to the factors listed in s 4(5). These include whether there is a likelihood of a dispute arising on the facts which makes it desirable for the proceedings to be heard by a full tribunal, and any views of any of the parties as to whether or not the proceedings ought to be heard by an Employment Judge alone or by a full tribunal.

Under the ETA 1996, s 4(3)(e), the parties can consent to a hearing by an Employment Judge alone. In *Sogbetun v Hackney LBC* [1998] ICR 1264, the claimant's complaint of unfair dismissal was heard, with the consent of the parties, by an Employment Judge sitting alone. It was clear from the claim form and response that there were going to be issues of fact to be resolved in the case. It was held by the EAT that the decision to allow the case to be tried by an Employment Judge alone (even with the consent of the parties) was perverse because of the factual issues that had to be determined. The hearing was therefore a nullity. The EAT accordingly remitted the case for re-hearing by a properly constituted tribunal. However, in *Post Office v Howell* [2000] IRLR 224, the EAT held that, even if a failure by an Employment Judge to consider exercising his power under s 4(5) amounts to a failure to perform a mandatory obligation, it constitutes an irregularity and does not go to jurisdiction. It follows that any decision made by the Employment Judge sitting alone is not a nullity. However, in the present case, it was likely that the lay members of the tribunal would have been of considerable assistance in resolving questions of fact and so the case was remitted for hearing by a full tribunal.

In *Gladwell v Secretary of State for Trade and Industry* [2007] ICR 264 (EAT), Elias P pointed out (at [46]) that the default position for cases falling within s 4(3) is that the case is to be heard by an Employment Judge alone unless he directs otherwise having had regard to the factors set out in subs (5). His Lordship said that there was nothing wrong in the tribunal office operating a standard practice that all cases in that category are listed before an Employment Judge alone but the parties are given an opportunity of making representations as to why a full panel should be constituted ([47]). His Lordship went on to say that it is important that the Employment Judge who hears the case should have regard to the possibility that the situation may have changed from when the original decision to have the matter heard by an Employment Judge alone was taken ([48]). There is no legal duty for the judge at the substantive hearing to invite any observations from the parties, although it would usually be prudent to do so ([49]). Brief reasons for the decision should be given, but failure to give reasons for not departing from the usual rule is not an error of law, unless the issue has been raised explicitly by one of the parties ([50]). His Lordship also noted that there may be some cases (especially where the parties are unrepresented) where the Employment Judge should actively consider exercising the discretion even where the issue has not been raised by the parties ([52]). The fact that the parties have positively agreed to the Employment Judge sitting alone will preclude a successful challenge unless the case is manifestly one where a panel should have been constituted whatever the views of the parties. However, in almost all cases, the failure of the parties to object when given the opportunity (especially where they are legally represented) will make a perversity challenge impossible to sustain ([53]). Sometimes it will be clear once the case is ready for trial that the area of factual dispute is such that a panel should be constituted. However, the Employment Judge reviewing the matter at the hearing is entitled to take account of the fact that there will be extra costs and delay, and perhaps additional difficulties for witnesses, if the matter is then adjourned ([54]).

In *Rabahallah v BT plc* [2005] IRLR 184 (EAT), during the course of proceedings, one of the lay members of the tribunal became unavailable. The claimant was asked to consent to the case continuing with a two-member tribunal. It was held that a party who is asked to consent to a case continuing before an employment tribunal consisting of the Employment Judge and one lay member is entitled to know whether the remaining lay member comes from the panel of employers' representatives or the panel of employees' representatives.

4.9.2 Preparation for the hearing

The President of the Employment Tribunals (England and Wales) has issued a notice (see *Harvey*, W. 746) saying that where a party is legally represented, the lawyer should prepare a bundle containing all correspondence and other documents on which they intend to rely at the hearing, arranged in correct sequence and numbered consecutively. Whenever practicable, there should be an agreed bundle (that is, the parties produce a joint bundle of documents). In any event, a list of documents should be sent to the other party. Three sets of documents should be made available for use by the three members of the tribunal. It should be added that a copy of the bundle ought to be available for use by witnesses when giving evidence.

4.9.3 Representation

ETA 1996, s 6 provides that a person may appear in person or else be represented at an employment tribunal by: (a) counsel or a solicitor; (b) a representative of a trade union or an employers' association, or (c) any other person whom the party desires to represent him. It should be noted that legal aid is not available to cover representation before employment tribunals.

In *Astles v AG Stanley Ltd*, 14 October 1996, unreported, the claimant failed to attend the hearing but his representative did. The EAT held that in such a case the tribunal had no right to refuse to hear the evidence.

In *Bache v Essex County Council* [2000] IRLR 251, the Court of Appeal held that an employment tribunal has no power to prevent a representative chosen by a party from acting on behalf of that party. Similarly, in *Dispatch Management Services (UK) Ltd v Douglas* [2002] IRLR 389, the claimants in an unfair dismissal claim were represented by solicitors who had previously acted for the employer in relation to certain business matters; the employer sought an order that the claimants should obtain different representation, on the ground of conflict of interest. However, the EAT held that an employment tribunal does not have power to interfere with a party's choice of representation and so cannot dismiss a party's representative from the case and require them to obtain different representation.

4.9.4   The conduct of the hearing

Rule 41 provides that the tribunal may 'regulate its own procedure and shall conduct the hearing in the manner it considers fair, having regard to the principles contained in the overriding objective'. Moreover, the tribunal should 'seek to avoid undue formality'. The rule goes on to make specific provision for the tribunal itself to 'question the parties or any witnesses so far as appropriate in order to clarify the issues or elicit the evidence' and to make it clear that the tribunal 'is not bound by any rule of law relating to the admissibility of evidence in proceedings before the courts'.

The members of the tribunal will generally have taken their seats in the room where the hearing takes place before the parties enter. Advocates remain seated while addressing the tribunal or questioning witnesses.

[handwritten margin note: Seated oral evidence/advocacy]

Normally, in an unfair dismissal case, the tribunal will consider the question of liability first and only go on to consider remedies if it finds in favour of the claimant. If the tribunal proposes to adopt this course, the parties should be informed so that the evidence called is restricted to the issue of liability. If no indication is given, the parties should ascertain which course the tribunal proposes to adopt. In *Thorne v Riverside Centre Ltd* (EAT, 22 November 2000, unreported), the claimants were dismissed on grounds of redundancy as a result of restructuring. Both claimed unfair dismissal. At the hearing, the employment tribunal concluded that the claimants had been unfairly dismissed because there had been inadequate consultation prior to dismissal. The tribunal then went on to consider the issue of remedies without informing the appellants that the liability and remedies would be dealt with at the same hearing. The EAT held that the tribunal had erred in law by not giving the parties the opportunity to call evidence and to make submissions on the issue of remedies because it had failed to make clear that it intended to deal with both liability and remedies at the same hearing. Accordingly, the case was remitted to the tribunal to hear and adjudicate upon the question of remedies anew. In *Abegaze v Shrewsbury College of Arts and Technology* [2009] EWCA Civ 96, [2010] IRLR 238, it was held that, while it is never ideal when the composition of the tribunal hearing liability differs from that hearing remedies, the change in composition does not go to the question whether there can be a fair trial (*per* Elias LJ, at [45]).

In an unfair dismissal case, the claimant has to prove that there was a dismissal. If the respondent denies that there was a dismissal (as where, for example, the claimant is alleging 'constructive dismissal'), this matter is dealt with first, with the claimant presenting the evidence of dismissal and the respondent then calling evidence to refute this. In most cases, however, the fact of dismissal is not in dispute. If the respondent admits dismissing the claimant, it is for the respondent to show that the dismissal was for a fair reason. The respondent's case is, therefore, presented first.

The respondent (or their representative) makes a short opening speech and then calls evidence. Each witness is examined in chief by the respondent, cross-examined by the claimant and re-examined by the respondent. The claimant (or their representative) then makes an opening speech and calls evidence. Each witness is examined in chief by the claimant, cross-examined by the respondent and re-examined by the claimant. The claimant then makes a closing speech; this is followed by the respondent's closing speech.

It should be borne in mind that members of the tribunal may ask questions of the parties and their witnesses if they wish to do so.

It is possible for a submission of no case to answer to be made in an employment tribunal case. However, such submissions will rarely be appropriate. In *Logan v Commissioners of Customs and Excise* [2003] EWCA Civ 1068, [2004] IRLR 63, the employment tribunal dismissed the claim following a submission of no case to answer by the respondent. Ward LJ (at [19]) said that it should be rare for a submission of no case to answer to be made to an employment tribunal, and even more rare for the submission to succeed. The court said that the law on this topic is accurately summarised in *Clarke v Watford Borough Council* (EAT, 4 May 2000, unreported), *per* HHJ Clark, at [19]:

(1) There is no inflexible rule of law and practice that a tribunal must always hear both sides, although that should normally be done. (2) The power to stop a case at 'half-time' must be exercised with caution. (3) It may be a complete waste of time to call upon the other party to give evidence in a hopeless case. (4) Even where the onus of proof lies on the [claimant], as in discrimination cases, it will only be in exceptional or frivolous cases that it would be right to take such a course. (5) Where there is no burden of proof, as under s 98(4) of the Employment Rights Act, it will be difficult to envisage arguable cases where it is appropriate to terminate the proceedings at the end of the first party's case.

Ward LJ added that the fourth proposition applies not only in discrimination cases but also in cases of constructive dismissal.

Although r 41 provides that the strict rules of evidence do not apply, where a party is legally represented, leading questions will generally not be permitted where the questioning relates to matters which are in dispute between the parties. Furthermore, in *Snowball v Gardner Merchant Ltd* [1987] ICR 719, Sir Ralph Kilner-Brown (at p 722) said that 'a tribunal must not ignore or totally disregard the well-established principles of law with reference to the admissibility of evidence'. As far as hearsay evidence is concerned, the tribunal is entitled to receive such evidence unless it 'could in some way adversely affect the reaching of a proper decision in the case' (see *Coral Squash Clubs v Matthews* [1979] ICR 607, at p 611). In any event, an advocate should bear in mind that hearsay evidence has a lower probative value than direct evidence.

Any correspondence which is 'without prejudice' is inadmissible, even in a tribunal (*Independent Research Services v Catterall* [1993] ICR 1; *Portnykh v Nomura International plc* [2014] IRLR 251).

In *Aberdeen Steak Houses Group v Ibrahim* [1988] ICR 550, at p 557, the following points were made by Wood J:

- It is for the party, not the tribunal, to decide the order in which witnesses are called.

- It is the duty of the parties, not the tribunal, to see that all relevant evidence is called.

- Allegations of dishonesty should not be sprung on a party at the last moment; if this happens, an adjournment may be necessary in the interests of justice.

- A party stating that no evidence will be called will usually be bound by that statement.

- Tribunals must admit any evidence that may be probative of any issue relevant to the case.

In *De Keyser v Wilson* [2001] IRLR 324 (EAT), Lindsay P (at [36]) gave detailed guidance on the use of expert witnesses in employment tribunals. In particular, there is encouragement to use a single joint expert wherever possible, as in the High Court and County Court.

In *Digby v East Cambridgeshire District Council* [2007] IRLR 585 (EAT), HHJ Clark said (at [12]) that a tribunal 'has a discretion, in accordance with the overriding objective, to exclude relevant evidence which is unnecessarily repetitive or of only marginal relevance in the interests of proper, modern day case-management. However, that discretion must be exercised judicially. It may properly be challenged on appeal on *Wednesbury* principles. The guiding principle is to ensure justice between the parties.' It follows that it is open to a tribunal 'exercising its case management powers, to keep the evidence and cross-examination within reasonable bounds' ([19]).

In *Hak v St Christopher's Fellowship* [2016] IRLR 342, the EAT gave guidance on deciding whether an interpreter is necessary, holding that 'a useful test for a tribunal to consider while making such an assessment ... is to ask whether the litigant's command of language is sufficient to enable him to give the best account to the tribunal which he would wish to give relating to the matters in dispute' ([45]).

It should be borne in mind that the tribunal is empowered to strike out a claim or response on the grounds that the manner in which the proceedings have been conducted by or on behalf of the claimant/respondent has been scandalous, unreasonable or vexatious (see r 18(7), discussed at **4.6.5.2**). Where a representative behaves in an aberrant and offensive manner, it is necessary for the tribunal to make serious endeavours to defuse the situation before aborting the hearing, only striking out the claim/response if it is proportionate to do so (*Bennett v Southwark LBC* [2002] IRLR 407).

The tribunal must not conduct its own research into issues related to case before it. In *East of England Ambulance Service NHS Trust v Sanders* [2015] IRLR 277, the tribunal conducted some research on the Internet. The EAT ruled that this is not permissible. Langstaff J, at [29], said that r 41 does not 'allow a Tribunal to make enquires on its own behalf into evidence which was never volunteered by either party. The Tribunal may, in an appropriate case, ask the parties whether they have thought about particular evidence or even, possibly, whether in an appropriate case the parties or one of them would wish an adjournment in order to obtain it. But it is not ... for the Tribunal itself to investigate the evidence and rely upon its own investigations.'

4.9.5 Failure to attend

Rule 47 of the Employment Tribunal Rules provides that:

If a party fails to attend or to be represented at the hearing, the Tribunal may dismiss the claim or proceed with the hearing in the absence of that party. Before doing so, it shall consider any information which is available to it, after any enquiries that may be practicable, about the reasons for the party's absence.

In *Roberts v Skelmersdale College* [2003] EWCA Civ 954, [2003] ICR 1127, the case was adjourned (at the employee's request) on medical grounds. The employee subsequently claimed that he did not receive notification of the new hearing date until five days before that date. The employee did not attend the hearing, and the tribunal disposed of the matter in his absence. The employee appealed against that decision. The Court of Appeal held that the tribunal has a very wide discretion in dealing with cases where a party fails to attend. The Rules do not impose on tribunals a duty, of their own motion, to investigate the case before them or to be satisfied on the merits that the respondent has established a good defence to the claim of the absent claimant (*per* Mummery LJ, at [15]). The Rules only require the tribunal to consider the documents before it (*Roberts v Skelmersdale College, per* Mummery LJ, at [16]). In *Yarrow v Edwards Chartered Accountants* (EAT, 8 July 2007, unreported), HHJ Clark ruled that where a party does not attend the hearing, the employment tribunal has a wide discretion in determining how far it will investigate the merits of the case before dismissing a claim. However, the tribunal (under r 27(6)) must, before dismissing an absent party's claim, consider any information which the parties have made available.

In *Duffy v George* [2013] EWCA Civ 908, [2013] IRLR 883, the tribunal had to deal with a sexual harassment case in which the complainant did not wish to attend the hearing, because she was afraid of being cross-examined by the respondent (who was unrepresented). The Court of Appeal said that, in a case such as this, a pre-hearing review should take place in order to address (i) whether the tribunal was satisfied by evidence that the claimant had grounds for, and was fearful of attending the *inter partes* hearing to be cross-examined by the appellant; (ii) if so, whether the tribunal should dispense with an *inter partes* hearing; (iii) if so, whether the tribunal should hold separate hearings at which each party gave their evidence in the absence of the other; and (iv) if so, whether the parties should be invited to submit in advance questions for tribunal to put to the other party at the separate hearing (*per* Mummery LJ, at [42]).

4.9.6 Use of electronic communications

Rule 46 of the Employment Tribunal Rules provides that a hearing may be conducted (in whole or in part) by 'use of electronic communication (including by telephone) provided that the Tribunal considers that it would be just and equitable to do so and provided that the parties and members of the public attending the hearing are able to hear what the Tribunal hears and see any witness as seen by the Tribunal'.

4.10 Orders, judgments and reasons

Rule 49 of the Employment Tribunal Rules provides that, where a tribunal is composed of three persons, any decision may be made by a majority; if it is composed of two persons the Employment Judge has a second or casting vote.

Rule 61(1) stipulates that, where there is a hearing, the tribunal may either announce its decision at the hearing or else reserve it to be sent to the parties, as soon as practicable, in writing. If the decision is announced at the hearing, a written record, in the form of a judgment if appropriate, must be provided to the parties as soon as practicable (r 61(2)).

As well as ordering a remedy in favour of a successful claimant (such as, for example, compensation for unfair dismissal), an employment tribunal is also able to impose a financial penalty. Section 12A(1) of the Employment Tribunals Act 1996 (inserted by the Enterprise and Regulatory Reform Act 2013) provides that, where an employment tribunal determining a claim involving an employer and a worker 'concludes that the employer has breached any of the worker's rights to which the claim relates', and also 'is of the opinion that the breach has one or more aggravating features', then the tribunal may order the employer to pay a penalty to the Secretary of State (whether or not it also makes a financial award against the employer on the claim). The penalty must be at least £100 but not more than £5,000 (subs (3)). The tribunal must have regard to the employer's ability to pay both when deciding whether to impose a financial penalty and, if so, how much (subs (2)).

4.10.1   The duty to give reasons

Rule 62(1) of the Employment Tribunal Rules requires the tribunal to give reasons for its decision on any disputed issue, whether substantive or procedural (including any decision on an application for reconsideration or for orders for costs, preparation time or wasted costs). Where the decision is given in writing, the reasons must also be given in writing; where the decision is announced at a hearing, the reasons may be given orally at the hearing or reserved to be given in writing later (r 62(2)). Where reasons are given orally, the Employment Judge will announce that written reasons will not be provided unless they are asked for by any party, either at the hearing itself or by a written request presented within 14 days of the sending of the written record of the decision; if no such request is received, the tribunal will provide written reasons only if requested to do so by the Employment Appeal Tribunal or a court (r 62(3)).

The extent of the reasons which must be given is governed by r 62(4) and (5): the reasons given for any decision should be 'proportionate to the significance of the issue and for decisions other than judgments may be very short'; in the case of a judgment, the reasons should:

identify the issues which the Tribunal has determined, state the findings of fact made in relation to those issues, concisely identify the relevant law, and state how that law has been applied to those findings in order to decide the issues.

Where the judgment includes a financial award, the reasons should identify, by means of a table or otherwise, how the amount to be paid has been calculated.

In *Bangs v Connex South Eastern Ltd* [2005] EWCA Civ 14, [2005] IRLR 389, the Court of Appeal held that, in exceptional cases, unreasonable delay in promulgating an employment tribunal's decision might be properly treated as a serious procedural error or material irregularity, thereby giving rise to a question of law within ETA 1996, s 21(1). This will only be the case, however, if the court is satisfied that the delay in promulgating the decision created a real risk that the parties had been deprived of the benefit of a full and fair trial.

In *Kwamin v Abbey National plc* [2004] IRLR 516 (EAT), Burton P (at [10]) said that three and a half months should be the maximum time after the end of a case for preparation and promulgation of all but the most complicated and lengthy judgments; beyond that time there is, in the absence of proper explanation, culpable delay. Where there is delay in the delivery of the decision, the question is whether the delay made the decision, or part of it, 'unsafe' ([12]). The longer the delay, the more scrutiny is required ([15.4]). The deference afforded to employment tribunals as an 'industrial jury' and finders of fact would be the less when it is suggested that there have been errors by the tribunal by virtue of the delay ([15.5]).

In *Tran v Greenwich Vietnam Community* [2002] IRLR 735, Sedley LJ (at [17]) said that the obligation on the tribunal is to explain *how* it got from its findings of fact to its conclusions. This may be done 'economically', but simply to recite the background and the parties' contentions and then to announce a conclusion is not sufficient. In *Williams v J Walter Thompson Group Ltd* [2005] EWCA Civ 133, [2005] IRLR 376, Mummery LJ (at [30]) said that, although employment tribunals must always make clear findings of fact on all relevant issues and give reasons for their conclusions on disputed questions of fact, it is not normally necessary to rehearse the evidence at great length or to include long verbatim quotations from background documents. The relevant principles were summarised in *Burmis v Governing Body of Aylesford School* (EAT, 3 October 2008, unreported), where HHJ Clark said (at [4]) that r 30(6) requires a tribunal, having identified the issues in the case, to provide a succinct chronological statement of the facts found, explaining where necessary why factual conflicts in evidence have been resolved by the tribunal in the way that they have. There must be a concise statement of the law. Finally, the tribunal has to demonstrate its reasoning, applying the law to the facts as found, and explaining its conclusions on the issues raised.

In *Bansi v Alpha Flight Services* [2007] ICR 308 (EAT), HHJ Serota, QC (at [22]) said:

In our opinion it is certainly good practice, where parties are legally represented in employment tribunals, for advocates to ask the tribunal to amplify its reasoning where it is considered that there has been a material omission in its findings of fact or in its consideration of the issues of fact and law before it. Where reasons are given ex tempore the application should be made at the time. If reasons are given in writing the request should be made as soon as possible after the reasons are received. We would encourage advocates to seek clarification from the employment tribunal promptly in any case where there might otherwise be an appeal based on alleged insufficiency of reasons. It is much easier for tribunals to deal with requests for clarification when they are fresh in their minds and the amplification of insufficient reasons and findings will save the parties time and expense and may in some cases obviate the need for an appeal and subsequent remission of the case.

This *dictum* was cited with approval by the EAT in *Royle v Greater Manchester Police Authority* [2007] ICR 281.

In *Albion Hotel (Freshwater) Ltd v Maia E Silva* [2002] IRLR 200, the appeal was based on the fact that the tribunal's decision was based on case law on which neither party had made submissions. HHJ Serota, QC (at [35]) said that, where a tribunal 'considers that an authority is relevant, significant and material to its decision, but has not been referred to by the parties, it should refer that authority to the parties and invite their submissions before concluding its decision. Failure to do so may amount to a breach of natural justice and of the right to a fair hearing.' In the present case, the uncited authorities had played a significant part in the decision; this meant that there had been 'significant procedural unfairness' and so the matter was remitted to the employment tribunal to hear submissions on the authorities not referred to the parties. However, in *Stanley Cole (Wainfleet) Ltd v Sheridan* [2003] EWCA Civ 1046, [2003] IRLR 885, Ward LJ said that the real question, in a case where the decision refers to case law not cited by the parties, is 'whether what happened was seriously irregular and unfair' ([28]). Where it is alleged that proceedings were unfair because the tribunal had referred to an authority which the parties had not had the opportunity to consider, that authority must be shown to be central to the tribunal's decision and not peripheral to it ([31]). Thus, the authority has to alter or affect the way the issues were addressed to a significant extent, so that it could 'truly be said by a fair-minded observer that the case was decided in a way which could not have been anticipated by a party fixed with such knowledge of the law and procedure as it would be reasonable to attribute to him in all the circumstances'. The vital question is whether it would have made any difference to the outcome of the case if the parties had been armed with the authority in question ([38]). Similarly, in *Clark v Clark Construction Initiatives Ltd* [2008] EWCA Civ 1446, [2009] ICR 718, Sedley LJ (at [5]) said that tribunals have an obligation to give reasons which are 'candid, intelligible, transparent and coherent'. His Lordship went on to say (at [11]) that 'a tribunal's determination is not vitiated by reference to uncanvassed authorities if these have not been central to and influential in the eventual decision'.

4.11 Enforcement of monetary awards

In nearly all cases where there is a finding of unfair dismissal, the tribunal awards compensation rather than ordering reinstatement or re-engagement. Under ETA 1996, s 15(1), any sum payable in pursuance of a decision of an employment tribunal is recoverable as if it were payable under an order of the County Court. It follows that the various enforcement mechanisms which exist in the County Court are available to enforce monetary awards made by employment tribunals.

4.12 Reconsideration of judgments

Rule 70 of the Employment Tribunal Rules provides that a tribunal, either on its own initiative or on the application of a party, may reconsider any judgment where it is necessary in the interests of justice to do so. On reconsideration, the original decision may be confirmed, varied or revoked. If the decision is revoked, it may be taken again. Unless it is made in the course of a hearing, an application for reconsideration must be presented in writing (and copied to all the other parties) within 14 days of the date on which the written record of the original decision was sent to the parties, or within 14 days of the date that the written reasons were sent (if later), and must set out why reconsideration of the original decision is necessary (r 71).

Any application for reconsideration will be considered by an Employment Judge. If the judge considers that 'there is no reasonable prospect of the original decision being varied or revoked', the application will be refused; otherwise, the tribunal will send a notice to the parties setting a time limit for any response to the application by the other parties and seeking the views of the parties on whether the application can be determined without a hearing. This notice may set out the judge's provisional views on the application (r 72(1)). Unless the application is refused, the original decision will be reconsidered at a hearing unless the Employment Judge considers, having regard to any response from the parties, that a hearing is not necessary in the interests of justice. If the reconsideration proceeds without a hearing the parties will be given a 'reasonable opportunity' to make further written representations (r 72(2)).

Where practicable, an application for reconsideration, and any reconsideration pursuant to that application, should be considered by the Employment Judge who made the original decision or who chaired the full tribunal which made it, as the case may be. Where that is not practicable, another Employment Judge will deal with the application or, in the case of a decision of a full tribunal, the reconsideration will be carried out by such members of the original tribunal as remain available (r 72(3)).

It is also possible for reconsideration to take place on the tribunal's own initiative. In that case, the tribunal must inform the parties of the reasons why the decision is being reconsidered (r 73).

Rule 69 contains a 'slip rule'. It enables an Employment Judge at any time to correct 'any clerical mistake or other accidental slip or omission in any order, judgment or other document produced by a Tribunal'.

4.13 Calculation of time limits

Rule 4 of the Employment Tribunal Rules governs the calculation of time limits. Rule 4(1) provides that:

Unless otherwise specified by the Tribunal, an act required by these Rules, a practice direction or an order of a Tribunal to be done on or by a particular day may be done at any time before midnight on that day. If there is an issue as to whether the act has been done by that time, the party claiming to have done it shall prove compliance.

Where the time specified for doing an act ends on a day other than a working day (i.e. on a Saturday or a Sunday, or a public holiday), the act is done in time if it is done on the next working day (r 4(2)).

Rule 4(3) stipulates that, where an act is to be done within a certain number of days of or from an event, 'the date of that event is not be included in the calculation'. The rule gives this example, based on the requirement that a response has to be presented within 28 days of the date on which the respondent was sent a copy of the claim: if the claim was sent on 1 October, the last day for presentation of the response is 29 October.

Under r 4(4), where an act is to be done 'not less than a certain number of days before or after an event', the date of that event is not be included in the calculation. This example is given, based on the requirement that a party wishing to present representations in writing for consideration by a tribunal at a hearing must do so not less than seven days before the hearing: if the hearing is fixed for 8 October, the representations must be presented no later than 1 October.

By virtue of r 4(6), where time is specified by reference to the date when a document is sent to a person by the tribunal, the date when the document was sent will, unless the contrary is proved, be regarded as 'the date endorsed on the document as the date of sending or, if there is no such endorsement, the date shown on the letter accompanying the document'.

To prevent misunderstandings, r 4(5) says that, where the tribunal imposes a time limit for doing any act, the last date for compliance should, wherever practicable, be expressed as a calendar date.

Rule 5 empowers the tribunal to alter time limits:

The Tribunal may, on its own initiative or on the application of a party, extend or shorten any time limit specified in these Rules or in any decision, whether or not (in the case of an extension) it has expired.

It should be noted that this power applies to time limits under the Rules or in a tribunal decision, and so does not give a tribunal a general power to override statutory time limits.

4.14   Service of documents

Rule 85(1) provides that documents may be delivered to the tribunal by post, by direct delivery to the appropriate tribunal office, or by electronic communication. Under r 86(1), documents may be delivered to a party by post, by direct delivery to that party's address, by electronic communication, or by being handed personally to that party (if that party is an individual and if no representative has been named in the claim form or response) or to any individual representative named in the claim form or response, or (at a hearing) to any person identified by the party in question as representing them at the hearing. By virtue of r 87, documents should be sent to non-parties at any address for service which they may have notified, or else at any known address or place of business in the UK or, if the party is a corporate body, at its registered or principal office in the UK.

Rule 90 provides that a document delivered in accordance with r 85 or r 86 shall, unless the contrary is proved, be taken to have been received by the addressee '(a) if sent by post, on the day on which it would be delivered in the ordinary course of post; (b) if sent by means of electronic communication, on the day of transmission; (c) if delivered directly or personally, on the day of delivery.'

Under r 91, a tribunal may treat any document as delivered to a person, notwithstanding any non-compliance with the rules on service, if satisfied that the document in question, or its substance, has in fact come to the attention of that person.

4.15   Costs orders and preparation time orders

Rule 76(1) of the Employment Tribunal Rules empowers a tribunal to make a costs order or a preparation time order.

4.15.1   Costs orders

Rule 74(1) defines 'costs' as meaning 'fees, charges, disbursements or expenses incurred by or on behalf of the receiving party (including expenses that witnesses incur for the purpose of, or in connection with, attendance at a Tribunal hearing)'. In *Ladak v DRC Locums Ltd* [2014] IRLR 851, the EAT ruled that costs can include expenses related to in-house lawyers.

Under rule 75(1), a costs order is an order which requires one party (the 'paying party') to make a payment to another party (the 'receiving party') in respect of the costs that the receiving party has incurred while legally represented or while represented by a lay representative, or in respect of a tribunal fee paid by the receiving party; or to another party or a witness in respect of expenses incurred, or to be incurred, for the purpose of, or in connection with, an individual's attendance as a witness at the tribunal. For these purposes, being legally represented means having the assistance of a person with a right of audience in the courts, including where that person is the receiving party's employee; being represented by a lay representative means having the assistance of someone without such a right of audience (r 74(2)).

4.15.2   Preparation time orders

A preparation time order is an order which requires one party (the 'paying party') to make a payment to another party (the 'receiving party') in respect of the receiving party's preparation time while not legally represented. For these purposes, 'preparation time' means time spent by the receiving party (including by any employees or advisers) in working on the case, except for time spent at any final hearing (r 75(2)).

It should be noted that a costs order in respect of the costs of legal representation or lay representation and a preparation time order cannot both be made in favour of the same party in the same proceedings (r 75(3)).

4.15.3   Criteria for making a costs order or preparation time order

Under r 76(1), a tribunal:

may make a costs order or a preparation time order, and shall consider whether to do so, where it considers that:

> (a) a party (or that party's representative) has acted vexatiously, abusively, disruptively or otherwise unreasonably in either the bringing of the proceedings (or part) or the way that the proceedings (or part) have been conducted; or
>
> (b) any claim or response had no reasonable prospect of success.

Under r 76(2), a tribunal may also make a costs order or a preparation time order where a party has been in breach of any order or Practice Direction, or where a hearing has been postponed or adjourned on the application of a party.

In *Barnsley Metropolitan Borough Council v Yerrakalva* [2012] IRLR 78, Mummery LJ (at [41]) said that the 'vital point in exercising the discretion to order costs is to look at the whole picture of what happened in the case and to ask whether there has been unreasonable conduct by the claimant in bringing and conducting the case and, in doing so, to identify the conduct, what was unreasonable about it and what effects it had'.

Many parties who appear before tribunals are unrepresented. In *AQ Ltd v Holden* [2012] IRLR 648, HHJ Richardson said (at [32]) that the tribunal:

must take into account whether a litigant is professionally represented. A tribunal cannot and should not judge a litigant in person by the standards of a professional representative. Lay people are … likely to lack the objectivity and knowledge of law and practice brought by a professional legal adviser … Further, even if the threshold tests for an order for costs are met, the tribunal has discretion whether to make an order. This discretion will be exercised having regard to all the circumstances. It is not irrelevant that a lay person may have brought proceedings with little or no access to specialist help and advice.

The power to make a costs order in respect of an adjournment applies only to the costs resulting from the adjournment and not to costs which would have been incurred in any event (*Cooper v Weatherwise (Roofing and Walling) Ltd* [1993] ICR 81 (EAT)).

Rule 76(3) provides that where, in proceedings for unfair dismissal, a final hearing is postponed or adjourned, the tribunal must order the respondent to pay the costs incurred as a result of the postponement or adjournment if the claimant has expressed a wish to be reinstated or re-engaged which was communicated to the respondent not less than seven days before the hearing, and the postponement or adjournment was caused by the respondent's failure, without a special reason, to adduce reasonable evidence as to the availability of the job from which the claimant was dismissed or of comparable or suitable employment.

Rule 76(4) provides that a tribunal may make a costs order in respect of a tribunal fee paid by the receiving party where a party has paid a tribunal fee in respect of a claim or application and that claim or application is decided in whole, or in part, in favour of that party. Under r 76(5), a tribunal may make a costs order in respect of expenses incurred for the purpose of an individual's attendance as a witness on the application of a party or the witness in question, or on its own initiative, where a witness has attended or has been ordered to attend to give oral evidence at a hearing.

4.15.4 Applying for a costs order or preparation time order

A party may apply for a costs order or a preparation time order at any stage up to 28 days after the date on which the judgment finally determining the proceedings in respect of that party was sent to the parties. However, no such order may be made unless the paying party has had a reasonable opportunity to make representations (in writing or at a hearing) in response to the application (r 77).

4.15.5 Amount of costs orders and preparation time orders

The amount of the order is governed by r 78. A costs order may:

(a) order the paying party to pay the receiving party a specified amount, not exceeding £20,000, in respect of the costs of the receiving party;

(b) order the paying party to pay the receiving party the whole or a specified part of the costs of the receiving party, with the amount to be paid being determined by way of detailed assessment carried out either by a county court in accordance with the Civil Procedure Rules, or by an Employment Judge applying the same principles;

(c) order the paying party to pay the receiving party a specified amount as reimbursement of all or part of a tribunal fee paid by the receiving party;

(d) order the paying party to pay another party or a witness, as appropriate, a specified amount in respect of necessary and reasonably incurred expenses connected with an individual's attendance as a witness; or

(e) if the paying party and the receiving party agree as to the amount payable, be made in that amount.

Under r 78(2), where the costs order includes an amount in respect of fees charged by a lay representative, the hourly rate applicable for the fees of the lay representative is limited to £33 (increased on 6 April each year by £1).

The limit of £20,000 applies only to a costs order made under para (a).

The amount of a preparation time order is governed by r 79. Under r 79(1), the tribunal must decide the number of hours in respect of which a preparation time order should be made, on the basis of information on time spent provided by the receiving party, and the tribunal's own assessment of what it considers to be a 'reasonable and proportionate amount of time to spend on such preparatory work, with reference to such matters as the complexity of the proceedings, the number of witnesses and documentation required'. The prescribed hourly rate is £33, increasing on 6 April each year by £1 (rule 79(2)).

4.15.6 Wasted costs orders

Rule 80(1) empowers a tribunal to make a wasted costs order against a representative in favour of any party ('the receiving party') where that party has incurred costs:

(a) as a result of any improper, unreasonable or negligent act or omission on the part of the representative; or

(b) which, in the light of any such act or omission occurring after they were incurred, the Tribunal considers it unreasonable to expect the receiving party to pay.

The costs so incurred are 'wasted costs'. For these purposes, a 'representative' is defined as 'a party's legal or other representative or any employee of such representative', but it does not include 'a representative who is not acting in pursuit of profit with regard to the proceedings'. A person acting on a contingency or conditional fee arrangement is considered to be acting in pursuit of profit (r 80(2)).

Under r 80(3), a wasted costs order may be made in favour of a party whether or not that party is legally represented and may also be made in favour of a representative's own client. However, a wasted costs order cannot be made against a representative where that representative is representing a party in his or her capacity as an employee of that party.

Rule 81 provides that a wasted costs order may order the representative to pay the whole or part of any wasted costs of the receiving party, or disallow any wasted costs otherwise payable to the representative (including an order that the representative repay to its client any costs which have already been paid). The amount to be paid, disallowed or repaid must be specified in the order.

Under r 82, a wasted costs order may be made by the tribunal on its own initiative or on the application of any party. A party may apply for an order at any stage up to 28 days after the date on which the judgment finally determining the proceedings as against that party was sent to the parties. A wasted costs order cannot be made unless the representative has had a reasonable opportunity to make representations (in writing or at a hearing) in response to the application or proposal.

4.15.7   Ability to pay

Rule 84 stipulates that, when deciding whether to make a costs order, preparation time order or wasted costs order, the tribunal 'may have regard to the paying party's (or, where a wasted costs order is made, the representative's) ability to pay'. Despite the use of the word 'may', it is submitted that regard should always be had to the financial circumstances of the paying party.

In *Kopel v Safeway Stores plc* [2003] IRLR 753, the EAT held that an offer to settle the case can be taken into account in deciding whether to make a costs order. However, failure by a claimant to achieve an award in excess of the rejected offer should not by itself lead to an order for costs. Before the rejection becomes a relevant factor in the exercise of its discretion regarding costs, the employment tribunal must first conclude that the conduct of the claimant in rejecting the offer was 'unreasonable' (*per* Mitting J, at [18]).

In *Nicolson Highlandwear Ltd v Nicolson* [2010] IRLR 859, the EAT held that the Employment Judge was wrong to approach the matter of costs on the basis that it is open to a claimant to pursue an unfair dismissal claim purely for the purpose of obtaining a declaration that he was unfairly dismissed. In the present case, where the claimant had been dismissed for fraud and was awarded no compensation, 'the only conclusion open to the employment judge was that the claimant acted unreasonably in bringing the claim at all' (Lady Smith, at [41]). It should be noted that this decision of the EAT seems to be inconsistent with *Telephone Information Services Ltd v Wilkinson* [1991] IRLR 148, where the EAT held that it was not unreasonable for a claimant to proceed with a claim in order to obtain a declaration of unfair dismissal, even though he had been offered adequate financial compensation.

In *Gee v Shell UK Ltd* [2002] EWCA Civ 1479, [2003] IRLR 82, the Court of Appeal had to consider whether, and if so in what circumstances, it was appropriate for an employment tribunal to point out to a claimant that failure of the claim might lead to an adverse costs order. It was held that an employment tribunal should only give a costs warning where there was a real risk that an order for costs would be made against an unsuccessful claimant at the end of the hearing (*per* Scott Baker LJ, at [21]). The tribunal must be particularly careful not to place unfair pressure on a litigant who is unrepresented ([21]). Moreover, an order for costs is very much the exception rather than the rule ([22]). The ultimate question, however, is whether the effect of the costs warning by the tribunal is to deprive the claimant of a fair hearing ([29]) by putting unfair pressure on the claimant to withdraw the claim ([30]).

In *Iron and Steel Trades Confederation v ASW Ltd* [2004] IRLR 926, the EAT said that there is no rule of practice which says that where a case had gone through a preliminary hearing, costs would only be awarded in exceptional circumstances. However, it is a relevant factor, when deciding whether a claim has been brought unreasonably, that the case has been sifted through or considered at a preliminary hearing (*per* Burton P, at [7] and [8]).

In *McPherson v BNP Paribas SA* [2004] EWCA Civ 569, [2004] IRLR 558, Mummery LJ (at [30]) said that where a tribunal is minded to make a costs order against a claimant who has withdrawn their claim, the crucial question is whether, in all the circumstances, the claimant has conducted the proceedings unreasonably, not whether the withdrawal of the claim was in itself unreasonable. His Lordship went on to reject the argument that particular costs can only be awarded if attributable to the unreasonable conduct in question, holding that the employer does not have to prove that specific unreasonable conduct by the claimant caused particular costs to be incurred ([40]).

For a short article on costs, see Twiss, 'Costs in the Employment Tribunal' (2004) 154 *NLJ* 1816–17.

4.16 Restrictions on disclosure

Rule 50 of the Employment Tribunal Rules enables the tribunal, at any stage of the proceedings (on its own initiative or on application) to make an order with a view to preventing or restricting the public disclosure of any aspect of those proceedings so far as it considers necessary in the interests of justice or in order to protect the ECHR rights of any person. When considering whether to make such an order, the tribunal must 'give full weight to the principle of open justice and to the Convention right to freedom of expression' (r 50(2)).

Under r 50(3), an order under r 50 may include:

(a) an order that a hearing that would otherwise be in public should be conducted, in whole or in part, in private;

(b) an order that the identities of specified parties, witnesses or other persons referred to in the proceedings should not be disclosed to the public;

(c) an order for measures preventing witnesses at a public hearing being identifiable by members of the public.

Rule 50(4) provides that any party, or other person with a legitimate interest, who has not had a reasonable opportunity to make representations before an order is made may apply, in writing, to the tribunal for the order to be revoked or discharged.

4.17   Appeals to the Employment Appeal Tribunal

See generally the Employment Appeal Tribunal Rules 1993 (SI 1993/2854) (EAT Rules 1993) and the *Practice Direction (Employment Appeal Tribunal: Procedure)*. Under s 28(2) of the Employment Tribunals Act 1996, the EAT proceedings are heard by a judge alone. However, a judge may direct that proceedings are to be heard by a judge and either two or four appointed members, or with the consent of the parties, either one or three appointed members (subs (3) and (4)).

Appeal lies to the EAT on 'any question of law arising from any decision of, or arising in any proceedings before, an employment tribunal' (ETA 1996, s 21(1)).

By virtue of the Employment Tribunals and the Employment Appeal Tribunal Fees Order 2013 (SI 2013/1893), a fee of £400 is payable by an appellant following receipt of a notice of appeal by the Employment Appeal Tribunal, and a fee of £1,200 is payable following notification of a direction by the Employment Appeal Tribunal for an oral hearing to dispose finally of proceedings (arts 13 and 14).

4.17.1   Points of law

A point of law arises where:

- the tribunal wrongly construed or applied a statutory provision; or
- the tribunal has reached a decision which no reasonable tribunal could reach on the facts of the case (that is, the decision is perverse within the meaning of the test laid down for judicial review in *Associated Picture Houses Ltd v Wednesbury Corporation* [1948] 1 KB 223). This includes a finding of fact unsupported by evidence or based on a clear misdirection in law (cf *Piggott Brothers & Co Ltd v Jackson* [1991] IRLR 309 (CA)).

In *Bangs v Connex South Eastern Ltd* [2005] EWCA Civ 14, [2005] IRLR 389, the Court of Appeal held that it is not incompatible with art 6 of the ECHR for domestic legislation to limit the right of appeal from an employment tribunal to questions of law only.

In *British Telecommunications plc v Sheridan* [1990] IRLR 27, the Court of Appeal held that the only grounds of appeal are error of law or perversity of decision. A misunderstanding or misapplication of the facts falling short of perversity cannot be used as a separate ground of appeal. The same applies to the EAT's jurisdiction to interfere with the employment tribunal's discretion on interlocutory matters (*Ashmore v British Coal Corporation* [1990] 2 QB 338 (CA)); in *Adams v West Sussex County Council* [1990] IRLR 215 (EAT), Wood J (at [16]) said that the EAT would have to consider whether the order made was one within the powers given to the tribunal, whether the tribunal's discretion has been exercised within guiding legal principles, and whether the exercise of the discretion could be regarded as perverse in the *Wednesbury* sense.

The Court of Appeal and the EAT have repeatedly said that the decision of a tribunal should not be reversed merely because the appellate court would not have come to that decision on the facts. As Waite P said in *Royal Society for the Protection of Birds v Croucher* [1984] IRLR 425, at [26]:

> We have to remember that it is our duty loyally to follow findings of fact by an [employment] tribunal ... and that cases must be very rare indeed where we take upon ourselves to reach the conclusion that a tribunal has arrived at a result not tenable by any reasonable tribunal properly directed in law.

The *Practice Direction* makes it clear that the notice of appeal 'must clearly identify the point(s) of law which form(s) the ground(s) of the appeal' (para 3.5). It goes on to say that it is not enough merely to assert something general, such as 'there was no evidence to support the decision' or 'the decision was one that no reasonable tribunal could have reached and was perverse': full particulars of the matters relied on to support such general grounds must be given (para 3.8). Furthermore, the notice of appeal can be amended only with permission of the EAT (para 3.10).

It is only in exceptional cases that the EAT will permit an appellant to raise a point of law which was not raised in front of the employment tribunal (*Kumchyk v Derby County Council* [1978] ICR 1116). Similarly, the respondent will not usually be allowed to raise a point of law which was not relied on before the tribunal (*Wilson v Boston Deep Sea Fisheries Ltd* [1987] ICR 526). In *Glennie v Independent Magazines Ltd* [1999] IRLR 719 (CA), Laws LJ (at [18]) said that a new point ought only to be permitted to be raised in exceptional circumstances; if the new issue goes to the jurisdiction of the tribunal that may be an exceptional circumstance, but only if the issue raised is a discrete one of pure law requiring no or no further factual inquiry.

In *Secretary of State for Health v Rance* [2007] IRLR 665, the EAT confirmed that there is a discretion to allow a new point of law (that is, one not raised at the employment tribunal) to be argued in the EAT. However, this discretion is exercised only in exceptional circumstances; it is even more exceptional to exercise the discretion where fresh issues of fact would have to be investigated (*per* HHJ McMullen, QC, at [50]). In *Bennett v Governing Body of Pennoweth School* (EAT, 22 July 2008, unreported) it was held that the essential ingredients of allowing a new point to be taken are: (a) that it is a discrete point which does not require further evidence on remission, particularly a point going to jurisdiction; and (b) it must be a 'knockout point' (*per* HHJ Clark, at [15]).

In *Wileman v Minilec Engineering Ltd* [1988] ICR 318, the EAT held that it is only appropriate to admit fresh evidence (that is, evidence not called at the employment tribunal) if that evidence satisfies three criteria:

- it could not have been obtained with reasonable diligence for use at the tribunal hearing; and
- it would have had an important influence on the result of the case; and
- it is apparently credible.

Another potential ground of appeal is that of bias on the part of the employment tribunal. The general test for bias is whether the reasonable observer present at the hearing, not being a party, or associated with a party, to the proceedings but knowing the issues, would reasonably gain the impression of bias (*Peter Simper & Co Ltd v Cooke* [1986] IRLR 19, *per* Peter Gibson J, at [10]).

In *Riverside Restaurants Ltd t/as Harry Ramsden v Tremayne* (EAT, 12 December 1995, unreported), HHJ Clark said that there are two main ways in which a tribunal member may give the appearance of bias by his conduct during the proceedings: giving a preliminary or tentative indication of a view on an issue in the case (for example, in an attempt to save time or promote agreement) may be seen as the expression of a concluded view on issues which are relevant to the case; attempting to prevent unnecessary prolixity or repetitious questioning may result in preventing legitimate and necessary cross-examination. Where a party is unrepresented, all necessary assistance should be given to that party by the Employment Judge, but the Employment Judge must be careful not to cross the line and assume the role of advocate (a point emphasised in *Drysdale v Department of Transport (Maritime and Coastguard Agency)* [2014] EWCA Civ 1083, [2014] IRLR 892, where the Court of Appeal, at [49], said that the 'appropriate level of assistance or intervention is constrained by the overriding requirement that the tribunal must at all times be, and be seen to be, impartial as between the parties, and that injustice to either side must be avoided').

In *Southwark London Borough Council v Jiminez* [2003] EWCA Civ 502, [2003] IRLR 477, Peter Gibson LJ (at [40]) said that if a tribunal chooses to indicate its thinking before the hearing is concluded, the parties should be left in no doubt that such expressions of view are only provisional and that the tribunal remains open to persuasion.

4.17.2 Procedure

The appeal is commenced by serving a standard form notice on the EAT. Under the EAT Rules 1993, r 3(3), where written reasons were requested orally at the hearing or in writing within 14 days of the date on which the written record of the judgment was sent to the parties, or where judgment was reserved and given in writing by the tribunal, the appeal notice must be served within 42 days of the date when the written reasons for the tribunal's decision were sent to the appellant. Where written reasons were not requested and judgment was not reserved by the tribunal, time starts to run from the date on which the written record of the judgment was sent to the parties. In the case of an appeal from an order of an employment tribunal, the appeal notice must be served within 42 days of the date of the order. The 42-day time period for appealing to the EAT starts to run from the date when the decision was put into the post by the employment tribunal, not the date when it would have been delivered in the normal course of post (*Gdynia American Shipping Lines (London) Ltd v Chelminski* [2004] EWCA Civ 871, [2004] IRLR 725). In *Sian v Abbey National plc* [2004] IRLR 185, the EAT had made the point that this is so even if the decision is not delivered. Burton P (at [15]) reasoned that 42 days is a lengthy period which allows for any risk of delay in the post. His Lordship added (at [17]) that any potential unfairness against a party who does not in fact receive the decision can be resolved by the application of the ordinary discretion to grant an extension of time to be granted if appropriate.

In *Kanapathiar v London Borough of Harrow* [2003] IRLR 571, the EAT pointed out that a notice of appeal that is not accompanied by the necessary documents (including the claim form, the response and the employment tribunal's reasoned judgment) is not a valid notice of appeal.

Time runs even if the question of remedy and assessment of compensation were adjourned by the tribunal or an application has been made to the tribunal for a review of its decision (*Practice Direction*, para 5.4).

Where the time limit has expired, it is open to the would-be appellant to seek an extension of time. An extension will be granted only if there is a good excuse for the delay (*Practice Direction*, para 5.7). In *United Arab Emirates v Abdelghafar* [1995] ICR 65,

Mummery P said (at [25]) that 'it is incumbent on the applicant for an extension of time to provide the court with a full, honest and acceptable explanation of the reasons for the delay'. His Lordship went on to say (at [30]) that 'the questions which must be addressed by the Appeal Tribunal … on an application for an extension are: (a) What is the explanation for the default?; (b) Does it provide a good excuse for the default?; (c) Are there circumstances which justify the Tribunal taking the exceptional step of granting an extension of time?'. The Court of Appeal adopted the same approach in *Aziz v Bethnal Green City Challenge Co Ltd* [2000] IRLR 111. In *Jurkowska v Hlmad Ltd* [2008] EWCA Civ 231, [2008] IRLR 430, the Court of Appeal ruled that the introduction into the EAT Rules 1993 of the overriding objective, to deal with cases justly, does not mean that the EAT must adopt a more relaxed approach to the extension of the 42-day time limit for appealing, and that the principles set out in *Abdelghafar* remain good law (although they are simply guidelines and every case will turn on its facts). The decision whether to extend time is pre-eminently a discretionary one for the judge. In the ordinary run of cases, it will be necessary for a good excuse for the delay to be shown (*per* Rimer LJ, at [17]). However, even if the explanation does not amount to a good excuse, there may be exceptional circumstances which nonetheless justify an extension ([19]). However, it will only be in 'rare and exceptional' cases that it will be appropriate to extend time ([20]). The EAT is clearly reluctant to extend time. In *O'Cathail v Transport for London* [2012] IRLR 1011, the appellant lodged the supporting papers a day late. Mummery LJ (at [26]) said that the 'length of the delay is a material factor, but the crucial issue is whether there was a good excuse for that delay, rather than whether the delay was long or short', and that the appellant 'did not get all the documents in on time, because he left lodging his appeal till the end of the period for appealing; and that obviously carries with it the risk that things can go wrong without having enough time left to correct them'.

Once the EAT receives a notice of appeal it sends it to the respondent, who has to indicate whether the appeal will be contested. In *Slingsby v Griffith Smith Solicitors* (EAT, 10 February 2009, unreported), HHJ Burke, QC said (at [22]) that the strict principles which apply to the grant of an extension of time for the institution of an appeal do not apply to the grant of an extension of time for the delivery of an answer. Even if the explanation for the delay does not amount to a good excuse, there might be exceptional circumstances that justify an extension of time ([35]).

In *Atos Origin IT Services UK Ltd v Haddock* [2005] IRLR 20 (EAT), the issue arose as to whether the employer was precluded from appealing on the basis that no notice of appearance had been entered at the employment tribunal, as required by the Employment Tribunal Rules. It was held that there is nothing in statute or case law to prevent the EAT from hearing an appeal by a respondent who has not entered a notice of appearance (*per* Mitting J, at [18]).

Under r 3(7) of the EAT Rules, if it appears to a judge or the Registrar that a notice of appeal 'discloses no reasonable grounds for bringing the appeal', or 'is an abuse of the Appeal Tribunal's process or is otherwise likely to obstruct the just disposal of proceedings', the would-be appellant is notified that no further action will be taken on the appeal. In such a case the would-be appellant may apply for an oral hearing, usually before a different judge (r 3(10)). In *Barke v SEETEC Business Technology Centre Ltd* [2005] EWCA Civ 578, [2005] IRLR 633, the Court of Appeal held that the EAT, when considering an appeal made on the grounds that the employment tribunal has failed to consider relevant matters and has given insufficient written reasons, has power to invite an employment tribunal to amplify its reasons before determining an appeal. The court approved the decision of the EAT in *Burns v Consignia plc (No 2)* [2004] IRLR 425. It should also be noted that para 3.7 of the *EAT Practice Direction* says that if it appears to the judge or Registrar that a notice of appeal gives insufficient grounds of, or lacks clarity in identifying, a point of law, the judge or Registrar may postpone any decision under r 3(7) pending the appellant's amplification or clarification of the notice of appeal, or further information from the employment tribunal. The process whereby the EAT invites an employment tribunal to amplify its reasons has come to be known as the *Burns-Barke* procedure. In *Woodhouse School v Webster* [2009] EWCA Civ 91, [2009] IRLR 568, Mummery LJ (at [26] and [27]) observed that this:

procedure is available where the EAT considers that there is possibly an inadequacy in the ET's reasons for its decision. The EAT may, before it finally decides the appeal, refer specific questions to the ET at the preliminary hearing of the appeal, requesting it to clarify or supplement its reasons where no reasons were given or where the reasons given were inadequate. The purpose of the procedure is to give the ET the opportunity of fulfilling its duty to provide adequate reasons for its decision without the inconvenience that might be involved in the EAT allowing a reasons challenge to the ET decision under appeal and having to remit the case to the ET for a further hearing ... [T]he ET can be asked before the hearing of the appeal to supply, if it is possible to do so, the reasons for which the request is made. It is not, however, desirable for the ET to do more than answer the request. The ET should not, for example, advance arguments in defence of its decision and against the grounds of appeal.

It is open to any of the parties to the appeal to seek a copy of the note of evidence taken by the Employment Judge, but such an order will be made only if the EAT is satisfied that the notes are necessary for the purpose of arguing the point of law raised by the appeal (*Practice Direction*, para 9.1ff). In *Hawkins v Ball and Barclays Bank* [1996] IRLR 258, the EAT refused to accept that such notes become necessary automatically upon an allegation of perversity being raised (*per* Keene J, at [15]).

Paragraph 16.2 of the *EAT Practice Direction* requires all parties to provide skeleton arguments for use in the appeal. Paragraph 16.3 stipulates that the skeleton argument 'should be concise and should identify and summarise the point(s) of law, the steps in the legal argument and the statutory provisions and authorities to be relied upon, identifying them by name, page and paragraph and stating the legal proposition sought to be derived from them. It is not, however, the purpose of the skeleton argument to argue the case on paper in detail.' Under para 16.6, the appellant's skeleton argument must be accompanied by a chronology of events relevant to the appeal which, if possible, should be agreed by the parties.

Paragraph 17 covers the citation of authorities before the EAT. Paragraph 17.6 says that 'reference should be made to no more than 10 authorities unless the scale of the appeal warrants more extensive citation', and that the cases relied upon 'should set out legal principle, rather than be merely illustrative of an application of it. Parties must be prepared to justify more extensive citation of authority.'

Paragraph 11.8ff of the *Practice Direction* provides for Preliminary Hearings, the purpose of which is to determine whether the appeal has a reasonable prospect of success or there is some other compelling reason why the appeal should be heard. If not, the appeal is dismissed at that stage (para 11.16); if satisfied that there is a reasonably arguable point of law, the EAT will give appropriate directions to enable the case to proceed to a full hearing.

It is open to the appellant to seek permission to amend the notice of appeal (para 3.10 of the *Practice Direction*). In *Khudados v Leggate* [2005] IRLR 540, it was held that, when considering an application to amend a notice of appeal, the starting point is the overriding objective to deal with cases justly (*per* Judge Serota, QC, at [79]). The merits of the proposed amendment alone cannot be a determining factor in the decision as to whether permission to amend should be given ([87]). Applications to amend should be made as soon as the need for the amendment is known ([82(a)]). No amendment can properly be entertained unless it at least raises a point of law which gives the appeal a reasonable prospect of success, or where there is some other compelling reason for the appeal to be heard ([85]). Account should also be taken of the extent to which the amendment, if allowed, would cause any delay ([86(c)]); whether allowing the amendment will cause prejudice to the opposite party, and whether refusing the amendment will cause prejudice to the applicant by depriving him of fairly arguable grounds of appeal ([86(d)]).

In *Jones v Governing Body of Burdett Coutts School* [1998] IRLR 521 (CA), it was held that the EAT had been wrong to exercise its discretion to allow an employee to amend the notice to appeal to raise a point which had been (incorrectly) conceded by his representative at the original tribunal hearing. The discretion to allow a new point of law to be raised, or a conceded point to be re-opened, on appeal should be exercised only in exceptional circumstances. This is especially so if the effect would be to raise issues of fact which were not fully investigated by the employment tribunal (*per* Robert Walker LJ, at [20]).

At the hearing of the appeal the parties may represent themselves, or be legally represented, or be represented by anyone else of their choosing. It should be noted that legal aid to cover advocacy before the EAT is available only to the extent that the proceedings concern contravention of the Equality Act 2010 (Legal Aid, Sentencing and Punishment of Offenders 2012, Sch 1, Pt 3, para 20).

4.17.3 Decision of the EAT

The EAT has the following powers:

(a) to dismiss the appeal;

(b) to allow the appeal and substitute its own decision for that of the employment tribunal; or

(c) to allow the appeal and remit the case to the same tribunal, or to a different tribunal, either for a complete rehearing or for further consideration of a particular point.

The EAT must remit the case back to the original, or a differently constituted, employment tribunal unless either it concludes that the legal error cannot have affected the result, or else it is able to conclude itself what the result must have been without the error. In *Jafri v Lincoln College* [2014] EWCA Civ 449, [2014] IRLR 544, Laws LJ (at [21]) said that:

The EAT's function is (and is only) to see that the Employment Tribunal's decisions are lawfully made. If therefore the EAT detects a legal error by the Employment Tribunal, it must send the case back unless (a) it concludes that the error cannot have affected the result, for in that case the error will have been immaterial and the result as lawful as if it had not been made; or (b) without the error the result would have been different, but the EAT is able to conclude what it must have been. In neither case is the EAT to make any factual assessment for itself, nor make any judgment of its own as to the merits of the case; the result must flow from findings made by the Employment Tribunal, supplemented (if at all) only by undisputed or indisputable facts. Otherwise, there must be a remittal.

Underhill LJ observed (at [47]) that 'even where more than one outcome is indeed possible, there is in my view no reason why the EAT cannot still decide the issue if the parties agree; and in an appropriate case they should be strongly encouraged to do so'.

The Court of Appeal reiterated this suggestion in *Burrell v Micheldever Tyre Services Ltd*, [2014] EWCA Civ 716, [2014] IRLR 630, and also observed that, 'even where remittal is necessary, the EAT, mindful of the overriding objective, may limit the scope of the remittal, for example by identifying issues or limiting or forbidding further evidence. It may also save further expense by remittal to the same rather than a fresh tribunal, subject to the constraints which govern that choice' (*per* Maurice Kay LJ, at [20]).

In *Kuznetsov v Royal Bank of Scotland plc* [2017] IRLR 350, Elias LJ said (at 22] that 'if the ET has erred in law, it is not for the EAT to substitute its decision for that of the ET save in exceptional cases'. His Lordship added (at para 34) that he would 'strongly encourage' the EAT to seek the consent of the parties in advance where the possibility of remission is likely to arise, given that remission is currently required in the absence of the consent of both parties.

An order for the payment of costs can be made by the EAT only in exceptional cases: for example, where the EAT considers that the proceedings were unnecessary, improper, vexatious, or misconceived, or that there has been unreasonable delay or other unreasonable conduct in bringing or conducting the proceedings (EAT Rules 1993, r 34A(1)). In particular, costs may be ordered where a party has not complied with a direction of the Appeal Tribunal, has amended the notice of appeal or answer (as the case may be) or has caused an adjournment of proceedings (r 34A(2)). Rule 34C enables the EAT to make a wasted costs order against a party's representative (costs caused by an improper, unreasonable or negligent act or omission on the part of any representative).

In *Gill v Humanware Europe Ltd* [2010] EWCA Civ 799, [2010] IRLR 877, Smith LJ pointed out that 'a wasted costs order can be made only if the improper or unreasonable or negligent conduct complained of results in wasted costs ... The test ... should be the usual test of causation' ([34]). In other words, the test is whether, but for the actions complained of, the party seeking costs would have avoided some expense and, if so, how much.

In *Horizon Security Services Ltd v Ndeze* [2014] IRLR 854 (EAT), HHJ Eady said that, whilst the EAT was generally a 'no costs' jurisdiction (and so the usual rule in civil proceedings, that costs followed the event, did not generally apply), account must now be taken of the introduction of tribunal fees: 'the general expectation had to be that a successful appellant would be entitled to recover the sums paid from a respondent who had actively sought to resist the appeal'. In *Goldwater v Sellafield Ltd* [2015] IRLR 381, the EAT ruled that fees are not recoverable if not paid by the appellant (in that case, the fees had been paid by the appellant's trade union).

4.17.4 Review of EAT decision

The EAT can, like an employment tribunal, be asked to review its own decision, and it may review a decision on its own initiative (see r 33). A review may take place, for example, where 'the interests of justice require such review' (r 33(1)(c)).

4.17.5 Further appeal

Further appeal (again on a point of law only) lies to the Court of Appeal and thence to the Supreme Court. In *Sukul-Lennard v Croydon Primary Care Trust* [2003] EWCA Civ 1192, The Times, 14 August 2003, the Court of Appeal held that where an applicant has appealed against a decision of an employment tribunal and the EAT refuses a full hearing, the Court of Appeal has the power to order that the appeal from the employment tribunal go back for a full hearing by the EAT.

4.18   Settling employment tribunal cases: alternative dispute resolution

Rule 3 of the Employment Tribunal Rules provides that:

A Tribunal shall wherever practicable and appropriate encourage the use by the parties of the services of ACAS, judicial or other mediation, or other means of resolving their disputes by agreement.

One of the advantages of a settlement agreement is that the recoupment provisions do not apply (see **Chapter 7**). Another advantage is that the parties can agree to things that the tribunal has no power to order. In an unfair dismissal case, a tribunal can only order reinstatement/re-engagement or compensation; the tribunal cannot, for example, order the respondent to provide the claimant with a reference. Where a settlement agreement does include provision of a reference, the precise terms of the reference should be incorporated into the agreement.

An employment tribunal case can be settled in three ways: through ACAS; by the parties drawing up a settlement agreement; or with the approval of the employment tribunal.

4.18.1   ACAS-conciliated settlements

An ACAS-conciliated settlement operates to bar further proceedings before the employment tribunal. See ERA 1996, s 203(2)(e)), which provides that this bar applies where a conciliation officer has taken action to promote settlement of the claim. In *Allma Construction Ltd v Bonner* [2011] IRLR 204, the claimant was offered £1,000 by the employer's representative to settle his unfair dismissal claim. The solicitor informed an ACAS officer that this was acceptable. The following day, the claimant changed his mind about accepting the offer, and said he would only settle the case for £5,000. The employer argued that the case had already been settled. The EAT said that s 203 covers 'any action taken by an ACAS officer in relation to the claim' (Lady Smith, at [26]). The fact that the ACAS officer had communicated the claimant's acceptance was enough to satisfy the statutory requirement that he had 'taken action' to promote settlement of the claim and so to oust the jurisdiction of the tribunal.

However, an ACAS-conciliated agreement can be set aside if, for example, there has been a material misrepresentation (that is, one which would be actionable at common law or in equity) by a party to the settlement (*Greenfield v Robinson*, 16 May 1996, unreported (EAT)).

4.18.2   Settlement agreement between parties

The parties may come to an agreement without involving ACAS or the employment tribunal, but only if the requirements of ERA 1996, s 203, are met.

Under s 203(3) a settlement agreement must satisfy six requirements:

(a) the agreement must be in writing;

(b) the agreement must relate to the particular proceedings;

(c) the employee 'must have received advice from a relevant independent adviser as to the terms and effect of the proposed agreement and, in particular, on its effect on his ability to pursue his rights before an employment tribunal'. A 'relevant independent adviser' is defined in s 203(3A)) as meaning:

(i)   a qualified lawyer,

(ii) a trade union official who has been certified in writing by the trade union as competent to give advice and who is authorised to do so on behalf of the trade union, or

(iii) a person who works at an advice centre (whether as an employee or a volunteer) and who has been certified in writing by the centre as competent to give advice and who is authorised to do so on behalf of the centre.

[Under subs (3B)(a), a person cannot be a 'relevant independent adviser' if he is employed by or is acting in the matter for the employer or an associated employer.]

(d) the adviser must be covered by insurance or by an indemnity provided for members of a profession or professional body;

(e) the agreement must identify the adviser; and

(f) the agreement must state that the conditions regulating settlement agreements under the Act are satisfied.

The agreement may be effected by an exchange of letters or by a formal contract or deed. It is enforceable by means of a contract action in the County Court or High Court. In *Rock-It Cargo v Green* [1997] IRLR 581, the EAT held that a valid settlement agreement (that is, one which satisfies ERA 1996, s 203(3)) is enforceable by a tribunal under its breach of contract jurisdiction (Employment Tribunals Extension of Jurisdiction (England and Wales) Order 1994). The employee can therefore bring a tribunal claim for any money which is due under that agreement (*per* Kirkwood J, at [16]).

An agreement which satisfies the requirements of ERA 1996, s 203, is binding whether made before or after a claim form has been presented (*Bennett v De Vere Hotels Ltd* (EAT, 30 November 1995, unreported). However, an employment tribunal has jurisdiction to determine whether an otherwise valid settlement agreement is unenforceable because it was entered into on the basis of a misrepresentation (*Industrious Ltd v Vincent* [2010] IRLR 204 (EAT)).

If the agreement does not satisfy the requirements of s 203, then it is worthless. In *Riverside Health Authority v Chetty* (EAT, 6 March 1996, unreported), for example, the EAT upheld a decision not to strike out unfair dismissal applications where the claimants had accepted sums of money 'in full and final settlement' of their claims but the settlement agreement did not comply with s 203. The case was remitted to the tribunal. The Employment Judge made an order requiring the claimants to repay to the employer the sums they had received under the settlement. The case returned to the EAT (*sub nom Chetty v Riverside Health Authority*), and the EAT held that the Employment Judge had exceeded his jurisdiction.

In *Sutherland v Network Appliance Ltd* [2001] IRLR 12, the claimant had entered into a written agreement with his employer, which provided that he would receive compensation 'in full and final settlement of any claims [which he might have] arising out of [his] employment or its termination'. He subsequently brought a claim against the employer alleging unfair dismissal and various breaches of contract. The question was whether the agreement prevented the tribunal from entertaining his contractual claims. He contended that his statutory and contractual rights could not be severed and, since the agreement contravened ERA 1996, s 203(1), the agreement was void in its entirety, thereby entitling him to proceed with the contractual claims. It was held that s 203 provides that agreements are only void to the extent that they offend the provisions of s 203. Therefore, the agreement was void only in so far as it precluded the claimant from pursuing his statutory claims. Had Parliament intended that contractual claims be given the protection afforded to statutory claims by s 203, it would have made express statutory provision, both in respect of claims in the employment tribunal and claims in the ordinary civil courts.

In *Hinton v University of East London* [2005] EWCA Civ 532, [2005] IRLR 552, Smith LJ said (at [33]) that, in order to comply with s 203, the settlement agreement must identify the particular or potential claims to be covered either by a generic description (such as 'unfair dismissal') or by reference to the section of the statute giving rise to the claim. Mummery LJ (at [24]) said that, if actual proceedings are compromised, it is good practice for the particulars of the proceedings and of the particular allegations made in them to be inserted in the settlement agreement in the form of a brief factual and legal description. If the compromise is of a particular claim raised which is not yet the subject of proceedings, it is good practice for the particulars of the nature of the allegations and of the statute under which they are made or the common law basis of the alleged claim to be inserted in the settlement agreement in the form of a brief factual and legal description (Mummery LJ, [25]). However, in *McWilliam v Glasgow City Council* [2011] IRLR 568, the EAT held that, in order for a settlement agreement to relate to a 'particular complaint', the complaint does not necessarily have to refer to an existing tribunal claim, or even be a claim that has been articulated to the employer. Rather, it is sufficient that there is 'an expression of dissatisfaction about something' (Lady Smith, at [28]). Moreover, the EAT held in the same case that there is no requirement that the independent adviser must offer a view on whether or not the deal on offer for accepting a compromise is a good one, or whether or not the adviser thinks that the employee should accept it (at [35]).

4.18.3   Withdrawal of claims

It is possible for the claimant simply to withdraw the claim. Rule 51 of the Employment Tribunal Rules states that, where a claimant informs the tribunal, either in writing or in the course of a hearing, that a claim (or part of it) is withdrawn, the claim (or part) comes to an end, subject to any application that the respondent may make for a costs, preparation time or wasted costs order. Where a claim (or part of it) has been withdrawn, the tribunal issues a judgment dismissing it (with the effect that the claimant cannot commence a further claim against the respondent raising the same, or substantially the same, complaint) unless either the claimant, at the time of withdrawal, expresses a wish to reserve the right to bring a further claim and the tribunal is satisfied that there would be legitimate reason for doing so, or else the tribunal believes that to issue such a judgment would not be in the interests of justice.

4.18.4   Consent orders

Rule 64 of the Employment Tribunal Rules provides that, if the parties agree in writing, or orally at a hearing, upon the terms of any order or judgment the tribunal may, if it thinks fit, make such order or judgment (which is to be identified as having been made by consent).

A consent order will often take the form of a *Tomlin* order. This is an order in which the terms of the agreement reached by the parties are set out in a schedule to the order.

The order itself merely stays the proceedings, subject to 'liberty to apply' to the tribunal if problems are encountered in carrying out the terms of the agreement. If the terms of the agreement are not complied with, the party seeking to enforce the agreement can go back to the tribunal to seek an order in the terms of the agreement between the parties (to the extent that the agreement concerns matters that the tribunal can deal with, namely reinstatement/re-engagement and compensation up to the statutory maximum); see, for example, *Milestone School of English Ltd v Leakey* [1982] IRLR 3. In so far as the agreement provides for things which the tribunal cannot order, enforcement would have to be through the civil courts by means of a contract claim.

4.18.5   ACAS arbitration scheme

There is an alternative to bringing an employment tribunal case. The ACAS Arbitration Scheme was established by Part II of the Employment Rights (Dispute Resolution) Act 1998 (ER(DR)A 1998).

The Scheme can be used where an employee has a claim for unfair dismissal (or a claim arising out of flexible working legislation) where:

(a) there are no jurisdictional questions, for example, whether there was a dismissal, or whether the employee has the necessary length of service to bring a claim;

(b) the case does not raise any complicated legal issues; and

(c) both the employer and the employee agree to arbitration.

Each party signs an Arbitration Agreement, either through ACAS (a Conciliated Agreement) or via an independent adviser (a Settlement Agreement). Once the agreement is signed, the claim can no longer be heard by an employment tribunal. ACAS then appoints an arbitrator (the parties normally having no choice of arbitrator); the arbitrator fixes a date and venue for the hearing.

Each party should submit a written statement of their case to the arbitrator prior to the hearing; this will be copied to the other side. Supporting documentation may also be produced.

There is no set format for the hearing: the procedure to be followed is set by the arbitrator, who can question the parties and any witnesses (both parties can call witnesses). The parties can bring anyone of their choosing to represent their case (and are liable for any fees or expenses incurred by any representative they appoint). All parties are given an opportunity to state their case, and the arbitrator will help if one of the parties has difficulty setting out their case. However, there is no cross-examination of witnesses.

In reaching a decision on the fairness of the dismissal, the arbitrator takes account of: the ACAS Code of Practice on Disciplinary and Grievance Procedures and the ACAS Guide: *Discipline and Grievances at Work*, together with his or her own knowledge and experience of good employment relations, and the evidence in the case.

If the arbitrator finds that the dismissal was unfair, reinstatement, re-engagement or compensation may be awarded. As in a tribunal, in coming to this decision the arbitrator will take into account the views of the parties and what is practicable and just. Any compensation will be calculated in a similar way to the tribunal. The award is binding, enforceable by the courts but confidential to the parties and ACAS. There is only a very limited right of appeal.

5

The contract of employment

5.1 Introduction: the nature of the contract of employment

Employment law is full of terminology which is technical in nature. Terms include 'worker', 'employee', 'employer', 'contractor' and 'end service user' to illustrate a few. The distinctions between some of these terms are extremely important.

To determine the level of protection provided by law, an individual's 'employment status' is very important. There are four statuses: employee (enjoys the greatest protection), worker (enjoys limited protection), self-employed (is not protected by statutory employment law) and the new 'employee shareholder' status as governed by s 205A Employment Rights Act 1996 (which is beyond the scope of this manual).

'Employee' is a phrase reserved solely for a person employed under a contract of employment with his or her employer, with the status of employee, meaning that he or she obtains the protection of the rights contained within the Employment Rights Act 1996 (ERA 1996) (including unfair dismissal and redundancy payment entitlement), among other measures. Please note, as stated below, that Part II of ERA 1996 and several other statutory provisions do apply to those with 'worker' status. The contract of employment confers rights which may exceed the basic statutory baseline, and differentiates the status of employees from others.

The relationship between employer and employee is based on the common law of contract. The ERA 1996, s 230(1), defines 'employee' as 'an individual who has entered into or works under ... a contract of employment'. 'Contract of employment' itself is defined as 'a contract of service or apprenticeship, whether express or implied, and (if it is express) whether oral or in writing' (s 230(2)). Thus the statutory definition refers back to the case law surrounding the concept of 'contract of service' (undefined by statute).

Although a contract of employment is the normal employment relationship, many workers are either independent contractors or have different contractual relationships. These would include the self-employed and the majority of agency workers.

5.1.1 The distinction between contracts of service and contracts for services

Put simply, a contract of service is a contract of employment which means that the person working under this arrangement is an employee. A contract for services does not confer employee status and is generally the arrangement for contracting a self-employed worker.

The distinction between the two is still significant for establishing vicarious liability, the issue in many of the earlier cases. It is interesting to note that, as the law on employee status for the purposes of employment rights has been subject to change, common law liability has followed suit, as illustrated by *Hawley v Luminar Leisure Ltd*

[2006] IRLR 817. However, it is noted that the wider scope within vicarious liability is born from important policy considerations and is not easily applied in employment cases. Hence as a result of *Viasystems (Tyneside) Ltd v (1) Thermal Transfer (Northern) Limited (2) S & P Darwell Limited (3) T Hall and Day t/a CAT Metalwork Services* [2005] EWCA Civ 1151, it is possible for an individual to have two employers for the purposes of vicarious liability, but not for the purposes of employment rights/protection. The distinction may also be important for tax and National Insurance purposes, protection under certain provisions of the Health and Safety at Work etc. Act 1974 (HASAWA), entitlement to statutory sick pay, statutory maternity pay and the jobseeker's allowance, and protection of wages should the employer become insolvent. The main significance, however, for the majority of employment tribunal cases is that unfair dismissal, redundancy payments and many other employment protection measures are only available to employees—those with a contract of employment. Note that the discrimination legislation, certain provisions of Part II of the ERA 1996 and many recent measures flowing from obligations established by European Directives, such as the National Minimum Wage Act 1998 (NMWA 1998) are extended to other workers.

5.1.1.1   The evolving test for the distinction

The earliest legal test was that of 'control'. It is a notion that dates back from the time when the employment relationship was considered to be one of master and servant. A worker had a contract of employment, if he or she was subject to the command of the employer in the manner of the work. This test assumes detailed supervision by the employer or his or her agents, and clearly became inadequate in the case of employers taking on highly skilled employees whose work they were unqualified to control. The classic example is a surgeon. A high degree of employee autonomy existed within these relationships which were clearly perceived by the parties to constitute contracts of employment.

A response to this inadequacy came in *Stevenson Jordan & Harrison Ltd v Macdonald & Evans* [1952] 1 TLR 101. The Court of Appeal introduced another criterion: the extent to which a worker was integrated into the employer's organisation—the 'integration' test. So, looking back at our example of a surgeon, although the employer may not be qualified to supervise closely the quality of the surgeon's work, he or she would be fully integrated into the employer's organisation (the NHS trust or hospital employing him or her). The difficulty lay in the lack of definition of this concept for future application. 'Integration' was a very abstract concept and it was often unrealistic to apply any one test to the complex situation represented by most employment relationships.

The approach most generally adopted today is to avoid treating any single test as conclusive and to weigh up all the relevant factors. This approach was first adopted by the High Court in *Ready Mixed Concrete (South East) Ltd v Minister of Pensions & National Insurance* [1968] 2 QB 497. The case concerned the employer's liability for the social security contributions of drivers working for Ready Mixed Concrete (RMC). The drivers' relationship with RMC was such that they purchased the lorry from RMC, wore an RMC uniform and undertook to work for no one but RMC. They had some day-to-day autonomy, for example, subcontracting the driving, but RMC retained a considerable degree of control.

The test established by McKenna J involved three questions:

(a) Did the worker work in return for remuneration?

(b) Was there sufficient control for the relationship to be one of master and servant?

(c) Were other terms consistent with it being a contract of service?

On the facts the court found that there was no contract of employment, particularly because (c) was not satisfied, most of the terms suggesting a contract for services.

For a contract of employment to exist it is generally required that the worker provide services personally, as illustrated by *Staff Sentinel v Potter* [2004] IRLR 752. However, in *MacFarlane v Glasgow City Council* [2001] IRLR 7, the Employment Appeal Tribunal (EAT) held that a worker who was able to arrange a substitute from a list approved by the employer could still be considered an employee, but it is submitted that this is a very rare case indeed. It is usually the case that an employee's duty is non-delegable.

Where the situation is that of a majority shareholder and/or director of a company who is seeking, usually upon the company's insolvency, to be treated as an employee, then the approach in *Secretary of State for Business, Enterprise and Regulatory Reform v Neufeld* [2009] EWCA Civ 280, should be followed, which imposes a number of other steps to the multifunctional test discussed in this chapter. This follows the approach in *Clark v Clarks Construction Ltd* [2008] ICR 63S.

5.1.1.2 What factors may be considered?

Control

This is part of the irreducible minimum required to establish a contract of employment (*Montgomery v Johnson Underwood Ltd* [2001] IRLR 269) although the degree of control may vary. The employer should at least retain 'ultimate authority' over the employee in the performance of work, even if the individuals may have day-to-day control of their own work, as the EAT in *White v Troutbeck SA* [2013] IRLR 286 stated: 'the key question is whether there is, to a sufficient degree, a contractual right of control over the worker. The key question is not whether in practice the worker has day-to-day control of his own work.' Despite being a concept dating back to notions of 'master and servant', it is still referred to in leading judgments as an essential requirement to this day, including the difficult issue of agency workers, as shown by *Bunce v Postworth Ltd t/a 'Skyblue'* (2005) IRLR 557. In deciding that a member of a limited liability partnership (LLP) could not be a 'worker', Lord Justice Elias stated: 'the very concept of employment presupposes as a matter of sociological fact a hierarchical relationship whereby the worker is to some extent at least subordinate to the employer' (*Clyde & Co LLP v Bates van Winkelhof* [2012] IRLR 992). The notion of being subordinate essentially is a matter of control.

Self-description and the implied contract doctrine

Parties drafting contracts may assume that their description of the employment relationship will be binding. However, the courts will go far to reject a self-description which flies in the face of the underlying reality and employ a test of substance rather than form (the first significant example of this is *Young and Woods v West* [1980] IRLR 201). The reasons for this are clear; individual workers may agree to accept a label suggested by an employer seeking to avoid granting employee status without an awareness of the consequences of so doing. This has been considered in the Court of Appeal in *Protectacoat Firthglow Ltd v Szilagyi* [2009] IRLR 365, where Lady Justice Smith stated: 'the court must look at the substance, not the label'.

The Supreme Court in *Autoclenz Ltd v Belcher & Ors* [2011] UKSC 41 considered the issue of whether employment status could exist when (following findings of fact by the employment tribunal) the reality of the situation was at odds with the contractual documents signed by the parties. Lord Clarke, giving the only judgment, approved the approach that 'the question in every case is … what was the true agreement between the parties' and that 'the relative bargaining power of the parties must be taken into account in deciding whether the terms of any written agreement in truth represents what was agreed and the true agreement will often have to be gleaned from all the circumstances of the case'.

In *Catamaran Cruisers Ltd v Williams* [1994] IRLR 386, W had been required by his employer to become an independent contractor. The Inland Revenue had refused to recognise this and continued to treat him as an employee. He therefore set up a private company which contracted with the appellants to provide his services. When his services were no longer required the issue of unfair dismissal arose. The tribunal found that there was no change whatsoever in W's terms of employment apart from the method of payment. For example, he was still entitled to holiday pay and sick pay. The EAT endorsed the tribunal's view that he was still an employee.

There had been a doctrine of 'implied contracts' with a number of cases giving assistance to both claimants and respondents. This has been in response to a number of cases where companies have sought to rely on a triangular relationship between worker, employment agency and end user to evade employment protection extended to employees. The Court of Appeal in *Dacas v Brook Street Bureau* [2004] IRLR 358 has indicated that even where there is no express contract a tribunal must consider whether there is an implied contract. Where the essential elements of control and mutual obligation (see later) exist, a contract of employment can be implied. However, this case appears to be something of a 'high watermark', since subsequent decisions have diluted this principle.

Elias P in *James v Greenwich BC* [2007] IRLR 168 has suggested that there should be a necessity for the implied contract; in other words, it should only be implied if it is the only way of making the relationship work.

Further, in *Cable & Wireless plc v Muscat* [2006] IRLR 354, the Court of Appeal, in a decision applying and examining *Dacas*, found that Mr Muscat had employment status on the basis of the business reality of his situation. It merits some detailed exposition. He had been employed directly by a company called Exodus Internet Ltd, who then told him he would have to provide his services by means of a limited company. He was then dismissed from his employment and his company (E-Nuff Comms Ltd) was engaged. Exodus was then sold to the appellants. The appellants provided him with a laptop computer and a mobile telephone and paid the bills. He was described as an employee within the departmental structure and given an employee number. However, he continued to submit invoices for his services through E-Nuff. Eventually the appellants decided not to deal with any contractors directly and advised Mr Muscat to enter into a contract for services with Abraxas Ltd, which he did. Abraxas' only involvement was payment of Mr Muscat's bills. When Mr Muscat's services were later dispensed with by the appellant, he sought to claim unfair dismissal, which caused the issue of employment status to be raised. It was stated: 'The essentials of a contract of employment are the obligation to provide work for remuneration and the obligation to perform it, coupled with control. It does not, in our view, matter whether the arrangements for payment are made directly or indirectly.'

There is clearly some discrepancy between the judgments in *Dacas*, *James* and *Muscat*. As a result, there is much scope for argument by claimants and respondents.

Consistency and details of relationship
The details of the arrangements between workers and their respective companies are highly relevant. Where workers are paid a regular wage or salary, where they have sick pay and paid holidays, where they work on the employer's premises, with the employer's plant and equipment, they are more likely to be considered employees (since all of these

arrangements are consistent with a contract of employment). None of these, however, is conclusive. In *Nethermere (St Neots) Ltd v Taverna and Gardiner* [1984] ICR 612, for example, machinists who worked from home were held to be employees. Further, a worker who applied for an advertised job and, following an offer of the same job, was then asked to sign a tender to supply services in *Ministry of Defence HD Defence Dental Service v Kettle* EAT 21/1/2007, was held to be an employee, since the method by which the relationship came into being could only be consistent with an employment relationship.

Economic reality

This particular factor was introduced by the High Court in *Market Investigations Ltd v Minister of Social Security* [1969] 2 QB 173. Here a part-time market researcher was able to decide her working hours but otherwise did everything according to the employer's instructions. In concluding that she was an employee, Cooke J interpreted the test as whether she was in fact *in business on her own account*. This test involves examining the level of financial risk on both sides, since generally an entrepreneur in business on their own account risks losing either capital or profits if the venture falters. Such risk tends not to exist for an employee (other than the possible future loss of a source of income). If she was in business on her own account, and thus economically independent of her employer, her contract would be one for services. If not, the contract would probably be one of service. In this case the latter was true even though the contract itself described her as an independent contractor.

This test was further considered by the Privy Council in *Lee Ting-Sang v Chung Chi-Keung* [1990] ICR 409. Here a skilled craftsman worked for a number of different employers. It might be thought that this would lead to the conclusion that he was in business on his own account. However, Lord Griffiths distinguished between 'a skilled artisan earning his living by working for more than one employer as an employee and … a small businessman venturing into business on his own account as an independent contractor with all its attendant risks'. In this case the fact that the worker gave priority to the work of this, his main employer, helped to underpin the economic reality of the relationship as one of employment.

The periods of employment in *Chung* were also substantial. Where, by contrast, individual contracts rarely last for more than one day, as in the case of *Hall v Lorimer* [1994] IRLR 171, the court is more likely to find self-employment.

In *Tiffin v Lester Aldridge LLP* [2012] IRLR 391 the Court of Appeal held that fixed share partners in a limited liability partnership are not employees. For two recent cases considering whether an individual was in business on his account, please refer to *Pimlico Plumbers Ltd v Smith* [2014] UKEAT/0495/12/DM and *Hospital Medical Group Ltd v Westwood* [2012] EWCA Civ 1005.

Mutual obligation

The factors considered so far have addressed the nature of the relationship between the contracting parties, but the doctrine of consideration imposes one other requirement. This is that there must be mutual obligation between the parties. As stated by Mr Justice Langstaff in *Cotswold Developments Construction Ltd v Williams* [2006] IRLR 181: 'mutual obligations are necessary for there to be a contract [of employment] at all' and that 'a contract under which there is no obligation to work could not be a contract of employment'. It can be fairly stated that mutuality of obligations has become the most significant of the factors (*Carmichael v National Power plc* [2000] IRLR 43). The most recent guidance on this issue can be found in the EAT's decision in *Drake v Ipsos Mori UK Ltd* [2012] IRLR 973.

Mutuality of obligations can be identified at two levels, which have been explained by Freedland (*The Contract of Employment*, Clarendon, 1976, pp 21–2) as follows:

At the first level there is an exchange of work for remuneration. At the second level there is an exchange of mutual promises of future performance. The second level—the promises to employ and to be employed—provides the arrangement with its stability and its continuity as a contract. The promises to employ and to be employed may be of short duration or may be terminable at short notice; but they still form an integral and most important part of the contract. They are the mutual undertakings to maintain the employment relationship in being which are inherent in any contract of employment.

This was the basis of the analysis in *McLeod v Hellyer Brothers Ltd* [1987] IRLR 232. Trawlermen entered a separate contract for each voyage. They worked exclusively for the same employer and had done so for a number of years. The Court of Appeal found that each time a new voyage was about to be undertaken there was no mutual obligation to offer the fresh contract and to agree to work. Therefore, regardless of the nature of the individual contracts, there was no 'umbrella contract' covering the longer period over which they had been working. In *Hellyer*, the court accepted that each individual contract could be one of employment. This has not always been the view of the courts. In *O'Kelly v Trusthouse Forte* [1983] ICR 728, the applicant was a 'regular casual' wine waiter. He worked for no one other than THF, and in practice always worked for them when requested and they gave him priority when work was available. However, there was no mutuality of obligation. The Court of Appeal held that not only did this prevent an 'umbrella' contract from arising, but also meant that each individual contract was one for services.

These decisions stand in contrast to that in *Nethermere (St Neots) Ltd v Taverna and Gardiner* [1984] ICR 612. This case concerned homeworkers who in practice regularly accepted the work offered to them. They were under no contractual obligation to do so, nor was the employer obliged to offer it to them. However, the Court of Appeal accepted the tribunal finding that the long-standing relationship that had developed had established an 'umbrella' contract of employment. The EAT came to a similar decision on facts which were hard to distinguish from *O'Kelly* in *Four Seasons Ltd v Hamarat* (1984), unreported (EAT 369/84).

In both cases a common thread is of both parties in practice working together regularly even though there is no contractual obligation so to do. This is at the least a matter of convenience for the employer, who does not wish to recruit new staff regularly. For most employees it is a matter of economic necessity to accept whatever jobs are offered. It has been argued (*per* Sir John Donaldson MR in *O'Kelly*) that this indicates that the regularity of the relationship may be attributed to market forces. A different view is seen in *Nethermere* where Stephenson LJ saw no reason 'why well-founded expectations of continuing homework should not be hardened or refined into enforceable contracts by regular giving and taking of work over periods of a year or more'.

The mere fact of an employer not being obliged to provide work is not always fatal to the finding of a contract of employment. In *Wilson v Circular Distributors Ltd* [2006] IRLR 38, a relief area manager was required to cover area managers during holidays and sickness absences, despite the contract expressly stating 'there will be occasions where no work is available'. Judge D Serota, QC stated: 'it is the absence of mutual obligations that is crucial. It is not sufficient for there to be an obligation of the employer to provide work. There has to be an absence of an obligation of the employer to provide work and an absence of obligation on the part of the employee when work is offered to accept that work.'

It is important to note that a small amount of discretion or choice in the hands of either the worker or company is not enough to extinguish a mutuality of obligations. In *Cornwall District Council v Prater* [2006] IRLR 362, a home tutor was referred pupils by the local authority. The council was not obliged to offer her pupils and she was not obliged to take them. However, once she had agreed, she was obliged to complete her commitment to that particular child and the council was obliged to provide work until that assignment ended. The fact that during each period of work she was obliged to teach and the council was obliged to pay was sufficient for a contract of employment to exist.

Conclusion

The contrasting decisions in relation to this issue have led to legal uncertainty and the general conclusion that each case will turn on its facts. The question of whether a contract is one of employment or for services is nearly always a mixed question of law and fact. As the EAT only has jurisdiction to hear questions of law (see **4.17**) it cannot overturn an employment tribunal's finding of fact unless it is perverse. Thus these cases do not operate as precedents to a significant degree, but identify possible arguments to raise at tribunal. The finding of either a contract of service or contract for services will often depend on the interaction of the factors stated in this section.

It is possible that the principle stated by the European Court of Justice in *Fenoll v Centre d'aide par le travail 'La Jouvene'* [2016] IRLR 67 will expand the eligibility of UK individuals to be considered employees and workers. In that case, it was stated that an employment relationship occurs where 'for a certain period of time a person performs services for and under the direction of another person in return for which he receives remuneration', a wide and generous definition.

The case of *Consistent Group Ltd v Kalwak* [2007] IRLR 560 is an example of an agency case where no implied contract with the end user was found, which relied upon 'self description' (a detailed consideration of the terms of a written agreement which included a number of attempts to exclude employee status), mutual obligations (here there were limited powers to delegate work) and control (one key feature of this case was the high degree of control exerted by the agency). Mr Justice Elias in this case found that the workers were employed by the agency and stated: 'Tribunals should take a sensible and robust view of these matters in order to prevent form undermining substance.'

Useful guidance has been provided by the Court of Appeal in *McMeechan v Secretary of State for Employment* [1997] IRLR 353. Waite LJ points out that cases involving casual or temporary workers tend to be capable of analysis in terms of both the overall relationship and individual engagements. Both may need to be analysed. Most cases involving statutory protection concentrate on the overall relationship because the claimant must show a two-year continuing contract to establish tribunal jurisdiction (for unfair dismissal and redundancy payments), unless employment was commenced before 6 April 2012. In *McMeechan* the applicant merely sought from the Secretary of State payment for his last engagement on the insolvency of the agency, so it was the most recent engagement which was relevant. Parties should therefore apply their factual analysis to the overall relationship or the most recent engagement, depending on what remedy is sought.

In *Carmichael v National Power plc* [2000] IRLR 43, casual tour guides could not be required to work if they did not want to. Although the Court of Session had found an implied term that the parties would provide and accept a reasonable amount of work this was held by the House of Lords to be insufficient to establish mutual obligation. The House of Lords was of the view that unless the parties to an agreement had agreed that a document or series of documents was intended to constitute an exclusive record of their agreement, any question arising as to the nature or terms of the contract was a question of fact to be determined upon consideration of all the evidence, including written documents, oral statements and conduct.

The only situation where the question of the existence of a contract of employment appears to be a question of law, and thus subject to appeal, is where it is purely a matter of interpreting documents (*Davies v Presbyterian Church of Wales* [1986] ICR 280). This is rare in normal employment situations, so the issue will normally remain one for argument on the facts before the tribunal.

Although terms implied by the parties' conduct may be used in the *construction* of a contract (see **5.2.4**), the Court of Appeal has rejected the use of terms implied from conduct to *establish the existence* of a contract of employment (*Stevedoring & Haulage Services Ltd v Fuller* [2001] IRLR 627).

It should be clear from the discussion above that for general questions of employment law, 'employee' status is not defined by statute. One important exception is in discrimination cases. Under s 83 Equality Act 2010, employment can also include 'a contract personally to do work'. The definition cannot be complied with where an unfettered right of substitution exists (and is exercised) and a lack of control (*Halawi v WDFG UK Ltd t/a World Duty Free* [2015] IRLR 50 (CA)). In this context, the meaning of 'employee' is an issue of EU law as a result of *Jivraj v Hashwani* [2011] UKSC 40.

Please note that as a result of reg 8 of the Fixed Term Employees Regulations 2002, an employee continuously employed on a series of fixed-term contracts for four years or more is automatically deemed to be a permanent employee (unless the continued use of fixed-term contracts can be justified). This obviously has important consequences in relation to unfair dismissal and redundancy as dealt with in **Chapter 6** of this manual.

5.1.2   Other categories of worker

5.1.2.1   Directors and other office holders

Where someone works as the temporary holder of an office which will continue after he or she has departed he or she will not normally have a contract of employment. Examples include directors of companies, police and prison officers, the clergy and persons holding public office.

A complication arises where the term 'director' is used to describe senior managers who are really employees. Guidelines for distinguishing the two were laid down in *Eaton v Robert Eaton Ltd* [1988] ICR 302. As referred to at **5.1.1.1**, the case of *Secretary of State for Business, Enterprise and Regulatory Reform v Neufeld* [2009] EWCA Civ 280 gives guidance on the method of determining employee status of a director/majority shareholder. A director will generally be an office holder, and therefore not an employee, unless there is evidence to suggest employee status, for example:

- description such as 'managing director';
- precise employment contract;
- payment by salary rather than fee;
- actual work done.

Those holding public sector offices which are controlled largely by statutory provisions may have the alternative remedy of judicial review under the Civil Procedure

Rules (CPR) 1998, Pt 54, available to them instead of relying on tribunal remedies (*Malloch v Aberdeen Corporation* [1971] 1 WLR 1578). The courts will be reluctant to allow this where the terms are fundamentally contractual in nature (*R v East Berkshire Health Authority, ex p Walsh* [1985] QB 152), but may where the terms are statutory in origin (*R v Secretary of State for the Home Department, ex p Benwell* [1985] QB 554).

For an exposition of the distinction between employee and office holder, see *Percy v Church of Scotland Board of National Mission* [2006] IRLR 195 (HL), where the status of a minister of religion was considered. This was further considered in *New Testament Church of God v Stewart* [2008] IRLR 134. The question will greatly depend on the facts of the individual case.

5.1.2.2   Civil servants

The ability of the Crown to dismiss its servants at will had often led to the conclusion that they do not have contracts of employment. This view (see *R v Civil Service Appeal Board, ex p Bruce* [1988] ICR 649) was rejected by the Divisional Court in *R v Lord Chancellor's Department, ex p Nangle* [1991] IRLR 343. The court found that the parties had the intention to create legal relations, and that a contract of employment did exist (rendering judicial review an inappropriate remedy). Civil servants are entitled, anyway, to most statutory employment protection measures (see ERA 1996, s 191). The Crown's power of dismissal at will means, however, that civil servants may not complain of wrongful dismissal (for the distinction between unfair and wrongful dismissal, see **Chapter 6**).

5.1.2.3   Agency workers

The diverse circumstances of agency workers make any general conclusions difficult to draw. Some work for a number of agencies. Others have a continuing relationship with one, which may provide sick pay and holiday pay, provisions normally associated with a contract of employment. Among these workers will be those who regularly change the employer for whom they work and others who work for the same employer for long periods.

Earlier cases in this area had tended to rely on an analysis of the contractual terms. This usually led to the conclusion that the contract with the agency is not one of employment (*Wickens v Champion Employment* [1984] ICR 365). However, agency contracts are often drafted so that the end user has no express contractual relationship with the worker. This would free the end user from responsibility for workers' statutory rights, often the motivation for using agency staff. At the same time, the characteristics of the worker's relationship with the agency (for example, a lack of control) usually mean that the worker cannot be seen as an employee of the agency. This may be consistent with the circumstances of workers who regularly change the end user for whom they work, but for those who work for the same end user for significant periods of time it appears to undermine the employment protection policies of successive governments.

This issue came before the Court of Appeal in *Dacas v Brook Street Bureau* [2004] IRLR 358, as discussed in **5.1.1.2** under 'Self description and the implied contract doctrine'. A cleaner, supplied by an agency, but working for the same end user for four years, claimed unfair dismissal. Her contract expressly stipulated that there was no contract of employment with either the agency or the end user. There was no mutual obligation between her and the agency, and the agency exercised no control over her work. The conclusion based on a contractual analysis that she was employed by neither was (*per* Sedley LJ) 'simply not credible'. The Court of Appeal analysed the factual situation and held that the end user exercised effective control over the worker and both were under a mutual obligation to provide and undertake work. Thus, in the face of an express contractual provision that there was no contract of employment the Court of Appeal held that one was implied and (*per* Mummery LJ) that this would 'accord with practical reality and common sense'.

The *Dacas* decision has been subject to some undermining by the EAT in *James v London Borough of Greenwich* [2007] IRLR 168, where Mr Justice Elias stated: 'it will be a rare case where there will be evidence entitling the tribunal to imply a contract between the worker and end user.' However, *Dacas* remains good authority.

The end user may attempt to prevent such implication of terms by providing in the written contract that it constitutes the complete agreement between the parties. This will not be conclusive where the facts show that it does not contain the entire bargain between the parties (*Royal National Lifeboat Institution v Bushaway* [2005] IRLR 674 (EAT)).

Thus, evidence of sufficient control and mutual obligation should lead the tribunal to infer a contract of employment even where no express contract exists. Whether this will be applied beyond the context of agency work and what length of employment relationship will be sufficient to establish such an implied contract is a matter to be worked out in future court decisions. If the *Dacas*, as opposed to the *James*, approach is confirmed, one consequence is likely to be the reduction of the use by employers of agency staff, as one benefit (ability to dismiss without consequence) may no longer be available.

There have been cases where the court has found a contract of employment with the agency (*McMeechan v Secretary of State for Employment* [1997] IRLR 353). This is distinguished in the Court of Appeal decision in *Bunce v Postworth Ltd t/a Skyblue* [2005] IRLR 557. Whereas in *McMeechan* the contract had provided that the worker should accept instructions from both agency and end user, in *Bunce* the contract provided for control by the end user alone. This narrow distinction enabled the Court of Appeal to maintain the *Dacas* approach towards the contractual relationship with the agency, but leaves workers who cannot establish a contract of employment with the end user unprotected. Where the agency exercises a high level of control, a contract of employment may be found to exist (*Consistent Group Ltd v Kalwak* [2007] IRLR 560).

Where the worker is employed by the agency, he or she will be protected by legislative provisions contained within the Agency Workers Regulations 2010 (SI 2010/93), Employment Agencies Act 1973 (EAA 1973), Employment Act 2008 (EA 2008) and their attendant regulations. These are beyond the scope of this book.

5.1.2.4 'Worker' status

The Working Time Regulations 1998 (SI 1998/1833), (WT Regs) (covering maximum working hours and minimum rights to annual leave), NMWA 1998 and Part Time Workers (Prevention of Less Favourable Treatment) Regulations 2000 (SI 2000/1551) (PTW Regs) extend protection to a category of person labelled a 'worker'. This was to ensure basic protection for a wider range of people than employees. 'Worker' is defined as anyone working under a contract of employment or any other contract to perform personally any work or services, except to a professional client or business customer. There is therefore a gap between employee status and worker status. In *James v Redcats (Brands) Ltd* [2007] IRLR 296, the EAT found that being self-employed is compatible with worker status. Similarly, in *Redrow Homes (Yorkshire) Ltd v Wright* [2004] IRLR 720, bricklayers who were sub-contractors were held to be 'workers', since they were obliged to perform work personally.

In determining whether a given individual is a worker or is in business on his/her own account, the tribunal will apply a test of substance and not form similar to cases of employee status. Hence, a written contract unequivocally stating a person was in business on his/her own account was not necessarily a complete or reliable definition of the nature of the relationship in *Boss Projects LLP v Bragg* (UKEAT/0330/13/SM).

The Court of Appeal in *Pimlico Plumbers v Smith* [2017] IRLR 323, disregarded the declaration within the contract documentation stating Mr Smith was 'an independent contractor of the company, in business on your own account' because the rest of the contract did not reflect that reality. The contract set out provisions on working time, conduct, availability for work, procedures and even appearance at work on plumbing jobs. The fact that Mr Smith's right of substitution was only a conditional one and the requirement to be available to work a minimum of 40 hours a week, along with the factors set out above, led the Court of Appeal to conclude Mr Smith was a worker.

Despite its status as only a non-binding Employment Tribunal decision, the judgment in *Aslam & Farrar and others v Uber* [2017] IRLR 4 is an illuminating one, clearly explaining the law and issues in determining worker status.

5.1.3 Illegality in the contract of employment

This most commonly arises where there has been a fraud on the Inland Revenue. Since it is a well-known principle at common law that an illegal contract is usually void, illegality in a contract of employment can make it unenforceable. As a result, the tribunal may refuse to accept jurisdiction in unfair dismissal cases (and in other cases where the existence of a contract is a prerequisite of bringing a claim) upon discovery that the contract is tainted with illegality.

The tribunal has, however, sometimes been willing to accept discrimination cases as the existence of a valid contract is not a requirement for their jurisdiction (*Hall v Woolston Hall Leisure Ltd* [2000] IRLR 578 (CA)). This liberal approach is being extended to unfair dismissal where, in *Enfield Technical Services Ltd v Payne* [2008] EWCA Civ 393, it was held that an illegal contract must consist of 'misrepresentation, some attempt to conceal the true facts of the relationship'.

A contract which is illegal since its inception, such as one entered into by an illegal immigrant, as in *Hounga v Allen & Anor* [2012] EWCA Civ 609, is not one which can be relied upon, even in a discrimination claim.

The Court of Appeal in *Colen v Cebrian (UK) Ltd* [2004] IRLR 210 has held that tribunals should enquire into the claimant's involvement in the illegality. According to Waller LJ, 'If at the date of the contract the contract was perfectly lawful and it was intended to perform it lawfully, the effect of some act of illegal performance is not automatically to render the contract unenforceable … the question is whether the method of performance chosen and the degree of participation in that illegal performance is such as to "turn the contract into an illegal contract".' It is also possible to sever the unlawful elements of performance according to *Blue Chip Trading Ltd v Helbsevi* [2009] IRLR 128.

A somewhat niche decision of the EAT on illegality is *Secretary of State for Justice v Betts & Ors* UKEAT/0284/16/DA where the contracts were found to be ultra vires, but the claimants were still held to be workers for the purpose of employment protection.

5.2 Terms of the contract of employment: statutory, express and implied terms

There is no requirement for a contract of employment to be in writing and so the contract of employment comes into existence when the offer of a job is accepted by the new employee.

It may be that the performance of the obligations under the contract is not to commence until some time in the future (after a period of notice with an existing employer has been worked out, for example). The contract, nevertheless, already exists, and remedies may be immediately available in appropriate situations (see *Sarker v South Tees Acute Hospitals NHS Trust* [1997] IRLR 328 at **5.7.2**).

In many cases, therefore, there will be little more than a brief oral agreement, with little mention of detailed terms. ERA 1996, s 1, requires employers to provide employees with a written statement of the terms of their contract within two months of the start of that employment. This statement, however, is not a contract, although it may be valuable evidence of the terms of the contract (see **5.2.3**).

Please see **5.9** for a specimen statutory written statement of terms.

There are a number of different sources of terms of the contract of employment.

5.2.1 Statutory sources

It should be noted that where the contract of employment is silent on an issue and employment legislation confers upon the employee a certain right, then that statutory right will prevail. However, these employment rights do not achieve the status of contractual terms. By contrast, a number of statutory sources imply specific clauses into contracts of employment.

Section 66 of the Equality Act 2010 implies an equality clause into all contracts of employment (see **Chapter 10**).

NMWA 1998 provides minimum levels of pay (see **5.5**).

In April 2016, a National Living Wage will prescribe hourly pay for workers and employees over the age of 25. Please see **5.5** for details.

WT Regs make provisions in respect of hours of work and holidays (see **5.6**).

Other statutory provisions affecting the contract of employment include the Teaching and Higher Education Act 1998 (THEA 1998), ss 32 and 33 (which entitles 16- and 17-year-olds to paid time off for education and training) and the Public Interest Disclosure Act 1998 (PIDA 1998). This, popularly known as the 'Whistleblowers' Act, protects against victimisation or dismissal for disclosing in good faith certain information which it is in the public interest to disclose. The cap on compensatory awards (see **7.5.8**) does not apply.

As a result of s 153 of the Small Business, Enterprise and Employment Act 2015, exclusivity clauses in so-called 'zero-hours' contracts have been prohibited.

5.2.2 Express terms

The terms of a contract may be expressed in writing, thus providing clear evidence of them, or may be orally agreed. Thus in *Hawker Siddeley Power Engineering Ltd v Rump* [1979] IRLR 425, the employee entered into an oral agreement that a written term in the contract he had signed, entitling the employer to send him anywhere in the country, would not apply to him. This had the effect of varying the written contract, and the employer was unable to enforce it. (Although such a wide ranging 'mobility clause' would anyway be unenforceable for having an unreasonable scope in the present day.)

Such disputes are questions of fact for the employment tribunal and thus not appealable. Where contractual terms are expressed entirely in writing their interpretation becomes a matter of law and thus an issue on which an appeal can be made (*Davies v Presbyterian Church of Wales* [1986] ICR 280).

Where the contract is in writing and is clear and comprehensive, the parole evidence rule will apply and the courts will not generally admit external evidence to aid interpretation (see *Nelson v British Broadcasting Corporation* [1977] ICR 649). On the other hand, where there are gaps or inconsistencies in the written contract, such external evidence may be admitted. This was the case in *Pedersen v Camden London Borough Council* [1981] ICR 674, where the Court of Appeal permitted reference to the job advertisement to clarify an ambiguity as to the type of work P was expected to perform. In general, therefore, extrinsic evidence is admissible to clarify an unclear written contract, or to augment an incomplete one. It will not be available to interpret or restrict a clear, complete one. The EAT in *Allen v TRW Systems* [2013] UKEAT 0083/12/1701 was prepared to hold that a policy contained in a staff/employee handbook was capable of being incorporated into the contract of employment despite omission from the statement of terms. In that case the policy had been reimpressed in a works council agreement, employee handbook and various correspondence. Hence the evidence which may be considered by the tribunal can potentially be wide.

Department of Transport v Sparks [2016] ICR 695 (CA) provides useful guidance on determining whether provisions are capable of being incorporated into the contract (where, perhaps, they are contained in a staff handbook or new policy). The questions to be considered are:

a) The document in question (what is its character, does it confer rights, how is it expressed).

b) The effect and importance of the disputed provision.

c) Is it 'apt for incorporation'?

This case is relevant to policy documents, staff handbooks, sickness absence procedures, etc.

In relation to the ability of an employee to challenge any terms of the contract of employment, the Court of Appeal in *Commerzbank AG v Keen* [2007] IRLR 132, have excluded the possibility of relying upon the Unfair Contract Terms Act 1977 (UCTA 1977), since the employee is not dealing with his or her employers 'as a consumer' (as required by UCTA 1977, s 3).

For guidance on the issue of whether an express term can be subject to a 'limiting' implied term and on implying terms generally, see *Ali v Petroleum Company of Trinidad and Tobago* [2017] UKPC 2.

5.2.3   The written statement of terms and conditions of employment

Although there is no requirement for a contract of employment to be in writing the law recognises that employees need to be aware of some of the essential terms of employment. As a result (by virtue of the Employment Rights Act 1996 (ERA 1996), s 1) all employees are entitled to a copy of their written particulars within two months of the start of their employment. This document is referred to in practice as either a 'written statement', the 'written particulars of employment' or a 'section 1 statement'. Although it is not a contract itself, it is persuasive (but not conclusive) evidence of the terms of the contract (*Robertson & Johnson v British Gas Corporation* [1983] IRLR 302 (CA)). Thus in *System Floors (UK) Ltd v Daniel* [1982] ICR 54, the written statement said that D's employment began on 19 November, a date which gave him sufficient continuity to claim unfair dismissal. All the other evidence, however, pointed to a later date. The EAT accepted this evidence, and thus concluded that he was ineligible to claim unfair dismissal.

The employer may substitute a written statement which refers to a document containing the details themselves. This must be reasonably accessible to employees covered by it, for example, on a notice board (ERA 1996, s 2(3)). For an example of a statutory written statement, see **5.9**.

What must the written particulars contain?
ERA 1996, s 1(3) provides that the employer must:

(a) Identify the parties.

(b) Specify the date when the employment began. This is the day referred to in the contract, rather than the first day of actual work. Thus a contract 'commencing on 1 May 1982' commences on that date even though it was a Saturday and the employee did not actually turn up until 4 May after the intervening bank holiday (*General of the Salvation Army v Dewsbury* [1984] ICR 498).

(c) Specify the date on which the employee's period of continuous employment began. This might include earlier employment with an associated employer, with a partnership before its reorganisation, etc. For full details see **6.3**.

Section 1(4) provides for the statement to include the following:

(a) The scale or rate of remuneration, or the method of calculating remuneration.

(b) Intervals at which remuneration is paid.

(c) Terms relating to hours of work (including any relating to normal working hours). This is important for calculating a week's pay, the basis of many assessments of quantum.

(d) Terms and conditions relating to:
  (i) holiday entitlement, including treatment of public holidays and holiday pay,
  (ii) incapacity due to sickness or injury,
  (iii) pensions and pension schemes.

(e) The length of notice required on either side to terminate the contract.

(f) The job title.

(g) Where employment is temporary, its expected duration (and where the employment is for a fixed term, the date when that employment is to end).

(h) The place of work, any mobility provisions and the employer's address.

(j) The particulars of any collective agreements which directly affect the terms of the contract.

(k) Where the employee is required to work outside the UK for over a month:
  (i) the period of work outside the UK,
  (ii) the currency for payment,

(iii) additional pay and benefits in return for working overseas,

(iv) terms and conditions relating to the employee's return to the UK.

(l) whether a contracting out certificate is in force (under the Pensions Schemes Act 1993 (PSA 1993)).

All these particulars must be contained or referred to in one document. Further, if no particulars are to be entered in relation to the content at (a)–(l), that fact must be stated (ERA 1996, s 2(1)).

Section 3(1), dealing with disciplinary and grievance procedures, requires the statement to include a note:

(a) Specifying disciplinary rules or referring to an accessible document which does so. (The accessible document may be part of a staff handbook or a separate disciplinary or grievance procedure. If employers do not wish such procedures to become contractual, the statement should make it clear that they are not.)

(b) Specifying:

(i) a person to whom the employee can apply if dissatisfied with a disciplinary decision relating to him,

(ii) a person to whom the employee should apply to seek redress of a grievance, and the appropriate procedure.

The statement must contain these particulars except for those required by s 1(4)(d)(ii) (iii), s 1(4)(e) and s 3(1), where reference to other accessible documents may be used.

Where changes occur in any terms the employer must provide an amended statement at the earliest opportunity, and never later than one month after the change, as required by ERA 1996, s 4.

Enforcement

ERA 1996, s 11, provides for a reference to an employment tribunal either where no statement has been given or where there is a dispute as to the contents of a statement. The tribunal may declare what terms should have been included. Despite the repeal of a number of the provisions of EA 2002, s 38 has survived, preserving the right to claim an award of two or four weeks' pay for a failure to provide written particulars of employment.

Although it does not have the power to enforce performance of the terms thus determined, its decision is *res judicata*. Thus where a statement makes no reference to paid holidays, and a tribunal declares that the employee was entitled to 25 days' paid holiday each year, this may not be questioned in a subsequent action to recover arrears of holiday pay.

This process of determining what terms should exist where they are absent or disputed was clarified in *Mears v Safecar Security Ltd* [1983] QB 54 (CA). The employment tribunal must fill any gaps and resolve any disputes. In so doing it should first see whether a term had been agreed orally, but not written down. Here it may need to resolve conflicting evidence. A term may be obvious from another term which has been agreed and written down. Thus an employee whose job title was 'night watchman' could not resist a finding that his hours of work, even if not expressly recorded, took place at night-time.

If these approaches do not help, the employment tribunal should consider how the contract has worked in practice. If an employee has regularly worked a particular pattern of hours without dissent, this will be evidence of the contractual term in respect of hours.

Finally (although *obiter*), the Court of Appeal suggested that where there is insufficient evidence to use any of these methods the tribunal should import the term it thinks *should* have been agreed, and, generally, resolve doubts in favour of the employee.

The relationship between contract and written statement

Where the employer provides both a written contract and a statutory statement, the latter cannot override the former (*Robertson v British Gas Corporation* [1983] ICR 351). Indeed, when, as in this case, the differing statutory particulars were introduced at a later stage they merely constituted an attempt at a unilateral variation of the contract. As any variation must be consensual, they had no effect.

How can the statutory written particulars be distinguished from a written contract?

Where the employee signs a document acknowledging receipt of his statutory particulars this is no more than evidence that the employer has complied with his obligations. Where, however, the acknowledgement describes the particulars as a contract of employment, the employee's signature is taken to indicate his assent to the statement actually being his contract. This was the case in *Gascol Conversions Ltd v Mercer* [1974] ICR 420.

Thus the written statement will be evidence of the express terms of the contract. Most contracts, however, are much more detailed and complex than compliance with s 1 requires. The Advisory, Conciliation and Arbitration Service (ACAS) Code of Practice on Disciplinary and Grievance Procedures (2004) (<http://www.acas.org.uk>) recommends inclusion of a variety of other information. This, however, has no statutory force, and it is common for employers to give little extra information as to contractual terms, just as it is for workers to take on employment very casually. Thus contracts may exist where relatively few terms have been expressly agreed. It therefore becomes necessary to look elsewhere for contractual terms.

5.2.4   Implied terms

As with ordinary common law contracts, contracts of employment often require terms to be implied to ensure they are workable, practical and complete. However, because the consequences of implication are very different, the courts will only imply a term into a contract of employment if necessary.

The basic principle may be seen in *Sagar v H. Ridehalgh & Son Ltd* [1931] 1 Ch 310. Deductions were made from a weaver's pay for bad work. Such deductions were normal and well established in that industry, although S had not been expressly informed of them when entering the contract. The Court of Appeal held that such a term could be implied provided it was 'reasonable, certain and notorious'. Actual knowledge by the individual affected was not necessary. (It should be noted that deductions from pay are now subject to the ERA 1996, Pt II and S's employers would not now be able to make the deduction in such circumstances.)

Courts are prepared to consider collective agreements as indicative of the appropriate term to imply, even where they are not technically incorporated (*Howman & Son v Blyth* [1983] ICR 416).

The concept of implication is used:

- to import terms where the contract is silent; and
- to assist the courts in interpreting terms which are unclear.

5.2.4.1 When might terms be implied?

The more detailed and precise a contract is, the less will the court be prepared to imply a term on an issue not mentioned in the contract (*Reid v Rush & Tompkins plc* [1990] ICR 61 (CA)). Contracts of employment, however, often require implied terms in order to operate effectively.

An example is the question of mobility clauses (see further **6.11.4.3**). The contract often says nothing about where the employee is to work. This is often of significance in redundancy situations. If the worker whose existing job disappears, refuses a transfer which was permissible within the terms of his contract, he is not redundant. If he refuses one which was not within the terms of the contract, he is redundant. If there is no express term, the court will have to imply a term.

In *O'Brien v Associated Fire Alarms Ltd* [1968] 1 WLR 1916, the employee was told to work 120 miles away, a justification being that the area was still administered by his district office. The Court of Appeal implied a term into the contract that he could only be expected to work a reasonable distance from home. He was not, therefore, obliged to agree to the move, and could receive a redundancy payment if there was no further work for him at his old place of work.

This type of term will not be reasonable in all situations. In *Stevenson v Teesside Bridge Engineering Ltd* [1971] 1 All ER 296, a steel erector employed in bridge building was required to move when work on the existing bridge was finished. It was held that, given the nature of the employment, it was not unreasonable to expect this degree of mobility.

Thus, the precise term which will be implied may rest on concepts of reasonableness, and an attempt to meet the demands of industrial relations reality. In so doing, implied terms may lead to radical reinterpretation of express terms. In *United Bank Ltd v Akhtar* [1989] IRLR 507, the contract entitled the employer to insist on the employee working anywhere in the country. He was told to move from Leeds to Birmingham at short notice, with no financial assistance. The EAT held that this involved breach of an implied term that employers will not, without reasonable and proper cause, conduct themselves in a way likely to destroy or seriously damage the relationship of confidence and trust. In this case, this implied term overrode the express terms of the contract. Note that this does not introduce an implied term that the employer should act reasonably, as to do so would contravene the rule in *Western Excavating (ECC) v Sharp* [1978] QB 761 (see **6.4.1.3**). This was emphasised in *White v Reflecting Roadstuds* [1991] IRLR 331 by the EAT, overruling a tribunal decision that there had been a constructive dismissal because the employer had acted unreasonably. The employer's action must effectively prevent the performance of the contract or damage the employment relationship in the way suggested in *Akhtar*.

Implied terms may be used to add flesh to the bones of express terms. In *Cosslett Contractors Ltd v Quinn* (1990) 413 IRLIB 15 it was held that where an employee was asked to work away from his usual workplace there would be an implied term that all expenses, losses, etc. incurred would be reimbursed.

5.2.4.2 What terms will typically be implied?

There is no simple list of terms which will be implied and this is something of a growth area. It is often of significance in establishing whether a resignation may be perceived as a constructive dismissal (see **6.4.1.3**). There is scope for applying the concept of reasonableness to argue for any particular filling of a gap in the express terms of a contract. It is convenient to consider the duties of the employer and employee separately.

5.2.4.3   Employer's duties

To pay wages or salary

This will normally be clear from the express words of the contract. It is implied, how-ever, that the employer need only pay where the employee is ready and willing to per-form the contractual obligations. An employer may therefore deduct a proportion of salary in appropriate circumstances.

In *Miles v Wakefield Metropolitan District Council* [1987] AC 539, a registrar taking industrial action refused to work Saturdays. This reduced his normal 37-hour week by three hours. His employers deducted 3/37ths of his normal salary. The House of Lords held that they were quite entitled so to do, as the employee had failed to provide con-sideration for that part of the contract.

The Court of Appeal has gone further in *Wiluszynski v Tower Hamlets London Borough Council* [1989] ICR 493. Here the employee refused to respond to requests from council-lors, while being prepared to do the rest of his work. The employer told him in advance that this was not acceptable and that if he did come to work his work would be seen as voluntary. In the event he was allowed to perform the remainder of his duties. The employer was nevertheless entitled to refuse payment altogether. The distinction is the employer's clear refusal to accept partial performance.

To provide work

In general the employer is under no obligation to provide work (see *Langston v Amal-gamated Union of Engineering Workers (No 2)* [1974] ICR 510). As long as the employer pays the employee, the employee may be kept in a state of 'idleness' (*Turner v Sawdon* [1901] 2 KB 653). There are certain exceptions. A right to work can be established by three factors as a result of the decision in *William Hill Organisation Ltd v Tucker* [1998] IRLR 313: the nature of the post (which must be specific and/or unique), the nature of the skills required (here the skills required frequent exercise to assure their 'sharpness') and the terms of the contract.

Where the employee is a pieceworker, there is a general implication that he or she must be provided with work, otherwise he or she can earn nothing. This will not, however, entitle employees to payment where, for example, the machine breaks down (*Devonald v Rosser & Sons* [1906] 2 KB 728). Similar arguments apply to those who earn a commission.

In *Bosworth v Angus Jowett & Co Ltd* [1977] IRLR 374, a sales director was held to be entitled to work to protect his professional reputation. This is easier to argue for high-status employees with reputations to protect.

Of co-operation, respect and fair treatment

Some examples are set out below.

The employer should not make it more difficult for the employee to perform his or her work. Thus in *Wetherall (Bond St W1) Ltd v Lynn* [1977] IRLR 333, the employer humiliated a manager in front of his subordinates. It was held that this undermined his authority and made it more difficult for him to perform his job. This constituted a breach of contract by the employer, enabling the employee to resign and claim con-structive dismissal.

There should be no unjust discrimination against the employee. In *F. C. Gardner Ltd v Beresford* [1978] IRLR 63, the employee resigned as being the only worker who had not been given a pay rise for two years. It was held that, as there were no grounds on which this treatment could be justified, it was a breach of contract. The EAT implied a term that the employer would not treat the employee capriciously in respect of pay.

The employer should observe appropriate standards of personal behaviour. In *Isle of Wight Tourist Board v Coombes* [1976] IRLR 413, a director said his secretary 'was an intolerable bitch on a Monday morning' in front of other employees. This was held to constitute a breach of this implied term.

Duty of care, and to provide a safe system of work etc

The common law basis of this duty extends from a duty to provide safe (competent) fellow employees, adequate plant and premises and a safe system of work, as established by *Wilsons & Clyde Coal Co Ltd v English* [1938] AC 57. This duty should be read alongside the statutory duties imposed by HASAWA.

It is likely that with the abolition of strict liability for breach of statutory duty under health and safety regulations as a result of s 69 of the Enterprise and Regulatory Reform Act 2013, this implied term will become more significant in the field of accident at work personal injury claims.

Although there is now a smoking ban in all British workplaces, *Waltons and Morse v Dorrington* [1997] IRLR 488 is significant in that, by finding the employer in breach of this implied term by not providing a smoke-free environment, the courts were willing to accept that an employer would be required to provide a working environment reasonably suitable for the performance of contractual obligations.

The courts have extended this term to include ensuring that references are not negligently prepared (see *Lawton v BOC Transhield Ltd* [1987] ICR 7).

Duty of mutual trust and confidence

The House of Lords has formally recognised this duty in *Malik v BCCI* [1997] IRLR 462. Here, employees had suffered a handicap on the labour market as a result of the corrupt dealings of their employer and were awarded damages reflecting this. Lord Nicholls overruled *Addis v Gramophone Co Ltd* [1909] AC 488 which laid down the principle that wrongful dismissal damages cannot cover losses caused through injury to feelings, the manner of the dismissal or the fact that dismissal itself makes finding another job more difficult.

The Court of Appeal has subsequently sought to limit the effect of *Malik*. In *French v Barclays Bank plc* [1998] IRLR 646 (CA), the court refused to accept that *Malik* had allowed recovery of damages for mental distress. Moreover, in *Johnson v Unisys Ltd* [1999] IRLR 90 (CA), where the applicant sought damages for wrongful dismissal claiming that he had suffered a breakdown as a result of the manner of his dismissal, the claim was rejected on the basis that *Malik* does not apply where there is an express dismissal.

However, these authorities serve to obscure the true import of the term of mutual trust and confidence.

The term was reformulated in *Baldwin v Brighton & Hove City Council* [2007] IRLR 232, which held that in order to demonstrate breach an employee must show conduct 'which, objectively considered, is likely to seriously undermine the necessary trust and confidence in the employment relationship'.

Examples of breach accepted by the case law are extremely wide ranging. In *Western Excavating v Sharp* [1978] IRLR 27 (CA), (a key authority for constructive unfair dismissal cases) physical or verbal abuse and sexual harassment were recognised as breaches. In *Post Office v Strange* [1980] IRLR 515, an extremely harsh and unfair disciplinary penalty was accepted as a breach. The categories of incident or behaviour are not closed.

Breach of this implied term is significant in constructive (unfair) dismissal since the conduct of the employer causes the employee to resign, and by reason of ERA 1996, s 95(1)(c), the tribunal may be able to treat this as dismissal of the employee (see generally **Chapter 6** and specifically **6.4.1.3**).

Care for employees' economic well-being

The Court of Appeal has concluded that there is no general duty of reasonable care for an employee's economic well-being (*Crossley v Faithful & Gould Holdings Ltd* [2004] IRLR 377), unless the employer has undertaken responsibility for advice (*Lennon v Commissioner of Police of the Metropolis* [2004] IRLR 385). To imply a general duty would be to 'impose an unfair and unreasonable burden on employers' (*per* Dyson LJ).

Duty to indemnify employee

The employer must indemnify the employee for expenses and liabilities incurred by the employee in the course of his employment (*In re Famatina Development Corporation Ltd (00431 of 1912)* [1914] 2 Ch 271). In that case, the employee, a consulting engineer made inquiries into the value of his employer's properties and options. He reported that the managing director had made contracts for worthless properties, had made misleading reports, and had arranged for certain secret commissions. The managing director then brought an action for libel and slander against the consulting engineer, the claim being eventually dismissed. The greater part of the employee's costs proved irrecoverable, and he now sought to recoup them following the liquidation of the company. The Court of Appeal held that in fact everything the employee had done was in pursuance of his duties as agent, and under the settled rules of agency; as a result, he was entitled to indemnity and reimbursement.

Duty to take reasonable care in giving references

There is no implied term requiring an employer to provide a reference for an employee (*Lawton v BOC Transhield Ltd* [1987] IRLR 404). Further, there is no statutory obligation on an employer to provide a reference for an employment. Therefore, an employee cannot take any action for the non-production of a reference.

In the case of unlawful discrimination, however, where a reference is refused for discriminatory reasons this may be actionable (*Coote v Granada Hospitality Ltd* [1999] ICR 100, ECJ). However, in that case, the employee had previously complained of discrimination, such a complaint constituting a 'protected act' and as a result, the failure to provide the reference became an act of 'victimisation'. Matters are somewhat complicated by the current wording of s 108(7) Equality Act 2010, which is subject to conflicting authorities; *Rowstock Ltd v Jessemey* [2012] UKEAT 0112/12/0503 and *Akwiwu & anor v Onu* [2013] UKEAT 0283/12/0105. The only legal issues arise in relation to the content of references provided.

Where a reference is provided, the House of Lords has decided that a duty of care may exist not only to the recipient of the reference but also to its subject (*Spring v Guardian Assurance plc* [1994] 3 All ER 129). The content of the reference should be 'true, accurate and fair' (*Bartholomew v London Borough of Hackney* [1999] IRLR 246). Furthermore, in *TSB Bank plc v Harris* [2000] IRLR 157, it was held that mentioning in a reference complaints which had not been drawn to the employee's attention could constitute breach of the implied term of trust and confidence. The drafting of references therefore requires considerable care. Employers should tell the employee first what the reference will contain.

Where a reference letter or telephone reference seeks to mention allegations of misconduct which were not subject to full investigation (here because they were discovered after the employee's departure), provided the remarks are merely cautionary and properly indicate the lack of investigation, there will be no liability following *Jackson v Liverpool City Council* [2011] IRLR 1009.

Employers may find themselves liable in relation to comments made post termination of employment about a former employee as a result of the extension of negligent misstatement (following the principles in *Hedley Byrne & Co Ltd v Heller and Partners Ltd* [1964] AC 465) in *McKie v Swindon College* [2011] IRLR 539 where those comments are 'not in fact supported by any evidence'. Since in that case there had been damage (the loss of employment), the damage was 'eminently' foreseeable, and the former employment relationship gave rise to the necessary proximity, it was 'fair, just and reasonable' to impose a duty of care.

5.2.4.4   Employee's duties

To give personal service

Since the contract of employment creates a personal relationship, in the majority of cases, performance is not delegable. The employee will be expected to perform his or her duties personally.

To obey reasonable and lawful orders

The law recognises an employer's prerogative which allows the employer to require employees to do things which are not specified in the contract, provided that they are both lawful and reasonable (*Laws v London Chronicle Ltd* [1959] 2 All ER 285). Many employers have included express terms to perform reasonable duties on request to avoid difficulties.

Honesty

The duty of honesty involves actions by employees which are not serious enough to constitute the dishonesty offences of theft and fraud. It is sometimes considered part of the employee's duty of mutual trust and confidence. There is, however, no implied term in an employment contract requiring an employee to disclose his or her own misconduct (*The Basildon Academies v Amadi & Fox* UKEAT/0343/14/RN).

To exercise reasonable care and skill

The employee has a duty to take reasonable care in the way he or she works, so as not to cause loss to the employer or injury to others. Employees will be in breach of this term should their duties be performed negligently or incompetently.

In *Lister v Romford Ice & Cold Storage Co Ltd* [1957] AC 555, the House of Lords held that the employee was liable to indemnify the employer after a vicarious liability claim. Note that in practice insurance companies have undertaken not to pursue such an indemnity.

An employee who claims to have a particular skill must have that skill and exercise it in his or her work.

To act in good faith at work (duty of fidelity and good faith)

Equitable principles have influenced this area of the contract of employment, requiring the employee to act honestly in relation to his employment. Particular duties have been identified as follows:

(a) Not to make undisclosed profits (see *Boston Deep Sea Fishing & Ice Co v Ansell* (1888) 39 ChD 339).

(b) Not to misuse the employer's property (for example, borrowing from the till, see *Sinclair v Neighbour* [1967] 2 QB 279).

(c) Not to misuse confidential information. Information, whether trade secrets or customer lists, may be expressly identified as confidential by the employer or may be obviously confidential (*Faccenda Chicken Ltd v Fowler* [1987] Ch 117). The employer must provide specific evidence that the information is its own secret rather than the knowledge, etc. acquired by the employee to use at his or her discretion (*FSS Travel and Leisure Systems v Johnson* [1998] IRLR 382). Public policy may override this principle, where disclosure is to the Inland Revenue or a regulatory body, see *Re a Company's Application* [1989] ICR 449. Note that the Public Interest Disclosure Act 1998 protects 'whistleblowers' from detriment or dismissal as a result of making 'a protected disclosure'. The law is to be found in ERA 1996, ss 47B and 103A.

It is to be noted that the duty of fidelity is not a fiduciary duty. The Court of Appeal in *Ranson v Customer Systems plc* [2012] IRLR 769 specifically ruled this out with Lewison LJ characterising the duty as 'no more than an obligation loyally to carry out the job that the employee agreed to do'.

Duty on an employee to work flexibly

In *Luke v Stoke on Trent City Council* [2007] IRLR 305 the EAT has stated: 'There is no reason in principle why a tribunal should not find an implied term in a contract of employment that an employee may be obliged to perform duties which go beyond or are different from those expressly required by the contract or to perform them at a different workplace.' However, such a finding can only be made in accordance with the normal strict rules governing the implication of terms.

Not to compete with the employer while employed

This can sometimes be considered part of the duty of good faith and fidelity discussed in this section. When considering this duty, the courts have attempted to strike a balance between protection of the employer and the employee's liberty to undertake spare-time activities—see Lord Greene MR's judgment in *Hivac Ltd v Park Royal Scientific Instruments Ltd* [1946] Ch 169, and contrast *Sanders v Parry* [1967] 1 WLR 753 and *Nova Plastics Ltd v Froggatt* [1982] IRLR 146. Please note many contracts of employment contain express non-competition or restraint of trade clauses, as discussed briefly at **5.8.1**.

Patents

Inventions made in the course of employment belong to the employer, who has the right to patent them (Patents Act 1977 (PA 1977), s 39). Section 40 gives an employee a limited right to compensation. Section 41(1) provides that this will be a 'fair share having regard to all the circumstances of the benefit which the employer has derived, or may reasonably be expected to derive, from the patent'.

The employer's implied duty of care and the express terms of the contract

Where the express terms of a contract entitle the employer to require action which could foreseeably damage the employee's health this appears to involve a breach of the duty of care. In *Johnstone v Bloomsbury Health Authority* [1991] 2 WLR 1362, a hospital doctor could be required to work up to 48 hours' overtime on top of a 40-hour working week, which he claimed could foreseeably injure his health. The Court of Appeal distinguished between terms giving the employer optional rights (as here, where the employer chose whether to impose the requirement) and those giving absolute rights. An employer exercising a discretion which broke the duty of care would be in breach of that duty. However, had there been an express term to work that overtime every week, this would have overridden the implied duty of care.

5.3 Terms of the contract of employment: incorporated terms

It is common for contracts of employment or statutory written statements to make reference to other documents in order to specify the terms which will apply. The provision in ERA 1996, s 2(2), allowing employers to meet the Act's requirements by referring the employee to another document, encourages this tendency.

The types of document most commonly referred to are collective agreements, works rules and disciplinary procedures. Thus, if a written contract provides that 'in cases of disciplinary action staff are subject to the company's disciplinary code, a copy of which is available from your section supervisor', the provisions of the disciplinary code will become terms of the employee's contract. (Please also refer to Express Terms at **5.2.2** earlier.)

This may also happen without express reference if circumstances are such that the incorporation of the disciplinary procedure may be implied. So, for example, where it is well known that disciplinary matters are always dealt with through the official procedure and this is readily accessible to employees, for example, by being available on a noticeboard, or staff handbook, an employment tribunal may feel able to imply the incorporation of the procedure.

Contrasting decisions have concerned the incorporation of Equal Opportunities Policies. In *Grant v South West Trains Ltd* [1998] IRLR 188, the Queen's Bench Division refused to incorporate provisions of a policy which was held to be stated in 'very general, even idealistic terms'. By contrast the EAT in *Secretary of State for Scotland v Taylor* [1997] IRLR 608 held the Scottish Prison Service's Equal Opportunities Policy to be a contractual document. There is no clear basis for distinguishing these cases, so employers may find themselves bound by the terms of such policies.

When considering whether a disciplinary policy was incorporated into the contract of employment, the High Court in *Hussain v Surrey & Sussex Healthcare NHS Trust* [2011] EWCA 1670 (QB) held that the factors to be considered were: the importance of the provision to the contractual working relationship, the level of detail prescribed by the provision, the certainty of the provision and whether it is workable. This principle is likely to be applicable to all questions of incorporation.

One area of dispute is the status of matters set out in documents such as a 'staff handbook' where the contract is silent on the status of such a handbook. Employees will often have only such a handbook as guidance to their employers' practices and expectations, and will rely heavily on the material. They would be surprised if such material was not contractually binding. Employers on the other hand, if wishing to be bound, would have put such material in the contract in the first place! Employers can attempt to rely on the doctrine of intent to create legal relations to evade such material becoming incorporated into the contract of employment. However, the courts will examine the wording of the disputed material carefully. If the statement in dispute is in the flavour of a statement of aspiration on the part of the employer, it will fall short of being contractually binding. However, contractual effect will be the likely consequence 'if, by their nature and language, they are apt to be contractual terms' and this will particularly be the case if the statement is 'put in clear terms of entitlement' as held by the Court of Appeal in *Keeley v Fosroc International Ltd* [2006] IRLR 961. In *Bateman v Asda Stores Ltd* [2010] IRLR 370, the EAT was prepared to incorporate a very wide variation clause from the staff handbook into the contract of employment, even though at least one employee suffered financial loss. The clause said that the employer 'reserved the right to review, revise, amend or replace the contents of this handbook'. Please refer to the remarks made at **5.2.2** and particularly on the case of *Allen v TRW Systems*.

In cases of unfair dismissal and discrimination, if an employer has a written policy or procedure which is distributed to staff, then that employer will generally be expected to follow such guidelines, regardless of whether the document is incorporated into the contract of employment or not. Therefore, the issue of incorporation will not in such cases be a vital one. However, much litigation on the issue of incorporation of terms involves the incorporation of collective agreements.

What is the legal status of a collective agreement?

These are agreements made between a trade union (or unions) on one hand and an employer (or employers) on the other. They range from local agreements affecting just one plant to national agreements covering workers in widely varying jobs, employed by different employers and represented by different trade unions.

There is a common law presumption (*Ford Motor Co Ltd v Amalgamated Union of Engineering & Foundry Workers* [1969] 2 QB 303), reinforced by the Trade Union and Labour Relations (Consolidation) Act 1992 (TULR(C)A), s 179(4), that collective agreements are not binding contracts. This may only be overridden by a clear written statement to the contrary. This is rarely done. Thus the collective agreement is not a contract itself, but its provisions may be incorporated into individual contracts between employer and employee.

The contents of a collective agreement

A collective agreement may contain terms which are purely concerned with the collective relationship (for example, an agreement that where a dispute arises a particular union official may insist on a meeting with a particular manager). It may contain terms which affect the individual's employment contract (for example, an increase in pay in return for a promise to abandon a specific restrictive practice).

To study the incorporation of collective agreements into individual contracts of employment we must consider five problems:

- How is a collective agreement incorporated?
- When do collectively agreed terms become incorporated?
- Which provisions of the collective agreement are incorporated?
- How are conflicts between provisions of different collective agreements resolved?
- How are collectively agreed provisions interpreted?

5.3.1   How is a collective agreement incorporated?

5.3.1.1   Express incorporation

Where there is an express provision in the contract of employment or in the written statement of terms referring to a collective agreement, the collective agreement or the parts referred to will be incorporated. Thus in *National Coal Board v Galley* [1958] 1 WLR 16, G's contract of employment provided that his wages were regulated by the national and county wage agreements, which required him to work such days or part days each week 'as may reasonably be required'. The contract also stated that 'this contract of service shall be subject to those agreements and to any other agreements relating to or in connection with or subsidiary to the wages agreement and to statutory provisions for the time being in force affecting the same'. The Court of Appeal held that this was incorporated into his individual contract and that he could therefore be required to work weekends (a reasonable requirement).

The reference to the collective agreement must indicate some intention to incorporate. In *Stewart v Craig Shipping Co Ltd* [1979] ICR 713, the reference (in a letter of appointment) was in the following terms: 'The terms and conditions set out in the national maritime board agreements have been taken into account in the above consolidated figure.' This was held not to incorporate the national agreement referred to, but merely to provide information as to how the figure referred to in the letter was arrived at.

Once a collectively agreed provision becomes incorporated into an individual contract it becomes a legally enforceable term of that contract even though the collective agreement itself is not legally binding (*Marley v Forward Trust Group Ltd* [1986] ICR 891).

Furthermore, once this process of incorporation takes place, a subsequent termination of the collective agreement does not terminate those provisions of it which became contractual terms. In *Robertson v British Gas Corporation* [1983] ICR 351, the contract of employment referred to a bonus scheme established by collective bargaining. The employer subsequently withdrew from that part of the collective agreement, and attempted unilaterally to terminate the bonus scheme. In the Court of Appeal, Ackner LJ held that the original contract contemplated alterations to, but not an absence of, the bonus scheme. Therefore the unilateral termination of the scheme simply left the last tariff in force. Kerr LJ added that alterations to the scheme were effective, as they were done by agreement, but that its termination was not, as it had not been agreed. Therefore the employers were obliged to continue paying under the bonus scheme.

In *Burroughs Machines Ltd v Timmoney* [1977] IRLR 404, the collective agreement (entered between the employers' union and a federation of which the employer was a member) provided that the employer could suspend guarantee payments if work stopped because of industrial action in a federated plant. The employer then left the federation. There was a strike in the employer's own factory. The employee argued that, as the plant was technically no longer a federated plant, guarantee payments were still payable. However, the guarantee pay scheme had become incorporated into individual contracts, and thus the collectively agreed provisions concerning the scheme were likewise incorporated. The Court of Session held that the employer therefore retained the right to suspend guarantee payments if there was a strike in their own plant.

Where there is no express reference to a collective agreement it is still common to find employees working on trade union-negotiated rates and conditions. How does incorporation take place in these circumstances?

5.3.1.2   Agency

It has been argued that a trade union is acting as the agent of employees who are its members, with the employer (or employers' association) acting as the third party. While this is superficially attractive, it fails to account for the normal practice that where employees work to collectively agreed terms they do so whether or not they are members of the union. Non-members are entitled to the same contractual terms as members. A supposed agency relationship cannot explain this. In *Holland v London Society of Compositors* (1924) 40 TLR 440, concerning an agreement between two unions, it was held that the union acted as principal, not as its members' agent. It is better therefore to ignore this argument unless there is a clear agreement establishing the union as agent of its members. In *Burton Group Ltd v Smith* [1977] IRLR 351, at p 353, Arnold J said:

There is no reason at all why, in a particular case, union representatives should not be the agents of an employee to make a contract, or to receive a notice, or otherwise effect a binding transaction on his behalf. But that agency so to do does not stem from the mere fact that they are union representatives and that he is a member of the union; it must be supported in the particular case by the creation of some specific agency.

5.3.1.3   Implied incorporation

A better explanation of incorporation where there is no express reference is to fall back on the courts' willingness to imply incorporation. This can be done when there is evidence of a regular practice or custom of incorporating collective agreements, or where it is obvious that incorporation has taken place. Thus where there has been a long tradition of working to the collectively agreed terms, or where this is the general expectation of the parties, incorporation may be implied. Other evidence supporting incorporation could include a high proportion of trade union membership. Where the contract makes no express reference to the collective agreement the question of incorporation will turn on the evidence. The general test is whether incorporation by custom and practice is 'reasonable, certain and notorious' (*Henry v London General Transport Services* [2001] IRLR 50). Tribunals attempt to arrive at conclusions which fit their view of industrial relations common sense, and arguments should be formulated with this in mind.

5.3.2   When do collectively agreed terms become incorporated?

A collective agreement may stipulate the date at which its terms are to take effect. Where there is a sufficiently established custom that the contract will incorporate collectively agreed terms they should become incorporated at that time, and will thus become enforceable by either party. Where no such stipulation has been made a date of commencement may be implied.

Thus a change in the terms of individual contracts may occur without the parties to those contracts taking active steps to agree to them. This view is supported by *Brand v LCC*, The Times, 28 October 1967, where the employer's attempt to challenge the incorporation of a collectively agreed provision on the grounds that it had not been implemented was rejected by the County Court. The relevant terms were held to have been incorporated automatically. By contrast, however, in *Dudfield v Ministry of Works*, The Times, 24 January 1964, a government-imposed 'pay pause' intervened between the date of concluding the collective agreement and its implementation. The employer successfully argued that the collectively agreed terms were not enforceable against him until he had taken the steps of implementing them. This decision may have been influenced by its specific policy connotations, and this may be a ground for distinguishing it.

In most situations, both parties' assent will be implied by their conduct in continuing to work and to provide work and payment once the terms of the new collective agreement have been made available.

If incorporation has taken place, the incorporated terms will be binding on employees whether or not they are aware of them. This is to meet the needs of industrial common sense. In *Gray Dunn & Co Ltd v Edwards* [1980] IRLR 23, Lord McDonald held that employers who recognise a union for collective bargaining and enter into a detailed agreement are entitled to assume that all union members know of it and are bound by it. He said, at p 24: 'There could be no stability in industrial relations if this were not so.'

Incorporated terms will normally be binding on employees whether or not they are members of the union which negotiated the agreement.

A decision on these problems is *Lee v GEC Plessey Telecommunications* [1993] IRLR 383, where a collective agreement, expressly incorporated by the statutory statement, provided for enhanced severance payments on redundancy. The employer issued new statements which did not mention the collective agreement and subsequently purported to withdraw the severance terms and replace them with less favourable terms. The employees issued a writ. While action was pending, the union negotiated a settlement providing for future severance payments to be the subject of negotiation. The employees sought a declaration that the original severance terms continued in their contracts of employment. This was opposed by the employers who claimed that no consideration had moved from the employees, thus the original terms were not binding; that the employers were entitled to alter the terms unilaterally; and that the settlement with the union was incorporated into individuals' contracts. The High Court granted the declaration requested, rejecting the employers' contentions. The employees continuing to work and not pursuing a pay claim was sufficient consideration. The employers had no right to vary the contract unilaterally. The new settlement was not incorporated as the union was not authorised to act as agent of the employees and the new statement made no provision for incorporation.

5.3.3 Which provisions of the collective agreement are incorporated?

Collective agreements are concerned:

- with the collective relationship (that between the trade union and the employer); and
- with terms and conditions of employment of union members.

It is only these latter provisions which should be incorporated into the contract of employment. However, the two elements of the collective agreement are sometimes difficult to disentangle, a problem which is exacerbated by the imprecise language of many collective agreements.

The distinction has been attempted in the cases. See, for example, *Gallagher v Post Office* [1970] 3 All ER 712 and *British Leyland UK Ltd v McQuilken* [1978] IRLR 345. In *McQuilken*, under a collective agreement concerned with the closure of a plant the employer gave skilled employees a choice of retraining or redundancy. M had originally chosen redundancy but then changed his mind. The employer, refusing to allow this, argued that this provision of the collective agreement was inappropriate for incorporation. This view was accepted by the court, which took the view that the collective agreement 'was a long-term plan dealing with policy rather than the rights of individual employees'. This was consistent with the Privy Council decision in *Young v Canadian Northern Railway Co* [1931] AC 83, but is difficult to reconcile with the later decision of *Joel v Cammell Laird (Ship Repairers) Ltd* (1969) 4 ITR 206. Here a similar agreement was held to be incorporated into J's contract. The main distinguishing factor was that this provision had already been implemented on many occasions, whereas in *McQuilken* the provision in question had not been implemented before.

It is perhaps better to think in terms of the appropriateness (or otherwise) for incorporation of a collectively agreed term. This may be illustrated by the majority and minority judgments of the Court of Appeal in *Camden Exhibition & Display Ltd v Lynott* [1966] 1 QB 555. The majority held that the term (that overtime would not be restricted) was incorporated. The issue was whether an overtime ban called by shop stewards was an inducement to breach of contract. The majority view was that the term meant that the union would not restrict overtime, and also that the employees would not 'officially or unofficially impose a collective embargo'. This interpretation appeared appropriate for incorporation. Russell LJ (dissenting) took the view that the term was limited to a collective procedural matter, that in effect individuals could arrange their own overtime without the union imposing a ceiling. This, he thought, was not appropriate for incorporation into the individual contract.

The High Court decision in *Kaur v MG Rover Group Ltd* [2004] IRLR 279 indicates the current approach of the courts. The collective agreement included the provision: 'there will be no compulsory redundancy'. K was threatened with redundancy and sought a declaration that she had a contractual right not to be made redundant. This was granted on the grounds that the provision needed to be read in the context of other provisions in the collective agreement requiring flexible working and other co-operative measures by employees, and was thus regarded as suitable for incorporation, even though there was an express contractual term allowing the employer to dismiss for any reason.

5.3.4   How are conflicts between provisions of different collective agreements resolved?

The major area of conflict is that between national and local collective bargaining. It is common for national collective agreements to be followed by local agreements whereby variations to suit local needs or to achieve local improvements are sought. These local agreements are generally those which are actually followed. However, the courts have usually held that the national agreements only are incorporated.

In *Loman v Merseyside Transport Service Ltd* (1967) 3 KIR 726, the question concerned the length of the contractual working week. The national agreement guaranteed a minimum wage on the basis of a 41-hour week. The local agreement guaranteed a minimum wage on the basis of a 68-hour week. Employees refusing to accept the local agreement were to be moved to other jobs. In spite of this the Divisional Court held that the local agreement was not intended to be binding, but was 'in the nature of a gentleman's agreement for ironing out local difficulties and providing an incentive for co-operation'.

A contrasting decision is *Saxton v National Coal Board* [1970] 5 ITR 196. The issue here was whether the working week involved five or seven days' work. The national agreement, which was expressly incorporated by the statutory written statement, provided for a five-day week. S, however, had worked a seven-day week consistently for over 20 years. The Divisional Court was prepared to imply a local agreement which would take precedence over the national agreement, even though there was no formal record of its existence. A distinguishing factor here was the existence in the national agreement of a statement providing for the union to enter into local agreements to arrange for workers in S's category to undertake additional shifts. Some such provision may be necessary if local agreements are to be enforced.

Another factor which makes *Loman* an unreliable precedent is the courts' willingness to give effect to the most recent agreement in time (see *Clift v West Riding County Council*, The Times, 10 April 1964).

5.3.5   How will collectively agreed provisions be interpreted?

In general the courts adopt a flexible approach. In *Burroughs Machines Ltd v Timmoney* [1977] IRLR 404, the employer had been a member of a federation which had negotiated a collective agreement providing that there would be no guarantee payments when workers were laid off because of industrial action in a federated plant. The employer then left the federation. There was a strike in the employer's own factory. Their employees sought guarantee payments as the plant was technically no longer a federated plant. However, the court held that the agreement should be interpreted flexibly, not rigidly or technically, and thus saw the term 'federated plant' as including the employer's own factory in these new circumstances.

5.4 Variation of terms

5.4.1 Consensual variation

Contract principles at common law require agreement before any term can be varied, and consideration for the variation. However, in the context of employment, it is rare for there to be explicit written agreement to variations or any change in the remuneration received. In practice the employee's continued working under the new terms is taken to represent both assent and consideration. In *FW Farnsworth Ltd v Lacy* [2013] IRLR 198, the employee received an amended contract containing higher pay, other benefits, and a restrictive covenant upon successful promotion. He did not sign and return it, and the question was whether the covenant was impliedly accepted. It was held, relying upon *Solectron Scotland v Roper* [2004] IRLR 4, that the acceptance of the new terms had occurred since the employee applied for new benefits which could be taken as acceptance of the legal incidents of the new definition of his relationship with his employer.

There is no need for variations to be in writing, but ERA 1996, s 4, requires the employer to give written notice of variations within one month. As with the written statement this may be done by reference. This reference may be to a general document such as a collective agreement. In general, the courts accept that subsequent versions override earlier ones, and that agreement is indicated by the parties continuing to work and pay wages (the wage–work bargain).

It is to be noted that EU law, specifically Directive 91/533/EEC, requires that changes in details as to essential parts of the contract, such as remuneration, must be recorded in writing within one month of such a change coming into effect.

However, problems arise where individuals or local groups negotiate a personal or local variation. Frequently this variation will not be documented. Does this vary the contractual position as laid out in the written statement?

In *Simmonds v Dowty Seals Ltd* [1978] IRLR 211, the written statement said that hours of work were 7.30 am to 5.30 pm. S entered into an informal agreement with his supervisor to transfer to the night shift. This continued for four years. The written particulars were never varied and the arrangement was probably never communicated to the personnel department. The supervisor had acted beyond his powers, but S was unaware of this. When the employer transferred S to the day shift, he resigned and claimed constructive dismissal. The EAT held that the agreement with the supervisor had varied the contract, as he had ostensible authority. Therefore the employers were acting in breach in transferring S to the day shift, and his constructive dismissal claim succeeded.

5.4.1.1 Does the signing of a standard contract constitute an effective variation?

In *Hawker Siddeley Power Engineering Ltd v Rump* [1979] IRLR 425, R had signed a standard contract containing a mobility clause whereby he could be required to work anywhere in the UK. He then agreed verbally with his manager that, due to his wife's illness, he would only be required to work in the South. He later signed a new copy of the original standard contract. The employer argued that even if the verbal agreement had varied the original contract, it had been varied again by his signing the standard agreement. The EAT held that signing the new statement did not vary the verbal agreement as R had not been warned that it was changing an important element of his contract.

5.4.2 Unilateral variation

Problems sometimes arise out of attempts by one party unilaterally to vary the contract. The basic principle is that no variation is effective without agreement, and will, indeed, constitute a breach of contract.

5.4.2.1 What will constitute agreement?

An employee may find that his or her employer wishes (for reasons of cost or otherwise) to make changes to working conditions. It may be a change to the overall hours worked or the time of day when such hours are worked, for example. The employer may need to effect changes immediately. As a result, the employee may be faced with a 'take it or leave it' situation. What response will be sufficient to constitute acceptance?

In *Marriott v Oxford & District Cooperative Society Ltd* (*No 2*) [1970] 1 QB 186, M was demoted with a drop in pay. He worked under protest for three or four weeks then resigned and claimed redundancy pay. The employer claimed that he had accepted the variation by working to the new terms. The Court of Appeal held that a unilateral change by the employer had broken the contract and terminated it. Four weeks' work under protest was insufficient to show that he had accepted the new contract. M was therefore entitled to redundancy pay. Note that the concept of constructive dismissal now provides a statutory basis for a similar outcome (although the acceptable length of time before resignation is likely to be far shorter), see **6.4.1.3**.

An employee must make up his mind soon. In *Western Excavating* (*ECC*) *Ltd v Sharp* [1978] QB 761, at p 769, Lord Denning MR said:

[The employee] must make up his mind soon after the conduct of which he complains: for, if he continues for any length of time without leaving, he will lose his right to treat himself as discharged.

The length of time necessary to indicate acceptance will be whatever time is reasonable in the circumstances. The redundancy payments legislation gives employees a four-week trial period to see if an alternative job is suitable (ERA 1996, s 141). In *Turvey v C. W. Cheyney & Son Ltd* [1979] ICR 341, the EAT held that this was meant to improve on the common law, and in *Air Canada v Lee* [1978] IRLR 392, eight weeks were allowed, representing a 'reasonable' common law period plus the statutory four weeks. (See further **6.11.5.2**.)

The view expressed in earlier cases, that the unilateral variation was a termination of the original contract, has been rejected in more recent decisions. It is now seen as a breach which leaves the contract intact and gives the employee a choice of resigning and claiming constructive dismissal, or arguing that the original terms of the contract still apply.

In *Burdett-Coutts v Hertfordshire County Council* [1984] IRLR 91, the employer attempted to impose a wage cut on school dinner ladies. It was put in the form of a variation in the terms of the contract. The High Court held that as the women did not accept this variation they could sue for arrears of wages up to the time the employer formally terminated the contract.

This was an action for breach of contract. The approach of tribunals where similar circumstances have led to an unfair dismissal claim provides a contrast. In *Gilham v Kent*

County Council (*No 2*) [1985] ICR 233, a case with similar facts except that the dinner ladies had refused to accept the variation and were sacked for so refusing, it was held that the employer's breach of the nationally agreed terms did not automatically mean that the dismissal for refusing to accept the variation was unfair. The tribunal had to assess the 'reasonableness' of the employer's behaviour. (See also **6.4.1.3.**)

The length of time an employee has to object to the new terms and whether the variation is sufficiently serious to constitute a breach will be a matter of fact for the court or tribunal to decide in each case.

5.5   National minimum wage and National Living Wage

A 'National Living Wage' will, from April 2016, prescribe a minimum hourly rate of pay for workers and employees over the age of 25. From April 2017 the rate will be £7.50 per hour, rising to £9.00 an hour in 2020. For employees and workers under 25 and until the National Living Wage comes into force, the National Minimum Wage and the National Minimum Wage Act 1998 (as amended) will continue to apply.

It is important to note that the legislation protects this broad class of 'worker' and is not confined merely to employees. This wider defined group includes homeworkers and workers provided by agencies (such as temporary workers or 'temps'). The rates are updated annually, and at the time of writing the October 2015 rates have not been published.

The Act must be read alongside a number of statutory instruments, however, the most essential is the National Minimum Wage Regulations 1999 (SI 1999/584) (NMW Regs).

Workers aged between 18 and 20 are entitled to at least £5.60 an hour, workers between 16 and 17 are entitled to a minimum of £4.05 per hour and apprentices in the first year of apprenticeship are entitled to £3.50 an hour. These minima take effect from 1 April 2017, and are likely to be increased in April 2018. There are some exceptions (such as those working outside the UK, certain workers in family businesses or live-in domestic workers, and those undergoing work experience as trainees on certain government schemes or as a compulsory element in undergraduate courses).

Significantly, NMWA, s 17 provides that:

(1) If a worker who qualifies for the national minimum wage is remunerated for any pay reference period by his employer at a rate which is less than the national minimum wage, the worker shall be taken to be entitled under his contract to be paid, as additional remuneration in respect of that period, the amount described in subsection (2) below.

(2) That amount is the difference between—

(a) the relevant remuneration received by the worker for the pay reference period; and

(b) the relevant remuneration which the worker would have received for that period had he been remunerated by the employer at a rate equal to the national minimum wage.

(3) In subsection (2) above, 'relevant remuneration' means remuneration which falls to be brought into account for the purposes of regulations under section 2 above.

In other words, the entitlement to be paid the minimum wage is statutorily implied into the contract. The result is that the worker has available to him or her all the usual civil remedies for breach of contract (both in the civil courts and employment tribunal) and other statutory rights will take the minimum wage into account where the level of remuneration is concerned. Notably, all workers paid less than the minimum wage will be able to complain of an unauthorised deduction (see **5.7.4**) in the employment tribunal, which is advantageous given the simplicity of the process.

The Act provides for enforcement by government agencies (for example, the Inland Revenue) and for criminal penalties.

Workers are entitled to access their records and have the right not to be victimised (in other words suffer detrimental treatment) for asserting their rights under this legislation in good faith under NMWA, s 17. Workers, in addition, if dismissed for asserting their rights for receiving the minimum wage, have been granted protection by NMWA, s 25 (which introduces ERA 1996, ss 104A and 105A). As a result, it is automatically unfair to dismiss a worker for seeking to be paid the minimum wage (or to select such an employee for redundancy), or to dismiss an employee as a consequence of prosecution, or to dismiss to avoid paying the minimum wage.

It should be noted that where a worker is required to be 'on call', that worker will not be entitled to be paid the minimum wage for anything other than the time spent working, even though the time spent at work on call will count for the purpose of the WT Regs (as amended); *South Manchester Abbeyfield Society Ltd v Hopkins* [2011] IRLR 300.

5.6   Hours and holidays

The WT Regs were introduced to implement the Working Time Directive (No 93/104) (WTD). The Regulations and Directive sought to impose limits on time worked and to introduce base line entitlements to annual leave in order to safeguard the health and safety of workers. The Regulations have been subject to a number of amendments (namely SI 1999/3372, SI 2001/3256 and SI 2003/1684) to clarify the uncertain wording of the original provisions. Readers are referred to *Harvey on Industrial Relations and Employment Law*.

The Regulations apply to 'employees' and 'workers' (see **5.1.2.4**). The definition of 'working time' is a wide one, including time spent working, time spent by a worker carrying out his or her duties and time when the worker is at the employer's disposal. This was deliberate and intended to catch out situations where perhaps the worker was available for work but not required such as workers 'on call' or 'on standby'.

It is important to note that there are a number of special requirements for 'young workers' (those under the age of 18). These are beyond the scope of this book. Readers are referred to *Harvey on Industrial Relations and Employment Law*.

The basic limits, rights and duties are as set out in **5.6.1–5.6.4**.

5.6.1   Limit on weekly working time: the 48-hour week

In any 17-week period (the 'reference period'), no worker is permitted to work more than an average of 48 hours per week (reg 4). Employers are placed under a positive duty to take all reasonable steps to ensure this limit is not exceeded. 'On call' time is included (see *South Manchester Abbeyfield Society Ltd v Hopkins*, discussed at **5.5**).

The 'reference' period is a rolling 17-week period, unless an individual or collective agreement provides otherwise. In 'special case' activities (such as work in security or surveillance, broadcasting, tourism, hospitals or prisons), this can be extended to

26 weeks. Further, if there is a workforce or collective agreement and it is necessary for objective or technical reasons, the period can be extended from 17 weeks up to 52 weeks.

It is possible for an individual worker to opt out of the limit, but a worker must agree in writing that the limit will not apply to him or her, and such agreement is terminable by any worker by giving not less than seven days' notice in writing (reg 5). Employers are obliged to keep an up to date record of workers agreeing to opt out, or an opt-out agreement will no longer be binding. Workers cannot be forced to sign opt-out agreements, and are protected from any detrimental treatment for refusal (any dismissal caused by such a refusal will also be automatically unfair) (see ERA 1996, s 45A and s 101A).

Contravention of the limit can result in action by local authorities and the Health and Safety Executive (HSE), which can ultimately include criminal proceedings. Claims by workers for breach of statutory duty are possible in the civil courts. Further, any workers refusing to work over 48 hours per week are protected from detriment and dismissal caused by their refusal will be automatically unfair (see ERA 1996, s 45A and s 101A). In *Barber v RJB Mining (UK) Ltd* [1999] IRLR 308, the High Court has held that employees may also seek a declaration and injunction restraining their employer from requiring them to work an average of over 48 hours per week.

5.6.2   'Rest breaks' and 'rest periods'

5.6.2.1   Daily rests

Each day a worker is entitled to a 'rest period', this is defined as an 11-hour period of 11 consecutive hours (in other words, an employer cannot seek to grant a number of breaks totalling 11 hours). This is subject to a few small exceptions: where workers are in special case activities (see **5.6.1**), where working time is 'unmeasured', where the worker is changing shift and the end of one shift and beginning of the next shift are not separated by 11 hours.

In addition, a worker is entitled to a 'rest period' (of 20 minutes) in any working day over six hours. There is no requirement that this break be subject to remuneration. This break should be uninterrupted and taken away from the worker's work station (see reg 12). The Department of Trade and Industry Guidance states that this break should be taken during the working day and should not be simply tacked on to the start or end of the day.

Employers must allow workers to take these daily rests, but are not under any positive obligation. They do not have to ensure the breaks are taken. The failure to grant rest breaks would appear only to become achievable once the worker has exercised his or her right and there has been a refusal of permission: *Miles v Linkage Community Trust Ltd* [2008] IRLR 602, a case which has troubled some commentators.

Individual workers cannot opt out of the daily rest break or daily rest period. Provided that an equivalent period of 'compensatory' rest is given, a collective or workplace agreement can modify these entitlements.

5.6.2.2   Weekly rest

Each week a worker is entitled to a rest period of not less than 24 consecutive hours in each 7-day period. This rest period should be uninterrupted. The daily rest and weekly rest periods should be taken consecutively.

However, an employer may choose to average the 7-day reference period over 14 days. This allows for either two uninterrupted rest periods (each of not less than 24 hours) in each 14-day period or one uninterrupted rest period of not less than 48 hours in each 14-day period.

Opt out

Individual workers cannot opt out of the weekly rest period. Provided that an equivalent period of 'compensatory' rest is given, a collective or workplace agreement can modify this entitlement.

5.6.2.3   Remedies

3 month time limit

A worker who has not been permitted to take his or her rest breaks and/or rest periods or whose employer has failed to provide equivalent compensatory rest may bring a claim in the employment tribunal. The claim must be brought within a time limit of three months starting from the act or omission of which the worker complains. The remedies available to the tribunal are a declaration of the claimant's rights and/or an award of compensation. Compensation is calculated as an amount which is just and equitable, having regard to the employer's default and the loss sustained by the worker as a consequence of such default.

5.6.3   Annual leave rights

5-6 weeks

All workers were initially, on commencement of the WT Regs, entitled to four weeks' annual leave. This has been increased to its current level of 5.6 weeks. This is a right to take leave and employers are not permitted to pay workers in lieu of their right (with the exception of the ability to pay accrued holiday pay on termination of employment). The entitlement to annual leave commences with the work in question.

The annual leave entitlement may be met by employers including public holidays and employees are only entitled to take public holidays if their contract so provides (*Campbell & Smith Construction Group Ltd v Greenwood* (2001) IRLB 667, 10).

The leave year is calculated either with reference to the contract of employment, the date of commencement of employment or from 1 October (since the Regulations first came into force on 1 October 1998). The Regulations stipulate that leave may be taken only in the leave year in which it is due (which restrains employers from preventing an employee from taking leave in a given year and carrying it over to the next). This has been confirmed in *Lyons v Mitie Security Ltd* [2010] IRLR 288.

The worker wishing to take leave is required to comply with obligations to give notice to his or her employer. Generally, the notice must be given twice as many days in advance of the proposed duration of the leave (so to take two days' leave, the notice must be given four days in advance). The employer can require an employee to take leave (provided notice is given) and can issue a notice requiring a worker not to take leave on particular days. These notice rights are subject to modification or exclusion subject to a valid collective or workplace agreement.

A worker prevented from taking annual leave due to long-term ill health causing them to be on sick leave is entitled to carry over untaken annual leave whether a prior request is made or not as a result of *NHS Leeds v Larner* [2012] IRLR 825 (CA). Generally, however, workers are expected to take their annual leave within the relevant leave year.

In *Lock and another v British Gas Trading Ltd (No. 2)* [2016] IRLR 946 (CA), holiday pay must include compensation for any results-based commission.

5.6.3.1   Remedies

To enforce his or her rights, the employee must bring a claim before the employment tribunal.

The claim must be brought within a time limit of three months starting from the act or omission of which the worker complains. The remedies available to the tribunal are a declaration of the claimant's rights and/or an award of compensation. Compensation is calculated as an amount which is just and equitable, having regard to the employer's default and the loss sustained by the worker as a consequence of such default. However, where the claimant's claim is for accrued holiday entitlement on termination of employment, the tribunal orders payment by the employer of the amount due to the claimant.

5.6.4   Night working

The relevant terms are defined in the WT Regs, reg 2(1) thus:

'night time', in relation to a worker, means a period—

(a) *the duration of which is not less than seven hours, and*

(b) *which includes the period between midnight and 5 a.m.,*

which is determined for the purposes of these Regulations by a relevant agreement, or, in default of such a determination, the period between 11 p.m. and 6 a.m.;
'night work' means work during night time;
'night worker' means a worker—

(a) *who, as a normal course, works at least three hours of his daily working time during night time, or*

(b) *who is likely, during night time, to work at least such proportion of his annual working time as may be specified for the purposes of these Regulations in a collective agreement or a workforce agreement.*

Night workers must not work more than eight hours on average per 24-hour period by virtue of reg 6(1) over a 17-week 'reference' period. A special category of night worker under reg 6(7) whose work involves special hazards or heavy physical or mental strain are subject to a simple eight-hour nightshift limit every 24 hours. Night workers are entitled to a free health assessment before commencing night work.

It is to be remembered that the WT Regs are intended to safeguard the health and safety of workers. As a result, the provisions relating to night work have expectations that risk assessments have been carried out, and in addition, that night workers have the opportunity for regular health assessments.

5.7   Breach of the contract of employment

There are a number of ways in which the contract of employment may be terminated. A number of these methods would not result in any legal dispute between the parties: an accepted resignation by the employee, termination agreed between the parties.

Where an employer is bringing a contract of employment to an end, in all likelihood their action will constitute a dismissal (see **6.4.1** for terminations by the employer which constitute dismissal). This would leave the employer potentially vulnerable to claims for unfair dismissal (which is fully dealt with in **Chapter 6**) or the claim in breach of contract known as 'wrongful dismissal'. Section **6.4.2** deals with terminations where there is no dismissal (such as frustration).

However, the contract may be breached in other ways such as the failure to pay wages and/or breach of an express or implied term. In some circumstances where such a breach occurs, the employee may wish to resign and claim constructive (unfair) dismissal, in which case readers are referred to **Chapter 6**. However, in some cases, the employee may only wish to take action in respect of remedying the breach of contract.

5.7.1   Jurisdiction of the employment tribunal

Previously, the formal civil courts system (the County Court and High Court) was the only forum for breach of contract claims. However, the Employment Tribunals Extension of Jurisdiction (England and Wales) Order 1994 (SI 1994/1623) (ETEJO) allows tribunals to hear breach of contract claims. The claim must arise or be outstanding on the termination of employment; be one over which the County Court or High Court would have had jurisdiction; and be one covered by ETA 1996, s 3(2). This in effect covers claims for damages for breach of the contract of employment or any contract connected with employment, claims for sums due under such a contract and claims for sums in pursuance of enactments relating to such contracts. Claims relating to personal injuries, living accommodation, intellectual property, restraint of trade or of confidentiality are excluded from the tribunal jurisdiction. Remedies other than damages are available only through the County Court or High Court.

The maximum tribunal award is £25,000, and the claim does not need to be linked with any other complaint (for example, of unfair dismissal or redundancy). Therefore, employees are not subject to the stricter procedural and evidential demands required for formal litigation in the civil courts under the CPR. Of particular benefit is the more relaxed regime on costs. However, those entering litigation must consider carefully the full value of their claim. Given that the statutory limit for recovery in the employment tribunal for breach of contract claims is £25,000, in the case of high-value wrongful dismissal claims, it is not possible to claim up to £25,000 in the employment tribunal and then any remainder above this limit in the High or County Court. This exclusion upon second proceedings is as a result of the Court of Appeal's judgment in *Fraser v HLMAD Ltd* [2006] IRLR 687.

Note that where the employer is insolvent, employees rank with preferential creditors (Insolvency Act 1986 (IA 1986), s 386 and Sch 6).

Employees considering a breach of contract claim should note that the employer may make a counterclaim. Moreover, that counterclaim may survive even if the original claim is rejected (for example, for being out of time) (*Patel v RCMS Ltd* [1999] IRLR 161 (EAT)).

The regulations do not remove this jurisdiction from the County Court or High Court. Therefore, where an employee fails to take steps until after the three-month limitation period for a tribunal claim, or wishes to claim more than £25,000, the County Court or High Court route is still available, the usual six-year limitation period applying, and there being no financial limit to jurisdiction.

This development enables tribunals to consider all the issues arising out of most dismissal cases. In particular, complaints about failures to pay wages in lieu of notice which do not fall within the technical requirements of ERA 1996, ss 13–27 (which now contain the relevant provisions of the Wages Act 1986 (WA 1986), see **5.7.4**), may be resolved by the tribunal, avoiding the need for a separate County Court claim for wrongful dismissal. The concept of wrongful dismissal, however, continues and should be understood (see **5.7.3**).

5.7.2   When will a remedy be available?

Following normal common law principles, the contract of employment comes into existence when a firm offer is unconditionally accepted, even if the date of starting work is at some time in the future. Thus in *Sarker v South Tees Acute Hospitals NHS Trust* [1997] IRLR 328, the applicant (Ms Sarker) had accepted a job offer which was confirmed and a starting date established. Before that date, however, the respondent withdrew the offer and the applicant complained of wrongful dismissal. The ETEJO provides (by art 3(c)) for tribunal jurisdiction where 'the claim arises ... on the termination of the employee's employment'. The EAT held that this related to the termination of the employment contract, whether or not work had actually started and Ms Sarker could therefore make her claim. It should be noted that employees who have not yet started work may therefore claim unfair dismissal for inadmissible reasons, there being no requisite period of continuous employment (see **6.3**) as well as breach of contract.

5.7.3   Wrongful dismissal

This arises where an employee claims to have been dismissed without the requisite period of notice. Employees are entitled to notice unless guilty of 'gross misconduct'. Wrongful dismissal claims do not attempt to query the quality of the decision to dismiss and are limited to the notice entitlement of the employee in question. In practice, unfair dismissal and wrongful dismissal are frequently claimed together by claimants.

5.7.3.1   What is meant by 'gross misconduct'?

Since an employer can dismiss without notice (also known as 'summary dismissal') for gross misconduct and escape liability for wrongful dismissal, the distinction between mere misconduct and gross misconduct is an important one.

A disciplinary code forming part of or attached to the contract may define or give examples of gross misconduct. In *Dietman v Brent London Borough Council* [1988] IRLR 299, D was dismissed for 'gross negligence'. It was held that although this could constitute gross misconduct it had to be considered in light of the agreed disciplinary provisions. In this case all the examples were of criminal offences. Therefore gross negligence was not gross misconduct.

Where there is no such provision the court will decide, considering that gross misconduct is that which would justify summary dismissal with neither warnings nor notice. Frequently, any act which would constitute a criminal offence will be accepted as gross misconduct.

In *Dunn v AAH Ltd* [2010] IRLR 709 gross misconduct was said to be conduct 'so undermining the trust and confidence which is at the heart of a contract of employment that the employer should no longer be required to retain the employee ... but should be entitled to accept ... the contract ... had been repudiated in its essence'. The employer must not delay in responding; *McCormack v Hamilton Academical Football Club* [2012] IRLR 108.

Wrongful dismissal is in a somewhat anomalous position to unfair dismissal in that summary dismissal may be justified by facts discovered subsequent to the dismissal (*Boston Deep Sea Fishing v Ansell* [1888] 39 ChD 339). However, where there is an agreement to make payment in lieu of notice, that payment becomes a debt accrued to the employee despite subsequently discovered gross misconduct as stated by the Court of Appeal in *Cavenagh v William Evans* [2012] IRLR 679.

5.7.3.2   What period of notice must be given?

The statutory minimum periods are as follows (ERA 1996, s 86(1)):

Length of service	Period of notice
Less than 4 weeks	None
4 weeks	1 week
2–12 years	1 week per full year worked
More than 12 years	12 weeks

ERA 1996, s 86(2), provides that an employee must give one week's notice of termination after one month's employment.

These statutory minima may be increased by the contract. If so, the contractual notice provisions will determine the remedy for the employee. The courts may occasionally imply a longer period of notice entitlement (*Hill v C. A. Parsons & Co Ltd* [1972] Ch 305—seniority and long service gave greater entitlement at common law). (See **6.1.2.1**.)

5.7.3.3   Payments in lieu of notice

The employer may meet notice requirements by giving pay in lieu (ERA 1996, s 86(3)). In other words, the employee receives payment for the requisite notice period, but is not required to work out his or her notice.

Where the contract provides for the employer to make payment in lieu of notice, the payment is an emolument rather than compensation and is therefore taxable (*EMI Group Electronics Ltd v Coldicott* [1999] IRLR 630 (CA)). In such circumstances there is no duty on the dismissed employee to mitigate loss (*Abrahams v Performing Right Society* [1995] IRLR 486 (CA)), and thus the payments in lieu are payable even if the dismissed employee has found alternative employment. Where the contract makes no such provision, a claim for a payment in lieu is for damages, not debt, the payment is not taxable and the normal rules of mitigation apply. The same is true where the contract allows the employer the choice as to whether or not to make a payment in lieu and the employer chooses not to do so (*Cerberus Software v Rowley* [2001] IRLR 160 (CA)).

HM Revenue and Customs (HMRC) publishes up-to-date guidance on payments in lieu of notice online. It has suggested that some non-contractual payments in lieu of notice may be emoluments and thus attract tax. This will particularly be the case if they are made as a matter of course (for example to a number of employees being made redundant) rather than as a discretion exercised afresh in every case. Readers are referred to the Employment Income Manual which can be found at <http://www.hmrc.gov.uk/manuals/eimanual>. Specific material on payments in lieu of notice are currently available at EIM12975-79 on the HMRC website. The duty to mitigate generally requires the dismissed employee simply to take reasonable steps to find alternative employment. It is not generally unreasonable for a wrongfully dismissed employee to refuse to return to work for his or her employer (but see the exceptional case of *Wilding v British Telecom Communications plc* [2002] IRLR 524 (CA) which provides guidance as to how the tribunal should assess whether the employee has acted reasonably).

The remedy in a wrongful dismissal claim is damages to cover the cost of a payment in lieu. It is not permissible to include a claim for the manner of the dismissal, consequent psychiatric injury or losses caused by it becoming thereby more difficult to find another job. This reflects the position in unfair dismissal, where no compensation for injury to feelings is available (as a result of the House of Lords' judgment in *Dunnachie v Kingston Upon Hull District Council* [2004] UKHL 36). See **Chapter 7** for a detailed exposition of the principles for awarding damages for unfair dismissal. Damages for wrongful dismissal may not include an element for loss of the chance to make an unfair dismissal claim (*Harper v Virgin Net Ltd* [2004] IRLR 3 90 (CA)). However, the damages awarded can go far beyond the lost pay during the notice period. In *Horkulak v Cantor Fitzgerald International* [2004] IRLR 942 the claimant, if not wrongfully dismissed, would have been eligible for a substantial 'discretionary' bonus. The Court of Appeal found an implied term that such a discretion would be exercised genuinely and rationally, and thus awarded a considerable sum.

5.7.4   Failure to pay wages: ERA 1996, Pt II remedies

ERA 1996 repealed the Wages Act 1986, but re-enacted its provisions in Part II (ss 13–27). In essence this provides employees with a system of debt collection through the employment tribunal, rather than an ordinary breach of contract claim. It will be the proper basis for a claim when a deduction occurs in the absence of a dismissal or where over £25,000 is sought through a tribunal claim. It is worth noting that there is no provision for counterclaim under ss 13–27, whilst there is under a common law breach of contract claim brought before the tribunal.

Generally, where a deduction would have been unlawful either at common law (*Home Office v Ayres* [1992] IRLR 52) or under the Act, the tribunal may make an appropriate declaration and order repayment or other financial adjustment. Problems, however, have arisen with the definition of 'wages' and of 'deduction'.

5.7.4.1   Wages and deductions

Section 27 provides that 'wages' means any payments from employer to employee in connection with the employment, including any fee, bonus, commission, holiday pay or other emolument referable to the employment, whether payable under the contract or otherwise, and also covering payments made by order of an employment tribunal or statutory schemes such as guarantee pay, sick pay or maternity pay. It excludes advances of wages as a loan, payments of expenses, pensions, redundancy payments and payments made to an employee in a different capacity. This is a broad definition. The main question which has arisen with it is whether a payment in lieu of wages is included. This was resolved by the House of Lords in *Delaney v Staples* [1992] 1 All ER 944. Lord Browne-Wilkinson's analysis is helpful here. He identified four situations:

(a) An employer gives proper notice of termination to his or her employee, tells the employee that he or she need not work until the termination date and gives him or her the wages attributable to the notice period in a lump sum. In this case (commonly called 'garden leave') there is no breach of contract by the employer. The employment continues until the expiry of the notice; the lump sum payment is simply advance payment of wages.

(b) The contract of employment provides expressly that the employment may be terminated either by notice or, on payment of a sum in lieu of notice, summarily. In such a case if the employer summarily dismisses the employee he or she is not in breach of contract provided he or she makes the payment in lieu. But the payment in lieu is not a payment of wages in the ordinary sense since it is not payment for work to be done under the contract of employment.

(c) At the end of the employment, the employer and the employee agree that the employment is to terminate forthwith on payment of a sum in lieu of notice.

Again, the employer is not in breach of contract by dismissing summarily and the payment in lieu is not strictly wages since it is not remuneration for work done during the continuance of the employment.

(d) Without the agreement of the employee, the employer summarily dismisses the employee and tenders a payment in lieu of proper notice. This is by far the most common type of payment in lieu and this case falls into this category. The employer is in breach of contract by dismissing the employee without proper notice. However, the summary dismissal is effective to put an end to the employment relationship, whether or not it unilaterally discharges the contract of employment. Since the employment relationship has ended, no further services are to be rendered by the employee under the contract. It follows that the payment in lieu is not a payment of wages in the ordinary sense since it is not a payment for work done under the contract of employment.

The tribunal jurisdiction allows claims under all four of the outlined situations to be dealt with in the tribunal. Claim forms, however, should still distinguish between the ERA 1996, ss 13–27 and common law claims such as wrongful dismissal.

Section 14 prescribes the situations in which employers may lawfully make deductions from wages. The four categories are:

- Deductions authorised by statute (for example, a deduction from earnings order imposed by a court).

- Justified deductions provided for by the contract of employment, either by a written term of that contract or notified to the employee in writing.

- Deductions expressly authorised in writing by the employee (for example, trade union subscriptions or payments into a pension scheme).

- Deductions from retail employees to cover till or stock shortages (note that these are limited to 10 per cent of pay deducted in respect of any working day).

A question which has come before the courts is whether a complete failure to pay a sum can fall within the term 'deduction'. This was also resolved in *Delaney*, where Ms Delaney's claim was for non-payment of holiday pay and commission as well as the payment in lieu of notice discussed at **5.7.3.3**. The House of Lords held that the non-payments of wages due did constitute deductions, thus enabling her to recover these sums through the tribunal.

New situations regularly arise where the tribunals have to decide, on the facts, what constitutes wages and what constitutes a deduction. Thus, in *Saavedra v Aceground Ltd t/a Terrazza Est* [1995] IRLR 198, the employer unilaterally decided to retain part of the service charge which was added to customers' bills. This had previously been distributed among the staff. The EAT held that the service charge, although the property of the employer, did constitute 'wages'. The unilateral decision to retain part of it constituted an unlawful deduction.

Where a discretionary bonus has been declared a refusal to pay it will constitute a deduction of wages under these provisions (*Farrell Matthews & Weir v Hansen* [2005] IRLR 160).

5.7.4.2   The uses of ERA 1996, Pt II (ss 13–27)

Part II claims constitute a significant proportion of employment tribunal cases. Most are relatively simple debt-collection cases, but the provisions may also be combined creatively with other claims. Thus, in *Whent v T. Cartledge Ltd* [1997] IRLR 153, the applicants' contract included the term: 'your rate of remuneration ... will be in accordance with [the collective agreement] as amended from time to time'. After a transfer covered by the TUPE Regulations (see **6.3.2.5**) the transferee employer de-recognised the applicants' union for collective bargaining purposes. The applicants sought a declaration under what is now ERA 1996, s 11 that their pay was still to be established by the collective agreement from time to time in force. They combined this with a claim under what is now ERA 1996, s 23, that the employer had made unlawful deductions by failing to increase their pay when the collective agreement increased pay levels. The EAT accepted both arguments.

5.7.5   Remedies for other breaches of contract

5.7.5.1   The use of damages claims

Breaches other than failure to give the requisite notice may occur. These may either be condoned by the other party, or if sufficiently serious may lead to a dismissal or resignation. They are normally dealt with by an employment tribunal in an unfair dismissal hearing. Where, however, the employee is ineligible to claim unfair dismissal a claim for breach of contract may be an alternative.

Where a failure to comply with contractual procedures prevents the employee from acquiring the necessary continuity to bring an unfair dismissal claim, it had been thought that a wrongful dismissal claim could include damages for the loss of this chance (*Raspin v United News Shops Ltd* [1999] IRLR 9). This has been rejected by the Court of Appeal in *Harper v Virgin Net Ltd* [2004] IRLR 390 (see **5.7.3.3**).

Another situation where a claim for breach of contract may be advisable is illustrated in *Rigby v Ferodo Ltd* [1988] ICR 29, where the employer unilaterally reduced the employee's wages entitling the employee to terminate the contract because of the employer's breach. The employee was entitled to damages for the breach of contract for the whole period of the breach, and not just for the contractual period of 12 weeks during which the employer could have lawfully terminated the employee's contract. (See also *Burdett-Coutts v Hertfordshire County Council* [1984] IRLR 91.) Thus there may be sound reasons for not accepting an employer's repudiation of the contract of employment and keeping the contract alive, damages being the measure of the loss suffered by the employee.

5.7.5.2   The use of equitable remedies

We will consider first the use of these remedies by employers, then by employees.

Use by employers

The main concern of employers is to avoid the disclosure of confidential information by employees and to protect themselves from unfair competition. Protection is normally achieved by the introduction of restrictive covenants into the contract of employment or by the use of 'garden leave' clauses. (For a fuller discussion on restrictive covenants and protection of confidential information, see **5.8.1**.) In *D v P* [2016] IRLR 355, the Court of Appeal stated that an injunction should be the starting point in considering a remedy for breach (or anticipatory breach) of a restraint of trade clause, subject to questions of validity. Where parties enter into a contract of employment freely and with open eyes, the employee 'should ordinarily be held to their bargain', an injunction being justified as 'the damage potentially sufferable by a covenantee such as D by a breach of the relevant restraint will usually be unquantifiable and will rarely, if ever, provide the covenantee with an adequate substitute for an injunction'.

However, delay in seeking relief, particularly if motivated by tactical considerations will result in refusal (*Legends Live Ltd v Harrison* [2017] IRLR 59).

'Garden leave' clauses are a contractual measure which enable the employer to continue to retain and pay employees during a long period of notice while not requiring them to work. Since the employee will therefore be unable to work elsewhere for this period, he or she will be unable to work for a competitor company. An employer wishing to have such protection should insert an express term in the contract of employment to this effect, since it makes enforcement a simpler process (there is no complication in proving the term and the likelihood of contrary implied terms being upheld is lessened). However, where the contract of employment identifies a right to work conferred on the employee, the garden leave clause will fail (*Hill v Tucker* [1999] ICR 291).

As discussed at **5.8.1**, the validity of restrictive covenants will be tested under the normal principles relating to contracts in restraint of trade. A restrictive covenant will either be set aside as void for being in restraint of trade or, if found to be valid, will be enforced in full by means of an injunction. The courts will not rewrite the covenant. There is, however, no such restriction on the interpretation of garden leave clauses. This is because the effect of a restrictive covenant is to prevent the employee from earning a living, whereas when garden leave clauses are enforced, the employee does not suffer financial loss. It is notable that the courts are prepared to grant injunctive relief for a shorter period than the garden leave clause specifies. In *Provident Financial Group plc and another v Hayward* [1989] IRLR 84, the court was willing to grant an injunction for a shorter period than that agreed, thus effectively varying the contract. The court will exercise its discretion in deciding to what extent the clause should be enforced.

The contrast between restrictive covenants and garden leave clauses came into focus in the Court of Appeal decision in *Armstrong and others v Credit Suisse Asset Management Ltd* (1996) 549 IRLB 13. The employer had used both a 12-month garden leave clause and post-termination restrictive covenants preventing competition for six months. The High Court enforced the restrictive covenants, but (halfway through the 12 months) declined to enforce the remainder of the garden leave period. The Court of Appeal refused the employees' appeal against the injunction enforcing the restrictive covenants, rejecting their argument that the time spent on garden leave could be set off against the restrictive covenant. Neill LJ did, however, recognise that, in exceptional cases, the fact that a long period of garden leave had elapsed could lead the court to refuse to enforce a restrictive covenant. This would presumably be done where it was not in the public interest for there to be further restrictions on the activities of the employees.

Use by employees

We have seen that dismissal may be in breach of contract by a failure to provide proper notice, or by a failure to comply with procedural requirements. In either case the breach does not terminate the contract unless the employee accepts it as doing so. In *Jones v Lee* [1980] ICR 310 a teacher at a Catholic school who had married a divorcee was dismissed in breach of the contractual dismissal procedure. The breach complained of was a denial of her right to make representations to the education committee of the local authority, whose ratification was necessary for any dismissal. The Court of Appeal granted her an injunction preventing dismissal until the procedures were complied with.

Jones v Lee is a comparatively rare example of an equitable remedy in an employment case. Enforcement by specific performance or injunction is not generally available

(Trade Union and Labour Relations (Consolidation) Act 1992 (TULR(C)A 1992), s 236) although there have been exceptions: see *Warner Brothers Pictures v Nelson* [1937] 1 KB 209; *McClelland v Northern Ireland General Health Services Board* [1957] 1 WLR 594; *Hill v C. A. Parsons & Co Ltd* [1972] Ch 305; *Evening Standard Co Ltd v Henderson* [1987] ICR 588). The cases discussed in the rest of this section distinguish this principle.

It is to be noted that whilst an employee may be able to obtain injunctive relief as a result of the breach of a contractually binding disciplinary procedure, damages cannot be recovered as a result of the Supreme Court's consideration of a damages claim in *Edwards v Chesterfield Royal Hospital* and *Botham v Ministry of Defence* [2012] IRLR 129.

In *Hughes v London Borough of Southwark* [1988] IRLR 55, social workers at the Maudsley Hospital were told to work in an understaffed area office three days a week. They successfully sought an injunction preventing the employer from implementing this unilateral variation of their contract. Here, the High Court was applying the Court of Appeal's view, in *Powell v Brent London Borough Council* [1988] ICR 176, that the object of the traditional refusal to enforce the contract of employment was to avoid forcing people to employ or work for those in whom they had lost confidence. Where there remains confidence, an injunction may be granted.

In *Ali v Southwark London Borough Council* [1988] ICR 567, Ms Ali sought an injunction restraining the employer from hearing a disciplinary charge other than according to the contractual disciplinary procedure (promises of confidentiality made this impossible to implement). The court refused to grant it as the employer had lost confidence in the employee on reasonable grounds on the evidence before it, and if the employer was finally found to have acted unfairly, damages would be an appropriate remedy.

In *Alexander v Standard Telephones & Cables Ltd* [1990] ICR 291, the same argument was used to refuse an injunction restraining dismissal until the contractual redundancy procedure was complied with. The High Court held that the fact that the employee had been selected for redundancy indicated that the employer could not have complete confidence in him. An opposing view was expressed by the Court of Session in *Anderson v Pringle of Scotland Ltd* [1998] IRLR 64, where, in the absence of evidence of mistrust, Lord Prosser rejected the view that preferring other employees implied loss of confidence. This view is preferable, not only in logic, but because it enables the courts to hold employers to their contractual procedures in redundancy cases.

In other contexts the courts seem increasingly willing to grant equitable relief. In *Wadcock v London Borough of Brent* [1990] IRLR 223, a social worker refused to comply with the demands of a reorganisation. He was dismissed in breach of the contractual disciplinary procedure. The High Court held that, as the procedure could only be gone through if the employee remained in employment, damages were not an adequate remedy. The employer objected that it had lost confidence in the employee as he was refusing to obey instructions and had discussed the matter with clients. In spite of this the judge granted an interlocutory injunction, observing that W's doing so was 'lamentable but perhaps understandable'. In return, W had to undertake to obey orders at work, on which basis the judge considered his continued employment tenable.

In *Robb v London Borough of Hammersmith & Fulham* [1991] IRLR 72, the High Court granted an injunction even though the employer had lost trust and confidence in the employee's ability to perform his job. The dismissal had been admittedly in breach of contract, and the injunction would, in effect, require the employee to be suspended on full pay until the contractual requirements had been performed. The argument that continuing trust and confidence was essential was expressly rejected, and 'workable' substituted as a criterion. As the employee was not seeking to return to his duties an injunction in this case would be workable and should be granted.

The Court of Session has gone further in *Stacey Ann Dow Pursuer against Tayside University Hospitals NHS Trust Defenders* (2006) SCLR 865, in granting an interdict against dismissal other than through the contractual mechanisms even though the relationship of mutual trust had broken down.

Note that a freezing injunction may be available to protect the assets of a respondent to proceedings in the employment tribunal (*Amicus v Dynamex Friction Ltd* [2005] IRLR 724).

5.8 Other contract-related matters

5.8.1 Restrictive covenants

These are provisions in a contract of employment which purport to impose restrictions on employees once they have left the employment. The starting point is that such provisions are prima facie void unless justifiable in all the circumstances (*Nordenfelt v Maxim Nordenfelt Guns and Ammunition Co* [1894] AC 535 (HL)). However, this principle has been balanced by a recognition that employers have legitimate interests to protect and that reasonable restrictions will be permitted. That balance has been considered in case law.

An employer may have a legitimate interest to protection in respect of:

* his customers, suppliers and other trade connections;
* his workforce;
* confidential information and trade secrets.

However, an employer does not have an unrestricted right to protect himself or herself from competition.

5.8.1.1 Customers, suppliers and other trade connections

Whether or not information of this type can be protected will generally depend on whether it stems from the work of the employer or the employee. If it is information built up by the customer contacts (and personal skills and characteristics) of the employee, it will not be protected (see *Cantor Fitzgerald (UK) Ltd v Wallace* [1992] IRLR 215 (QBD)). Where, by contrast, there is insufficient customer contact by the individual employee concerned, the employer may have a legitimate interest to defend (*Dawnay, Day & Co Ltd v De Braconier D'Alphen* [1997] IRLR 442 (CA)). More recent consideration of whether an employee can be prevented from dealing with 'any customer' of the employer can be found in *WRN Ltd v Ayris* [2008] IRLR 889. Use of email contact lists is considered in *Hays Specialist Recruitment (Holdings) Ltd and another v Ions and another* [2008] IRLR 904.

5.8.1.2 Workforce

Many industries face senior employees setting up in competition and poaching favoured colleagues. The Court of Appeal had doubted whether this was an appropriate area for protection (*Hanover Insurance Brokers Ltd v Schapiro* [1994] IRLR 82). However, subsequently, in *Dawnay, Day & Co. Ltd v de Braconier d'Alphen* [1997] IRLR 442 the Court of Appeal endorsed the High Court's recognition that an employer had an interest in maintaining a stable workforce. The court enforced a one-year no-poaching covenant in respect of senior managers, but rejected as too wide a clause covering all employees.

5.8.1.3   Confidential information

In *Thomas Marshall (Exports) Ltd v Guinle* [1978] IRLR 174, Megarry VC suggested the following test:

- Does the owner think disclosures would be injurious to him or her or advantageous to rivals or others?
- Does the owner believe that it is still confidential (that is, that it has not already become public knowledge)?
- Are those beliefs reasonable?
- The information must be judged in the light of the practices of the particular trade or industry concerned.

The Court of Appeal in *Faccenda Chicken Ltd v Fowler* [1986] 1 All ER 617 suggested that information should be protected:

if it can properly be classed as a trade secret or as material which, while not properly to be described as a trade secret, is in all the circumstances of such a highly confidential nature as to require the same protection as a trade secret.

The court also recognised that information may be expressly identified as confidential by the employer or may be obviously confidential.

The concept of trade secret itself received further attention from the Court of Appeal in *Lansing Linde Ltd v Kerr* [1991] 1 All ER 418 where Butler-Sloss LJ observed:

[W]e have moved into the age of multinational businesses and worldwide business interests. Information may be held by very senior executives which, in the hands of competitors, might cause significant harm to the companies employing them. 'Trade secrets' has, in my view, to be interpreted in the wider context of highly confidential information of a non-technical or non-scientific nature, which may come within the ambit of information the employer is entitled to have protected, albeit for a limited period.

A further guide (based on the views of the House of Lords in *Herbert Morris Ltd v Saxelby* [1916] 1 AC 688) distinguishes between 'objective' and 'subjective' knowledge. A client list would fall into the former category and thus be regarded as the employer's property even though it was in the departing employee's mind. It can be distinguished from the employee's own skills and aptitudes (even if developed in that employment) which would be that employee's subjective knowledge and not susceptible to protection by a restrictive covenant (see *SBJ Stephenson Ltd v Mandy* [2000] IRLR 233 (QBD)).

These are helpful guidelines, but considerable doubt remains as to the circumstances in which information may legitimately be protected.

5.8.1.4   How extensive may the restraint be?

In competition cases the courts will consider the geographical area within which competition is prohibited, and the period of time for which the restraint continues. The type of work undertaken by the employee, particularly where specialised or skilled, can also be an issue. A lifetime ban has been acceptable in the past where the geographical restriction was limited (seven miles from Tamworth in the case of a solicitor was held to be reasonable in *Fitch v Dewes* [1921] 2 AC 158). In some cases, such a geographical area may not be seen as acceptable, as demonstrated by *Allen Janes LLP v Johal* [2006] IRLR 599).

A 12-month ban may be overturned if it extends throughout the United Kingdom (a dry-cleaning company director, in *Greer v Sketchley Ltd* [1979] IRLR 445 (CA)), whereas it was upheld in *Norbrook Laboratories Ltd v Adair* [2008] IRLR 878. The courts will be prepared to examine the nature of the work, extent of competition, risk to employer, client contract and relationships in its consideration. As a result, in *Croesus Financial Ltd v Bradshaw & Bradshaw* [2013] EWHC 3685 (QB), the pattern of annual contact with clients by financial advisers justified a 12-month restraint duration. Where client contact is direct, increasing the risk to the employer, executives were validly restrained for 12 months in *Baker Tilly UK Holdings Ltd v Clough* [2013] EWHC 3616. Please note the seniority of the role will be material, as a junior trader in *Associated Foreign Exchange Ltd v Abbassi* [2010] EWHC 1178 could not be restrained for such a period of time, the restraint clause being void.

In *Coppage v Freedom Security Limited* [2013] IRLR 970, the Court of Appeal was particularly persuaded to accept a six-month restraint against a former director, Sir Bernard Rix, noting '… if the restraint period is as short as six month, that must be a powerful factor in assessing the overall reasonableness of the clause.'

The court will consider the availability of work for the employee were the restrictive covenant to be upheld. The court will seek to protect the employer's legitimate interests, but will not seek to prevent the employee from being able to earn a living at all. It is likely that when *Fitch v Dewes* was decided, the employment market for solicitors was such that the employee could easily have worked elsewhere, allowing the employer firm to maintain its client base. However, in *Allen Janes LLP v Johal*, a six-mile radius of the employer's office in High Wycombe was criticised thus: 'an area clause which is not limited to the clients of the claimant is wider than is necessary to protect the claimant's legitimate interests.' Rather surprisingly in *Merlin Financial Consultants Ltd v Cooper* [2014] ILR 610, a one-year restraint of the whole of the United Kingdom was upheld as the financial services market is 'a single geographical market'.

The courts will also consider the status of the employee. A more senior employee may be more considerably restrained than a junior employee. This flows from the more real damage likely to be done by competition from the senior employee which makes this a legitimate interest to protect.

The courts will look at the factual context of the restriction. In *Office Angels Ltd v Rainer Thomas* [1991] IRLR 214, the Court of Appeal rejected a covenant restraining a branch manager from setting up an employment agency within 1,000 metres as this covered most of the City of London.

Restrictive covenant clauses do not retain their effect indefinitely. The restriction may become unenforceable as the status or responsibilities of the employee evolve, as found in *Patsystems v Neilly* [2012] IRLR 979.

It is important to remember that the only basis for enforcing a restrictive covenant is that it protects a legitimate interest of the employer. The courts have been prepared to consider the employer's business need of recruiting and replacing departing staff, as illustrated by *Re-Use Collections Ltd v Sendall* [2015] IRLR 226, where a three-month restraint, representing the time which would be needed to replace the relevant employees, was upheld. If it is ineffective in so doing it will be struck down as it is a restraint of trade without the justification for permitting it.

This creates a difficulty for those drafting restrictive covenants. If they go beyond legitimate protection (either by being too extensive geographically or in time, or in seeking to protect something not legitimate to protect), the covenant may be struck down. If they restrain an employee from doing something he or she is not in a position to do anyway, they may be struck down. As Lady Justice Arden noted in *ProActive Sports Management Ltd v Rooney* [2012] IRLR 241, the boundary between unenforceable and acceptable contracts is 'an uncertain and porous one'. The inequality of bargaining power, access to legal advice, age and sophistication in financial and contractual matters may be relevant factors.

5.8.1.5   The court's discretion

These cases involve the court exercising its equitable jurisdiction and consequently its discretionary powers. Generally, when faced with a restrictive covenant which is held to be void, the court will strike it down. It will not re-write the covenant in order to make it acceptable.

However, some relief may be available if the offending element of the covenant may be properly severed from the remainder. This may be acceptable if severance leaves the severed parts intact. In *Business Seating (Renovations) Ltd v Broad* [1989] ICR 729 the covenant purported to extend to an associated company. While this was void it could be severed, leaving intact the protection for the company for which the employee had worked.

Moreover, in construing the meaning of the covenant the court may be prepared to cut down a literal meaning in order to achieve the parties' intentions. Thus in *Hollis & Cov Stocks* [2000] IRLR 712 the Court of Appeal had to consider a covenant restricting a solicitor from 'working' within 10 miles for 12 months. This was certainly too wide. However, the court was prepared to construe the provision as meaning 'working as a solicitor' and enforce that as a proper restriction.

Where such an appeal to the intentions of the parties is not available, the court will not sever objectionable elements or 'read down' the terms to make them acceptable. See *Wincanton Ltd v Cranny and SDM European Transport Ltd* [2000] IRLR 716 (CA), where the employer had clearly hoped to be able to enforce a very broad restriction.

Drafters may seek to avoid these problems by including a provision such as 'in the event that any restriction shall be found to be void but would be valid if some part thereof were deleted such restrictions shall apply with such modifications as may be necessary to make them valid or effective'. The courts may give some limited effect to such a provision. For an illustration, see *Hinton & Higgs (UK) Ltd v Murphy and Valentine* [1989] IRLR 519 (CS).

5.8.1.6   The effect of repudiatory breach

Where the employer is in repudiatory breach of the contract of employment the employee will be freed from obligations under the contract and any restrictive covenant will be discharged (*General Billposting Co Ltd v Atkinson* [1909] AC 118 (HL)). This is most likely to arise in situations of constructive dismissal (see **6.4.1.3**) and wrongful dismissal (see **5.7.3**).

Where the employee breaks a fundamental term of the contract he or she will not be able to claim that the contract is thus at an end as to do so would be to take advantage of his or her own default (*Thomas Marshall (Exports) Ltd v Guinle* [1978] IRLR 174 (ChD)).

5.8.1.7   Remedies

Where breach of a valid restrictive covenant is established, the normal remedies for breach of contract are available. However, damages are rarely what the employer seeks. An injunction is the normal remedy sought and, given the short period for which most valid covenants run, most applications are for interim injunctions, where the normal criteria established in *American Cyanamid Ltd v Ethicon Ltd* [1975] AC 396 will apply. The court may depart from the *American Cyanamid* principles if the conditions required in *Office Overload v Gunn* [1977] FSR 39 (CA) apply; although this will be a rare situation following *Lawrence David Ltd v Ashton* [1991] 1 All ER 385 (CA). The employer must also show that the breach of the covenant is causing actual or potential harm (*Jack Allen (Sales and Service) Ltd v Smith* [1999] IRLR 19).

In the relatively rare cases where an employee seeks a remedy, a declaration as to whether the restrictive covenant is void may be available.

5.8.2   Negligence

It had been usual for an employee who suffers some form of injury or illness as a result of his employers failing to safeguard his safety to rely on the statutory duties owed by employers under HASAWA or the numerous Health and Safety Regulations. However, s 69 of the Enterprise and Regulatory Reform Act 2013 has closed the door on this type of strict liability claim. Workers or employees will now have to rely on the common law. In respect of the law of contracts of employment, employees will need to rely on implied terms. For example, the employee may rely on the implied term obliging the employer to provide a safe place of work (as set out at **5.2.4.3**). However, it is still possible for the employer to be in breach of the duty of care and thereby be liable for negligence.

Whether action is brought under the common law of negligence or as breach of an implied term of the contract of employment establishing the same standards (*Waters v Metropolitan Police Commissioner* [2000] IRLR 720 (HL), the employer will be personally liable for breach and vicariously liable for breaches by those appointed to perform that duty.

It is generally accepted that the employer is required to provide:

- a competent staff;
- adequate material; and
- a proper system and effective supervision.

Recent recognition of the damage caused by stress at work has led to the High Court expanding the scope of the employer's duty to provide a safe system of work (*Walker v Northumberland County Council* [1995] IRLR 35) where a senior social worker suffered a nervous breakdown through excessive workload. He returned to work on a promise of assistance which was not made available. The employer was held liable for the further damage he suffered as the earlier experience had made the subsequent injury foreseeable. In *Cross v Highland and Islands Enterprise* [2001] IRLR 54, the Court of Session held that this duty obliges employers not to subject employees to conditions (for example, overwork, or regular bullying) which reasonably foreseeably could cause psychiatric injury or illness. In *Walker* the House of Lords recognised a similar duty where victimisation or harassment causes physical or psychiatric injury.

The Protection from Harassment Act 1997 (PHA) applies to the employment relationship. In *Majrowski v Guy's and St Thomas's NHS Trust* [2005] IRLR 340 the Court of Appeal held that an employer could be vicariously liable for employees' acts of harassment provided that they were sufficiently connected with the employment. In *Veakins v Kier Islington Ltd* [2010] IRLR 132 (CA), a female electrician bullied by her female supervisor was held to be able to rely on PHA in claiming against her employer provided that the conduct complained of 'is oppressive and unacceptable, albeit the court must keep in mind that it must be of an order which "would sustain criminal liability"'. The standard of 'oppressive and unacceptable' behaviour was also used in *Rayment v Ministry of Defence* [2010] IRLR 768 in the High Court. These judgments extend the prospect of employer liability from that which previously existed following *Conn v Council of the City of Sunderland* [2008] IRLR 324. This is an independent cause of action from the developing case law on harassment in the context of the discrimination legislation (for which see **8.5**).

Liability for references and negligent misstatement is also possible, see **5.2.4.3**.

5.8.3   Will industrial action constitute a breach of contract?

The question of whether an employee is in breach of his or her contract commonly arises in the context of industrial action. Industrial action is a breach of contract if it means that the employee fails to carry out his or her obligations. Strike action is clearly such a breach. It will not, however, terminate the contract. The action will be seen as a repudiatory breach of contract (*Simmons v Hoover Ltd* [1977] QB 284) to which the employer may respond by accepting the repudiation, or not as he chooses. The strike does not involve the employees resigning in any way. Therefore if the employer accepts the repudiation this will constitute a dismissal (*London Transport Executive v Clarke* [1981] IRLR 166) (see also **Chapter 6**).

5.8.3.1   Do other forms of industrial action constitute breach?
Overtime ban
If overtime is a contractual requirement, then a ban will constitute a breach of contract. Otherwise it will not.

Go-slow
This is probably a breach of an implied term that employees should work at normal speed (see also the *ASLEF* case discussed at 'Work to rule').

Work to rule
In theory this looks like careful compliance with the contract and therefore not a breach. However, in *Secretary of State for Employment v ASLEF (No 2)* [1972] 2 QB 455, the Court of Appeal held a work to rule to constitute a breach of contract. Train drivers were working to rule. The rulebook had been developed over many years. It was complex and partially outdated. In practice it was usually ignored as complete compliance would disrupt the timetable. The work to rule involved a careful compliance with rules with the object of disruption. Lord Denning MR held that the rulebook (in this case) was not incorporated into the drivers' contracts, but was merely guidance as to how to carry out the contract. There was an implied duty to interpret rules in a way which does not cause disruption.

Withdrawal of goodwill
In the *ASLEF* case Lord Denning MR expressly disapproved the view that there was an implied term that the employee must actively assist the employer in his objects. Thus a withdrawal of goodwill will not be a breach, provided the employee does not disrupt the undertaking.

Selective strike
This arises where, for example, a union arranges for key workers alone to withdraw their labour, resulting in others having no work to do. Do those who are thus made idle have a right to be paid?

In *Chappell v Times Newspapers Ltd* [1975] ICR 145, selective strike action had been organised. The employers said they would treat all members as having dismissed themselves. The non-striking workers sought an injunction against the termination of their employment. As individuals, they had not participated in any disruptive action. They had merely refused to undertake the work of those on strike. The Court of Appeal refused an injunction on the equitable ground that the workers did not come to the court with clean hands.

Where an employer takes no such steps, workers idle in such circumstances may be entitled to payment.

5.9   Specimen statutory written statement of terms of employment

The following specimen statement meets the requirements of ERA 1996, s 1, and is appropriate for a salaried employee whose employment is not covered by collective bargaining.

TERMS OF EMPLOYMENT

From: *[Employer]*

To: *[Employee]*

The following particulars constitute the terms of your employment as at *[date]*, given pursuant to Part I of the Employment Rights Act 1996.

1. Your employment with *[employer]* commenced on *[date]*. No employment with any previous employer is to count as part of your present employment.

2. You are employed as an [   ] at *[employer]*'s Head Office at *[address]*. Your duties are set out in [*refer to job description or staff handbook etc.*] and in addition to those duties, you may be required to carry out other or additional duties as necessary.

3. Your rate of pay is £[   ] per annum/per month/per week, payable weekly/ monthly in arrears. (*If necessary, give details of when payments will be made, eg, 'on the 26th of each month' or 'on the Tuesday following the week you have worked'.*)

4. You are required to work [   ] hours per week. Your normal working hours are between [   ] and [   ] Monday to Friday, with a break of one hour for lunch each day. (*Add, if applicable, information relating to overtime, eg: 'You may be required to work reasonable amounts of overtime, in which case you will be entitled to time off in lieu, to be taken at a time agreed by you and your section supervisor' or 'You may be required to work reasonable amounts of overtime at the rate of time and a half' or 'You may be required to work reasonable amounts of overtime, however this will not be subject to further remuneration'.*)

5. You are entitled to [*insert appropriate number, the minimum allowable being 5.6*] weeks' paid holiday a year [*including/in addition to*] public holidays. (*Reference should be made to any written guidance such as: 'Detailed holiday regulations are available for inspection in the personnel office/are contained in the staff handbook'. Alternatively, main points should be stated, such as when the leave year runs from and to, how much notice of leave booking is required, whether leave can be taken during the notice period, etc ...*)

6. If you are unable to attend work through sickness or injury you should contact Human Resources or your Line manager [delete as appropriate] immediately. (*Reference should be made to any written guidance such as 'Full regulations are available for inspection in the personnel office/contained in the staff handbook'. Alternatively, the main points should be stated, such as for what period will full sick pay be paid, when medical certificates should be provided.*)

7. Your employer operates a pension scheme in respect of your employment, details of which are [*available for inspection in the personnel office/contained in the staff handbook*].

8. (a) You are obliged to give a minimum period of [*one/two/three*] [*weeks/months*] notice to terminate your employment.

(b) If you are in breach of your contract you may be dismissed without notice.

[(c) In other cases you will be entitled to a minimum period of notice as follows:

(i) [   ] week's notice for any period of continuous service up to two years;

(ii) [   ] week's notice for each complete year of continuous service between two and 12 years;

(iii) [   ] weeks' notice where your continuous employment exceeds [   ] years.] (*If silent, the position will be the statutory notice under s 86(1) ERA 1996*)

[9. If you have any grievance relating to your employment you should in the first instance raise it with your section supervisor.]

[10. The disciplinary rules are [*available for inspection in the personnel office/ contained in the staff handbook*]. If you are dissatisfied with any disciplinary decision relating to you, you should first apply to your section supervisor. Detailed procedures for disciplinary matters are available [*for inspection in the personnel office/contained in the staff handbook*].]

Dated _____   Signed _____
                          (Company
                          Secretary/Supervisor/Manager/Director)

Acknowledgement by employee

I acknowledge receipt of a copy of this written statement.

Dated_____   Signed _____ (Employee)

[9] and [10] are optional, as there is no longer any obligation to use the statutory procedures due to their repeal. Employers are now no longer obliged to offer procedures for the resolution of grievances or to follow any mandatory procedure for disciplining employees (although the process may be considered in an unfair dismissal or discrimination claim which may result).

Unfair dismissal and redundancy

6

6.1 An overview: the background to unfair dismissal and redundancy

6.1.1 Introduction

Unfair dismissal remains the most important form of employment protection legislation in terms of volume of case law, public awareness and persistent influence on personnel practices. This right has existed since the Industrial Relations Act 1971 (IRA 1971). Despite the introduction of anti-discrimination legislation to ensure equal pay and eliminate race and sex discrimination in the 1970s and the subsequent broadening of protection to cover disability, age, religious beliefs, sexual orientation, gender reassignment and the introduction of restrictions on working time and a minimum wage, unfair dismissal continues to make up the majority of employment tribunal claims. The relevant statutory provisions relating to unfair dismissal are to be found in Part X of the Employment Rights Act 1996 (ERA 1996), as amended.

Compensation upon dismissal by reason of redundancy is provided by Part XI of ERA 1996 and is intended to compensate a long-serving employee for the loss of his or her security of employment.

6.1.2 Common law

All employees work to a contract of employment, although the terms of that contract may be express or implied, agreed in writing or orally. This is radically different from a contract for services under which self-employed people work (see **5.1** for further guidance). Breach of the contract of employment is discussed at **5.7**. Damages for a breach of the employment contract are limited at common law to the loss suffered by the injured party by the failure to comply with the terms of that contract. As with any other contract at common law, damages for termination of a contract of employment will be limited to the loss suffered by the failure to comply with the terms of that contract: a dismissal without notice will therefore give a right to claim damages in lieu of the notice period provided under the contract (or to be implied) but no more. This is covered in detail under wrongful dismissal at **5.7.3**.

It was the inadequacy of damages at common law for most employees (most will work to notice periods of 12 weeks or less) that led to the introduction of redundancy compensation in the Redundancy Payments Act 1965 (RPA 1965) and subsequently to the introduction of remedies for unfair dismissal in the IRA 1971.

Though employment tribunals have jurisdiction to determine complaints relating to redundancy payments, unfair dismissal and breach of contract (see the precedents at **11.3** for a sample claim under this jurisdiction), the contractual damages which might be due by reason of an employer's breach of the contract of employment are very different (both in terms of the approach to liability and in respect of the calculation of damages) to questions of entitlement to a statutory redundancy payment and to cases of unfair dismissal.

A claim under common law for the breach of the employment contract upon its termination ('wrongful dismissal') is subject to no statutory cap (although employment tribunals can only award damages for breach of contract up to £25,000) and the employee does not have to meet a qualifying condition in order to claim damages at common law. For a fuller explanation see **5.7.3**.

Employees who are unable to make a claim for unfair dismissal may be able to sue for wrongful dismissal for breach of contract and will, in any case, have six years in which to bring a claim in the High Court or County Court, whereas a complaint of unfair dismissal must be brought within three months of the effective date of termination and a claim for statutory redundancy payment within six months.

It is important to note that a fair dismissal may still be a wrongful dismissal, and vice versa, and an employee may be able to seek an interim injunction to prevent a dismissal taking place in breach of a contractual disciplinary procedure (*Dietman v Brent LBC* [1988] IRLR 299 and *Irani v Southampton and South West Hampshire Health Authority* [1985] IRLR 203) or redundancy procedure (*Anderson v Pringle of Scotland Ltd* [1998] IRLR 64 (CS)). Frequently, a dismissed employee will combine claims for unfair dismissal and wrongful dismissal.

It had been the position that employees over the age of 65 lost the right to claim unfair dismissal and subsequently that dismissal upon reaching 'normal retirement age' was potentially fair. However, since the Equality Act 2010 and the Employment Equality (Repeal of Retirement Age Provisions) Regulations 2011, from 6 April 2011, an employer can only rely on a contractual retirement age which can be objectively justified. Please refer to **8.2.1** and **8.4.5** for further guidance.

6.1.2.1   Termination at common law

As indicated at **6.1.2**, all contracts of employment will be terminable lawfully upon notice, whether that notice period is express or implied. The right to terminate on notice at common law is not affected by whether the dismissal itself is fair or unfair.

If the contract of employment is silent on the question of the notice period, then at common law 'reasonable' notice must be given. Reasonable notice will depend upon the particular circumstances of the case—the status and length of service of the employee, the custom and practice within that employment or trade and any other relevant factors in each particular case (*Hill v C A Parsons & Co Ltd* [1972] Ch 305).

ERA 1996, s 86, provides for certain minimum periods of notice to be given by the employer to all employees, depending on their length of service (see **5.7.3.2**). Where there is no express provision in the contract indicating the parties' agreement to a particular period of notice, 'reasonable notice' will be deemed to be at least the statutory minimum provided by s 86.

During the period of notice the employee is entitled to be paid his or her average wages for any period where no work is provided by the employer or where the employee is absent through sickness, injury or due to absence on agreed holidays. No such wages are due, however, if he or she goes on strike after notice has been given (ERA 1996, s 91(2), which accords with the position at common law where no wages are due if an employee has withdrawn his or her labour by way of industrial action or strike).

An employer may choose to dispense with the employee's services and pay his or her wages or salary in lieu of notice and this may be a means used by an employer to keep the employee's obligations under the contract of employment alive while preventing him or her coming into the workplace ('garden leave'), although the contract must specifically allow for this. Another reason for doing this is to prevent the employee from working for competitors. The parties can, of course, agree a shorter period of notice and an employee may waive his or her right to notice or money in lieu of notice.

If it is the employee who is terminating the contract then, unless the contract of employment provides for a longer period of notice, ERA 1996, s 86 requires the employee to give the employer a minimum of one week's notice in all the circumstances. An employee who declines to work out the notice period provided under the contract of employment could be sued for breach of contract by the employer. In most cases, however, the employer will be able to provide cover for that employee or will be unable to show the loss sustained and, particularly where the notice period is short, it will rarely be worthwhile to seek damages against the employee. Quantification of loss is a particular difficulty for the employer.

If an employee works out his or her notice, the dismissal will be effective on its expiry. Similarly, if the contract is kept alive, although the employee is not required actually to come in and perform work for the employer, the dismissal will still not be effective until the end of the notice period. If an employee is dismissed summarily but paid monies in lieu of notice then the dismissal will be effective on the actual day the employee leaves the employment, not when the notice period would have ended.

6.1.2.2   Conduct justifying summary dismissal at common law

As with all contracts, a repudiatory breach of the employment contract by one party will enable the other to treat that conduct as having brought the contract of employment to an end thereby discharging the innocent party from all further obligations under the contract. The position is no different in employment law: gross misconduct on the part of an employee is likely to constitute such a repudiatory breach entitling the employer to treat the contract as having come to an end immediately and so dismiss the employee summarily, that is, without notice. (See **5.7.3.1** for more guidance on gross misconduct.) On the other hand, a breach of a fundamental term of the contract on the part of the employer will also enable the employee to treat the contract of employment as having come to an end immediately, thus entitling the employee to leave the employment and to seek damages for the employer's summary termination of the contract. (See **6.4.1.3** on constructive dismissal.)

In either case, whether the employer's or employee's conduct is serious enough to constitute a fundamental breach is a question of fact and will depend on the circumstances within which the employment relationship existed.

6.2   Unfair dismissal: introducing the basic right

ERA 1996, s 94(1) provides:

An employee has the right not to be unfairly dismissed by his employer.

The right not to be unfairly dismissed, and the corresponding right to complain of an unfair dismissal, is one provided by statute and only those who meet the terms of the statute can claim the benefit of this entitlement.

6.2.1   Employment under a contract of service

The right to complain of unfair dismissal (and the right to claim a statutory redundancy payment) is confined to those who are employed pursuant to a contract of employment: that is a contract of service (ERA 1996, s 230). Put simply, the person bringing a claim must be an 'employee'. See **Chapter 5** for an exposition of the test for employee status.

6.2.2   Exclusions from unfair dismissal protection

The following categories of employees working at particular jobs or in particular circumstances are excluded from the right provided by s 94 and may make no claim for unfair dismissal:

(a) Employees who have been continuously employed for less than two years where the date of commencement of employment is on or after 6 April 2012 are excluded from the right to claim unfair dismissal, unless the dismissal is for one of the prescribed automatically unfair reasons (see **6.9**) (ERA 1996, s 108(1) and see Unfair Dismissal and Statement of Reasons for Dismissal (Variation of Qualifying Period) Order 2012 (SI 2012/989)). The period of 'continuous employment' commences with the day on which the employee was due to start work under the contract of employment and ends with the effective date of termination (see **6.5**).

Any employee who has been employed for one week less than the qualifying period of one year and is dismissed is entitled to add to this computation the week's statutory notice to which he is entitled (ERA 1996, s 97(2)–(3)). However, an employee dismissed without notice for proven gross misconduct will not be able to rely upon this statutory extension, as their right to receive notice will have been lost.

(b) 'Employee shareholders' under s 205A Employment Rights Act 1996. Such employees are limited to claims for automatically unfair reasons and for discriminatory reasons under EA 2010.

(c) Employment as a master or member of the crew of a fishing vessel where the employee is paid by way of a share of the profits is also excluded (ERA 1996, s 199).

(d) Police officers and members of the armed forces are also excluded from the right (ERA 1996, ss 192 and 200 (as amended)).

(e) Any employment covered by a contractual dismissals procedure agreement under the provisions of ERA 1996, s 110 is excluded.

(f) Employees who work for foreign governments and other international organisations which enjoy diplomatic immunity can claim unfair dismissal only if that immunity is waived (but see the State Immunity Act 1978 (SIA 1978)).

(g) A Minister of the Crown may also issue a certificate that specified employment or a specified type of person be excluded from statutory employment protection for the purpose of safeguarding national security (ERA 1996, s 193, and see *Council of Civil Service Unions v Minister for the Civil Service* [1985] AC 374 (HL)).

(h) Persons dismissed in connection with a strike or lock-out: where the industrial action is *unofficial*, apart from some limited exceptional cases, the dismissed employee loses the right to claim unfair dismissal altogether (Trade Union and Labour Relations (Consolidation) Act 1992 (TULR(C)A 1992), s 237, as amended).

Since 1 October 2006, the exclusion of those over the age of 65 from the right to claim unfair dismissal has been abolished. Now, employers must objectively justify any contractual retirement age, as explained at **6.1.2**.

6.2.3   Note

(a) Unlike redundancy cases, no lower age limit applies in unfair dismissal claims.

(b) An illegal contract can render a contract of employment unenforceable and hence any unfair dismissal claim which is dependent upon that contract (*Hewcastle Catering Limited v Ahmed and Elkamah* [1992] ICR 26 (CA)). However, not every illegality in performance will turn a contract into an illegal contract, according to *Colen v Cebrian (UK) Ltd* [2004] IRLR 210 (CA). See **5.1.3** for further guidance.

(c) While there is a general prohibition on contracting out of the statutory right to claim unfair dismissal, there can be a valid settlement of a claim of unfair dismissal involving an Advisory, Conciliation and Arbitration Service (ACAS) Conciliation Officer where the employee has agreed to withdraw his or her complaint or where there is a valid compromise agreement (ERA 1996, s 203). See **11.4** for a case study involving such a compromise agreement.

(d) Where industrial action is taken which is not unofficial but is not 'protected' action within the meaning of the Trade Union and Labour Relations Act 1974 (TULRA 1974), s 238A, the employment tribunal retains jurisdiction to consider a complaint of unfair dismissal in certain circumstances (TULR(C)A 1992, s 238).

(e) The exclusion which applied to employees who ordinarily worked abroad which was contained in ERA 1996, s 196 was abolished by the Employment Relations Act 1999 (ERA 1999), s 32(3). Accordingly, the jurisdiction of the tribunal to consider complaints of unfair dismissal will be resolved on normal conflict of law principles. It is where it can be established that the employment relationship has much stronger connections with the UK and UK employment law than any other country such that Parliament would intend such an employee to be able to claim unfair dismissal per the EAT in *Dhunna v Creditsights* [2012] UKEAT/0246/12/LA.

6.3 Continuity of employment

The concept of 'continuous employment' is significant both in determining whether an employee is entitled to unfair dismissal protection and in computing benefits. An employee must have continuous employment of at least two years to have the right to claim unfair dismissal, where the date of commencement is on or after 6 April 2012 (see **6.2.2**). Periods of continuous employment are calculated and expressed in terms of years or months, commencing with the day on which the employee starts work under the contract of employment. If the contract starts on a non-working day (for example, a bank holiday) the period of employment will begin to run from that date, despite the fact that work does not begin until a later day (*General of the Salvation Army v Dewsbury* [1984] ICR 498).

6.3.1 Calculation of continuous employment

Continuity of employment is a statutory concept, governed by ERA 1996, Pt XIV, Ch I.

There is a legal presumption that continuity of employment exists. Provided that an employee can establish the date on which employment commenced, it is presumed to be continuous until the employer proves to the contrary (ERA 1996, s 210(5)). This presumption does not, however, apply where the employee has to prove some additional fact to link periods in the history of his or her employment, for example that there has been a relevant transfer of an undertaking from one employer to another (*Secretary of State for Employment v Cohen and Beaupress Limited* [1987] ICR 570 (EAT)).

Continuity of employment is a concept somewhat distinct from the contract of employment: an employee may change his or her place of work, job or terms and conditions of employment, provided that he or she remains with the same employer or works for an associated employer or different employers where there has been a transfer of the undertaking in which he or she works.

On the question of whether continuous employment starts on the day when the employee begins to carry out activities for the employer or a later date when the employment commences under the contract, in *Koenig v The Mind Gym* [2013] UKEAT/0201/12/RN it was determined by relying on the contract. Hence the contract will have relevance, depending on the factual circumstances.

6.3.2   Interruptions in work and preserving continuity

Continuity of employment will be broken if there is a gap of a week or more in the employee's history of employment and that employee is unable to show that he or she comes within the deeming provisions set out at **6.3.2.1–6.3.2.6**. These provisions apply only to those cases where the contract of employment no longer subsists: if the contract of employment continues then there is no gap in continuity which needs to be filled or bridged. Therefore, any absences from work covered by the contract of employment (which should always be carefully checked) are disregarded, such as annual leave.

The judgment of Langstaff P in *Welton v Deluxe Retail ((t/a) Madhouse)* [2013] IRLR 166 is instructive on this complicated issue.

6.3.2.1   Sickness or injury

Where an employee is absent through sickness or injury then, in addition to any contractual sick leave, the first 26 weeks of absence count towards continuity and there is no break (ERA 1996, s 212(3)(a) and (4)).

6.3.2.2   Temporary cessation of work

Where the employee is absent, with no subsisting contract, because there is a temporary cessation of work, continuity is preserved (ERA 1996, s 212(3)(b)). 'Temporary' means a period of absence which is relatively short in duration when contrasted with periods of work (*Berwick Salmon Fisheries Co Ltd v Rutherford* [1991] IRLR 203). The cessation may, however, be for a considerable period of time—it is to be viewed historically with the benefit of hindsight (*Fitzgerald v Hall, Russell & Co Ltd* [1970] AC 984 (HL)). There must be a cessation of work, not merely of work done by that employee; if the work is transferred from one employee to another there is no 'cessation' (*Byrne v Birmingham City District Council* [1987] IRLR 191). Regular patterns of gaps in an employee's work will not amount to temporary cessations: temporary in this sense means 'transient' (see *Ford v Warwickshire County Council* [1983] 2 AC 71 (HL)). Whether an individual absence is temporary or not, is, however, a question of fact for an employment tribunal to determine.

6.3.2.3   Absence by arrangement or custom

When an employee is absent from work by arrangement or custom, continuity is preserved (ERA 1996, s 212(3)(c)). A period of secondment to another employer can, under this provision, count towards continuity (*Wishart v National Coal Board* [1974] ICR 460). Equally this provision can cover working one week on, one week off (*Lloyds Bank Ltd v Secretary of State for Employment* [1979] ICR 258).

6.3.2.4   Strike or lock-out

In the event of a strike or lock-out continuity of employment is preserved but the days lost by the employee because of strike action or lock-out do not qualify for computation purposes; the employee neither gains nor loses, and that period is merely wiped from the history (ERA 1996, s 216).

6.3.2.5   Change of employer: transfer of business

At common law the termination of employment with one employer and the commencement of employment with another would mean that an entirely new contractual history had commenced unrelated to the previous relationship. A change in the identity of the employer at common law would necessarily mean the termination of the contract of (personal) service and the commencement of a new contract.

The continuity of employment provisions under the ERA 1996 draw upon that common law concept by stating that continuity will only apply to employment by one employer subject to the provisions of s 218. In reality the exceptions are extremely broad:

(a) Where an Act of Parliament causes one corporate body to replace another as the employer (ERA 1996, s 218(3)).

(b) Where the employer, not being a corporate body, dies and the personal representatives carry on the business (ERA 1996, s 218(4)).

(c) Where the employer is constituted by a partnership, personal representatives or trustees, and the composition of the organisation changes (for example, a partner retires and another is appointed) (ERA 1996, s 218(5)), although it may be useful to see the Court of Appeal decision in *Stevens v Bower* [2004] IRLR 957 on changes to a partnership.

(d) Where the employee is taken into the employment of an associated employer (ERA 1996, s 218(6)). 'Associated employer' is defined as any two employers where one is a company of which the other (directly or indirectly) has control or both being companies of which a third person (directly or indirectly) has control (ERA 1996, s 231).

(e) Where the employee of a local education authority moves from employment by that authority to employment by governors of a local education authority maintained school and vice versa (ERA 1996, s 218(7)).

(f) Where the trade or business or undertaking in which the employee is employed is transferred, continuity of employment is unbroken (ERA 1996, s 218(2)). Whilst this provision relates to continuity of employment, it should be read against the background of the more wide-ranging Transfer of Undertakings (Protection of Employment) Regulations 2006 (SI 2006/216) and the Acquired Rights Directives (77/187/EEC and 2001/23/EC), a summary of which appears at **6.3.2.6**.

6.3.2.6   Has there been a transfer of an undertaking covered by TUPE?

For these provisions to 'bite', the transfer in question must be the transfer of a business and not a mere transfer of assets (*Melon v Hector Powe Ltd* [1981] ICR 43 (EAT)). The Court of Appeal in *Millam v The Print Factory (London) 1991 Ltd* [2007] IRLR 526 suggests the mere fact that there has been a transfer of shares does not preclude that there has been a TUPE transfer, but this approach was not taken in *Brookes v Borough Care Services* [1998] IRLR 636.

To obtain the protection of TUPE 2006, the transfer must be a 'relevant transfer' within reg 3 of which there are two types; (a) a transfer of an economic entity (which retains its identity) from one legal person to another, and (b) a service provision change, under reg 3(1)(b). The approach to be adopted in determining the question whether or not there has been a transfer of an undertaking in any particular case has been led by decisions of the European Court of Justice (ECJ) relating to the Acquired Rights Directive (EEC Directive 77/187), and it is a question of fact to be determined in the circumstances of each individual case. The old jurisprudence is to be followed since the introduction of TUPE 2006 and its wording follows that of the major authorities such as the

Spijkers decision. Therefore, in deciding whether or not the economic entity (the undertaking or business) in question has retained its identity, regard should be had to:

all the facts characterised in the transaction in question, including the type of undertaking or business, whether or not the business's tangible assets such as buildings and moveable property are transferred, the value of its intangible assets at the time of the transfer, whether or not the majority of its employees are taken over by the employer, whether or not its customers are transferred and the degree of similarity between the activities carried on before and after the transfer and the period, if any, for which those activities were suspended . . . All these circumstances are merely single factors in the overall assessment which must be made and cannot therefore be considered in isolation. (*Spijkers v Gebrouders Benedik Abattoir CV* (Case 24/85) [1986] ECR 1119 (ECJ))

Further, the undertaking in question must be a 'stable economic entity' (*Rygaard v StroMolle Akustik A/S* (Case C-48/94) [1996] IRLR 51 (ECJ)). This issue has been considered by the Court of Appeal in *Balfour Beatty Power Networks Ltd v Wilcox* [2007] IRLR 63 (which also considers the clarity of distinction between an asset-reliant and labour-intensive business).

An undertaking for these purposes does not, however, have to fit any strict tests—it can be, for instance, of any size and can even consist of merely one employee (*Schmidt v Starund Leih Kasse der Sruheren Ämter Bourdesholen, Kiel und Cronshagen* (Case C-392/92) [1995] ICR 237 (ECJ)).

The approach of the domestic courts and tribunals has been broad (consistent with the purpose of the Acquired Rights Directive, that is, to protect the rights of employees on a transfer of a business). See, in particular, *Dines v Initial Healthcare Services* [1995] ICR 11 (CA) and *Isles of Scilly Council v Brintel Helicopters Ltd* [1995] ICR 249 (EAT). In *BSG Property Services v Tuck* [1996] IRLR 134 (EAT), it was held that the additional 'single economic entity' requirement of the *Rygaard* case should not be widely applied and, in reality, added nothing to the existing approach.

The decision of the ECJ in *Süzen v Zehnacker Gebäuldereinigung GmbH Krankenhausservice* (C-13/95) [1997] IRLR 255 would, however, suggest that a more restrictive approach is to be taken and that the transfer of a service contract is not a transfer of a part of a business within the Acquired Rights Directive 'if there is no concomitant transfer of significant tangible or intangible assets or the taking over by the new employer of a major part of the workforce, in terms of their numbers and skill, assigned by his predecessor to the performance of the contract'. The ECJ decision on this point in *Abler v Sodexho MM Catering Gesellschaft* [2004] IRLR 168 considers the 'asset-reliant' and 'labour-intensive' business distinction and, as stated in this section, see the Court of Appeal's decision in *Balfour Beatty Power Networks Ltd v Wilcox* [2007] IRLR 63.

The Court of Appeal in *Betts and others v Brintel Helicopters and another* [1997] ICR 792 took the restrictive approach of the *Süzen* case; however, subsequent domestic case law has continued to take a more liberal and purposive approach (see *Cheesman and others v Brewer* [2001] IRLR 144 (EAT), *RCO v Unison* [2002] ICR 751 (CA) and *ECM (Vehicle Delivery) Service Ltd v Cox* [1999] IRLR 559 (CA)).

For guidance on what constitutes a service when considering a 'service provision change', see *Pannu v Geo W King (in liquidation)* [2013] IRLR 193. Appellate guidance on service provision changes can be found in *Enterprise Management Services Ltd v Connect-Up Ltd* [2012] IRLR 190.

For the employee to be automatically transferred from one employer to another upon the transfer of an undertaking, he or she must have been employed 'immediately before' the transfer in question. In considering this requirement, however, a wide and purposive interpretation of the Regulations has meant that employees will be held to be employed 'immediately before the transfer' if they would have been so employed but for a dismissal which relates to the transfer itself (*Litster v Forth Dry Dock and Engineering*

Co [1990] 1 AC 546 (HL)). The decisive moment will be when the person responsible for carrying on the business becomes the *de facto* employer, not when the formal transfer is completed if this occurs later (*Berger & Busschers v Besselsen* [1990] ICR 396 (ECJ)). Equally a transfer may be effected by a series of two or more transactions and may take place whether or not any property is transferred to the transferee by the transferor employer. Employees have the right to object to the automatic transfer of contracts of employment to a new employer although such an objection will amount to a termination of the contract of employment without there having been a dismissal.

Employers will not be able to avoid TUPE obligations by refusing to take on the workforce in labour-intensive undertakings. Tribunals will be astute in looking behind deliberate 'TUPE avoidance' in this regard (*see ADI (UK) Ltd v Willer* [2001] IRLR 542 (CA)).

As discussed at **6.9**, a dismissal by reason of a transfer of an undertaking will be automatically unfair unless it is for an economic, technical or organisational reason, in which case the fairness or otherwise of the dismissal will be subject to the same considerations as arise in normal unfair dismissal cases. Dismissals of employees by reason of *a* business transfer (as distinct from *the* business transfer) where no buyer has been identified and no sale of the business is certain, may also be caught (see *Morris v John Grose Group Ltd* [1998] ICR 655 (EAT)). Transfer of undertakings is a complex issue of employment law and readers needing further guidance are referred to *Harvey on Industrial Relations and Employment Law*.

6.3.3   Continuity flowchart

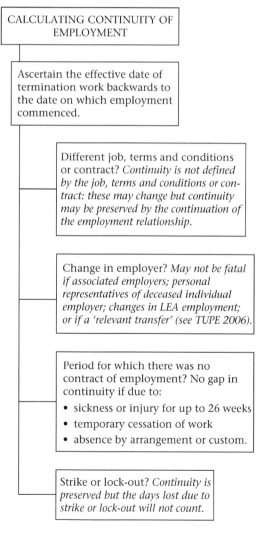

Figure 6.1 Continuity flowchart

6.4   Dismissal and termination of employment

6.4.1   Dismissal

For there to be an unfair dismissal, there must be a dismissal. ERA 1996, s 95, defines 'dismissal' as arising in three situations:

- termination by the employer, with or without notice;
- expiry of a fixed-term contract without renewal;
- constructive dismissal.

Where dismissal is in dispute, the burden of proof will be on the employee to establish this threshold to a claim of unfair dismissal.

6.4.1.1   Termination by the employer

It is a requirement that where the employee wishes to reply on dismissal by the employer, that dismissal should be communicated. In *Sandle v Adecco UK Ltd* [2016] IRLR 941, HHJ Eady QC stated: 'communication might be by conduct and the conduct in question might be capable of being construed as a direct dismissal or as a repudiatory breach, but it has to be something of which the employee was aware.'

With or without notice
In most cases the intention of the employer to dismiss, whether with or without notice, will be clear. Where there is no ambiguity in the language used by the employer, that is, where there is a clear and present intention to sever the employment relationship, then an employee is entitled to take the words used at face value (*Sothern v Franks Charlesly & Co* [1981] IRLR 278 (CA)).

Where there is ambiguity the intention is to be determined objectively: how would a reasonable observer, in those circumstances, view the employer's intention (*B G Gale Ltd v Gilbert* [1978] ICR 1149 (EAT)). Courts and tribunals have long recognised the special circumstances that may arise in the context of industrial relations and many cases have stressed the need to consider all the facts of the particular case (*Martin v Yeoman Aggregates Ltd* [1983] ICR 314 and *Sovereign House Security Services Ltd v Savage* [1989] IRLR 115 (CA)). This approach has even led to an implied right to 'retract' words of notice given in the heat of the moment (*Kwik-Fit (GB) Ltd v Lineham* [1992] ICR 183 (EAT)).

In *CF Capital plc v Willoughby* [2011] IRLR 985, the Court of Appeal had to consider if an unambiguous notice of dismissal could be withdrawn because it was given mistakenly. Generally speaking, notice cannot be withdrawn without consent unless special circumstances apply. Lord Justice Rimer stated that the special circumstances exception arose in 'heat of the moment' cases where notice was given orally (and often in bad temper). In the *Willoughby* case the notice was written and since it was intended to end her employment (and offer her agency terms instead), the special circumstances exception did not apply.

Variation of notice
The notice period, once initially agreed, can be varied. It was previously thought that this would have to be done in writing by a withdrawal of the original notice and the acceptance of a new notice period. However, as a result of *Palfrey v Transco plc* [2004] IRLR 916, the notice (that determines the effective date of termination) can be varied. The decision of the Employment Appeal Tribunal (EAT) was that an agreement to bring

forward the date of termination and shorten the notice period amounted to a with-drawal of the original notice of dismissal and the substitution of a shorter period.

Counter-notice

Once notice has been given by an employer, should an employee give counter-notice to terminate the employment earlier than the expiry of the employer's notice, the employee will still be regarded as having been dismissed by the employer and for the reason as originally given (ERA 1996, s 95(2)).

On the other hand, if it is the employee who gives notice initially but the employer subsequently (before the expiry of the notice period) dismisses without notice then this will constitute a dismissal by the employer (*Harris & Russell Ltd v Slingsby* [1973] ICR 454).

Pressured resignations

Where an employer 'invites' the employee to resign this will amount to a dismissal if, in fact, there is no real choice; the employee has really been given an instruction to leave (*Rasool v Hepworth Pipe Co Ltd* [1980] ICR 494 (EAT)). In *Sandhu v Jan de Rijk Transport Ltd* [2007] IRLR 519, the employee was invited to a meeting which he knew was to discuss his dismissal. The subject matter of the meeting was to discuss terms and reach an agreement. The Court of Appeal found that this was a dismissal since Wall LJ stated: 'Resignation, . . . implies some form of negotiation and discussion; it predicates a result which is a genuine choice on the part of the employee.' Furthermore, an agreement that the employee will 'resign' may well be void by reason of ERA 1996, s 203(1) which restricts the ability of employers and employees to contract out of the statutory provisions. See also *Igbo v Johnson Matthey Chemicals Ltd* [1986] ICR 505 (CA).

6.4.1.2   Expiry of a fixed-term contract without renewal

This is a dismissal for unfair dismissal purposes. Merely because a fixed-term contract contains a provision allowing for termination on notice by either side does not mean that it is not still a 'fixed term' (*Dixon v BBC* [1979] QB 546 (CA)).

Contracts to perform a specific task or function and contracts terminable on some future event are not fixed-term contracts as they have an indefinite or uncertain life (*Wiltshire County Council v NATFHE* [1980] IRLR 198).

As discussed at **5.1.1.2**, the Fixed Term Employees Regulations 2002 apply, confer-ring in certain circumstances rights on fixed-term workers who have worked for 4 years or more.

6.4.1.3   Constructive dismissal

(See the precedents at **11.5** for a sample claim of constructive unfair dismissal.)

'Constructive dismissal' is a creature of statute, where ERA 1996, s 95(1)(c), states that an employee will be treated as dismissed where 'the employee terminates the contract under which he is employed (with or without notice) in circumstances in which he is entitled to terminate it without notice by reason of the employer's conduct'.

Where the employee resigns when entitled to do so by reason of the employer's con-duct, that conduct constitutes a repudiation of the contract which the employee accepts by resigning. The crux of the matter is to determine the nature of the prior conduct of the employer which entitled the employee to resign. For statutory purposes the con-tract is terminated by the employer (not necessarily unfairly) (*Savoia v Chiltern Herb Farms Ltd* [1982] IRLR 166).

The leading case is *Western Excavating (ECC) Ltd v Sharp* [1978] QB 761 where the Court of Appeal held that the employer must be in breach of contract for a claim of constructive dismissal to succeed. The test for constructive dismissal is purely contractual and not that of unreasonableness which is far too indefinite. In adopting a more stringent, contractual and objective approach, the Court of Appeal indicated that the statute distinguished between dismissal and unfairness, and that in what is now s 95 'terminate' and 'entitled' had a legal and therefore contractual flavour. Moreover, the employer's conduct does not have to be intentional or in bad faith before it becomes repudiatory.

In a constructive dismissal case an employment tribunal is seeking to establish whether the employer's conduct is clearly a fundamental breach of one of the terms and therefore sufficiently important to be a repudiation by the employer. The Court of Appeal in *Pederson v Camden London Borough Council* [1981] ICR 674 has held that this is a question of mixed fact and law, so that the EAT will rarely alter a tribunal's decision on this point. This concept of constructive dismissal was further endorsed in *Woods v WM Car Services (Peterborough) Ltd* [1982] IRLR 413.

Whether the conduct complained of is a repudiatory breach is to be judged under an objective test as a result of *Buckland v Bournemouth University Higher Education Corporation* [2010] IRLR 445 (CA) rather than a range of reasonable responses test. This was further endorsed in *McBride v Falkirk Football & Athletic Club* [2012] IRLR 22 where an argument that an autocratic style was the norm in football clubs was rejected, the EAT stating: 'An employer cannot pray in aid that he and others in his industry treat all employees badly and therefore treating an employee badly cannot amount to a breach of the duty to maintain trust and confidence.' As stated by Lord Hughes in *Grewals (Mauritius) Ltd v Koo Seen Lin* [2016] IRLR 638 (PC): '…the acid test is not whether the employer intended to dismiss; it is whether he has by his conduct, objectively judged, repudiated the contract."

Some examples of employer's actions leading to constructive dismissal include a unilateral change in employment terms (*McAndrew v Prestwick Circuits Ltd* [1988] IRLR 514), a breach of an express term of the contract or going beyond its scope (*Simmonds v Dowty Seals Ltd* [1978] IRLR 211) and a failure to follow a contractually binding disciplinary procedure (*Post Office v Strange* [1981] IRLR 515). On what constitutes the conduct of the employer, see *Hilton International Hotels (UK) Ltd v Protopapa* [1990] IRLR 316. Repudiatory breach could be of an implied term as well as an express one (for example, *British Aircraft Corporation Ltd v Austin* [1978] IRLR 332), and the EAT both before and after *Western Excavating (ECC) Ltd v Sharp* has readily implied new terms into contracts of employment whereby fresh duties such as reasonable courtesy, tolerance and respect towards the employee, have been imposed upon the employer. (See further *United Bank Ltd v Akhtar* [1989] IRLR 507 and *White v Reflecting Roadstuds* [1991] IRLR 331.) This tends to outmanoeuvre the contractual approach in the latter situation and may (although should not) be a replacement for the 'unreasonable conduct' test (see **5.2.4**).

As a result of the 'last straw' doctrine established in *Lewis v Motorworld Garages Ltd* [1985] IRLR 465, an employee may argue that there is a series of breaches by the employer which taken together constitute a fundamental breach (even though the breaches taken in isolation may not be a fundamental breach). This has been subject to further guidance in *London Borough of Waltham Forest v Omilaju* [2005] IRLR 35 where it was stated that when recognising if the act complained of is the final straw, its 'essential quality is that, when taken in conjunction with the earlier acts on which the employee relies, it amounts to a breach of the implied term of trust and confidence. It must contribute something to that breach although what it adds may be relatively insignificant.'

Obligations under the health and safety legislation have also been held to establish implied contractual terms (see *Waltons & Morse v Dorrington* [1997] IRLR 488 (EAT)), a case preceding the ban on smoking in public places but which gives contractual force to an employer's obligations under HASAWA 1974.

It had been held that a genuine, but mistakenly held view of the contract does not indicate of itself an intention on the part of the employer to break the contract, and thus is no ground for claiming constructive dismissal (*Frank Wright & Co (Holdings) Ltd v Punch* [1980] IRLR 217). This potentially restricts constructive dismissal by requiring employees to prove that the mistake was not genuine. The Court of Appeal expressed misgivings about this approach in *Financial Techniques (Planning Services) Ltd v Hughes* [1981] IRLR 32. In the circumstances it would be unwise to rely on the *Punch* doctrine, a position further endorsed in *Brown v JBD Engineering Ltd* [1993] IRLR 568.

If the employer announces an intention to break the contract at a future date, and the employee does not accept the anticipatory breach, it is open to the employer to retract the announcement and inform the employee that the contract will be performed. The employee will thus lose the right to claim constructive dismissal (*Norwest Holst Group Administration Ltd v Harrison* [1985] IRLR 240). Controversially, it has been held that where an employee is dismissed for refusing to accept new contractual terms, even with lawful notice, or actually resigns, this may still amount to a constructive dismissal (*Greenaway Harrison Ltd v Wiles* [1994] IRLR 380).

A claim of constructive dismissal in the employment tribunal presents certain practical problems for both the employer and employee. An employer should contest such a claim on the grounds:

- that there was no dismissal; and
- if there was a dismissal, that the actions taken were reasonable and fair.

To do otherwise may lead to a finding of constructive unfair dismissal because since no reason for dismissal is put forward the dismissal will be automatically unfair, as the employer has the burden of proving a potentially fair reason for dismissal (*Derby City Council v Marshall* [1979] IRLR 261).

The employee has to be sure that he or she has a strong case and should leave promptly showing that he or she has accepted the employer's repudiation as terminating the contract of employment. If the employee continues to work he or she may be treated as waiving the breach and cannot then bring a claim based on the employer's repudiation. In particular, the employee can be faced with difficulty if the employer makes life generally unpleasant for the employee, but no single episode of itself amounts to a fundamental breach. Yet if the employer is in breach, but the employee does not resign but subsequently alleges a further breach, the employment tribunal will consider the whole of the employer's conduct and not just the most recent incident which led to the resignation (*Lewis v Motorworld Garages Ltd* [1985] IRLR 465). An employee must eventually decide on his or her final course of action within a reasonable period of time, as he or she cannot work under protest for the employer indefinitely even if necessary for economic reasons (*W E Cox Toner (International) Ltd v Crook* [1981] IRLR 443).

The fact that the employee obtains a new job before leaving, will not, however, necessarily be fatal to his or her claim: the breach must be the effective cause of the employee's leaving, it need not be the sole cause (*Jones v F Sirl & Son (Furnishers) Ltd* [1997] IRLR 493 (EAT)). Provided the repudiatory breach 'played a part in the dismissal', it will be sufficient (*Wright v North Ayrshire Council* [2014] IRLR 4). Nor will it be fatal to a claim of constructive dismissal if the employee does not tell the employer the reason for leaving at the time (*Weathersfield Ltd v Sargent* [1999] IRLR 94 (CA)). *Wright v North Ayrshire Council* is significant in addition for establishing that the old approach of determining the principal reason for resignation is 'an error of the law' according to Mr Justice Langstaff.

A further difficulty for the employee is that he or she must be careful in avoiding causing damage to the employment relationship. In *RDF Media Group v Clements* [2008] IRLR 207, an employee in repudiatory breach of a mutual obligation was unable to rely on his employer's repudiatory breach. In *Aberdeen City Council v McNeill* [2010] IRLR 374, the EAT (Scotland) held that an employee guilty of misconduct (namely sexual harassment) was in prior repudiatory breach and hence was not entitled to terminate his contract by reason of his employer's conduct.

A finding of constructive dismissal completes only the first of the three decisions the employment tribunal must make, that is, that there was a dismissal. It must still decide whether the reason for the dismissal was potentially fair and a sufficient reason in the circumstances (ERA 1996, s 98(4)).

If an employee resigns with notice, he or she may present a claim before the notice has expired (ERA 1996, s 111, and see *Presley v Llanelli Borough Council* [1979] ICR 419).

6.4.2 Terminations which are not dismissals

6.4.2.1 Frustration

A contract of employment will be frustrated if its performance is rendered impossible by some intervening event which is not the fault of either party. However, if there is repudiatory conduct by either party there could be a dismissal.

The doctrine of frustration arising by operation of law may occur where there is long-term absence through accident or illness or imprisonment (*F C Shepherd & Co Ltd v Jerrom* [1987] QB 301). General guidance on the factors to be considered where frustration is in issue was suggested in *Egg Stores (Stamford Hill) Ltd v Leibovici* [1977] ICR 260 and in *Williams v Watsons Luxury Coaches Ltd* [1990] ICR 536. In *Four Seasons Healthcare Ltd v Maughan* [2005] IRLR 324, an employee's misconduct at work led to criminal proceedings. The employee's bail conditions precluded him from entering his workplace. In dealing with the issue of whether this could constitute frustration (the EAT concluded it did not), Judge Ansell gave some useful guidance on the doctrine as applicable to employment.

Particularly important will be the length of time the employee is likely to be away from work, and the length of time he or she has been employed and the need to obtain a replacement. However, the duration of the intervening or 'disabling' event is not conclusive. In *Gryf-Lowczowski v Hinchingbrooke Healthcare NHS Trust* [2006] IRLR 100, the duration of the disabling event (the suspension of nearly two years pending reskilling training for a consultant surgeon) was not determinative. It was held that the nature of the employment must be considered in addition. In practice, the party asserting frustration must show that there was no fault on his or her part, and the party against whom frustration is being asserted cannot rely on his or her own misconduct in response (*F C Shepherd & Co Ltd v Jerrom*).

6.4.2.2 Resignation

Provided that the resignation by the employee is not provoked by the employer's repudiatory conduct thus bringing the matter within ERA 1996, s 95(1)(c) (constructive dismissal), it will not constitute a dismissal. The words of resignation must be clear and unambiguous; otherwise the test will be what would the reasonable employer have understood by those words in that context (*Tanner v D T Kean Ltd* [1978] IRLR 110). A resignation must also be effective on an ascertainable date. Words of resignation spoken in the heat of the moment may be retracted, if this is done within a reasonable period of time, depending on the circumstances of the case (*Kwik-Fit (GB) Ltd v Lineham* [1992] ICR 183 (EAT)).

A resignation brought about by threat or duress by the employer will be a dismissal. Ultimately, whether an employee resigned or was dismissed is a question of fact for an employment tribunal. An employer terminating an employee's contract of employment, believing erroneously that the employee had resigned, will have dismissed the employee for a justifiable reason (*Ely v YKK Fasteners (UK) Ltd* [1993] IRLR 500).

6.4.2.3 Self-dismissal or constructive resignation

In *London Transport Executive v Clarke* [1981] IRLR 166, the Court of Appeal discounted the doctrine of constructive resignation whereby it was suggested that a breach of contract by the employee entitled the employer to treat the contract of employment as being terminated. In that situation, the employer has recourse to either the contractual or statutory disciplinary procedure.

If an employee leaves a job or commits a breach of contract, an employer must expressly or impliedly accept the repudiation, thereby constituting a dismissal. However, it is arguable that a resignation may be implied if an employee does not answer communications from the employer, goes to work for another employer or just disappears.

6.4.2.4 Consensual termination or mutual agreement

Clearly, if the contract of employment comes to an end due to some mutual agreement that it should do so there is no dismissal; the reason for such agreement is generally irrelevant, but it may go to establishing whether or not the agreement was genuine (*Birch v University of Liverpool* [1985] ICR 470). Mutual agreement whereby employment will finish when a future event occurs is not a consensual termination (*Igbo v Johnson Matthey Chemicals Ltd* [1986] ICR 505). There is still a likelihood of a dismissal where the parties agree to terminate when an employee is already under notice from the employer. Lastly, it should be noted that a person who volunteers for redundancy has volunteered to be dismissed.

6.4.2.5 Performance

If a person is employed for a specific task or job, then the contract of employment is discharged by performance when the object has been achieved, for example, writing a book (*Wiltshire County Council v NATFHE* [1980] IRLR 198).

6.4.2.6 Operation of law

A contract of employment may be terminated by automatic operation of law in accordance with company and partnership law.

6.5 Effective date of termination

6.5.1 Statutory definition

ERA 1996, s 97(1) provides that the effective date of termination can be:

- if the employment is terminated with notice, the date on which the notice expires; or

- if the employment is terminated without notice, the date on which the termination takes effect; or

- in the case of a fixed-term contract, the date on which the term expires.

In practice it is important to be accurate about the actual date of termination when, as a matter of law, the contract of employment comes to an end in order to establish:

- the qualifying period, that is, two years if employment commences after 6 April 2012;

- the date for calculation of compensation payments;

- when written reasons for dismissal may be sought;

- the employee's age (should exclusion be relevant and to assist calculating compensation);

- whether within the time limit for bringing a claim—generally three months for unfair dismissal and generally six months for redundancy payments (see **4.2**).

6.5.2 Determining the effective date of termination

When notice is given by an employer, unless the contract provides that such notice is to have immediate effect, it will take effect on the following day; *Wang v University of Keele* [2011] IRLR 524, regardless of the method by which the notice is given.

Where the employee is dismissed with notice the effective date of termination is the date on which the notice expires, or as in *Thompson v GEC Avionics Ltd* [1991] IRLR 488 when the employee's counter-notice expires on an earlier date. In any event notice of dismissal or counter-notice will not be effective until it has been received.

Where the dismissal is lawfully without notice, for example, summary dismissal for gross misconduct, the effective date of termination is the date on which the termination takes effect (*Stapp v The Shaftesbury Society* [1982] IRLR 326).

Where the dismissal is with notice but the employee is not actually required to work out that notice, the date of termination should be the date of the expiry of the notice. If, however, the dismissal is 'instant' but with payment of wages in lieu of notice, that is, damages as compensation for wrongful dismissal, the date of termination should be that last day on which the employee actually worked. In *Newman v Polytechnic of Wales Students Union* [1995] IRLR 72, the EAT said that the effective date of termination should be decided in a practical and common-sense way, having particular regard to what was understood by the parties at the time. *Adams v Alan Sankey Ltd* [1980] IRLR 416 suggests that the date of termination depends on the true construction to be placed on the dismissal and upon any correspondence involved.

In any event, the effective date of termination cannot be earlier than the date on which the employee receives knowledge of the dismissal (*McMaster v Manchester Airport plc* [1998] IRLR 112 (EAT)).

Where dismissal is communicated by post, the Court of Appeal have held the notice period commences when it is received by the employee having personally taken delivery of it, not when put in the post or the date of arrival (*Newcastle upon Tyne NHS Foundation Trust v Haywood* [2017] IRLR 629).

Where notice should have been given, the proper statutory minimum notice is added to the actual date of dismissal (ERA 1996, s 97(2)), except where summary and constructive dismissals are involved, or unless such extension is inapplicable by statute. This addition, however, does not apply to the award of compensation for unfair dismissal.

The effective date of termination in a constructive dismissal case is a question of law (*BMK Ltd and BMK Holdings Ltd v Logue* [1993] IRLR 477).

If dismissal results from the expiry of a fixed-term contract the date when the contract terminates is when the fixed term expires.

Where the employee is dismissed because of a strike or other industrial action even when notice is given, the effective date is the date on which the notice is given.

The courts have declined to extend the effective date of termination to cover periods during which an appeal against dismissal is being made under an internal disciplinary procedure (*West Midlands Co-operative Society v Tipton* [1986] AC 536 (HL)). This is the case even where an initial summary dismissal decision is, on appeal, changed to dismissal with pay in lieu of notice (*Rabess v London Fire and Emergency Planning Authority* [2017] IRLR 147 (CA)). This has a significant effect on the time limit for bringing a claim.

In **6.4.1.1** on the issue of variation of notice, it was noted as a result of *Palfrey v Transco plc* [2004] IRLR 916, that the notice (that determines the effective date of termination) can be varied. However, that is only as a result of changing the notice period. The effective date of termination itself is a matter of law and cannot be varied by the parties by agreement, following the judgment in *Fitzgerald v University of Kent at Canterbury* [2004] IRLR 300.

6.6 The reason for the dismissal

While the employee must prove that he or she was *dismissed,* the employer has the onus of proving the reason for the dismissal and that the reason is capable of being fair for the purposes of ERA, s 98(1) and (2) (*Smith v Glasgow District Council* [1987] IRLR 326). If the employer cannot prove a reason for dismissal, the dismissal is automatically unfair (*Adams v Derby City Council* [1986] IRLR 163). This matter has been considered in the context of a dispute between the parties on the reason (employer claiming misconduct, employee relying on protected disclosure) in *Kuzel v Roche Products Ltd* [2008] EWCA Civ 380, the burden being on the employer to show the reason since 'He knows what it is', *per* Mummery LJ.

The employment tribunal is charged with the responsibility of determining whether or not the employer's reason for dismissal is fair, on the set of facts known to the employer or the belief held by the employer at the time of dismissal which actually causes the employer to dismiss the employee (*W. Devis & Sons Ltd v Atkins* [1977] AC 931 and *Stacey v Babcock Power Ltd* [1986] QB 308).

The reason or reasons for the dismissal must be those that are uppermost in the mind of the employer, although the examination of the employer's reasoning will not stop at the giving of notice but will continue until the effective date of termination (see *Parkinson v March Consulting Ltd* [1998] ICR 276 (CA) and *Alboni v Ind Coope Retail Ltd* [1998] IRLR 151 (CA)). The employment tribunal must be astute in establishing that the reason is genuine and it must determine what the principal factor or impetus motivating the dismissal was. The importance of uncovering the 'real reason' for dismissal was highlighted in *ASLEF v Brady* [2006] IRLR 576 where it was accepted that a potentially fair reason for dismissal (in this case misconduct) could be used as a 'pretext' for dismissal.

The employer cannot dismiss for an insubstantial reason and then search for some reason such as misconduct to justify it (*W. Devis & Sons Ltd v Atkins* [1977] AC 931). This is to be compared with wrongful dismissal where this is permissible (*Boston Deep Sea Fishing & Ice Cov Ansell* (1888) 39 ChD 339). However, evidence discovered between the date of notice and an appeal can be relevant (*National Heart & Chest Hospitals Board of Governors v Nambiar* [1981] IRLR 196). As the House of Lords emphasised in *West Midlands Co-operative Society Ltd v Tipton* [1986] AC 536, an employer must properly consider matters which have come to light on appeal from the initial decision to dismiss and to his or her action in dismissing the employee.

6.6.1   Written reasons for dismissal

Under ERA 1996, s 92(1), when an employee is dismissed, either with or without notice, or upon the expiry of a fixed-term contract, he or she is entitled to receive, on request, a written statement of the reasons for the dismissal within 14 days. This statement is admissible in any proceedings before a tribunal or a court. To be so entitled an employee must have been employed for more than two years where the date of commencement of employment is on or after 6 April 2012 (see **6.2.2(a)** for details).

A complaint may be presented to an employment tribunal by an employee that the employer has unreasonably refused to provide such a written statement, or that the statement which has been provided is inadequate or incorrect. If the complaint is well founded, an employment tribunal or a court may make a declaration on what it finds were the employer's reasons for dismissal and make an award of two weeks' pay. (See generally the precedents at **11.3** and **11.8** in this regard.) The employee would need to show some attempt to request the written reasons before making a claim to the employment tribunal.

For a written statement under s 92 to be valid, it must be possible for anyone reading the statement to know the essential reasons for the dismissal (*Horsley Smith & Sherry Ltd v Dutton* [1977] IRLR 172).

6.6.2   Reasons for dismissal that are capable of being fair ('potentially fair reasons')

The employer not only has to establish the reason for the dismissal (or the principal reason if more than one) but also bears the burden of showing that it falls within *one* of the following categories of prima facie fair or potentially fair dismissals:

- it was related to the capability or qualifications of the employee for performing his or her work (ERA 1996, s 98(2)(a)); or

- it was related to the conduct of the employee (ERA 1996, s 98(2)(b)); or

- the employee has reached 'normal retirement age' (ERA 1996, s 98(ZA)) for cases where notice of dismissal was given before 5 April 2011 under transitional arrangements for abolition of the retirement age;

- the employee was redundant (ERA 1996, s 98(2)(c)); or

- the employee could not continue to work in that position without contravention of statutory provision or restriction (ERA 1996, s 98(2)(d)); or

- there was some other substantial reason (SOSR) of a kind such as to justify the dismissal of an employee holding the position which that employee held (ERA 1996, s 98(1)(b)).

'Capability' is assessed by reference to skill, aptitude, health or any other physical or mental quality (ERA 1996, s 98(3)(a)).

'Qualifications' means any degree, diploma or other academic, technical or professional qualification relevant to the position which the employee held (ERA 1996, s 98(3)(b)).

These 'potentially fair' reasons for dismissal (as they are known in practice) will be examined in more detail later. Once a potentially fair reason has been established by the employer, the tribunal turns to the reasonableness of the dismissal as set out at **6.7**.

6.7 Reasonableness of dismissal: 'fairness'

The question here is whether the employer acted as a reasonable employer could reasonably have done in all the circumstances of the case. The ERA 1996, s 98(4), provides that:

the determination of the question whether the dismissal is fair or unfair having regard to the reason shown by the employer—

(a) *depends on whether in the circumstances (including the size and administrative resources of the employer's undertaking) the employer acted reasonably or unreasonably in treating it as a sufficient reason for dismissing the employee, and*

(b) *shall be determined in accordance with equity and the substantial merits of the case.*

The burden of proof at this stage lies equally on both employer and employee. The way in which the tribunal looks at the issue of reasonableness varies with each different potentially fair reason for dismissal and therefore will be examined in detail under each separate heading.

Section 98(4) ERA 1996 has been clarified by case law. Specifically, the tribunal must not substitute its view for that of the employer. As a result, overall it must be remembered that the essential test is: did the employer act reasonably? It is not a question of would the employment tribunal members have acted as the employer did (*Grundy (Teddington) Ltd v Willis* [1976] ICR 323). In other words, the tribunal cannot substitute its decision for that of the employer. The importance of this principle has been reiterated in *London Ambulance Service NHS Trust v Small* [2009] IRLR 563 (CA).

The correct approach is for the employment tribunal to decide whether the employer's decision to dismiss fell within a 'band of reasonableness' (*Iceland Frozen Foods Ltd v Jones* [1982] IRLR 439 and *Boys and Girls Welfare Society v McDonald* [1996] IRLR 129 (EAT))—a test expressly approved by the Court of Appeal in *Foley v Post Office; HSBC Bank plc v Madden* [2000] ICR 1283, and which applies to the reasonableness of the employer's investigations as well as to the final decision to dismiss (see *Sainsbury's Supermarkets Ltd v Hitt* [2003] ICR 111 (CA)). (See **6.8.2** for investigation in the context of conduct dismissals.) Therefore the employer need only show that dismissal was within a band of reasonable responses open to them in order to escape liability.

Unfair dismissal claims are no longer heard by a bench, but are heard by a judge sitting alone. *Mitchell v St Joseph's School* [2013] UKEAT 0506/12/2604 provides useful guidance on what the tribunal's approach should be, with HHJ McMullen QC stating:

It is not a misuse of language to describe the hearing of a case of unfair dismissal for misconduct as a judicial review of the employer's procedure and decision. It remains to be seen whether the band of reasonable responses will be widened as a result of single judges deciding without the benefit of lay members' experience in industry.

Another concern of the tribunal is whether a fair procedure has been followed. For cases where the disciplinary action commenced between 1 October 2004 and 5 April 2009, compliance with the statutory dismissal and disciplinary procedures will be considered under ERA 1996, s 98A, but this is beyond the scope of this book. In all cases, however, the tribunal can consider the fairness of the procedure used by the employer more generally under ERA 1996, s 98(4). The tribunal can therefore look qualitatively at the procedures used by the employer beyond mere compliance with the statutory procedures. Issues such as natural justice, bias and conduct of fair hearings can all therefore be relevant.

More generally, a tribunal will consider the issue of reasonableness with regard to the service record of the employee and length of service. This can involve consideration of performance, disciplinary history, appraisals, etc. An important case dealing with the operation of reasonableness and confirming the importance of the length of service of the dismissed employee as a relevant factor is *Strouthos v London Underground* [2004] IRLR 636.

6.8   The 'potentially fair' reasons in detail and the application of reasonableness

The tribunal will, in an unfair dismissal case, consider:

(a) Was there a dismissal?

(b) Was the reason capable of being fair?

(c) Has the employer acted reasonably in treating it as a sufficient reason for dismissal?

See flowchart at **6.10** for clarification.

Another complication is that there are two versions of the ACAS Code of Practice 1 on Disciplinary and Grievance procedures; the April 2009 version is for current cases where the procedures do not apply. If your version is not dated on the cover, it is for when the procedures applied between 1 October 2004 and 5 April 2009. The tribunal is entitled to take the provisions of the Code of Practice into account in making its decision.

6.8.1   Capability or qualifications

The most common examples here relate to incompetence, inability, illness and lack of qualifications. Where appropriate, employment tribunals endeavour to adopt an objective approach.

In relation to lack of competence, the employer must meet the test set out in *McPhie and McDermott v Wimpey Waste Management* [1981] IRLR 316. It is to be noted that competence can overlap with conduct; the employee's failings may be due to an inherent lack of ability (incompetence), a lack of good attitude or diligence (conduct) or a refusal to perform to a required standard (conduct). It may be necessary to delve into the factual background to ascertain to what the employer's concerns with the employee relate.

When dismissing an employee on the ground of ill health, consultation is of the utmost importance (*East Lindsey District Council v Daubney* [1977] ICR 566), unless there are wholly exceptional circumstances (*Eclipse Blinds Ltd v Wright* [1992] IRLR 133). However, an employer does not necessarily dismiss an employee unfairly on ill-health grounds even if the employer was responsible for the illness which caused the dismissal (*London Fire and Civil Defence Authority v Betty* [1994] IRLR 390, although see also *Edwards v Governors of Hanson School* [2001] IRLR 733 (EAT), and *McArdie v Royal Bank of Scotland* [2007] EWCA Civ 806). It has, in *First West Yorkshire v Haigh* [2008] IRLR 182 (EAT), been held that it was unfair to proceed to a capability dismissal without first considering early retirement for ill health. Please note that the ACAS Code of Practice on

Disciplinary and Grievance Procedures does not apply to ill health dismissals (*Holmes v Qinetiq Ltd* [2016] IRLR 664).

Readers should note that in some instances, long-term ill health of an employee may lead to the employee being able to claim disability discrimination under the Equality Act 2010 in addition to unfair dismissal, provided he or she can come within the definition of disability (see **Chapter 8**).

One key issue which arises from the case law is that the employee must be made aware by the employer of any concern, must be given time to improve and be warned of the consequences of failing to do so.

6.8.2   Conduct

This can cover misconduct not only within employment, but also outside employment where this will affect the employee's ability or scope to do his or her work. Examples abound here and would include absenteeism without cause, commission of criminal offences, failure to obey lawful and reasonable orders, disobedience of disciplinary rules, wilful poor performance of duties and dishonesty.

However, when deciding if the potentially fair reason of conduct had been engaged, it is not necessary for the tribunal to find the employee culpable. Culpability is part of the consideration of fairness under ERA 1996, s 98(4) (*JP Morgan v Ktorza* [2016] UKEAT/0311/16).

6.8.2.1   Conduct: reasonableness

When analysing whether a conduct dismissal is fair, the tribunal will consider questions of substantive and procedural fairness. The substantive fairness will be determined by considering the investigation into misconduct (see the discussion on *BHS v Burchell* [1978] IRLR 379 which follows) and the decision-making process, having regard to the seriousness of the misconduct, length of service and overall work history of the claimant. Even in a gross misconduct case, it may well be the employer has 'a discretion to exercise' as illustrated by *Arnold Clark Automobiles Ltd v Spoar* [2017] IRLR 500.

An employment tribunal will consider the means whereby the decision to dismiss the employee was reached, bearing in mind the relevant version of the ACAS Code of Practice on Disciplinary and Grievance Procedures, particularly in cases of misconduct and incapability. The Code is not legally binding and so non-compliance does not make dismissal automatically unfair, but a failure to comply may reflect adversely on the employer. The employer does not have to operate his or her disciplinary, warnings and grievance procedures exactly as prescribed by the Code (see *Westminster City Council v Cabaj* [1996] IRLR 399 (CA)), but an employment tribunal will obviously wish to see that appropriate use is made of such procedures. Ultimately, there is a requirement that internal (domestic) tribunals should act in good faith before making the decision to dismiss (see *Earl v Slater & Wheeler (Airlyne) Ltd* [1973] 1 WLR 51). Where the employee considers that the decision-maker is acting in bad faith, he or she must put it to the individual or panel (*Secretary of State for Justice v Lown* [2015] ALL ER (D) 205 (Dec)).

It is important that an employee knows of what he or she is accused, has a chance to explain, and is given a chance to improve in suitable cases. There should therefore be a full investigation and a proper hearing, ideally carried out by different people.

The employee has a statutory right to be accompanied to a disciplinary hearing or meeting under the Employment Relations Act 1999, s 10, and a failure to allow the attendance of the permissible accompaniment can be a factor for the tribunal to consider in unfair dismissal claims. It is to be noted that if a representative of an employee is refused by an employer, even if the refusal does not fall foul of s 10, it can still be held to be a breach of mutual trust and confidence, as found in *Leeds Dental Team Ltd v Mrs D Rose* UK EAT/0016/13.

Where the disciplinary hearing may have a 'substantial influence or effect' on the employee's right to practise his profession, the employee may have an additional right to legal representation as a result of *R (on the application of G) v Governors of X School* [2010] IRLR 222. The employee should have a right of appeal if he or she disagrees with any decision taken.

Where dismissal is a possibility the ACAS Code recommends a procedure of:

- first, formal action (which may result in an oral or written warning where the consequences of further default are made clear) (paras 19–22);

- a final written warning (para 24); and

- dismissal (although the Code advises the employer to consider alternative methods of 'punishing' the employee) (paras 25–26).

Any warning given should be clear, unambiguous and indicate the eventual outcome and the consequences of failure to comply. A warning which has expired, is ambiguous or is irrelevant may lead to a dismissal not being justified (*Bevan Ashford v Malin* [1995] ICR 453).

Employers cannot rely upon warnings indefinitely. They should expire after a specified period. The ACAS Code recommends that a final written warning should have a validity of 12 months. In *Diosynth Ltd v Thomson* [2006] IRLR 284 the Court of Session found that it was unreasonable for an employer to rely upon an expired warning since the employee 'was entitled to assume that the warning letter meant what it said, and that it would cease to have effect after one year', although whether it can be taken into account is a question of reasonableness (*Airbus UK v Webb* [2008] IRLR 309 (CA)).

An employer's reliance on previous warnings can only be challenged if given in bad faith or manifestly inappropriate (*Davies v Sandwell* [2013] EWCA Civ 135), a principle affirmed in *Way v Spectrum Property Care Ltd* [2015] EWCA 381. In *Davies v Sandwell*, the EAT stated that it is only in limited circumstances where a final written warning needs to be reconsidered. In fact, even where the final written warning related to long-term sickness absence in the case of a disabled employee, there was no obligation to reconsider that warning (*General Dynamics Information Technology Ltd v Carranza* [2015] ICR 169). The tribunal should not go behind any valid warning but can take into account the factual circumstances which gave rise to the warning (*Wincanton Group plc v Stone* [2013] IRLR 178). It is only when there are grounds for considering a final written warning to be manifestly inappropriate that a tribunal should enquire into whether it should have been given when examining a subsequent dismissal (*Simmonds v Milford Club* UKEAT/0323/12/KN).

In cases where crime arises at work, an employer only has to have a genuine belief to dismiss: the employer does not have to prove the case against the employee beyond reasonable doubt, as in a criminal court (*British Home Stores Ltd v Burchell* [1978] IRLR 379 and *W. Weddel & Co Ltd v Tepper* [1980] ICR 386). The *Burchell* 'test' has three elements:

- the employer must establish first the fact of its belief (the reason for the dismissal);

- that the employer had reasonable grounds for that belief; and

- that the employer had carried out a reasonable investigation in forming that belief.

Whilst *BHS v Burchell* is not a rigid rule of law, the tribunal will often consider its three limbs in forming its decision. The test is capable of a great deal of flexibility since the level of investigation which may be required by an employer will vary with the size of the employer, the seriousness of the offence and the quality of the evidence against the employee. The ultimate test is whether the employer's conduct (in investigating and disciplining the employee) falls within the range of reasonable responses of the reasonable employer in all the circumstances of the case (*Boys and Girls Welfare Society v McDonald* [1996] IRLR 129 (EAT)). Where the alleged misconduct would have an effect on the employee's reputation or ability to work in his or her chosen field, the degree of investigation will perhaps need to be higher since in such cases employers have been advised to 'take seriously their responsibilities to conduct a fair investigation' by Elias LJ in *Salford Royal NHS Foundation Trust v Roldan* [2010] IRLR 721. However, an employer is not required to investigate every line of defence put forward by an employee (*Shrestha v Genesis Housing Association Ltd* [2015] EWCA Civ 94).

Given the breadth of possibilities under the range of reasonable responses test, the range of evidence which may be relied upon by an employer will be correspondingly wide. In reasonable circumstances, an employer may use police statements as evidence as in *Rhondda Cynon Taf v Close* [2008] IRLR 868. Employers are cautioned to take care, however, where evidence can prove contradictory. In the *Roldan* case, the evidence of the employee and that of her accuser was in direct conflict. The employer chose to believe the accuser. The Court of Appeal warned employers about whether such a stance is reasonable, Elias LJ stating that an employer is 'not obliged to believe one employee and to disbelieve another' and that it may well be 'perfectly proper for the employer to say they are not satisfied they can resolve the conflict of evidence and accordingly do not find the case proved'. Unless there is good reason not to, an employer will be expected to investigate matters which support the account of an employee accused of gross misconduct, *per Stuart v London City Airport* [2012] UKEAT/0273/12/BA.

A warnings procedure will be inappropriate in cases such as gross misconduct warranting summary dismissal which is discussed in more detail at **5.7.3.1** and **6.1.2.2**. Otherwise the law on procedural unfairness in this context has been placed on a firm basis by the House of Lords in *Polkey v AE Dayton Services Ltd* [1988] AC 344, overruling *British Labour Pump v Byrne* [1979] IRLR 94. *Polkey* confirms the view that whether or not a dismissal is fair has to be judged by what the employer did, not on what the employer might have done.

Cases such as *Spink v Express Foods Group Ltd* [1990] IRLR 320 and *Louies v Coventry Hood & Seating Co Ltd* [1990] ICR 54 have emphasised the employee's right to know the case or the allegations made against him or her. Ideally, the employee should receive written notification of the employee's alleged conduct, which must be given before any disciplinary meeting. An overriding consideration is, however, if there are genuine reasons for a witness remaining anonymous or fears for an informant's safety should his or her identity be released, then an employee may be unaware of the source of the evidence without natural justice in this context being necessarily infringed. *Linfood Cash & Carry Ltd v Thomson* [1989] ICR 518 is the leading case on this point, setting out guidelines for employers in such cases. The case of *Ramsey v Walker's Snack Foods* [2004] IRLR 754 deals with the type of circumstances where the *Linfood* guidelines may be departed from.

It is established that any procedural defect must always be sufficiently serious to render a dismissal unfair, as *Fuller v Lloyds Bank plc* [1991] IRLR 336 indicates, where a failure to provide witness statements did not result in an unfair dismissal as the employee was fully aware of the allegations (see also *Hussain v Elonex plc* [1999] IRLR 420 (CA)). An overriding consideration is that, as the Court of Appeal in *Paul v East Surrey District Health Authority* [1995] IRLR 305 endorses, all employees of an employer must be treated consistently in disciplinary matters. Even so, there may be distinguishing features between cases, such as mitigating circumstances or the employee's attitude, which warrant similar misconduct being dealt with differently, provided that it is a reasonable response by the employer. Furthermore, in all hearings there is also an element of 'due process'—a delay of nine months was criticised in *Distillers Co (Bottling Services) Ltd v Gardner* [1982] IRLR 47.

Guidance was given to employers on the fair approach to a disciplinary hearing against an employee in *Clark v Civil Aviation Authority* [1991] IRLR 412, where the EAT said:

Explain the purpose of the meeting; identify those present; if appropriate arrange representation; inform the employee of the allegation or allegations being made; indicate the evidence whether in statement form or by the calling of witnesses; allow the employee and representative to ask questions; ask whether the employee wishes any witnesses to be called; allow the employee or the representative to explain and argue the case; listen to argument from both sides upon the allegations and any possible consequence, including any mitigation; ask the employee whether there is any further evidence or enquiry which he considers could help his case.

When examining the issue of procedural fairness in the case of *R (on the application of Bonhoeffer) v General Medical Council* [2012] IRLR 37, the Administrative Court stated: 'the more serious the allegation, the greater the importance of ensuring that the accused … is afforded fair and proper procedural safeguards' and 'the more astute should the courts be to ensure the trial process is a fair one.'

The *Clark* case demonstrates that a full and fair appeal hearing may remedy the defects of an original dismissal thus rendering the dismissal fair. Yet this would be of no avail if there were previous fundamental flaws involved, or if the appeal process was being used by an employer to cover earlier mistakes as indicated in *Sartor v P&O European Ferries (Felixstowe) Ltd* [1992] IRLR 271. What *Byrne v BOC Ltd* [1992] IRLR 505 decides is that in order to cure any procedural defect, the appellate process must be sufficiently comprehensive to remedy the deprivation of rights occurring at the disciplinary hearing. Those defects cannot be rectified by an appeal process where the person conducting the appeal can be considered a judge of his or her own cause. However, a review of the original decision can suffice (*Biggin Hill Airpot v Derwich* UKEAT/0043/15/DN).

Where an appeal is successful, it automatically revives the contract of employment, even if the decision is not communicated to the employee, as a result of *Salmon v Castlebeck Care (Teesdale) Ltd* [2015] IRLR 189.

Employers dealing with appeals against dismissal, if considering a sanction short of dismissal, must take care that they have the power to impose that penalty. In *Piper v Maidstone & Tunbridge NHS Trust* [2012] UKEAT/0359/12/KN, the appeal panel decided to impose a demotion requiring a transfer of work location which was rejected by the employee. As this required his consent, the EAT found this did not expunge the dismissal, allowing the employee's claim to continue.

An appeal in disciplinary proceedings (warnings, etc.) can only result in an increased penalty of the contract of employment allows it: *McMillan v Airedale NHS Foundation Trust* [2014] EWCA Civ 1031.

Furthermore, the fact that the employer operates a grievance procedure is not an adequate substitute for giving an employee the opportunity to explain before being dismissed for misconduct (*Clarke v Trimoco Group Ltd* [1993] IRLR 148).

In *Lock v Cardiff Railway Co Ltd* [1998] IRLR 358, the EAT stressed the need for employment tribunals to have regard to the ACAS Code of Practice in determining the fairness or otherwise of a dismissal.

6.8.3   Retirement

Until 6 April 2011 it had been a potentially fair reason to dismiss an employee upon reaching the compulsory retirement age, provided that certain procedures had been followed.

This compulsory retirement was possible once an employee had reached the 'normal retirement age'. However, the 'normal retirement age' was abolished as a result of the Employment Equality (Repeal of Retirement Age Provisions) Regulations 2011 (SI 2011/1069). An employer seeking to dismiss an employee upon reaching a certain age must show that the decision to do so can be objectively justified or risk liability for age discrimination under the Equality Act 2010; see **8.2.1** and **8.4.5** for further details.

6.8.4 Redundancy

The employer must prove the reason for dismissal, as already stated. In redundancy cases, the employer will have to show that the statutory definition of redundancy in ERA 1996, s 139 has been met. Once established, it is not necessarily the case that a dismissal for redundancy will automatically be fair, or that the employer will have acted reasonably in treating that reason as a sufficient ground for dismissal. (See the precedent at **11.4**.)

In *Williams v Compair Maxam Ltd* [1982] IRLR 83, the EAT suggested the following guidelines as sound current industrial relations practice in such circumstances:

(a) The employer will give as much warning as possible of impending redundancies so as to enable trade unions and employees to consider alternative solutions and to seek alternative employment.

(b) The employer will consult with the unions as to the best means by which the desired object can be achieved with as little hardship as possible. In particular, the criteria for selection should be agreed, and the actual selection should be made in accordance with those criteria.

(c) The criteria for selection should not depend solely on the opinion of the person making the selection, but should be capable of being objectively checked.

(d) The employer must ensure that the selection is made in accordance with the criteria, and will consider any representations made.

(e) The employer will ascertain whether there is any alternative employment which can be offered.

While these principles are obviously more appropriate for large firms or companies, especially where trade unions are involved, rather than small businesses, the weight of the case law indicates that all employers ignore the duty to consult on redundancies at their peril. Consultation should now cover the reasons for proposed redundancies, not just the methods of their implementation, as a result of the EAT ruling in *UK Coal Mining Ltd v National Union of Mineworkers (Northumberland Area)* [2008] IRLR 4. The size of the undertaking may affect the nature, formality or extent of the redundancy consultation (*De Grasse v Stockwell Tools Ltd* [1992] IRLR 269), but an employer should consult employees being dismissed for redundancy (*Ferguson & Skilling v Prestwick Circuits Ltd* [1992] IRLR 266). The consultation must be fair and genuine (*Rowell v Hubbard Group Services Ltd* [1995] IRLR 195), and employees and/or unions must be consulted over selection criteria for redundancy (*Rolls Royce Motor Cars Ltd v Price* [1993] IRLR 302), even if those concerned are content to dispense with these requirements which may require that the employee has access to information about the assessments of others under the selection criteria (*John Brown Engineering Ltd v Brown* [1997] IRLR 90 (EAT)) (and see further *Polkey v A E Dayton Services Ltd* [1988] AC 344). A perfunctory and insensitive consultation is likely to lead to make a redundancy dismissal unfair (*Thomas v BNP Paribas Real Estate Advisory & Property Management UK Ltd* [2016] UKEAT/0134/16/JOJ).

Clearly, to avoid a successful claim for unfair dismissal in this connection, good employers should consult trade unions and employees affected, consider alternative courses of action and adopt proper selection procedures for redundancy (for example, in the past 'last in, first out' (LIFO) was used although this may now fall foul of protection against age discrimination under the Equality Act 2010). Moreover, the existence of detailed criteria for selection for redundancy is insufficient unless they are applied fairly as between employees who prospectively face redundancy. Whilst employers have a high degree of flexibility in the selection criteria which may be used, care must be taken that they are not nebulous. In *Watkins v Crouch t/a Temple Bird Solicitors* [2011] IRLR 382, a criterion of 'the overall requirements of the business' was criticised for being 'so subjective . . . [in that it] might well be said not to satisfy the requirement for selection criteria to be sufficiently objective so as to eliminate . . . decisions being made on a basis which cannot withstand close scrutiny'. Finally, whether or not there should be an appeal procedure against redundancy selection for a dismissal to be fair has been considered, albeit inconclusively, in *Robinson v Ulster Carpet Mills* [1991] IRLR 348.

Matters are further complicated by the requirements of the information and consultation of the Employees Regulations 2004 (SI 2004/3426) (whose threshold is now five employees) and the statutory duty to consult under TULR(C)A 1992, s 188, where 20 or more employees are being made redundant. Redundancy volunteers are counted in deciding if the threshold is met (*Optare Group Ltd v TGWU* [2007] IRLR 931 (EAT)). Protective awards to employees are the consequence of non-compliance.

Redundancy selection criteria may also raise issues of sex and race discrimination in the context of unfair dismissal (*Brook v London Borough of Haringey* [1992] IRLR 478).

Further guidance on how redundancy law operates can be found at **6.11**.

6.8.5   Breach of statutory requirement

An employer cannot be expected to continue to employ an employee if such employment would break the law, for instance, where an employee is employed solely as a driver and is disqualified from driving under road traffic legislation (see, for example, *Appleyard v F M Smith (Hull) Ltd* [1972] IRLR 19). The employer must show that the statutory requirement had an effect on the work the employee was employed to perform and that there was no alternative work available. The disqualified driver could, for example, be redeployed to office work. In *Sutcliffe and Eaton v Pinney* [1977] IRLR 349, it was established that the employer must consult with the employee and consider alternative employment. Employers face criminal prosecution under the Asylum and Immigration Act 1996 (AIA 1996), s 8, for employing any person who does not have permission to work in the UK. Therefore, employers who dismiss an employee due to expiry of a work permit or other impediment to working legally in the UK can rely on this reason.

6.8.6   Some other substantial reason

This is a separate and distinct category of unfair dismissal: see *RS Components Ltd v Irwin* [1973] ICR 535. To demonstrate 'some other substantial reason' (or 'SOSR' as it is referred to in practice), the employer must show that the reason relied upon could, on the face of it, justify the dismissal. Whether the dismissal is fair is then subject to the tribunal's findings in relation to ERA 1996, s 98(4). As a result, the EAT found in *Willow Oak Developments Ltd t/a Windsor Recruitment v Silverwood* [2006] IRLR 28 that an employer who dismissed employees for refusing to sign restrictive covenants which the employment tribunal had found to be unlawful could constitute 'SOSR' since the reason was not 'whimsical or capricious'. The correct approach is for the reasonableness (legality) of the covenant to be considered when assessing the overall reasonableness of the dismissal under ERA 1996, s 98(4).

Generally, but not exclusively, this category has concerned sound commercial or business reasons for dismissing employees, as in *Hollister v National Farmers' Union* [1979] IRLR 238. Many cases involve the offering of new contracts of employment with less attractive terms, as in *St John of God (Care Services) Ltd v Brooks* [1992] IRLR 546. In any event it is a matter of balancing the disadvantage of any new contract for the employee against the benefit of the change to the employer (*Catamaran Cruisers Ltd v Williams* [1984] IRLR 386). (For employees refusing to adapt to change, see *Cresswell v Board of Inland Revenue* [1984] IRLR 190.) The tribunal will look at whether a reasonable employer would make the same changes to the contractual terms of the employee (*Chubb Fire Security v Harper* [1983] 311).

There is some connection with the principles governing contracts of employment here, as in exceptional cases, loss of trust and confidence can be SOSR (*Ezsias v North Glamorgan NHS Trust* [2011] IRLR 550).

The danger here is that this category has been used as a catch-all to underpin the managerial prerogative of employers, and may show a bias towards the employer rather than the employee. A notable example of this is *Perkin v St George's Healthcare NHS Trusts* [2005] EWCA Civ 1174, where the employee was fairly dismissed because of his personality despite his technical competence at his job. Ironically, it has been applied to reorganisational or quasi-redundancies within a business, leaving dismissed employees with neither redundancy payments nor unfair dismissal compensation (see *Hollister v National Farmers' Union*).

Where any type of reorganisation or variation of contracts is to be implemented, the employer will need to conduct consultation to avoid falling foul of the reasonableness test of ERA 1996, s 98(4).

SOSR has also been held to cover irreconcilable breakdowns between employees (*Treganowan v Robert Knee & Co Ltd* [1975] ICR 405 (QBD)) and dismissals at the behest of third parties (*Scott Packaging and Warehousing Co Ltd v Paterson* [1978] IRLR 166 (EAT)). Guidance on third-party pressure to dismiss can be found in *Henderson v Connect (South Tyneside) Ltd* [2010] IRLR 466, and it is to be noted that an employer is required to make some inquiry into the justification of the request (*Bancroft v Interserve* [2012] UKEAT 0329/12/KN).

The defence of 'economic, technical or organisational reason' under either TUPE 2006 or TUPE 1981 (as amended) comes within the SOSR category (ERA 1996, s 98(1)(b)). However, as a result of the Court of Session's judgment in *Hynd v Armstrong* [2007] IRLR 338, a transferor employer is unlikely to be able to rely on the transferee's reason for dismissal to establish an economic, technical or organisational reason.

Please note that the ACAS Code of Practice on Disciplinary and Grievance Procedures does not apply to SOSR dismissal (*Phoenix House Ltd v Stockman* [2016] IRLR 848).

6.9 Automatically unfair reasons for dismissal

6.9.1 Trade union membership or non-membership

The effect of TULR(C)A 1992, s 152, is that dismissal of an employee for refusing or failing to join a union in a closed-shop situation is automatically unfair. This applies principally to the post-entry closed shop. Meanwhile, TULR(C)A 1992, s 152(1), states that the dismissal of an employee will be unfair if the reason (or principal reason) was because the employee:

(a) was, or proposed to become, a member of an independent trade union; or

(b) had taken part, or proposed to take part, in the activities of an independent trade union at an appropriate time; or

(c) was not a member of any trade union, or of a particular trade union, or of one of a number of particular trade unions, or had refused, or proposed to refuse, to become or remain a member.

These reasons are known as 'inadmissible reasons', and where they exist an employment tribunal will have jurisdiction even where the normal period of continuous employment has not been established. In this context the reason for dismissal is the set of beliefs held by the employer which causes him or her to dismiss (*CGB Publishing v Killey* [1993] IRLR 520).

'Independent trade union' is defined in TULR(C)A 1992, s 5.

'An appropriate time' is defined in TULR(C)A 1992, s 152(2). The protection in s 152(1)(b) applies to trade union activities during the employment in question (*Bass Taverns Ltd v Burgess* [1995] IRLR 596) and not to previous activities in other employments. However, industrial action is specifically excluded. In fact, TULR(C)A 1992, s 137 makes it unlawful to refuse a person employment on grounds relating to union membership, thereby effectively removing pre-entry closed-shop restrictions.

In TULR(C)A 1992, s 152(1)(c), the proposal may be contingent, for example, the employee will leave the union if it takes certain action (*Crosville Motor Services Ltd v Ashfield* [1985] IRLR 475). For a restrictive interpretation of TULR(C)A 1992, s 152(1), see *Carrington v Therm-Astor Ltd* [1983] ICR 208, and, by analogy, *Associated Newspapers Ltd v Wilson* [1995] 2 AC 454 (HL). In *Wilson,* the House of Lords took a very narrow view of what it is to be a trade union member: penalising an employee for utilising the benefits of membership would not found a claim under s 152. This is to be contrasted with the far wider definition of trade union membership which forms the basis of the decisions in *Discount Tobacco & Confectionery Ltd v Armitage* [1990] IRLR 15; *Fitzpatrick v British Railways Board* [1991] IRLR 375 and *Speciality Care plc v Pachela* [1996] IRLR 248 (EAT) (although the approach of the House of Lords in *Wilson* was reaffirmed by the EAT in *NACODS v Gluchowski* [1996] IRLR 252).

Note that the qualifying period does not apply to the dismissal of an employee in this context (see TULR(C)A 1992, s 154).

6.9.2 Selection for redundancy—inadmissible reasons

Redundancy is a prima facie fair ground for dismissal, for example, where a company goes into liquidation. In that case an employee, if qualified, will simply wish to claim a redundancy payment. However, if the dismissal is alleged to be unfair, it may be on the basis of ERA 1996, s 98(2)(c), and the general test of reasonableness. However, it may be that the selection for redundancy was a dismissal which was automatically unfair (often described as an 'inadmissible reason') by virtue of TULR(C)A 1992, s 153 and ERA 1996, ss 99 and 105.

The following are the specific situations covered:

(a) The person has been selected because of trade union membership/activities/non-membership (see for example, *Britool Ltd v Roberts* [1993] IRLR 481, *Dundon v GPT Ltd* [1995] IRLR 403 and *O'Dea v ISC Chemicals Ltd* [1995] IRLR 599).

(b) Selection was because the person exercised his or her functions in health and safety cases or asserted a statutory right (and see **6.9.7**).

(c) The taking of leave for family reasons (see **6.9.3**) was the basis for selection.

The qualifying period and upper age limit for unfair dismissal will not apply to the dismissal of employees in this context.

6.9.3 Leave for family reasons

(See the precedent at **11.8**.)

See generally the Maternity and Parental Leave etc Regulations 1999 (SI 1999/3312), amended by SI 2002/2789, the Paternity and Adoption Leave Regulations 2002 (SI 2002/2788) and the Shared Parental Leave Regulations 2014 (S1 2014/3050).

Under ERA 1999 (as amended) a dismissal will be automatically unfair if the reason for dismissal is:

- because of or connected with pregnancy, childbirth or maternity; or
- by reason of ordinary, compulsory or additional maternity leave; or
- by reason of ordinary or additional adoption leave;
- by reason of parental leave;
- by reason of paternity leave;
- by reason of dependant's leave under ERA 1999, s 57A; or
- by reason of taking shared parental leave.

The dismissal of a *temporary replacement* when a woman wishes to return to work after a pregnancy can be justified if there is a substantial reason for it, subject to ERA 1996, s 98(4). Section 106(3) deals with a temporary replacement taken on because of suspension of the pregnant employee on medical grounds under either s 64 or s 66.

Note:

(a) There must be a causative link between the pregnancy and the dismissal (*Del Monte Foods Ltd v Mundon* [1980] IRLR 224), something that has been widely interpreted in practice (see *Clayton v Vigers* [1990] IRLR 177 and *Brown v Stockton-on-Tees Borough Council* [1989] AC 20 (HL)): the question being whether the employee's pregnancy precipitated and permeated the decision to dismiss (see *O'Neill v Governors of St Thomas More RCVA Upper School and another* [1996] IRLR 372 (EAT)).

(b) Pregnancy is within the remit of sex discrimination (see *Webb v EMO Air Cargo (UK) Ltd* [1994] IRLR 482).

6.9.4 Discrimination on unlawful grounds

For an employer to argue a dismissal is fair, as stated at **6.6.2**, the reason for dismissal must come within one of the categories of prima facie or potentially fair reasons under ERA 1996, s 98(2). Hence dismissal for say, gender (sex) or racial reasons cannot come within any of the potentially fair reasons and will be unfair. However, those who are dismissed in such circumstances should not place reliance on an unfair dismissal claim save in exceptional circumstances since this would impose qualifying conditions (such as being an 'employee', having two years' continuous service) and a cap on compensation. More advantageous would be a claim of discriminatory dismissal under the Equality Act

2010 (EqA 2010), s 39(2)(b), or discriminatory constructive dismissal under EqA 2010, s 39(7)(b). The EqA 2010 protects employees, contract workers, police officers, those working as partners in partnerships and LLPs, barristers/advocates and office-holders (although only employees enjoy the particular protection of s 39, with equivalent protection for the other categories appearing elsewhere in the EqA 2010). Discrimination on grounds of age, disability, pregnancy, maternity, race, religion/belief or lack of the same, sex and sexual orientation is covered by EqA 2010, s 4. Further guidance on this complex subject can be found in **Chapter 8**.

6.9.5   Transfer of Undertakings (Protection of Employment) Regulations 2006

To determine the question of whether there has been a transfer of an undertaking within the meaning of these regulations, see **6.3.2.6**.

(See the precedent at **11.6** for a sample claim involving TUPE.)

If a 'relevant transfer' (or a reason connected with it) is the reason or principal reason for the dismissal, then the dismissal is automatically unfair. This does not apply, however, where the reason or principal reason is an 'economic, technical or organisational reason entailing changes in the workforce' (commonly referred to as 'ETO'). This rule is as a result of TUPE 2006, reg 7. Protection is only achieved after two years' continuous employment. Guidance on such reasons can be found in *Meikle v McPhail (Charleston Arms)* [1983] IRLR 351 and *Trafford v Sharpe & Fisher (Building Supplies) Ltd* [1994] IRLR 325. In this situation there is a presumption that the dismissal was for 'some other substantial reason' (SOSR) in accordance with ERA 1996, s 98(1)(b). Hence it is presumed to be for a fair reason. It then remains for the employment tribunal to apply the test in s 98(4): did the employer act reasonably in treating it as a sufficient reason for dismissing the employee? Should this be the case, the employee can then claim a redundancy payment as redundancy comes within the ETO reason (*Gorictree Ltd v Jenkinson* [1984] IRLR 391). Further guidance on the operation of this defence can be found in *BSG Property Services v Tuck* [1996] IRLR 134 (EAT).

Changes in the workforce mentioned in this defence mean changes in the composition of the workforce: mere changes in the terms and conditions of individual members of the workforce are insufficient (*Berriman v Delabole Slate Ltd* [1985] IRLR 305). However, if the same employees are retained but they are required to do entirely different jobs, there is a change in the workforce under *Crawford v Swinton Insurance Brokers Ltd* [1990] ICR 85.

If it is a condition of the sale and transfer of a business that the transferor employer dismisses the workforce by reason of redundancy, should the transferee employer recruit replacement labour that does not necessarily make the dismissals unfair. The ETO defence may be available to the transferor employer (*Anderson v Dalkeith Engineering Ltd* [1985] ICR 66). Yet the transferee employer may be liable for unfair dismissal in this context, if it is a condition of purchase that the transferor employer dismisses the workforce as redundant before sale in an effort to ensure that the transferee employer does not inherit them (*Litster v Forth Dry Dock and Engineering Co* [1990] 1 AC 546). Furthermore, the ETO reasons must be reasons consequent upon transfer, otherwise the transfer would not be a reason for dismissal (see *D'Urso v Ercole Marelli Elettromeccanica Generale SpA* [1992] IRLR 136).

As discussed under 'Some other substantial reason' (at **6.8.6**) the Court of Session in *Hynd v Armstrong* [2007] IRLR 338 held that transferor employees will be unable to rely on the transferee's reason for dismissal to establish an ETO reason. A transferor can only rely upon a reason of their own to attempt to justify dismissal. TUPE is a complex area of employment law with frequent appellate decisions, so readers are referred to *Harvey on Industrial Relations and Employment Law* for further guidance.

6.9.6 Rehabilitation of Offenders Act 1974

To assist the rehabilitation of a person into society and in promoting employment prospects after the commission of a criminal offence, the Rehabilitation of Offenders Act 1974 (ROA 1974) provides that after the expiration of a period of time (which varies with the sentence or the order of the court) certain convictions will become 'spent'. Section 4(3)(b) provides that failure to disclose a spent conviction is not grounds for dismissing or excluding a person from any office, profession, occupation or employment. No sanction is provided, but if the only reason a person is dismissed is because he or she has a past conviction which is now spent, this would amount to an unfair dismissal. Many professionals, including lawyers, accountants, doctors, teachers, nurses, police and social workers, are exempt from these provisions.

6.9.7 Unfair dismissal in health and safety cases and for asserting a statutory right in the employment context

Regardless of length of service, etc., employees have the right not to be dismissed by reason (or principally by reason) of:

(a) His or her carrying out health and safety activities or for leaving the workplace in the event of serious and imminent danger (ERA 1996, s 100(1)).

(b) His or her bringing proceedings to enforce a statutory right or otherwise alleging that the employer had infringed such a right (ERA 1996, ss 104 and 104A). The rights in question are: any right conferred by the ERA 1996 where the remedy is by complaint to the employment tribunal; the right to statutory minimum notice under ERA 1996, s 86; the right to require the employer to cease deduction of union dues or political fund contributions under ERA 1996, ss 68 and 86; the right not to have action short of dismissal taken on union grounds under TULR(C)A 1992, s 146; the right to time off for union duties and activities under TULR(C)A 1992, s 170; and the rights conferred by the Working Time Regulations 1998 (WT Regs 1998).

Note: the employee does not actually have to establish an entitlement to the right in question, merely that he or she brought proceedings or alleged a breach of such an entitlement in good faith.

These rights have been extended to include:

- shop workers and betting workers who refuse to work Sundays (ERA 1996, s 101);
- employees who have asserted rights under the WT Regs 1998 (ERA 1996, s 101A), (although as a result of *McLean v Rainbow Homeloans Ltd* [2007] IRLR 14 (EAT), an employee was permitted to rely upon s 101A where he or she 'has refused to accede to a requirement that would have breached the regulations and that the dismissal is because of that refusal. The fact that the requirement would have breached the regulations does not, however, have to be the reason for the employee having declined to comply');
- trustees of occupational pension schemes (ERA 1996, s 102);
- employee representatives (ERA 1996, s 103), in the public interest;

- employees who have asserted rights derived from:
  - the National Minimum Wage Act 1998 (NMWA 1998) (ERA 1996, s 104A),
  - the Tax Credits Act 2002 (TCA 2002) (ERA 1996, s 104B),
  - the Flexible Working Regulations 2002 (FW Regs 2002) (ERA 1996, s 104C),
  - the Part-Time Workers Regulations 2000 (PTW Regs 2000).

Where such a reason constitutes the reason for selection in a redundancy case, the dismissal will also be rendered automatically unfair, see ERA 1996, s 105.

The qualifying period and the exclusion from protection otherwise resulting from reaching the normal retirement age are limitations on the right not to be unfairly dismissed that do not apply when one of the automatically unfair reasons for dismissal arises, see ERA 1996, ss 108 and 109.

6.9.8 Protection under the Public Interest Disclosure Act 1998

As a result of ERA 1996, s 103A, regardless of length of service, it is automatically unfair to dismiss an employee who has made or threatened to make a protected disclosure. Further, the selection for redundancy of such a person is automatically unfair where the reason for selection is the protected disclosure under ERA 1996, s 105.

In other words this legislation means protection for 'whistleblowers'. One area of confusion has been how the burden of proof should operate on the issue of reason for dismissal. This has been the subject of detailed guidelines in *Kuzel v Roche Products Ltd* [2008] EWCA Civ 380. It is important to note that in order to determine whether the disclosure is within the protection of the legislation, it is sufficient that the employee believes the matters disclosed amount to a criminal act or found a legal obligation, even if that belief is mistaken (*Babula v Waltham Forest College* [2007] IRLR 346 (CA)). However, as a result of *Cavendish Munro Professional Risks Management Ltd v Geduld* [2010] IRLR 38 (EAT), employees must ensure what is being communicated is 'information' (which will be protected) rather than making an 'allegation' which does not convey facts and will not qualify for protection.

The issue of causation in such claims should be treated in the same fashion as discrimination claims following *Fecit v NHS Manchester* [2011] IRLR 511 (EAT).

Whistleblowing cases involve complex legal issues so readers are referred to *Harvey on Industrial Relations and Employment Law*.

6.9.9 Unfair dismissal of strikers

By TULR(C)A 1992, s 238A, an employee dismissed for taking part in official (or 'protected') industrial action will be regarded as unfairly dismissed, provided that:

(a) the dismissal takes place within the period of 12 weeks beginning with the day on which the employee started to take the protected industrial action (s 238A(3)); or

(b) the dismissal takes place after the 12-week period but the employee had stopped participating in the action *before* the 12-week period expired (s 238A(4)); or

(c) the dismissal takes place after the expiry of the 12-week period and the employee continues to participate in such action *but* the employer has not taken such procedural steps as would have been reasonable for the purposes of resolving the relevant dispute (s 238A(5)).

6.9.10   Failure by the employer to comply with a requirement of the Dismissal and Disciplinary procedures as required by Employment Act 2002 and attendant regulations (SI 2004/752)

This type of automatically unfair dismissal only applies to dismissals where the disciplinary action commenced between 1 October 2004 and 5 April 2009, where the employee has one year's continuous service as a result of ERA 1996, s 98A. This topic is beyond the scope of this book, and readers are requested to research elsewhere, although it is not anticipated that many cases under this statutory framework remain unheard or unresolved.

6.10   Unfair dismissal flowchart

The flowchart at Figure 6.2 provides a general outline only and should not be relied upon without reference to the appropriate text (references in brackets) to practitioner works and the primary sources.

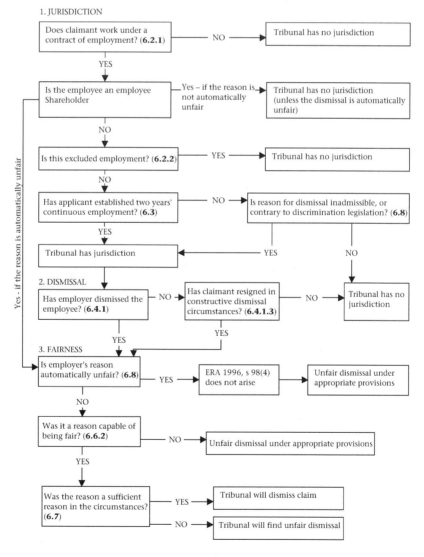

Figure 6.2 Unfair dismissal flowchart

6.11 Redundancy not involving unfair dismissal (ERA 1996, Pt XI)

Entitlement to a redundancy payment depends on whether the claimant was:

- an employee;
- in qualifying employment;
- for the qualifying period; and
- dismissed;
- for redundancy.

6.11.1 Qualifying employment

There are certain categories of employee who, although they would otherwise qualify for a redundancy payment, are precluded from making a claim (some are common with unfair dismissal), because of the nature of their employment or their situation:

(a) Share fishermen (ERA 1996, s 199(2)).

(b) Crown servants, office-holders for the purposes of the Superannuation Acts and those who are treated as civil servants for pension purposes (ERA 1996, s 159).

(c) Employees of a government of an overseas territory (ERA 1996, s 160).

(d) Domestic servants in a private household who are close relatives of their employer (ERA 1996, s 161).

(e) A person employed under a fixed-term contract for two years or more who, before the term expires, agrees in writing to exclude rights to a claim (ERA 1996, s 197) (although some commentators have argued that this might be contrary to the European Framework Directive on fixed-term work (99/70/EC)).

(f) Employees covered by an agreement made between an employer's organisation and a trade union for exemption from ministerial order on an application by both parties thereto (ERA 1996, s 157).

(g) In certain situations where the employee will be in receipt of an occupational pension (ERA 1996, s 158).

6.11.2 Qualifying employee

In order to qualify, the employee must have at least two years' continuous employment with the employer (ERA 1996, s 155), but excluding any week which began before the employee was 18.

For statutory provision for redundancy payments, the 'relevant date' for termination of employment is governed by ERA 1996, s 145. Its terms are broadly similar to those in ERA 1996, s 97, which deals with the concept of 'the effective date of termination' in unfair dismissal cases.

6.11.3 Dismissal for redundancy

By ERA 1996, s 136(1), a dismissal takes place if:

(a) the employer terminates the contract (with or without notice); or

(b) a fixed-term contract expires without being renewed; or

(c) the employee terminates the contract (with or without notice) in circumstances which are such that he or she is entitled to do so by reason of the employer's conduct.

A dismissal for redundancy can also occur if:

(d) the employment is terminated by the death, dissolution or liquidation of the employer, or the appointment of a receiver (ERA 1996, s 136(5)).

An employee who leaves employment prematurely, anticipating possible redundancies in the future, will not be dismissed from that employment and therefore will not be entitled to a redundancy payment (*Morton Sundour Fabrics Ltd v Shaw* (1967) 2 ITR 84), but cf the counter-notice provisions ERA 1996, s 142 and see *Pritchard-Rhodes Ltd v Boon and Milton* [1979] IRLR 19. Furthermore, it seems that the parties may suspend a redundancy notice if the employer anticipates that more work may arise. If this extra work does not materialise, the employee may reactivate the notice, even after its expiry date, and claim a redundancy payment (*Mowlem Northern Ltd v Watson* [1990] ICR 751).

6.11.4   Dismissal by reason of redundancy

A claim for a redundancy payment can only be made by an employee dismissed for redundancy. An employer can challenge a claim if it was not a genuine redundancy. If the reason is other than redundancy, it is for the employer to prove it. Should the employer do so, there will be no liability for a redundancy payment, but otherwise the statutory presumption of redundancy will prevail (ERA 1996, s 163(2)).

Under ERA 1996, s 139(1), a dismissal is because of redundancy if it is wholly or mainly attributable to:

(a) the fact that the employer has ceased, or intends to cease, to carry on the business for the purposes of which the employee was employed; or

(b) the fact that the employer has ceased or intends to cease to carry on that business in the place where the employee was employed; or

(c) the fact that the requirements of that business for employees to carry out work of a particular kind, or for employees to carry out work of a particular kind in the place where they were so employed, have ceased or diminished or are expected to cease or diminish.

In the past, the contractual approach seemed to predominate here, that is, not only what work was the employee actually doing, but also what could he or she be made to do (*Haden v Cowen Ltd* [1983] ICR 1), although even this was not to be applied in an overly technical or legalistic way (*Johnson v Peabody Trust* [1996] IRLR 387 (EAT)). However, the House of Lords has emphasised the need to look at the facts of the case, not just the contract (see *Murray v Foyle Meats Ltd* [1999] IRLR 562).

6.11.4.1   Business closure

This is generally a straightforward situation (although note the position on business transfers, see **6.3.2.5**). 'Business' is defined in ERA 1996, s 235(1).

6.11.4.2   Diminishing requirements for work of a particular kind

This can take a number of different forms. The employer may require fewer employees for existing work (*Carry All Motors Ltd v Pennington* [1980] ICR 806), or there is less work for current employees (*Chapman v Goonvean & Rostowrack China Clay Co Ltd* [1973] ICR

310). It is, however, relevant to ask whether there has been a cessation or diminution in the work actually performed by the employee(s) in question (*Shawkat v Nottingham City Hospital NHS Trust* [1999] IRLR 340 (EAT)).

For consideration of what may loosely be described as a 'redundancy situation' in this area, see *Hindle v Percival Boats Ltd* [1969] 1 WLR 174; *Lesney Products & Co Ltd v Nolan* [1977] IRLR 77; *Johnson v Nottinghamshire Combined Police Authority* [1974] 1 WLR 358 and *Murphy v Epsom College* [1985] ICR 80.

6.11.4.3 Relocation of employee

This may be caused by the employer moving the place of business or the employee being required to work elsewhere (whether close by or in another part of the country). The question is essentially one of construction of the individual employee's contract of employment, and whether, as a matter of law on the express terms or implied terms, the employer has contractual authority to instruct the employee to move. It may frequently involve the existence or otherwise of a mobility clause (see **5.2.3**). The relationship between redundancy and mobility clauses is explained in the recent authority of *Home Office v Evans* [2008] IRLR 59.

Where there is no express provision as to place of work, a mobility clause can be implied. If a contract of employment does not envisage an employee working in a new location (for example, Brighton rather than London), then prima facie the employee has a claim for a redundancy payment, and vice versa. In *Bass Leisure Ltd v Thomas* [1994] IRLR 104, a 'geographical' rather than a 'contractual' test for redundancy was preferred. The statutory definition of redundancy was fulfilled even though a mobility clause in a contract of employment could require the employee to work at other locations, when the place where the employee had worked had closed down, as in this case. This approach has been approved by the Court of Appeal in *High Table Ltd v Horst and another* [1997] IRLR 513, where it was stressed that the question involved a consideration of the factual circumstances of the case.

Whether an employer's moving the place of business is sufficient to constitute a redundancy situation is really a question of fact, depending on the distance involved and the consequent inconvenience for the employees concerned.

6.11.4.4 Transferred redundancy ('bumping')

This is where an employee is redundant and is moved to another position, thereby making the employee occupying *that* position redundant. The latter may then make a claim for a redundancy payment or unfair dismissal. In determining whether there is a redundancy, the tribunal applies the test in *Murray v Foyle Meats Ltd* [1999] UKHL 30. An employer must, of course, act reasonably in such a situation, and in an unfair dismissal case, the tribunal will go on to consider ERA 1996, s 98(4).

6.11.5 Employer's defences to a claim for a redundancy payment

The employer may deny that there was a dismissal, or that it was for redundancy, or indeed both.

6.11.5.1 Misconduct

Under ERA 1996, s 140(3), an employee, who has been given notice of dismissal by reason of redundancy, and who, while working out his notice, commits an act of misconduct sufficient to warrant summary dismissal and is dismissed, must have entitlement (or otherwise) to a redundancy payment determined by an employment tribunal. Provided that the summary dismissal was justified, the employment tribunal will then determine whether it is just and equitable for that employee to receive the redundancy payment in whole or in part.

A complication arises where the employee is given notice of dismissal by reason of redundancy, and afterwards and during the notice period takes part in a strike. Despite this being conduct which entitles the employer to terminate the contract without notice, the employee is not barred from receiving the whole of his redundancy payment (ERA 1996, s 140(2)). However, if an employee is on strike and is subsequently dismissed by reason of redundancy he or she will be disqualified from receiving a redundancy payment. The saving provision in s 140(2) does not then apply, because s 140(1) provides that the employee will not be entitled to a redundancy payment if the employer, being entitled to terminate the contract of employment, does so with or without notice: obviously a strike being in breach of contract falls into this category (*Simmons v Hoover Ltd* [1977] QB 284).

6.11.5.2   Offers of renewal of contract or suitable alternative employment

(See the precedent at **11.4**.)

Under ERA 1996, s 141, if the employer makes an offer (whether in writing or not) to the employee to renew the contract of employment, or to re-engage him or her under a new contract, which is effective on the expiry of the old contract or within four weeks thereafter, then s 141(3) states that if: (a) the provisions of that new contract as to capacity, place at which employed, and other terms and conditions of employment would not differ from the corresponding provisions of the previous contract; or (b) these terms and conditions do differ, but the offer constitutes an offer of suitable employment, and in either case the employee unreasonably refuses that offer, then he or she will not be entitled to a redundancy payment (*Curling v Securicor Ltd* [1992] IRLR 549).

Whether the offer is of suitable (alternative) employment is a question of fact and degree, and each case is assessed objectively. Naturally, such factors as the conditions of employment, hours of work, pay, holidays, fringe benefits, qualifications and experience are relevant considerations (see, for example, *Sheppard v National Coal Board* (1966) 1 ITR 177).

Is an employee's refusal of an offer to renew the old contract on the same terms or refusal of the offer of suitable alternative employment unreasonable? Here subjective issues affecting the employee may also be taken into consideration. Personal problems and difficulties, but not personal likes and dislikes, are relevant. Domestic hitches, the prospect of a ruined social life, absence of proper educational facilities for children, and awkward travel arrangements for work can be reasonable grounds for refusing such an offer (*Paton Calvert & Co Ltd v Westerside* [1979] IRLR 108). See also *Cambridge and District Co-operative Society v Ruse* [1993] IRLR 156, where it was held that an employee may reasonably refuse a suitable offer of alternative employment on the grounds of his or her personal perception of the job offered.

Trial period in new employment

Under ERA 1996, s 138, if the contract is renewed on the basis of new terms and conditions of employment, then the employee is entitled to have a four-week trial period, or such longer period as may be agreed between the parties, for the purpose of training the employee under the new contract. Any new agreement must be made before the employee commences work under the new contract. It must be in writing, indicate the length of the trial period and specify the terms and conditions of employment which will apply after the trial period. If, before or during the trial period, the new contract is terminated by either party, the employee will be treated as dismissed for the reason and on the date that his previous (old) contract of employment ended. ERA 1996, s 98, could permit a consideration of whether the dismissal during the trial period itself was fair or unfair (*Hempell v W. H. Smith & Sons Ltd* [1986] IRLR 95). However, if before or during the trial period the employee unreasonably terminates the contract, he or she will not be entitled to a redundancy payment by reason of his or her dismissal from the previous contract (ERA 1996, s 141(4)).

It may also be relevant to consider ERA 1996, s 138, in an unfair dismissal claim where redundancy is in issue (*Ebac Ltd v Wymer* [1995] ICR 466).

When the statutory trial period was introduced, the question arose whether it replaced the 'common law trial period' (whereby an employee had a reasonable period within which to decide whether or not to accept the repudiation by the employer, or to continue with the new contract which had been offered) which had been acknowledged as existing in cases of constructive dismissal. In *Air Canada v Lee* [1978] IRLR 392, it was firmly decided that the statutory period was in addition and consecutive to the common law period.

6.11.5.3 Transfer of business or undertaking

Continuity of employment when a business is transferred is preserved by ERA 1996, s 218(2) (see **6.3.2.5**), so that the transfer will not itself entitle employees to claim redundancy. Moreover, if the employee is later made redundant by the new employer, employment with the old employer will count for the purposes of qualification for and computation of a redundancy payment. This will apply even where there is a change in the employee's capacity (*Lord Advocate v De Rosa* [1974] ICR 480). Employees would only be able to claim redundancy payments where it would be reasonable to refuse the offer (s 141(2)).

The position under ERA 1996 is complemented by the TUPE 2006 Regulations, but this has not been without its difficulties.

See **6.3.2.5** and **6.8.5**.

6.11.6 Lay-off and short-time working

Even if there is no dismissal, an employee can claim a redundancy payment when there is a temporary cessation of the employer's business. Where the employee has been laid off or kept on short time for a consecutive period of four weeks, or for an aggregate period of six or more weeks within a period of 13 weeks, the employee can serve a written notice on the employer indicating that he or she intends to make a claim for a redundancy payment (ERA 1996, s 148(1)).

Lay-off is defined as a period when the employer does not provide work for the employee and as a result the employee is not entitled to any remuneration under the contract of employment (ERA 1996, s 147(1)). A period of short time is defined as where an employee's remuneration for any week is less than half a week's pay (s 147(2)). In this context the guarantee payment provisions in ERA 1996, Pt III should also be considered.

After the employee has served written notice on the employer under ERA 1996, s 148, if the employee wishes to terminate the contract, he or she must then give notice of termination (that is, contractual notice subject to a minimum of one week). On termination, the employee will be treated as redundant. To defeat the claim the employer must show that it is reasonably to be expected that the employee would be provided with work for at least 13 weeks without the prospect of being laid off or kept on short time, the period commencing within four weeks of the employee's notice under s 148. Any counter-notice must be served by the employer within seven days. Unless there is a contractual right to lay off staff or place staff on short time, the employer will be in breach of contract, and possibly liable to a claim for constructive dismissal (s 95(1)(c) and see **6.4.1.3**). Once it is shown that there has been a dismissal, it is open to the employee to claim unfair dismissal and/or a redundancy payment.

6.11.7 The collective handling of redundancies (Trade Union and Labour Relations (Consolidation) Act 1992, Pt IV, Chapter 2)

By TULR(C)A 1992, s 188(1), as amended, an employer proposing to dismiss as redundant 20 or more employees shall consult all persons who are appropriate representatives of any of the employees who are about to be dismissed. A period of 45 days is required for 100 or more redundancies and 30 days where the number is greater than or equal to 20 for proposals made on or after 6 April 2013. As set out at **6.8.4**, redundancy volunteers are counted in determining if the threshold required is met: *Optare Group Ltd v TGWU* [2007] IRLR 931, (EAT).

'Appropriate representatives' are defined by s 188(1B) as: (a) employee representatives elected by the employees; or (b) if the employees are of a description in respect of which an independent trade union is recognised by the employer, representatives of the trade union. Previously, where both types of representative were in existence, the employer could choose whom to consult.

The employer must comply with the requirements of the Information and Consultation of Employees Regulations 2004 which implements the Collective Redundancies Directive 98/59. Readers requiring further detail on either the Directive or the Regulations are referred to *Harvey on Industrial Relations and Employment Law*. However, commentators on employment law are concerned following the judgment in *Junk v Kuhnel* [2005] IRLR 310 that the UK legislation is out of line with the requirements of EU law.

Provided that the employer issues an invitation to hold elections for elected representatives early enough to provide for the election to be held before consultation should begin, no complaint of a failure to consult such representatives can be made (s 188(7A)), and the employer must give to each affected employee the information set out at ERA 1996, s 188(4). The consultation should be 'in good time' generally, but the Regulations above impose a timetable for larger employers.

By s 188(4), as amended, the employer has a duty to disclose to the appropriate representatives in writing the following:

(a) the reasons for the employer's proposals;

(b) the numbers and description of employees whom it is proposed to dismiss as redundant;

(c) the total number of employees of any such description employed by the employer at the establishment in question;

(d) the proposed method of selecting the employees who may be dismissed;

(e) the proposed method of carrying out the dismissal, with due regard to any agreed procedure, including the period over which the dismissals are to take effect;

(f) the proposed method of calculating the amount of any redundancy payment to be made (otherwise than in compliance with an obligation imposed by or by virtue of any enactment) to employees who may be dismissed.

On the operation of these revised provisions, see the useful guidance in *MSF v GEC Ferranti (Defence Systems) Ltd (No 2)* [1994] IRLR 113 and their wider implications in *Northern Ireland Hotel and Catering College and North Eastern Education and Library Board v NATFHE* [1995] IRLR 83.

In any consultation, the employer must consider any representations made by the representatives. Consultation must include ways of avoiding dismissals, reducing the numbers of employees to be dismissed and mitigating the consequences of dismissal, and must be undertaken by the employer with a view to reaching agreement with the representatives. 'Special circumstances' may excuse the employer from compliance with these responsibilities (s 188(7), as amended, and see *Clarks of Hove Ltd v Bakers' Union* [1978] ICR 1076 on the interpretation of this provision).

If there is a failure to consult, a trade union or an elected representative, in enforcing this *collective* right, can complain to an employment tribunal. Where there is no recognised trade union and no elected representative, an individual employee who has been made redundant can bring a complaint. Unless the tribunal finds that it was not reasonably practicable for the employer to comply, it will make a declaration as to the non-compliance and it may also make a *protective award*.

This is an award of remuneration for a protected period to cover those employees who were dismissed without consultation (s 189). The entitlement to payment is a week's pay for every employee to whom the award is made for each week of the protected period, and pro rata if the period is less than a week (s 190). The purpose of the protective award is to compensate the employee for the wages lost due to the employer's failure to consult, rather than as a method of punishing the employer for the default (*Spiller-French (Holidays) Ltd v Union of Shop, Distributive & Allied Workers* [1980] ICR 31). Provision is also made for the termination of employment during the protected period (s 191). Should an employer fail to pay an employee a protective award, in whole or in part, a complaint may be made to an employment tribunal (s 192(1)). If the tribunal finds the complaint well founded, it can order the employer to make good the deficiency (s 192(3)).

It should be noted that TUPE 2006 contains provisions for consultation with appropriate representatives in the event of a 'relevant transfer' (see **6.3.2.5** and **6.3.2.6**) being proposed, with a view to securing their agreement to the measures to be taken. This duty in certain circumstances overlaps with the duty under these statutory provisions and to a certain extent with the remedies available.

Regarding the financial provision and calculation of redundancy payments, see **7.9**. Contractual provision for redundancy may well exceed the statutory minima for redundancy payments. Where the contractual redundancy scheme clearly provides that it is to encompass the statutory entitlement, there will be no double compensation. If an employer routinely pays staff in excess of the statutory maximum, even if there is no contractual term in writing, the custom and practice doctrine can give rise to an implied term entitling employees to the enhanced redundancy payment as in the case of *Peregrine & Ors v Peacock Stores* [2014] All ER (D) 22.

6.12 Interaction of unfair dismissal and redundancy

The provisions indicated relate to ERA 1996 unless stated otherwise.

6.12.1 Redundancy

'Redundancy' is defined in s 139(1). Redundancy may occur where:

- a business closes down; or
- there are diminishing requirements for work of a particular kind; or
- the employee is relocated.

Redundancy is prima facie a fair reason (potentially fair reason) for dismissal (s 98). Therefore a number of outcomes are possible in an unfair dismissal and redundancy case:

(a) If the dismissal is reasonable both as regards choice and procedural fairness (s 98(4)), then the dismissal is fair but the employee is entitled to a redundancy payment.

(b) If the tribunal finds the dismissal was unreasonable under s 98(4), then the dismissal is unfair, and the claimant is entitled to the remedies available in unfair dismissal cases (see **Chapter 7**).

(c) If the tribunal finds the dismissal is unreasonable under TULR(C)A 1992, s 153, ERA 1996, ss 100 and 104 (dismissal for a trade union reason/in health and safety cases/assertion of statutory rights), then the dismissal is automatically unfair.

(d) If the employee is not in fact redundant within the statutory definition of redundancy (defined in s 139(1)):

   (i) then there will be an unfair dismissal, unless

   (ii) dismissal for a 'quasi-redundancy' reason which is capable of being 'some other substantial reason', one of the potentially fair reasons for dismissal under s 98(1)(b), in which case:

      (1) if the dismissal is reasonable under s 98(4), then the dismissal is fair, but no redundancy payment is payable since there is no redundancy;

      (2) if the dismissal is unreasonable under s 98(4), then the dismissal is unfair, and the claimant is entitled to the remedies available in unfair dismissal cases (see **Chapter 7**).

6.12.2 'Business reorganisation'

This can be brought within 'some other substantial reason' in s 98(1)(b), so it is prima facie fair (one of the potentially fair reasons for dismissal). As a result:

- If the dismissal is reasonable under s 98(4), then the dismissal is fair.
- If the dismissal is unreasonable under s 98(4), then the dismissal is unfair, and the claimant is entitled to the remedies available in unfair dismissal cases (see **Chapter 7**).
- If the ground cannot be established (that is, there is not 'some other substantial reason'), then the dismissal will be unfair, and the claimant is entitled to the remedies available in unfair dismissal cases (see **Chapter 7**).

6.12.3   Dismissal because of transfer of undertaking

TUPE 2006, reg 4, subject to certain exceptions, operates to transfer contracts of employment to the purchasing employer if the employee is employed at the time of the transfer. (See **6.3.2.6** on whether there has been a transfer of an undertaking.) This means any contractual notice entitlement, redundancy scheme, severance payment or dismissal procedure under the old employer will transfer to the new employer.

A dismissal of an employee (by the selling or purchasing employer) 'for a reason connected with the transfer' (which is a question of fact) will be automatically unfair under TUPE 2006, reg 7, unless it is for an economic, technical or organisational (ETO) reason entailing changes in the workforce, which is deemed to be a prima facie fair (potentially fair) reason for dismissal under s 98(1)(b), and so:

(1) If the dismissal is reasonable under s 98(4), then the dismissal is fair; or

(2) If the dismissal is unreasonable under s 98(4), then the dismissal is unfair, and the claimant is entitled to the remedies available in unfair dismissal cases (see **Chapter 7**).

Remedies for unfair dismissal and redundancy

7.1 Remedies for unfair dismissal

If a tribunal decides that the claimant has been unfairly dismissed, it can order (a) reinstatement, (b) re-engagement or (c) compensation. It must consider the three remedies in that order.

Reinstatement is an order that 'the employer shall treat the complainant in all respects as if he had not been dismissed' (Employment Rights Act 1996 (ERA 1996), s 114(1)). In other words he or she returns to his or her old job, with arrears of pay, pension rights, etc. by a date which the tribunal specifies. There may be no changes to contractual terms, although a tribunal may order appropriate changes to specific duties (*McBride v Scottish Police Authority* [2016] IRLR 633 (SC)).

Re-engagement is an order that 'the complainant be engaged ... in employment comparable to that from which he was dismissed or other suitable employment' (s 115(1)). The tribunal specifies the terms of employment (which may be with an associated or successor employer) and lays down a deadline for compliance. It should consider the practicability of re-engagement (*Lincolnshire County Council v Lupton* [2016] IRLR 576). A tribunal should not generally order re-engagement in respect of a specific job, although it may identify the nature of the proposed employment. Nor should it order re-engagement in significantly more favourable employment than the claimant would have obtained if reinstatement had been ordered (*Rank Xerox (UK) Ltd v Stryczek* [1995] IRLR 568).

By s 116(1) before making an order for reinstatement or re-engagement the tribunal must consider (a) the employee's wishes, (b) whether such an order is practicable and (c) whether it would be just, if the employee caused or contributed to the dismissal. The award of the tribunal is not rendered a nullity by a failure to follow this procedure, but 'the Employment Appeal Tribunal ought in appropriate cases to be very ready to send a case back for further hearing on remedies' (*per* Neill LJ in *Cowley v Manson Timber Ltd* [1995] IRLR 153). The question of practicability should be assessed at the time of the tribunal decision, not at the time of the dismissal (*King v Royal Bank of Canada Europe* Ltd [2012] IRLR 280).

The employer's failure to comply with an order under s 114 or s 115 for reinstatement or re-engagement may result in increased compensation (see **7.7**).

Compensation. Although financial compensation is intended to be the option of last resort (see the wording of s 112), in practice over 99 per cent of successful claims for unfair dismissal result in a monetary award. This is partly because many claimants are reluctant to seek reinstatement after making a successful employment tribunal claim. It may also be that tribunals are reluctant to grant the remedies, perhaps because they are unenforceable, or because of the traditional view that enforcement of a contract of service is inappropriate. The award usually consists of two elements:

- the basic award,
- the compensatory award.

Occasionally there may also be an additional award.

The most recent government statistics available (based on the 2015/16 Employment Tribunal and EAT Statistics) show that the median tribunal award for unfair dismissal was £7,332

7.1.1 Employment tribunal fees

The introduction of tribunal fees by the Employment Tribunals and Employment Appeal Tribunal Fees Order 2013 (SI 2013/1893) has been ruled void *ab initio* by the Supreme Court in R *(on the application of Unison) v Lord Chancellor* [2017] UKSC 51. The Lord Chancellor has announced that fees will no longer be required but new measures designed to recover some of the cost of employment tribunal litigation may be introduced.

7.2 Basic award

This is intended to compensate the employee for loss of job security. It represents a number of weeks' gross pay, calculated as follows (ERA 1996, s 119):

... the amount of the basic award shall be calculated by—

(a) *determining the period, ending with the effective date of termination, during which the employee has been continuously employed,*

(b) *reckoning backwards from the end of that period the number of years of employment falling within that period, and*

(c) *allowing the appropriate amount for each of those years of employment.*

(2) In subsection (1)(c) 'the appropriate amount' means—

(a) *one and a half weeks' pay for a year of employment in which the employee was not below the age of forty-one,*

(b) *one week's pay for a year of employment (not within paragraph (a)) in which he was not below the age of twenty-two, and*

(c) *half a week's pay for a year of employment not within paragraph (a) or (b).*

Note that:

(a) The weekly pay is gross wages, before deduction of tax, etc. A week's pay will include bonuses, allowances and commissions, but only if they are provided for by an express or implied term in the contract. It will not include the value of a company car (*Weevsmay Ltd v Kings* [1977] ICR 244). More generally, the calculation of a week's pay becomes complex when the employee's pay varies from week to week, or where overtime is involved (see ERA 1996, ss 220–229).

(b) It is subject to a limit (periodically raised) of £489. Dismissals before 6 April 2017 will be subject to the previous weekly maximum of £479.

£508 before 6ᵗʰ.4.19
£525 after 6ᵗʰ.4.19

(c) A maximum of 20 years' employment can be counted. Hence the maximum basic award is 30 × £489. (The maximum multiplier is 30 because each year of continuous employment over the age of 41 is worth 1½ weeks' pay.)

(d) The 'effective date of termination' in s 119 is defined in s 97. Whilst it is usually the date upon which the dismissal was to take effect, this will be extended to include the statutory period of notice to which the employee was entitled under s 86, if appropriate (see **6.5**).

(e) Only complete years are counted, for example, if the employee has worked 11 years, eight months, only 11 years will count.

A ready reckoner produced by the Department for Business, Innovation and Skills to assist with the calculation of redundancy payments is presented at **7.9** and, with an appropriate adjustment, may be applied to the calculation of the basic award.

7.3 Reductions in the basic award

The amount of a basic award, calculated as in **7.2**, may be reduced on the following grounds:

(a) Because the employee has received a redundancy payment. This reduction applies only where the dismissal was in fact by reason of redundancy. It is not enough that an employer *states* that the payment is by reason of redundancy, even if the employee accepts that description at the time (*Boorman v Allmakes Ltd* [1995] IRLR 553).

(b) Because the employer has made an *ex gratia* payment, if such a payment was referable expressly or impliedly to the basic award (see further **7.5.3**).

(c) Where the employee's conduct before dismissal 'was such that it would be just and equitable to reduce ... the basic award' (s 122(2)). This provision is equivalent to (but differently worded from) that for reducing the compensatory award in cases of contributory fault (see **7.5.1**). Note also that reductions under this heading are not generally made in a redundancy case (s 122(3)). Otherwise it is only in exceptional circumstances that the same reduction would not be made from both awards (*University of Sunderland v Drossou* [2017] UKEAT 0341–16–1306).

(d) Where the employee has unreasonably refused an offer of full reinstatement, the employment tribunal shall reduce the award to such extent as it considers just and equitable (s 122(1)).

The basic award cannot be reduced merely because the employee has suffered no financial loss (*Cadbury Ltd v Doddington* [1977] ICR 982). Nor can it be reduced because of a failure to mitigate (*Lock v Connell Estate Agents* [1994] IRLR 444). Both of these questions are relevant to the compensatory award.

The Employment Act 2002 (EA 2002), s 34(6) lays down a minimum basic award where dismissal is automatically unfair because the statutory dismissal and disciplinary procedure has not been completed as a result of fault by the employer. In these circumstances, the minimum basic award is four weeks' pay (subject to the statutory maximum for a week's pay—currently £489).

7.4 Compensatory award

This compensates the employee for the loss suffered as a result of dismissal, subject to a maximum award (see **7.5.8**). As to the burden of proof, the Employment Appeal Tribunal (EAT) has commented in *Barley v Amey Roadstone Corporation Ltd* [1977] IRLR 299 that:

although the burden of proof lies mainly upon the claimant, the evidential burden may well shift—and indeed usually will shift to the employer once the claimant has put forward some coherent, sensible suggestion as to what the result of the failure ... is likely to have been, and what would be likely to have happened had there been no failure.

The statutory basis for the compensatory award is to be found in ERA 1996, s 123, the most important parts of which read:

(1) *Subject to the provisions of this section and sections 124, 126, 127 and 127A(1), (3) and (4), the amount of the compensatory award shall be such amount as the tribunal considers just and equitable in all the circumstances having regard to the loss sustained by the complainant in consequence of the dismissal in so far as that loss is attributable to action taken by the employer.*

   ...

(4) *In ascertaining the loss referred to in subsection (1) the tribunal shall apply the same rule concerning the duty of a person to mitigate his loss as applies to damages recoverable under the common law.*

   ...

(6) *Where the tribunal finds that the dismissal was to any extent caused or contributed to by any action of the complainant, it shall reduce the amount of the compensatory award by such proportion as it considers just and equitable having regard to that finding.*

The compensatory nature of this award is key. Over-compensation should be avoided. In *Optimum Group Services plc v Muir* [2013] IRLR 339, a TUPE case, the claimant had brought an unfair dismissal claim against O and a number of potential transferees. One of these transferee employers settled the claim for £20,000. The tribunal, however, found that there had been no transfer and found in favour of the claimant against O. The compensatory award was assessed at £23,668, which was ordered to be paid in full in spite of the settlement. On appeal the EAT held that this was wrong as it would involve double recovery.

The statute and case law (see especially *Norton Tool Co Ltd v Tewson* [1972] ICR 501) suggest heads of claim for the compensatory award as outlined at **7.4.1–7.4.8**.

7.4.1 Immediate loss of wages

This covers the period from the effective date of termination (see **6.5**) to the date of the tribunal hearing. The wages in question are net of deductions of tax and National Insurance (contrast the basic award). They include regular bonuses and overtime, unless the employer can show that such overtime has ceased or diminished.

The tribunal's assessment of the loss will be the net amount which the employee would have earned minus the amount actually earned in fresh employment (if any).

What if the employee has a short period of unemployment after dismissal, and then gets a new job which pays more? The extra earnings in the later weeks must not be set off against the loss of earnings in the earlier weeks.

According to *Whelan v Richardson* [1998] IRLR 114, the tribunal should usually calculate the loss between the date of dismissal and the date that permanent alternative employment was obtained. The EAT reasoned that employees should not be discouraged from trying to mitigate their losses by taking temporary employment. Only the acquisition of permanent employment should therefore represent a cut-off point for the calculation of the compensatory award. In *Dench v Flynn & Partners (a firm)* [1998] IRLR 653, the Court of Appeal held that an employer's liability does not necessarily cease even when the employee gains new permanent employment. Where the new job came to an end after a period of a couple of months, part of the employee's loss thereafter might still be attributable to the original unfair dismissal, and could form part of the compensatory award.

If the reason why a claimant is unemployed is not the dismissal complained of, there will be no entitlement to compensation. Thus someone incapable of work through disability will not be able to recover compensation for the consequential lost pay. However, the receipt of incapacity benefit is not sufficient to trigger this consequence. In *Sheffield Forgemasters International Ltd v Fox* [2009] IRLR 192, the EAT points out circumstances in which a claimant may be entitled to incapacity benefit while also being able to do the job from which he had been dismissed. It was necessary for the tribunal to have evidence of actual incapacity. Here, the effect of receipt of incapacity benefit was simply that it had to be set off against the amount of compensation claimed.

7.4.2 Future loss of wages

The period in question for this head of loss begins immediately after the tribunal hearing. The crucial question in computing the loss is: does the employee have a job now? That is, at the date of the tribunal hearing.

(a) Assume that he or she does not. The tribunal needs to decide:

  (i) when the employee is likely to obtain a job; and

  (ii) what the wage is likely to be.

In deciding these questions, it will need to take into consideration the local job market, the employee's personal characteristics (for example, age, skills) and the likely duration of the job lost by the unfair dismissal (for example, whether redundancy was in any event likely). In addition, anticipated increases in wages must be taken into account. Once these issues have been considered, the tribunal multiplies the net weekly wage lost by the period of unemployment caused by the unfair dismissal, for example, 13 weeks at £300 per week, amounting to £3,900 future loss of wages.

The Court of Appeal has given guidance as to how that future date should be assessed. In *Wardle v Crédit Agricole Corporate and Investment Bank* [2011] IRLR 604 it was held that the proper approach is to estimate the date by which the prospects of obtaining an equivalent job were better than 50 per cent. In so deciding, the court disapproved the approach adopted by the tribunal, which had been to calculate future losses across the remainder of the claimant's career and then to reduce that by the likelihood (70 per cent in their estimation) that he would have found an equivalent job. Such a whole career loss approach would only be appropriate where there was no real prospect of the claimant ever achieving an equivalent job.

The approach of most tribunals to determining the period is 'broad brush'. Periods of zero, 12, 13, 26 and 52 weeks are statistically the most common, indicating a wish to fix on a round period of, for example, three, six or 12 months. However, where there is evidence which will help the tribunal to arrive at a period which is realistic in all the circumstances, this should be adduced.

If the tribunal does try to ascertain the likely future loss it should recognise that the task is inherently speculative. The significance of the proper approach is apparent in *Scope v Thornett* [2007] IRLR 155, where the tribunal concluded (on an admittedly speculative basis) that the claimant would have been likely to have been dismissed within six months anyway, and reduced her compensation accordingly. The EAT, on appeal, took the view that the exercise in speculation was wrong and that they should not have limited it in this way. By contrast, the Court of Appeal held that speculation was proper provided that there was an evidential base from which to work and remitted the case to the tribunal. Presumably, this principle applies equally to anticipating periods of unemployment as it did here to anticipating loss of the job from which she was dismissed. This principle was applied in *Cumbria County Council v Bates* [2013] UKEAT 0398/11/1308 where the EAT approved the consideration of evidence of the claimant's subsequent conviction for common assault (in a matter unrelated to the dismissal). This meant that the claimant would have been barred from teaching and indicated a cut-off date for the compensation assessment.

(b) What if the employee has started another job by the date of the hearing? If pay in the new job is equal to or greater than in the old, there is no future loss of wages, and hence no award under this head. On the other hand if the new wage is lower than the old, there will be a continuing loss to the employee which needs to be compensated under this heading. In determining this compensation the tribunal adopts a multiplier/multiplicand approach as in tort cases. The sum in question is the weekly shortfall in wages, multiplied by a reasonable estimate of how long that deficit will continue. (See *Adda International Ltd v Curcio* [1976] ICR 407 and *Cartiers Superfoods Ltd v Laws* [1978] IRLR 315.)

What if the claimant has acquired another job at lower wages, but with more attractive conditions, for example, shorter hours and longer holidays? There is no direct authority in the employment field, but in a personal injuries case (*Potter v Arafa* [1995] IRLR 317) the Court of Appeal has held that the plaintiff does not need to give credit for such benefits because 'shorter hours are not money, and longer holidays are not money' (*per* Staughton LJ at p 319).

7.4.3 Loss of fringe benefits

Contractual benefits come under this head, which covers both the immediate and future loss periods. Some examples:

(a) A company car. The value depends on the evidence placed before the tribunal, but it is common to use as a basis the AA guide. Nothing will be awarded where the car was solely for business purposes.

(b) Commission.

(c) Free food.

(d) Benefits under a share participation scheme.

(e) Loans. The valuation of a company's low interest loan is the difference between the interest on the particular loan and the market rate for a comparable loan.

(f) Accommodation. Similarly, if the employee enjoyed subsidised accommodation, the award should reflect a comparison between the cost of the subsidised housing and that of suitable alternative accommodation.

(g) Special travel allowances. But note that allowances paid free of tax should not be taken into account, since their function is to reimburse the employee for necessary expenses, and there should have been no profit.

(h) Bonuses, provided they are contractual. But Christmas gifts cannot be considered.

(i) Tips may be claimed, but tax should be deducted first.

(j) Holiday pay entitlement during the compensatory award period can be recovered.

(k) Medical insurance.

(l) Luncheon vouchers.

The list is not, of course, exhaustive, and this is pre-eminently an area on which careful instructions need to be taken on both sides.

7.4.4 Loss of pension rights

In accordance with the usual rule, the claimant must prove loss and its extent. This is a notoriously difficult heading to quantify. It is also potentially a most valuable head of claim. Where the employer provided a money purchase scheme calculation can be relatively simple; however, final salary schemes can be notoriously complicated to calculate. Some guidance is provided by guidance, *Employment Tribunals: Principles for Compensating Pension Loss*, 4th edn (London: The Stationery Office, 20017, available for free download at https://www.judiciary.gov.uk/wp-content/uploads/2015/03/principles-for-compensating-pension-loss-20170810.pdf.

This, known as the 'Principles', was prepared by a group of Employment Judges. It includes a helpful explanation of the different types of pension schemes likely to be encountered and case studies showing how the methods work. The Principles recognise that some cases are 'simple' and here, compensation will be based on the lost contributions that the employer would have made had it not been for the dismissal. This is likely to be applied where the dismissed employee was enrolled in a defined contribution scheme, or to defined benefit schemes where the period of loss is short (see The Principles 5.36–5.40). However, there are also 'complex' cases, typically involving defined benefit schemes where the period of loss is greater. These will be addressed by a 'seven steps' model (The Principles 5.54–5.61), using either Ogden tables or expert evidence.

If the parties do not have the necessary information to embark on these calculations, or if they are reluctant to undergo the cost of doing so until liability has been decided, the tribunal will assess the basic and compensatory award, ignoring pension rights. It will then put the matter back, if necessary, to a later date. This will enable a sum for loss of pension rights to be agreed or, failing that, determined by the tribunal.

Choice of which approach to use should be exercised with caution. In *Griffin v Plymouth Hospital NHS Trust* [2014] IRLR 962, the CA held that the simplified approach was inappropriate where the claimant had been a member of a final salary scheme but had moved to a new job with a money purchase scheme.

7.4.5 Loss of statutory protection

As a result of the unfair dismissal, the employee will have to work two years in a new job to acquire the right to a redundancy payment, or to found a claim for unfair dismissal (and entitlement will be lower since it is closely related to length of service). This is compensated for by an award which was calculated for several years at £100 (*S. H. Muffett Ltd v Head* [1987] ICR 1). In practice, the amount most frequently awarded now seems to be £350 (although £300 and £400 are also quite common).

7.4.6   Loss of the right to long notice

This is frequently lumped together with loss of statutory protection. It ought, however, to be regarded and assessed separately, as is clear from *S. H. Muffett Ltd v Head* [1987] ICR 1. Its basis is the right to service-related notice, stemming from ERA 1996, s 86. Hence an employee with 10 years' service is entitled to 10 weeks' notice. If he or she loses that job, that period of notice must be rebuilt. This loss may be reflected in the compensatory award. Thus in *Daley v A. E. Dorsett (Almar Dolls) Ltd* [1981] IRLR 385, the EAT awarded four weeks' net pay, being half the period of entitlement to notice after the employee's eight years' service. Tribunals frequently, however, refuse to make an award under this head, on the basis that it is too speculative. In *S. H. Muffett Ltd v Head*, the EAT agreed that 'it depends upon the double contingency that the dismissed employee will get a new job and, second, that he would be dismissed from that job before building up the same entitlement to the period of notice applicable to the first job'. Nonetheless, it stressed that the 'tribunal must use its knowledge of local conditions and consider the remoteness or otherwise of these contingencies'. Clearly they would not be so remote where there is 'wide scope for movement from one employer to another'.

In *Arthur Guinness Son & Co (Great Britain) Ltd v Green* [1989] ICR 241, it was stated that, by convention, the sum eventually arrived at under this head should never be more than six weeks' wages.

7.4.7   Manner of dismissal

In *Norton Tool Co Ltd v Tewson* [1972] IRLR 86, it was accepted that a sum might be awarded if the way the employee's sacking was handled made him or her less acceptable to a future employer (*John Millar & Sons v Quinn* [1974] IRLR 107). Similarly, *Norton Tool* was authority for the proposition that if the manner of dismissal causes the employee emotional upset and hinders the search for a new job, this can be included in the compensatory award. The manner of dismissal might also affect the claimant's ability to mitigate.

The wider question, however, was whether compensation for distress and hurt feelings could in themselves form part of the compensatory award for unfair dismissal. In *Johnson v Unisys Ltd* [2001] IRLR 279, the House of Lords gave some consideration to this question in dealing with a claim for wrongful (as opposed to unfair) dismissal. In a comment which was later held to be *obiter*, Lord Hoffmann said (of the compensatory award in unfair dismissal cases):

[In] *Norton Tool Co v Tewson* ... it was said that the word 'loss' can only mean financial loss. But I think that is too narrow a construction. The emphasis is upon the tribunal awarding such compensation as it thinks just and equitable. So I see no reason why in an appropriate case it should not include compensation for distress, humiliation, damage to reputation in the community or to family life.

These remarks caused some consternation among practitioners, as they were contrary to the long-standing principle set out in *Norton Tool*. There were various conflicting decisions on the issue at different levels, which culminated in the definitive statement of the law by the House of Lords in *Dunnachie v Kingston-upon-Hull City Council* [2005] IRLR 727. Their Lordships made it clear that compensation for unfair dismissal should only be payable in respect of identifiable financial loss. Damages for injury to feelings and psychiatric injury arising from an unfair dismissal cannot therefore be recovered.

7.4.8   Expenses of looking for work

These will include, for example, travel to interviews, buying publications which carry advertisements of suitable jobs, and the cost of moving house to take up a new job. In an appropriate case, the tribunal could award expenses incurred in a reasonable attempt to set up a new business (*Gardiner-Hill v Roland Berger Technics Ltd* [1982] IRLR 498). Claimants must provide evidence of any such expenses or attempts.

7.5   Adjustments to the compensatory award

Sections **7.5.1–7.5.10** discuss grounds for adjusting a compensatory award.

7.5.1   Contributory fault

The employment tribunal has the power under ERA 1996, s 123(6), to make a reduction in the compensatory award where the employee is thought to be at fault:

Where the tribunal finds that the dismissal was to any extent caused or contributed to by any action of the complainant, it shall reduce the amount of the compensatory award by such proportion as it considers just and equitable having regard to that finding.

The principle involved is analogous to a decision on contributory negligence in tort. The tribunal examines the employee's conduct and determines:

(a) Whether it has contributed to the dismissal—not to the unfairness of the dismissal. For example, if the dismissal is unfair because of a procedural defect the employee's conduct can still result in a reduction of award.

(b) To what extent it has contributed. This is expressed as a percentage, which is at the tribunal's discretion.

Note that:

(a) It is not open to the tribunal to reduce for contributory fault on the basis of misconduct discovered after the dismissal (*Soros and Soros v Davison and Davison* [1994] IRLR 264) (but the 'no difference rule' may be relevant here, see **7.5.6**).

(b) The tribunal should not reduce on this ground unless the employee's conduct was in some way blameworthy. It would not be just and equitable to do so.

(c) A tribunal can make a finding of 100 per cent contributory fault (see *W. Devis & Sons Ltd v Atkins* [1977] AC 931). If it does there is no compensatory award.

(d) The power to reduce the compensatory award for contributory fault under s 123(6) has an equivalent in relation to the basic award under s 122(2) (see **7.3**). Usually, deductions from the basic and compensatory awards go hand in hand. The tribunal may, however, make a reduction from the compensatory award only (*Les Ambassadeurs Club v Barinda* [1982] IRLR 5). Where reductions are made from both the basic and compensatory awards, they may be different (*Charles Robertson (Developments) Ltd v White* [1995] ICR 349, where 50 per cent was deducted from the basic award, and 100 per cent from the compensatory award) but this should be restricted to exceptional cases (*University of Sunderland v Drossou* [2017] UKEAT 0341–16–1306).

(e) Failure to exercise a right of appeal under the employer's internal procedure does not constitute contributory fault (*Hoover Ltd v Forde* [1980] ICR 239) (but see **7.5.7**).

(f) Failure to use a grievance procedure in a constructive dismissal situation may constitute contributory fault (*Wall v Brookside Metal Co Ltd* (1990) 421 IRLIB 9) (but see **7.5.7**).

(g) It is conceivable, although unusual, for contributory fault to be found in constructive dismissal cases (*Frith Accountants Ltd v Law* [2014] IRLR 510 (EAT)).

This is a crucial area in practice, and one where you need to develop your own judgment. In addition, two cases give instructive insights into the principles involved. In *Morrison v Amalgamated TGWU* [1989] IRLR 361, the Northern Ireland Court of Appeal held that: (1) the tribunal should take a broad common sense view of the situation; (2) that view should not be confined to the moment of dismissal; (3) the employee's conduct must have contributed to the dismissal; and (4) it must have been culpable, blameworthy or unreasonable.

In *Parker Foundry v Slack* [1989] ICR 686, A was dismissed for fighting with B. The employer considered A the aggressor and dismissed him. The tribunal held: (1) there was insufficient evidence to show A was the aggressor; (2) the dismissal was unfair; but (3) there was 50 per cent contributory fault. On appeal, it was argued that A's position should be compared with B, who had merely been suspended for two weeks without pay. The EAT held that the question was: what was the employee's share in responsibility for his dismissal? That had been the question asked by the tribunal, whose decision was therefore upheld.

Tribunals should take care not to make deductions on the basis that a settlement might have been achieved. In *Gallop v Newport City Council* [2013] IRLR 23 the tribunal inquired into a failed attempt to make a compromise agreement and reduced some elements of the compensatory award by 50 per cent as a result. This was held to be illegitimate by the EAT as these discussions were privileged.

The order in which deductions are made is important (see further **7.5.9**). In *Digital Equipment Co Ltd v Clements (No 2)* [1998] IRLR 134, the Court of Appeal considered the point at which a redundancy payment in excess of the statutory redundancy payment should be deducted in the calculation of the compensatory award. C had been dismissed on grounds of redundancy, receiving a contractual redundancy payment which exceeded the statutory entitlement by £20,685. His dismissal was held to be unfair, but the tribunal went on to find that if the employers had followed a fair procedure, there was a 50 per cent chance that he would have been dismissed. In assessing his compensatory award, the tribunal calculated his total loss of earnings and other benefits at

£43,136. From that figure, they first deducted the excess redundancy payment and then reduced the remaining sum by 50 per cent, to reflect their finding about his prospects if a fair procedure had been followed. That gave a figure of £11,225 to which the tribunal applied the statutory limit then in force, and made an award of £11,000. The employers appealed, arguing that the tribunal should have reduced the loss by 50 per cent first, giving a compensatory award of £21,568 from which the excess redundancy payment should then have been deducted, leaving an award of £833. The EAT upheld the appeal, but that decision was reviewed by the EAT on the ground that material decisions had not been considered. This led to the restoration of the decision of the tribunal. That was in turn appealed to the Court of Appeal, which held, in effect, that the employer's argument was correct. The court took the view that the intention of the statute was that payments made by employers which exceed the statutory redundancy payment should be deducted after the tribunal had decided the amount of the compensatory award.

7.5.2   Redundancy payment

Where a redundancy payment made by the employer exceeds the basic award payable, any excess will go to reduce the compensatory award (see ERA 1996, s 123(7) and *Rushton v Harcros Timber and Building Suppliers Ltd* [1993] IRLR 254).

7.5.3   *Ex gratia* payment

Where the employer has made a prior *ex gratia* payment to the employee, it will be deducted from the compensatory award in so far as it has not been deducted from the basic award (see *Chelsea Football Club & Athletic Co Ltd v Heath* [1981] IRLR 371). Thus, in *Quiring v Hill House International Junior School* (1989) 397 IRLIB 14, an *ex gratia* payment which would have been made in any event was not to be deducted from the compensatory award. It was a non-contractual bonus, which would have been paid at the end of the year. Its payment was therefore not referable to the dismissal.

7.5.4   Payment in lieu of notice

The situation to be examined is where the employer, having dismissed the employee, pays the employee to cover the notice period but without requiring the employee to work. A period of notice is, of course, usually a contractual and statutory right for the employee. Where such payment is made, there have been conflicting decisions as to whether the money paid in lieu of notice should be deducted from the compensatory award. The Court of Appeal held that it should be deducted in *Babcock FATA Ltd v Addison* [1987] IRLR 173. The basis of the decision is that the claimant is to be compensated for his or her immediate loss of wages (see **7.4.1**) from the date of dismissal to the date of hearing. This inevitably includes the period covered by money paid in lieu of notice. If there were no deduction for such money paid in lieu, therefore, there would be double compensation. The deduction may only be made, of course, from that part of the compensatory award which covers the period for which the payment in lieu of notice was made. The rest of the compensatory award remains payable by the employer.

There is a related question. If the employee is given pay in lieu of notice and gets another job and earns wages during the notice period, must credit be given for the sums earned by way of mitigation? In *Babcock*, it was held that such credit need only be given where the full wages for the notice period are in excess of what good industrial relations practice would require.

In *Hardy v Polk (Leeds) Ltd* [2004] IRLR 420, however, the EAT held that an employee who found new employment during what would have been his notice period was required to offset the earnings from the new employment against the compensatory award. The contrary position was adopted by a differently composed EAT in *Voith Turbo Ltd v Stowe* [2005] IRLR 229, which proclaimed the right of employment tribunals to shape good industrial relations practice and declined to follow *Hardy v Polk*. The employee was not required to give credit for his earnings during a period covered by payment in lieu of notice.

Some insight into these conflicts is offered by the Court of Appeal decision in *Burlo v Langley* [2007] IRLR 145. This suggests a limited approach to the question of tribunals applying the concept of good industrial practice in assessing compensation. The original statement in *Norton Tool* that tribunals should do so was limited to those facts, entitling the unfairly dismissed employee to full compensation for the notice period without having to account for earnings during the same period. This does not mean that an employee can claim full notice pay if it does not represent the loss actually incurred. Mummery LJ expressed the hope that these conflicting cases would be resolved soon by a House of Lords' decision.

7.5.5   Failure to mitigate

The employee has a duty to mitigate (see ERA 1996, s 123(4)). Crucially, the employee must take reasonable steps to get another job. In *Gardiner-Hill v Roland Berger Technics Ltd* [1982] IRLR 498, the claimant was dismissed as managing director of the respondent company at age 55. He tried to set up his own business. In the period of six and a half months between dismissal and hearing he earned only £1,500. The tribunal held that this did not represent a reasonable attempt to mitigate his loss. They reduced his compensation by 80 per cent to reflect their finding that he had spent 90 per cent of his time on the new business, rather than looking for alternative employment. But the EAT took the view that his actions were reasonable. In any event they disapproved of the tribunal making a percentage reduction (as is the usual and proper practice in the different situation of contributory fault), saying at p 500:

In order to show a failure to mitigate, it has to be shown that if a particular step had been taken, [the dismissed employee] would, after a particular time, on balance of probabilities have gained employment .... In fixing the amount to be deducted for failure to mitigate, it is necessary for the tribunal to identify what steps should have been taken; the date on which that step would have produced an alternative income and, therefore, to reduce the amount of compensation by the amount of the alternative income which would have been earned.

It is not necessary for dismissed employees to take the first job which comes along. If they wait, they may obtain better-paid employment. But, after a period of unemployment, it will become increasingly reasonable for the employee to accept a job at a lower rate of pay than before. The onus of proof of failure to mitigate is on the employer, in line with the standard common law rule (*Fyfe v Scientific Furnishings Ltd* [1989] ICR 648). The tribunal ought to ask the question: What if the claimant had had no hope of recovering compensation? If he or she had acted reasonably would the job have been accepted (assuming one was on offer)? Or would greater efforts have been taken to chase one? On the latter point, the claimant should be prepared to adduce evidence of efforts to find work, for example, visits to the Job Centre, looking at situations vacant, willingness to retrain, etc. Note that a failure to follow an internal appeals procedure is not a failure to mitigate (*William Muir v Lamb* [1985] IRLR 95 and *Lock v Connell Estate Agents* [1994] IRLR 444).

7.5.6   The *Polkey* principle and the 'no difference rule'

To understand the concept involved in the possible reduction under this head, see the decision in *Polkey v A. E. Dayton Services Ltd* [1988] AC 344.

The situation under examination is where the employment tribunal decides that the employer's decision to dismiss was unfair because of a defect in procedure. What if the employee would or might have been dismissed even after a fair procedure? If the tribunal decides that the employer's failure to follow a fair procedure did not affect the outcome, then it will be right to make no compensatory award at all. If the tribunal is in doubt about whether the employee would have been dismissed, then that doubt 'can be reflected by reducing the normal amount of compensation by a percentage representing the chance that the employee would still have lost his employment' (*per* Lord Bridge of Harwich at p 365, quoting Browne-Wilkinson J in *Sillifant v Powell Duffryn Timber Ltd* [1983] IRLR 91). This involves a prediction, and thus a percentage reduction, rather than considering whether, if the correct procedure had been followed, the dismissal decision might have been within the range of reasonable responses and thus fair (*Hill v Governing Body of Great Tey Primary School* [2013] IRLR 274). A percentage deduction should be identified.

In some cases, then, the application of a *Polkey* reduction will mean that compensation will be reduced to nothing, because the tribunal concludes that taking the proper procedural steps would have had no effect on the outcome—the claimant would still have been dismissed. In other cases, the tribunal reduces compensation by a percentage to reflect its view that dismissal would have been a likely outcome, even if the proper procedure had been followed.

The *Polkey* reduction is, however, limited to cases of procedural unfairness. It cannot apply where the dismissal is held unfair on substantive grounds. In *Steel Stockholders (Birmingham) Ltd v Kirkwood* [1993] IRLR 515, the claimant was dismissed for redundancy, and the tribunal held that his dismissal was unfair because the proper pool of employees from whom those to be made redundant were chosen was the entire workforce, rather than the two radial drillers on backshift duty (of whom Mr Kirkwood was one). The choice of a pool and the adoption of criteria for selection were not, said the EAT, procedural matters, but part of the substance of the decision. The possibility of a *Polkey* reduction therefore did not arise, since 'Lord Bridge's observations ... do not apply where the grounds for holding a dismissal unfair arise from the substance of the decision'.

Similar reasoning was adopted by the Court of Session in the Scottish case of *King and Others v Eaton Ltd (No 2)* [1998] IRLR 686. In that case, it was said that a distinction between unfairness which was 'merely procedural' and that which was 'genuinely substantive' was often of some practical use in deciding whether to apply the 'no difference' rule. If there had been a mere procedural lapse, it might be relatively straightforward to envisage what the course of events would have been if procedures had stayed on track. On the other hand, if what went wrong was more fundamental or 'substantive', and seems to have gone 'to the heart of the matter', it might be difficult to envisage what would have happened in the hypothetical situation of the unfairness not having occurred. In the instant case, there had been no consultation about the method and criteria adopted for redundancy selection. That cast doubt upon the method and criteria themselves. To ask what method and criteria would have been adopted if the employer had consulted was to embark on a sea of speculation. In such a situation, the tribunal was justified in refusing to consider whether the unfair act or omission 'made a difference'. The refusal to make a *'Polkey* reduction' was therefore upheld.

This reduction should, in principle, apply only to the compensatory award (see *Cadbury Ltd v Doddington* [1977] ICR 982). This view is reinforced by the leading judgment of the Lord Chancellor in *Polkey v A. E. Dayton Services Ltd* with which the rest of their Lordships agreed: 'injustice to the employee ... is not a necessary ingredient of an unfair dismissal, although its absence will be important in relation to a compensatory award' (at p 363). In *Taylor and Others v John Webster, Buildings Civil Engineering* [1999] ICR 561, the tribunal decided on a *'Polkey* reduction' of 40 per cent for the whole of the award made to three employees who had been unfairly dismissed, to reflect the chance that they would have been declared redundant anyway. The EAT decided that the 40 per cent reduction should not have been applied to either the basic award or a sum representing payment in lieu of notice, both of which the employees would have received in any event.

For the application of the principle where contributory conduct is also in issue, see *Rao v Civil Aviation Authority* [1994] IRLR 240. In any event it is clear from *Campbell v Dunoon and Cowal Housing Association* [1993] IRLR 497 that any reduction under this head is different from that made for contributory conduct under s 123(6). For the position in relation to the order in which deductions should be made, which can have a significant effect upon the size of the final award, see *Digital Equipment Co Ltd v Clements (No 2)* [1998] IRLR 134, **7.5.1** and **7.5.9**.

7.5.7   Adjustments under Employment Act 2008, s 3

Statutory policy is to encourage employers to carry out sound procedures when undertaking disciplinary action or dismissal and also to encourage employees to make full use of grievance and appeal procedures before bringing matters to the tribunal. The Employment Act 2008 (EA 2008), s 3, introduces s 207A into the Trade Union and Labour Relations (Consolidation) Act 1992 (TULR(C)A 1992), which provides a discretion to the tribunal to adjust an award where there has been unreasonable failure to comply with the standards established in the ACAS Code of Practice on Disciplinary and Grievance Procedures (<http://www.acas.org.uk/index.aspx?articleid=2174>). This permits the award to be increased or decreased by an amount the tribunal considers 'just and equitable' up to 25 per cent, depending on the tribunal's judgment of any procedural failure by either party. Note that this only applies to disciplinary situations and not (for example) ill-health dismissals (*Holmes v Qinetiq Ltd* [2016] IRLR 664).

7.5.8   The statutory maximum

ERA 1996, s 124, lays down that the compensatory award shall be subject to a maximum. The Unfair Dismissal (Variation of the Limit of Compensatory Award) Order

2013 (SI 2013/1949) introduces a new requirement that the award will be the lesser of the traditional maximum sum (currently £80,541 and updated annually on 6 April by statutory instrument) and 52 weeks' gross pay. Dismissals before 6 April 2017 will be subject to the previous maximum of £78,962.

£83682
| Now
v
£86 444

Note that the award is only reduced to this maximum after the appropriate deductions outlined at **7.5.1–7.5.8** have been made. This rule, which can be of considerable practical importance, flows from the wording of s 124(5):

The limit imposed by this section applies to the amount which the employment tribunal would, apart from this section, award in respect of the subject-matter of the complaint after taking into account—

(a) *any payment made by the respondent to the complainant in respect of that matter, and*

(b) *any reduction in the amount of the award required by any enactment or rule of law.*

An example of the difference in practice is provided by *McCarthy v British Insulated Callenders Cables plc* [1985] IRLR 94. The tribunal assessed compensation at £15,820. The employers made an *ex gratia* payment of £1,274. The maximum compensatory award at that time was £7,000. The tribunal reduced the award from £15,820 to £7,000 and then deducted £1,274, to give an award of £5,727. The EAT disagreed. It held the £1,274 should be deducted from £15,820. The resulting figure should then be reduced to £7,000.

It should be noted that the statutory maximum does not apply to certain claims, such as those under ERA 1996, s 103A (protecting whistleblowers). Here, claims may include considerable sums for future loss where the dismissed whistleblower can show serious problems in finding alternative employment (*Small v Shrewsbury & Telford NHS Trust* [2017] EWCA Civ 882, applying principles in the discrimination case *Chagger v Abbey National plc* [2010] IRLR 47, see **8.9.4.2**).

7.5.9 The order of deductions

The cases dealing with the order in which deductions ought to be made from the compensatory award have centred on contributory fault, and are dealt with in **7.5.1**. In accordance with the statute and the case law, the order in respect of the main steps is:

- calculate the total loss;
- deduct payments already made as compensation for dismissal (for example, *ex gratia* payments) other than enhanced redundancy payments;
- deduct sums earned since dismissal or sums which should have been earned if reasonable mitigating steps had been taken;
- deduct a percentage representing the chance that dismissal would have occurred anyway;
- make any adjustments required by EA 2008, s 3, for unreasonable failure to follow the ACAS Code of Practice;
- increase any compensation in respect of the employer's failure to provide written particulars of employment (EA 2002, s 38: see the note below);
- deduct contributory fault percentage;
- deduct any enhanced redundancy payment which exceeds the basic award;
- apply the statutory maximum (currently the lower of £80,541 or 52 weeks' gross pay).

Note: Reference is made in this summary to EA 2002, s 38. That section provides that tribunals must award compensation to an employee where, upon a successful claim being made under any of a number of jurisdictions (including unfair dismissal), it becomes evident that the employer was in breach of his statutory duty to provide full and accurate written particulars of employment. Reference should be made to EA 2002, Sch 5, for a list of the jurisdictions affected. The tribunal may award between two and four weeks' pay (subject to the statutory maximum currently in force) under this provision.

7.5.10 Recoupment

Part of the compensatory award will probably represent wages in respect of a period of unemployment. It is also likely that, in respect of that period, the claimant will have received jobseeker's allowance and/or income support. There is therefore reckoned to be an element of double compensation or unjust enrichment. This is prevented by 'recoupment'—the Government reclaims the allowance for the period from the effective date of termination to the date of the hearing. Current provisions may be found in the Employment Protection (Recoupment of Jobseeker's Allowance and Income Support) Regulations 1996 (SI 1996/2349). There have been conflicting decisions of the EAT as to whether incapacity benefit (which is not subject to recoupment) should be deducted from the compensatory award when the tribunal performs its calculations. In *Hilton International Hotels (UK) Ltd v Faraji* [1994] IRLR 267, the EAT held that incapacity benefit does not fall to be deducted. In *Rubenstein v McGloughlin* [1996] IRLR 557, it was held that one half of the incapacity benefit received should be deducted (cf personal injury awards). However, in *Puglia v C. James & Sons* [1996] IRLR 70, it was held that the amount received in incapacity benefit should be deducted in full. As Mummery J put it in *Puglia*, 'the present position is confused and uncertain'. In *Morgans v Alpha Plus Security Ltd* [2005] IRLR 234, the EAT held that the full amount of incapacity benefit which the claimant had received during the period of the award should be deducted. In coming to this conclusion, the EAT reasoned that there was no power for the tribunal to disregard receipts so that a claimant might recover a sum in excess of actual loss. The inconsistency between the decisions in *Rubinstein* and in *Puglia* would therefore be resolved in favour of *Puglia*. Since 2008 incapacity benefit has been replaced by Employment and Support Allowance.

The portion of the compensatory award which reflects wages for this period is known as the 'prescribed element'. The employment tribunal should, in giving its decision, identify the prescribed element and the period which it covers. The Department of Employment then works out the jobseeker's allowance or income support for that period, and serves a recoupment notice on the parties, specifying the amount reclaimed. The employer must pay this amount to the department and the balance to the employee.

There are limits to the prescribed element, and hence on recoupment:

(a) It applies only to the compensatory award.

(b) It applies only to loss up to the date of hearing, and not to future loss. (The sum awarded for post-tribunal loss will, however, affect *future* entitlement to jobseeker's allowance: Social Security (Unemployment, Sickness and Invalidity Benefit) Regulations 1983 (SI 1983/1598) as amended.)

(c) If compensation is awarded for a shorter period than that between dismissal and hearing, the prescribed element is restricted to that shorter period (*Homan v A1 Bacon Ltd* [1996] ICR 721).

(d) If the prescribed element is reduced by a percentage amount (because of the claimant's contributory conduct or under the *Polkey* principle) then the amount of benefits to be recouped will be reduced by the same percentage.

The phenomenon of recoupment has an important practical effect. Where the case is settled before a decision is made by the tribunal, the recoupment regulations do not apply. Hence both parties can benefit financially by settling before the tribunal makes a decision. This can be a considerable incentive to the parties to settle prior to (or even during) the hearing. It is not unknown for a tribunal, after deciding that the dismissal was unfair, to ask the parties to settle, thereby avoiding the recoupment regulations.

In negotiating a settlement, therefore, you should have the effect of recoupment in mind. For example, if the tribunal is likely to award £5,000, but recoupment will be £1,000, then a settlement over £4,000 will be of benefit to the employee. A settlement under £5,000 will benefit the employer. There is therefore a substantial band of common interest to assist negotiation.

7.6 Interest

An employment tribunal cannot make an award of interest, since the power to do so is reserved to courts of record by the Law Reform (Miscellaneous Provisions) Act 1934, s 3. In *Nelson v British Broadcasting Corporation (No 2)* [1980] ICR 110, it was held that:

- a tribunal is not a court of record; and
- the EAT cannot award interest since it is unable to grant to a claimant a remedy which the tribunal itself could not have granted.

There is an exception to the general rule that a tribunal cannot make an award of interest. It is able (and in some circumstances required) to do so in relation to discrimination cases (see **8.9.4**).

It is also worth noting that there may be circumstances where a tribunal may award an allowance for delayed payment (*Melia v Magna Kansei Ltd* [2006] IRLR 117). This reflects the power to make deductions to reflect the value of early receipt of future losses. The Court of Appeal holds that it is equally just to pay a premium for delayed payment.

The separate question arises of entitlement to interest after the tribunal has made an award. If an award is unpaid 42 days after the tribunal decision, then interest becomes payable, at the rate specified for the time being in accordance with the Judgments Act 1938, s 17 (Employment Tribunals (Interest) Order 1990 (SI 1990/479)).

7.7 Additional award

This comes into play if the employer fails to carry out an order to reinstate or re-engage an employee, where the tribunal has made such an order after a finding of unfair dismissal. It is a form of exemplary or punitive damages, and consists of an additional award of between 26 and 52 weeks' gross pay (subject to a maximum of £489 per week).

The tribunal needs to decide where to fix its award along the spectrum from 26 to 52 weeks. In doing so, it will receive some guidance from *Mabirizi v National Hospital for Nervous Diseases* [1990] ICR 281. In that case, the tribunal fixed the additional award to reflect:

- The employer's culpability in failing to reinstate despite an order to do so.
- Compensation for the employee for her arrears of wages.
- The employee's failure to mitigate her loss by trying to get another job.

The EAT upheld this approach. In particular, the last factor could legitimately be weighed in the balance in determining where in the range of the additional award should be fixed. Note that the approach here is different from the calculation where a failure to mitigate affects the compensatory award. As will be seen from the decision in *Gardiner-Hill v Roland Berger Technics Ltd* [1982] IRLR 498 (see **7.5.5**), the proper approach there is to fix a date after which the claimant's failure to mitigate affected loss. With the additional award, factors are being dealt with which enable a tribunal to fix a point on a spectrum which happens to be calibrated in weeks.

The employer can avoid the payment of an additional award by showing that it was not practicable to comply with the order for reinstatement or re-engagement (see ERA 1996, s 117(4)).

If the employer does reinstate or re-engage the employee, but does not fully comply with the tribunal's order, then the tribunal will make a further compensatory award to compensate the employee for the loss arising from the employer's failure to comply. This provision (see s 117(1)) is rather different from the additional award proper (under s 117(3)), which is not based on loss to the employee.

7.8   Breach of contract claims

We have already seen that the employment tribunal has jurisdiction to award damages of up to £25,000 for breach of contract claims arising on termination (see **5.7.1**). In addition, there may be circumstances where an unfair dismissal also constitutes breach of contract and where the consequences exceed the maximum award available, a claim in the normal courts may be worth pursuing.

In *Edwards v Chesterfield Royal Hospital NHS Foundation Trust/Botham v MoD* [2012] IRLR 129 a surgeon claimed £3.8 million as a result of a dismissal which was in breach of the contractual procedural requirements. At first instance the court applied the principle in *Johnson v Unisys* [2001] IRLR 279 which limits wrongful dismissal compensation to the notice period and prevents breach of the implied term of trust and confidence from overriding the statutory limits on compensation for unfair dismissal. The Court of Appeal allowed the claimant's appeal by distinguishing *Johnson v Unisys* in that it was an express, rather than an implied term which was broken. This entitled the claimant to compensation for all the losses he could show flowed from the breach of the disciplinary process. The Supreme Court (divided four to three) has subsequently held that this was wrong, as to permit recovery of such losses would be contrary to the limitations imposed by Parliament on the statutory unfair dismissal regime. If, however, an employee anticipates a breach of contractual procedures by the employer, an injunction may be available as this does not undermine the statutory approach to compensation.

7.9 Redundancy payments

If the employee is entitled to a redundancy payment (see **6.11**) then the amount of payment is calculated in accordance with ERA 1996, s 162. The calculation is similar (but not identical) to that laid down for the basic award by s 119.

The entitlement is to:

- one and a half weeks' pay for each year's continuous employment during the whole of which the employee was 41 or over;
- one week's pay for each such year during the whole of which the employee was between 22 and 40;
- half a week's pay for each year between 18 and 21.

Note that:

(a) The week's pay is gross, before deduction of tax, etc.

(b) It is the pay to which the employee is contractually entitled. It will cover bonuses, allowances and commission if covered by an express or implied term in the contract. It will not cover, for example, a company car or free accommodation (*Lawrence v Cooklin Kitchen Fitments Ltd* (1966) 1 ITR 398; *Weevsmay Ltd v Kings* [1977] ICR 244).

(c) There is a maximum to the weekly pay which can be reckoned (currently £489). [£508 as of April 2018]

(d) A maximum of 20 years' employment can be counted. Because, for an employee over 41, each year's service triggers off an entitlement to 1½ weeks' pay, the maximum redundancy payment is 30 × £489 = £14,670. [£15 240]

(e) Only complete years are counted.

Figure 7.1 is a ready reckoner produced by the Department for Business, Enterprise & Regulatory Reform for the calculation of redundancy payments. Note that it can also be applied to calculating the basic award in unfair dismissal cases, although you must bear in mind that years below the age of 18 may also be included in the calculation.

7.9.1 Collective redundancy rights: the protective award

Whenever advising on redundancy it is important to recall the requirement in TULR(C)A 1992, ss 188–189, which provides for collective consultation whenever 20 or more employees may be dismissed within a 90-day period. A failure to conduct such consultation gives affected employees a claim for a protective award. This is a punitive award, up to a maximum of 90 days' pay, reduced if the employer can show mitigating circumstances for its default (*GMB v Susie Radin Ltd* [2004] EWCA Civ 180, IRLR 400). It is payable in addition to any claim for a redundancy payment or unfair dismissal compensation. Guidance may be found in *Shields Automotive v Langdon and Brolly* [2013] UKEATS/0059/12/BI, where Langstaff P confirmed the punitive nature of the award and indicated the factors which should influence how it should be calculated.

Statutory redundancy pay table

Age	2	3	4	5	6	7	8	9	10	11	12	13	14	15	16	17	18	19	20
							Service (Years)												
17*	1																		
18	1	1½																	
19	1	1½	2																
20	1	1½	2	2½	-														
21	1	1½	2	2½	3	-													
22	1	1½	2	2½	3	3½	-												
23	1½	2	2½	3	3½	4	4½	-											
24	2	2½	3	3½	4	4½	5	5½	-										
25	2	3	3½	4	4½	5	5½	6	6½	-									
26	2	3	4	4½	5	5½	6	6½	7	7½	-								
27	2	3	4	5	5½	6	6½	7	7½	8	8½	-							
28	2	3	4	5	6	6½	7	7½	8	8½	9	9½	-						
29	2	3	4	5	6	7	7½	8	8½	9	9½	10	10½	-					
30	2	3	4	5	6	7	8	8½	9	9½	10	10½	11	11½	-				
31	2	3	4	5	6	7	8	9	9½	10	10½	11	11½	12	12½	-			
32	2	3	4	5	6	7	8	9	10	10½	11	11½	12	12½	13	13½	-		
33	2	3	4	5	6	7	8	9	10	11	11½	12	12½	13	13½	14	14½	-	
34	2	3	4	5	6	7	8	9	10	11	12	12½	13	13½	14	14½	15	15½	-
35	2	3	4	5	6	7	8	9	10	11	12	13	13½	14	14½	15	15½	16	16½
36	2	3	4	5	6	7	8	9	10	11	12	13	14	14½	15	15½	16	16½	17
37	2	3	4	5	6	7	8	9	10	11	12	13	14	15	15½	16	16½	17	17½
38	2	3	4	5	6	7	8	9	10	11	12	13	14	15	16	16½	17	17½	18
39	2	3	4	5	6	7	8	9	10	11	12	13	14	15	16	17	17½	18	18½
40	2	3	4	5	6	7	8	9	10	11	12	13	14	15	16	17	18	18½	19
41	2	3	4	5	6	7	8	9	10	11	12	13	14	15	16	17	18	19	19½
42	2½	3½	4½	5½	6½	7½	8½	9½	10½	11½	12½	13½	14½	15½	16½	17½	18½	19½	20½
43	3	4	5	6	7	8	9	10	11	12	13	14	15	16	17	18	19	20	21
44	3	4½	5½	6½	7½	8½	9½	10½	11½	12½	13½	14½	15½	16½	17½	18½	19½	20½	21½
45	3	4½	6	7	8	9	10	11	12	13	14	15	16	17	18	19	20	21	22
46	3	4½	6	7½	8½	9½	10½	11½	12½	13½	14½	15½	16½	17½	18½	19½	20½	21½	22½
47	3	4½	6	7½	9	10	11	12	13	14	15	16	17	18	19	20	21	22	23
48	3	4½	6	7½	9	10½	11½	12½	13½	14½	15½	16½	17½	18½	19½	20½	21½	22½	23½
49	3	4½	6	7½	9	10½	12	13	14	15	16	17	18	19	20	21	22	23	24
50	3	4½	6	7½	9	10½	12	13½	14½	15½	16½	17½	18½	19½	20½	21½	22½	23½	24½
51	3	4½	6	7½	9	10½	12	13½	15	16	17	18	19	20	21	22	23	24	25
52	3	4½	6	7½	9	10½	12	13½	15	16½	17½	18½	19½	20½	21½	22½	23½	24½	25½
53	3	4½	6	7½	9	10½	12	13½	15	16½	18	19	20	21	22	23	24	25	26
54	3	4½	6	7½	9	10½	12	13½	15	16½	18	19½	20½	21½	22½	23½	24½	25½	26½
55	3	4½	6	7½	9	10½	12	13½	15	16½	18	19½	21	22	23	24	25	26	27
56	3	4½	6	7½	9	10½	12	13½	15	16½	18	19½	21	22½	23½	24½	25½	26½	27½
57	3	4½	6	7½	9	10½	12	13½	15	16½	18	19½	21	22½	24	25	26	27	28
58	3	4½	6	7½	9	10½	12	13½	15	16½	18	19½	21	22½	24	25½	26½	27½	28½
59	3	4½	6	7½	9	10½	12	13½	15	16½	18	19½	21	22½	24	25½	27	28	29
60	3	4½	6	7½	9	10½	12	13½	15	16½	18	19½	21	22½	24	25½	27	28½	29½
61+	3	4½	6	7½	9	10½	12	13½	15	16½	18	19½	21	22½	24	25½	27	28½	30

Redundancy Payments Offices

Figure 7.1 Statutory redundancy pay table

7.10   Overlapping claims: a review

When an employee's contract of employment has been terminated by his or her employer there are three potential claims: a claim at common law for wrongful dismissal; more commonly a claim under ERA 1996, Pt X for unfair dismissal and a claim under ERA 1996, Pt XI for redundancy (excluding for present purposes the possibility of a claim for unlawful discrimination (see **8.1**), or under ERA 1996, Pt II (see **5.7.4**)).

7.10.1   Claim for wrongful dismissal and unfair dismissal

Both wrongful and unfair dismissal claims can be pursued provided that the employee is qualified to do so.

Note that:

(a) A wrongful dismissal will not always be unfair, and vice versa.

(b) In a case where no notice was given, damages for wrongful dismissal will only be awarded for wages in the lost notice period. Should the dismissal be unfair, compensation will at least extend to a basic award, and wages in the lost notice period and for the future may form part of the compensatory award.

(c) Although the Supreme Court in *Edwards v Chesterfield Royal Hospital NHS Foundation Trust/ Botham v MoD* [2012] IRLR 129 prevents claims for the breach of an employment contract recovering damages beyond what the statutory unfair dismissal regime permits (see **7.8**), *dicta* by Lord Dyson suggest that injunctive or declaratory relief may be available where there is evidence that the employer intends to act in breach of contractually binding procedures.

(d) The limitation period for bringing proceedings for wrongful dismissal in the courts is six years (unless the contract of employment is under seal, in which case it is 12 years). The deadline for an application in the employment tribunal is three months.

(e) It is not permissible to bring a wrongful dismissal claim in the employment tribunal and then seek to recover excess damages over the £25,000 limit through a fresh court action, even where that 'right' is expressly reserved in the ET1 (*Fraser v HLMAD Ltd* [2006] IRLR 687).

(f) The qualifying period for an action for unfair dismissal is generally two years, but any employee can bring an action for breach of contract, regardless of length of service.

The rule against double recovery means that an employee can recover any particular item of loss either as damages for wrongful dismissal, or as part of the compensatory award, but not both. Since damages for wrongful dismissal only cover the period of lost notice, it is only that part of the compensatory award on which the rule against double recovery can bite.

7.10.2   Claim for wrongful dismissal and redundancy

Similar considerations apply to a dismissal which is both in breach of contract, and by reason of redundancy (see **7.10.1**). However, a redundancy payment should not generally be deducted from damages for wrongful dismissal. For a review of the cases, see *Baldwin v British Coal Corporation* [1995] IRLR 139, where, exceptionally, there was a deduction.

7.10.3 Claim for unfair dismissal and redundancy

A situation can arise, as has been indicated, when a dismissal is both unfair and by reason of redundancy. Indeed an employee can pursue a claim for unfair dismissal and a claim for redundancy provided he or she is qualified to do so. The claims can be pursued in the same action in the alternative.

Compensation is likely to be higher for the unfair dismissal claim, which attracts both a basic award (equivalent to a statutory redundancy payment) and a compensatory award. Note that by ERA 1996:

(a) If the dismissal is by reason of redundancy and is unfair, but the right to a redundancy payment has been lost by reason of a suitable offer of renewal of contract or re-engagement being unreasonably refused by the employee, or where the employee is not deemed to be dismissed for the purpose of Pt XI (redundancy payments) of ERA 1996, the amount of the basic award is limited to two weeks' pay for Pt X (unfair dismissal) of ERA 1996 by reason of s 121.

(b) If the dismissal is by reason of redundancy and is unfair, but the right to a redundancy payment is not lost, then the basic award is reduced by the amount of the redundancy payment, whether in pursuance of ERA 1996, Pt XI or otherwise (s 122(4)). Where the basic award of compensation is reduced to nil in this way, any excess redundancy payment will reduce the compensatory award (s 123(7)). This situation should arise only when a non-statutory redundancy payment (contractual or otherwise) has created an excess.

(c) The amount of the basic award may also be reduced as an employment tribunal considers just and equitable if the dismissal was caused or contributed to by an act of the employee, or because he has unreasonably refused an offer of reinstatement, or because of his conduct before the dismissal (s 122). But no reduction in the basic award can be made on the grounds of contributory conduct if the reason for the dismissal was redundancy, unless the dismissal was unfair because of trade union membership or non-membership, in which case the excess over the ordinary basic award may be so reduced.

7.10.4 Claim for unfair dismissal, redundancy and wrongful dismissal

In theory these three claims could be pursued simultaneously as an employee who is dismissed unfairly, and by reason of redundancy, may also be dismissed in breach of the contract of employment thereby giving rise to a common law action for wrongful dismissal. The redundancy payment would reduce the amount of compensation for unfair dismissal which in its turn would reduce the amount of damages for wrongful dismissal. Multiple actions, in general, provide no additional monetary gain.

7.11 Penalties

In addition to paying the compensation as explained in this chapter, a respondent may be required by the tribunal to pay a penalty of between £100 and £5,000 where the breach of the worker's rights has been aggravated (Employment Tribunals Act 1996 s 12A(1), inserted by the Enterprise and Regulatory Reform Act 2013). This is a payment to the Secretary of State, not the claimant. (See **4.10**.)

7.12   Exercises

The table in Figure 7.2 provides a checklist for calculating compensation for unfair dismissal. The first part, headed 'basic award', can also be used for the calculation of redundancy payments.

The table is designed to assist you to make calculations and deductions in the appropriate order (see **7.5.1–7.5.4** and **7.5.9**).

7.12.1   Exercise 1

Using the table calculate the redundancy payment to which Jill, age 49, who has been working for her employer continuously for 17 years, is entitled. Her wages before tax are £300 per week.

7.12.2   Answer 1

(1) Insert '£300' at point A.

(2) The number of weeks' pay to which she is entitled is (8 × 1½) + (9 × 1) = 12 + 9 = 21; therefore insert '21' at point B.

(3) Perform the necessary multiplication (£300 × 21) and insert the answer ('£6,300') at point C.

(4) On the given facts, none of the amounts to be deducted from (a) to (e) applies. Hence insert the same amount ('£6,300') at point E.

7.12.3   Exercise 2

Using the table, calculate the unfair dismissal award to which Jack is entitled. After eight years' service at the age of 37, he was earning £490 gross (£370 net) per week. He received an *ex gratia* payment of £500 from his employer. Despite tremendous efforts he has been unable to get a job between the date of his dismissal (20 November 2017) and the employment tribunal hearing (12 March 2018). The tribunal decides that he was partly to blame for his dismissal, and assesses contributory fault at 50 per cent for the compensatory award (not the basic award). Further findings:

- He is likely to be unemployed for a further three months.
- There are no pension rights or benefits other than wages which need to be taken into account.
- He should receive £350 for loss of statutory protection.
- Any award for the loss of right to long notice would be too speculative.
- He incurred £35 expenses in seeking work.
- The *ex gratia* payment was, on the facts, referable to the basic award.
- Jack received £520 in jobseeker's allowance up to the date of hearing.

7.12.4   Answer 2

Basic award

(1) Insert '£489' at point A.

£

BASIC AWARD

Gross Wages assessed at £ ___*A*___ pw (Max £489)   *C*

for __*B*__ weeks)

Less

a) Unreasonable refusal of reinstatement

b) Conduct before dismissal/contributory fault assessed at ___%   *D*

c) Redundancy payment   *E*

NET BASIC AWARD

COMPENSATORY AWARD

1. PRESCRIBED ELEMENT

Loss of wages including taxable benefits to date of hearing (after allowing for failure to mitigate)

Net average lost wages £ ___*F*___ pw

From ___*G*___ to __*H*__ being a total of ___*I*___ weeks   *J*

and net average lost wages £ _____pw

From _____ to _____ being a total of _____weeks

Less

Earnings/money in lieu of notice   _____

Less

'*Polkey*' reduction assessed at _____ %

Conduct before dismissal/contributory fault assessed at ___*K*___ %   *L*

And/or

Adjustment (+ or -) under Employment Act 2008, s. 3 at _____ %   _____

NET PRESCRIBED ELEMENT   *M*

· ·

OTHER AND CONTINUING LOSS

1) Estimated future loss of wages after allowing for failure to mitigate

   Net average wages £__*N*__ pw for __*P*__ weeks.

2) Loss of other benefits

3) Loss of pension rights   *Q*

4) Loss of statutory protection   *R*

5) Loss of right to long notice

6) Expenses in looking for work   *S*

TOTAL (1-6, where appropriate)   *T*

Less

'*Polkey*' reduction assessed at _____ %

Conduct before dismissal/contributory fault assessed at ___*U*___ %   *V*

Less

Excess of redundancy payment over basic award   _____

Other payments by respondent referable to compensatory award

And/or

Adjustment (+ or -) under Employment Act 2008, s. 3 at _____ %

                                                                  _____

NET OTHER AND CONTINUING LOSS   *W*

· ·

NET COMPENSATORY AWARD (Not to exceed the smaller of £80,541

or one year's gross pay)   *X*

ADDITIONAL AWARD

Where Claimant not reinstated/re-engaged under ET order

Tribunal awards _____ weeks' gross pay at £_____pw   _____

NET BASIC AWARD: £ *Y*

NET COMPENSATORY AWARD: £ *Z*

NET ADDITIONAL AWARD: £ _____

GRAND TOTAL   £_*A A*_ Less recoupment of £ __*B B*__ = £ __*C C*__

Figure 7.2 Unfair dismissal assessment of compensation

(2) Insert '8' at point B.

(3) Perform the necessary multiplication (8 × £489: the statutory limit) and insert the answer ('£3,912') at point C.

(4) Insert '£500' at point D.

(5) Perform the necessary subtraction (£3,912 – £500) and insert the answer ('£3,412') at point E.

Compensatory award

(6) Insert '£370' at point F.

(7) Insert '23.11.17' at point G and '14.3.18' at point H.

(8) Insert '16' at point I.

(9) Perform the necessary multiplication (16 × £370) and insert the answer ('£5,920') at point J.

(10) Insert '50' at point K.

(11) Perform the necessary multiplication (£5,920 × 50%) and insert the answer ('£2,960') at point L.

(12) Perform the necessary subtraction (£5,920 – £2,960) and insert the answer ('£2,960') at point M.

(13) Insert '£370' at point N.

(14) Insert '13' at point P.

(15) Perform the necessary multiplication (13 × £370) and insert the answer ('£4,810') at point Q.

(16) Insert '£350' at point R.

(17) Insert '£35' at point S.

(18) Perform the necessary addition (£4,810 + £350 + £35) and insert the answer ('£5,195') at point T.

(19) Insert '50' at point U.

(20) Perform the necessary multiplication (£5,195 × 50%) and insert the answer ('£2,597.50') at point V.

(21) Perform the necessary subtraction (£5,195 – £2,597.50) and insert the answer ('£2,597.50') at point W.

(22) Perform the necessary addition (£2,960 + £2,597.50) and insert the answer ('£5,557.50') at point X.

(23) Insert '£3,412' at point Y.

(24) Insert '£5,557.50' at point Z.

(25) Perform the necessary addition (£3,412 + £5,557.50) and insert the answer ('£8,969.50') at point AA.

(26) Insert '£520' at point BB.

(27) Perform the necessary subtraction (£8,969.50 – £520) and insert the answer (£8,449.50) at point CC.

7.13   Problems

(A) Alan Aston had been employed by Basil Brushes for 21 years when he was dismissed on 6 April 2018—unfairly, as the tribunal decided. At the date of dismissal he was aged 58, and his gross pay was £500 p.w. (take-home pay £390 p.w.). Calculate his entitlement to a basic award.

(B) Cyril Canning was employed by Deadend Distribution for 11 years as a mechanic. At the time of dismissal he was 44. He was earning £440 p.w. gross (take-home pay £340 p.w.). He was given a total of £1,600 and told that £880 was redundancy pay and £720 was to compensate him for getting the sack. He was given five weeks' notice, which he worked out ending on 31 December 2017. Immediately after he left Deadend, he started a job with Eager Enterprises at £400 p.w. gross (take-home pay £300 p.w.). Any increases in wages at Eager are likely to be in line with the current inflation rate of 2 per cent, as are those at Deadend. Both firms have their annual pay award in October, six months after the tribunal hearing. Neither firm has an occupational pension scheme. At Deadend, he was paid £20 p.w. for 'travel and incidental expenses', not subject to tax. The job at Eager does not require him to travel and there is no such payment. Calculate the size of his award for unfair dismissal, assuming that the tribunal found no contributory fault or conduct to merit a decrease in the award, and that the date of the tribunal hearing was 30 April 2018.

(C) Sheila Sharkey was unfairly dismissed from her job as a personnel officer at the age of 28, after three years' service. Her salary was £29,000 a year (£23,000 after tax). She was given a redundancy payment of £1,674 and worked out her notice until 31 October 2017. On 1 December 2017, she started a new job at £32,000 a year (£25,800 after tax). During the month of November she received jobseeker's allowance totalling £300. At the tribunal hearing on 16 April 2018, it was decided that she had been unfairly dismissed, but that her own conduct was such that both the basic and compensatory awards should be reduced by 25 per cent. Fringe benefits in her new employment are equivalent to those in her old job; the pension scheme is much more attractive. Assess her award for unfair dismissal.

(D) Theresa Tucker was unfairly dismissed from her post as a systems analyst on 25 September 2017. She was then aged 36, and had been employed by the firm for seven years. She was given seven weeks' pay in lieu of notice, and told not to return to work. Her salary was £44,200 gross p.a. (£36,400 take-home). On 27 January 2018 Theresa received an offer of a job from another firm as a computer programmer to start the following Monday at a salary of £36,290 gross p.a. (£26,000 take-home). She refused this in the belief that she could get a job with a better salary and prospects. At the tribunal hearing on 16 April 2018, it was decided that:

(a) She had been unfairly dismissed.

(b) Her own conduct had made a 20 per cent contribution to her dismissal, and this deduction should be made from both the basic and compensatory award.

(c) It would have been reasonable for her to accept the job at a lower salary, and keep looking for another post with equivalent pay to that received in her old job.

(d) She could expect to find another job at a salary comparable to her old one, one year after her dismissal.

(e) Her lost pension rights should be assessed in total at £70,000.

(f) The company car which she had in her old job was worth £2,000 p.a.

(g) She had spent £100 looking for work.

(h) The circumstances were too speculative to make an award for loss of the right to long notice.

During her period of unemployment, Theresa had been in receipt of benefits totalling £1,000. Calculate her award and the prescribed element.

Discrimination in employment

8.1 Unlawful discrimination

The first point to understand is that there is <u>no general law prohibiting discrimination</u>. Indeed, discrimination is the essence of the task of those taking decisions about recruitment, promotion or the offering of training opportunities within employment, provided that the <u>criteria for discrimination</u> are <u>proper</u>: <u>experience</u>, <u>qualifications</u>, <u>motivation,</u> etc. By contrast there are the criteria which are made unlawful by legislation. These are known as protected characteristics and may be found in the Equality Act 2010 (EqA 2010), ss 4–12:

- Age (s 5);
- Disability (s 6);
- Gender reassignment (s 7);
- Marriage and civil partnership (s 8);
- Race (s 9);
- Religion or belief (s 10);
- Sex (s 11);
- Sexual orientation (s 12).

In addition there are provisions elsewhere which provide <u>protection</u> to <u>part-time</u> and <u>fixed-term workers</u>. Although not generally regarded as part of the discrimination legislation they adopt a similar analytical approach:

- Being a part-time worker (Part-Time Workers Regulations 2000 (PTW Regs 2000));
- Being a fixed-term employee (Fixed Term Employees (Prevention of Less Favourable Treatment) Regulations 2002 (FTE Regs 2002)).

This chapter will consider first some general principles and then explain the different protected characteristics. It will then consider the different ways in which unlawful discrimination may occur, before addressing proof and remedies.

Any introduction to discrimination law must address the significant change introduced by the EqA 2010. The previous situation was controlled by several different Acts and statutory instruments. The detailed provisions varied between different protected characteristics and the relevant tests and remedies could be affected by the way in which ET1 forms (see **4.1**) were drafted. Much of this was the result of the fact that many provisions were introduced by regulation under the European Communities Act 1973. Such regulations may only implement EU provisions. Given that, for example, the criteria for race discrimination in UK law were wider than those under EU law, the way in which a claimant identified his or her racial category could impact on which provisions applied. EqA 2010 does away with most of the anomalies which had developed over the years. Any remaining differences are, arguably, intended and are designed to reflect the inherent differences between the protected characteristics.

The basic concepts which underpin the 2010 Act are the same as those to be found in the legislation which it has replaced. In many cases no change is intended. Therefore the case law on the earlier provisions will, in many cases, continue to be relevant. Useful guidance is available from ACAS with three guides on equality at work (<http://www. acas.org.uk/index.aspx?articleid=1363>).

8.1.1   Equal opportunities

The implementation of anti-discrimination legislation must consider the past inequalities which led to the need for such legislation. The Treaty on the Functioning of the European Union (TFEU), art 157(4), permits positive action to address sex discrimination and similar principles are extended by the Directive. EqA 2010 implements these principles by allowing special provision to be made for persons who share a particular protected characteristic who, as a result, suffer a disadvantage, have different needs from others or who are under-represented in a specific activity. Thus, ss 158–159 provide that it will not be unlawful discrimination to take action designed to enable or encourage such persons to overcome or minimise that disadvantage or to participate in that activity. This may involve positive action in recruitment or making training available. Any such action must be proportionate.

The precise line between ensuring equality of opportunity for those suffering from an existing disadvantage and acting unlawfully in the interests of such people can be difficult to draw. What, for example, of a provision which allows an employer, when faced with two equally qualified candidates, to offer the job to the candidate whose gender is under-represented in that job category? The early approach of the European Court of Justice (ECJ) was restrictive. In *Kalanke v Freie Hansestadt Bremen* [1995] IRLR 660, such a provision was held to be contrary to the Directive (Equal Treatment Directive 76/207) then in force. Article 2(4) allowed 'measures to promote equal opportunity for men and women, in particular by removing existing inequalities which affect women's opportunities'. The ECJ perceived the provisions to provide for equality of outcome, not equality of opportunity, and thus held it to fall outside the protection of art 2(4). This decision was widely criticised and its effect has been minimised by the ECJ decision in *Marschall v Land Nordrhein-Westfalen* [1998] IRLR 39. This holds that such practices are not unlawful provided they do not override individual factors which would otherwise give a male candidate precedence. Subsequently a revised TFEU, art 157 (previously Treaty of Rome, arts 141(4) and 119), has authorised Member States to take measures to give specific advantages to compensate for disadvantages in pursuing vocational activities or professional careers. Guidance as to proper approaches may be found in *Re Badeck* [2000] IRLR 432 (ECJ).

Positive discrimination which falls outside these relatively narrow provisions will generally be unlawful (but see **8.7.2**).

8.1.2   Scope of the discrimination legislation

The legislation covers not only acts within employment, but also those preceding it (such as discriminatory behaviour in recruitment decisions and advertising). EqA 2010, s 108, provides explicitly for post-employment discrimination. It also applies to the

Recruitment

For training
Also for work placement
but not volunteering

provision of training opportunities, which are broadly defined. They include 'any form of education or instruction' which includes unpaid internships within the Government Legal Service (*Treasury Solicitor's Department v Chenge* [2007] IRLR 386 (EAT)). The decision suggests that this may apply to any work placement, even if unpaid, and the application to mini-pupillages in barristers' chambers may be of particular interest to readers of this book. This view receives support from the Supreme Court in *X v Mid Sussex Citizens' Advice Bureau* [2013] IRLR 146, which also rules that protection does not extend to volunteering.

Most employment discrimination claims are brought against the employer. The extent of liability is provided for by EqA 2010, s 109 and extends beyond the common law limits to vicarious liability (see *Unite the Union v Nailard* [2016] IRLR 906). The issue of vicarious liability for the discriminatory torts of fellow employees has arisen most commonly in harassment claims and is addressed in **8.5.4**. Moreover, there is nothing in the legislation to prevent a claim being brought against the employee carrying out the discriminatory act, whether or not the employer is also a respondent (*Barlow v Stone* [2012] IRLR 898).

Nothing in the Act prevents a claim by a corporate body (*EAD Solicitors LLP v Abrams* [2015] UKEAT 0054_15_0506).

8.1.3   Influence of EU law

It should already be apparent from the above that European Union (EU) law has had a significant impact on UK employment law in the related areas of discrimination and equal pay. If you are unfamiliar with the way in which European and domestic law interact you should read **Chapter 3**. Note that although the decision to leave the EU will affect the way in which EU provisions apply they will continue to have influence (see **3.4**). The developments of particular importance include the direct application of provisions of the TFEU and (for public sector employees) Directives; the interpretation of UK legislation in the light of EU provisions; the reference of problems (sometimes directly by tribunals) to the ECJ; and the importation of EU concepts into English jurisprudence. These are mostly dealt with in the text, but an example of the last may be seen in *Thomas v Chief Adjudication Officer* [1991] 2 WLR 886. The Court of Appeal applied the Social Security Directive 79/7 to discrimination in statutory invalidity benefits on the basis of the EU principle of proportionality. A discriminatory practice may only be justified if necessary to achieve some other legitimate goal. Moreover, the practice must be proportionate to the goal desired. Thus if the damage done is greater than the good achieved, or if the goal might be achieved in a non-discriminatory way, the practice may not be justified. This is applied equally to domestic legislation (*Mangold v Helm* [2006] IRLR 143) as to the decisions of employers. Moreover, recent UK legislation has adopted this concept, so, in delimiting the 'justification defence' for indirect discrimination EqA 2010, s 19(2)(d) provides: 'A cannot show it to be a proportionate means of achieving a legitimate goal'. Note that where a remedy exists under domestic law it is impermissible to seek the equivalent EU remedy (*Blaik v The Post Office* [1994] IRLR 280). This is only allowed when there is a discrepancy between the UK law and the EU law it purports to enact.

Legitimate and
proportionate

8.2   The protected characteristics

This section will explain the different protected characteristics.

8.2.1   Age

Age discrimination has been prohibited in UK law since 2006. EqA 2010, s 5, refers to persons 'of a particular age group' which means being defined by reference to a particular age or range of ages. This is not very precise. One difficulty is that decision-makers may make stereotypical assumptions about people of a particular age. Two decisions of the CJEU indicate the circumstances where this might be acceptable. In *Wolf v Stadt Frankfurt am Main* [2010] IRLR 244, a maximum recruitment age of 30 was accepted in the case of front-line fire-fighters. However, in *Vital Perez v Ayuntamiento de Oviedo* [2015] IRLR 158, a similar provision in respect of police officers was rejected as disproportionate. *Wolf* was distinguished on the basis of the different physical demands of the two jobs.

Age is unusual amongst the protected characteristics because there is an objective justification defence for direct discrimination (EqA 2010, s 13(2)). This operates differently from the justification defence in indirect discrimination claims (see **8.4.5**). According to the Supreme Court in *Seldon v Clarkson Wright and Jakes* [2012] IRLR 590, the only justifications which might be effective are those of a 'public interest' nature. Examples are achieving fairness between the generations and preserving dignity. Thus a compulsory retirement age may be justified in order to achieve a balanced and diverse workforce. However, there must be a real problem to be addressed. If the workforce is already balanced and diverse that justification will fail. This limitation on the justification defence is required by the terms of the Framework Employment Equality Directive 2000/78 even though the wording of s 13(2) is identical to that in s 19(2)(d) which provides for justification of indirect discrimination (see **8.4.5**). When *Seldon* was remitted for consideration, the EAT held that it was justifiable to choose 65 as a retirement age as opposed to any other age that might have had a less discriminatory effect (*Seldon v Clarkson Wright and Jakes (No 2)* [2014] IRLR 748). The principle in *Seldon* has been applied by the Court of Appeal in *Lockwood v Department of Work and Pensions* [2013] IRLR 941 where an enhanced redundancy payment for older workers was held to be justified by the social policy objective of providing older workers with a financial cushion to help with the greater financial problems they tend to face. It is worth noting the judgment of Rimer LJ, rejecting the EAT view that comparators of a different age could not be used, as their circumstances were so different. This, he said, was like arguing that a black claimant in a race discrimination case could not use white comparators as their circumstances were so different. The argument was circular.

Retirement may also be relevant where indirect age discrimination is claimed. In *Homer v Chief Constable of West Yorkshire Police* [2012] IRLR 601 the claimant could not attain the highest point on his pay scale because he did not have a law degree. As he was in the 60–65 age range he would not be able to complete a degree before his normal retirement date and therefore suffered a 'particular disadvantage'. EAT and CA decisions had held that this was not indirect age discrimination as the disadvantage was the result of his proximity to retirement. In essence it had been argued that he could have obtained a law degree at an earlier stage. The Supreme Court holds, instead, that, *per* Baroness Hale, 'a requirement which works to the comparative disadvantage of a person approaching compulsory retirement age is indirectly discriminatory on grounds of age.' Such a requirement may be justified on wider grounds than those applying to direct age discrimination.

8.2.2 Disability

Disability discrimination has been prohibited in UK law since the Disability Discrimination Act 1995 (DDA 1995). EqA 2010 provides for certain types of discrimination applicable only to disability. These will be addressed in **8.7**.

Definition

EqA 2010, s 6, defines disability as physical or mental impairment which has a substantial and long-term adverse effect on the ability to carry out normal day-to-day activities. Where a job requires specific physical activities (such as heavy lifting) it could be that an injury inhibits an employee from undertaking these tasks while not affecting day-to-day activities in the rest of his life. In *Banaszczyk v Booker Ltd* [2016] IRLR 273, the EAT held that lifting and moving goods at work were 'normal day-to-day activities' and, on that basis, the claimant was disabled. Each element of the s 6 definition requires some elaboration. Detailed Guidance is available from the Office for Disability Issues at <http://odi.dwp.gov.uk/docs/law/ea/ea-guide-2.pdf>.

8.2.2.1 Physical or mental impairment

While the concept of a physical impairment is seen as relatively simple, mental impairment is defined as including learning, psychiatric and psychological impairments. More generally, a claimant, although required to establish the fact of impairment, is under no obligation to establish the cause of the symptoms (*Millar v Inland Revenue Commissioners* [2006] IRLR 112 (CS)) and Guidance, para A3. Thus an obese person who could not show a physical or mental cause of his condition could still be regarded as disabled. The EAT held in *Walker v Sita Information Network Computing Ltd* [2013] All ER (D) 317 (May) that the tribunal should look at the effect of the condition. The CJEU has since confirmed that obesity is not a disability in itself, but if it causes a disability it does not prevent that disability from being protected (*Fag og Arbejde v Kommunernes Landsforening* [2015] IRLR 146).

No burden on claimant to show cause

Thank god →

8.2.2.2 Substantial adverse effect

It is the effect of the impairment on the individual, not the impairment itself, which must be substantial. Moreover, progressive conditions are covered by the legislation. Therefore if an employee suffers less favourable treatment because of contracting, for example, multiple sclerosis, which is currently having a minor effect but the prognosis suggests will have a greater effect, the Act will apply (Sch 1, para 8(1)).

EqA 2010, Sch 1, para 5(1), provides that a person may be treated as disabled in respect of an impairment that would be likely to have a substantial adverse effect were it not successfully controlled by treatment. The House of Lords has held that 'likely' means 'could well happen' rather than 'more probably than not' (*SCA Packaging v Boyle* [2009] UKHL 37).

Tribunals should adopt an inquisitorial approach and focus on what the claimant cannot do (or can do only with difficulty), rather than on what he or she can do. Thus in *Goodwin v The Patent Office* [1999] IRLR 4, a paranoid schizophrenic who heard voices was usually able to carry out his work to a satisfactory standard. The tribunal finding that he did not therefore suffer a substantial adverse effect missed the point. The condition did interrupt his concentration and this should have been the focus of their considerations.

Severe disfigurement will be treated as having a substantial adverse effect on the ability to carry out normal day-to-day activities (EqA 2010, Sch 1, para 3).

8.2.2.3 Long-term effect

This, in effect, means over 12 months or for the rest of the claimant's life. Conditions which may be characterised by periods of remission (such as cancer or multiple sclerosis) are included if recurrences are likely to take place over more than 12 months (Sch 1, para 2(2)).

8.2.2.4 Normal day-to-day activities

The Act does not define normal day-to-day activities but the Guidance, para D3 gives useful examples:

The usual

shopping, reading and writing, having a conversation or using the telephone, watching television, getting washed and dressed, preparing and eating food, carrying out household tasks, walking and travelling by various forms of transport, and taking part in social activities. Normal day-to-day activities can include general work-related activities, and study and education-related activities, such as interacting with colleagues, following instructions, using a computer, driving, carrying out interviews, preparing written documents, and keeping to a timetable or a shift pattern.

8.2.2.5 Addiction and impairment

Don't count

The Equality Act 2010 (Disability) Regulations 2010 (SI 2010/2128) provide (reg 3) that: 'addiction to alcohol, nicotine or any other substance is to be treated as not amounting to an impairment for the purposes of the Act'. However, in *Power v Panasonic UK Ltd* [2003] IRLR 151, a woman who was an alcoholic and suffered from depression was entitled to a remedy. The EAT held that the depression was an impairment and it did not matter how it had arisen. This is reflected in the Guidance, para A7.

8.2.3 Gender reassignment

s7 Gender reassignment

Case law (*P v S and Cornwall County Council* [1996] ICR 795) had extended the interpretation of the Sex Discrimination Act 1975 (SDA 1975) to include discrimination against transsexuals. EqA 2010, s 7(1), protects those who propose to undergo, are undergoing or have undergone gender reassignment. This does not require surgery (see EqA 2010, Explanatory Note 43).

EqA 2010, s 16, makes specific provision for those treated less favourably in terms of absences from work because of gender reassignment.

8.2.4 Marriage and civil partnership

Marital status has been protected since the implementation of SDA 1975. EqA 2010, s 8, extends protection to those in civil partnerships. However, the protection is narrowed to the extent that only being married or having a civil partner is protected. Less favourable treatment on grounds of being engaged, divorced or single appears to be lawful.

Section 8 does not protect those dismissed because they are married to a particular person (*Hawkins v Atex Group* [2012] IRLR 807, where H's husband, as CEO of the respondent, was instructed not to employ family members).

8.2.5 Pregnancy and maternity

Although SDA 1975 had been interpreted as preventing discrimination on grounds of pregnancy (given that only women could become pregnant) the law had become complex because employers who had discriminated against a woman on grounds of pregnancy had sought to defend themselves by claiming that a man who would be absent for a similar period would equally be dismissed. This was rejected by the ECJ in *Dekker v*

Stichting Vormingscentrum voor Jonge Volwassen (VJV-Centrum) Plus (Case 177/88) [1991] IRLR 27, on the argument that dismissal on grounds of pregnancy was direct sex discrimination. This side-stepped the normal need for a comparator. Furthermore, the Employment Rights Act 1996 (ERA 1996), s 99, provides that dismissal for pregnancy, childbirth or maternity leave is automatically unfair, ensuring that no qualifying period is required.

[margin note: Automatically unfair]

A further complication arises from a series of measures designed to assist those with family responsibilities (see **Chapter 9**). Specific rights and remedies may be available in appropriate circumstances.

EqA 2010, s 18(2)–(4), make it unlawful to treat a woman unfavourably because of pregnancy, illness suffered as a result of it, or maternity leave. This terminology avoids the need for a comparator. However, it may be necessary for the claimant to show that the reason for the unfavourable treatment fell within these categories (*Interserve FM Ltd v Tuleikyte* [2017] IRLR 615, where a blanket policy of treating all employees who had been absent without pay for three months as leavers was not inherently discriminatory).

[margin note: No comparator]

8.2.6 Race

The definitions under the Race Relations Act 1976 (RRA 1976) were the subject of considerable litigation and debate throughout the lifetime of that Act. Although EqA 2010, s 9, provides new definitions, much of the earlier case law will still be relevant. Section 9(1) provides that 'race' includes 'colour, nationality and ethnic or national origins'. Persons are protected if they are members of a 'racial group'. Racial groups may be defined broadly or narrowly. Thus 'Asian' may include such smaller groups as 'Pakistani', 'Sikh' or 'Indo-Chinese'. Any may constitute a racial group (s 9(4)).

Where the treatment complained of is because of immigration status (for example, being a vulnerable migrant worker) the Supreme Court has held that this does not constitute discrimination on grounds of nationality (*Taiwo v Olaigbe* and *Onu v Akwiwu* [2016] IRLR 719).

In *Mandla v Lee* [1983] 2 AC 548, the 'no turban' rule case, Sikhs were held to be indistinguishable from other north-west Indians by reference to colour, race, nationality or national origins (the definitions of 'race' then in force). If they were not a racial group then an indirect discrimination claim would fail. The House of Lords held that Sikhs were a racial group defined by their ethnic origins, a broader concept than the purely racial. Lord Fraser held (at p 562):

For a group to constitute an ethnic group in the sense of the Act of 1976, it must, in my opinion, regard itself, and be regarded by others, as a distinct community by virtue of certain characteristics. Some of these characteristics are essential; others are not essential but one or more of them will commonly be found and will help to distinguish the group from the surrounding community. The conditions which appear to me to be essential are these: (1) a long shared history, of which the group is conscious as distinguishing it from other groups, and the memory of which it keeps alive; (2) a cultural tradition of its own, including family and social customs and manners, often but not necessarily associated with religious observance.

His Lordship also identified further relevant, but not essential characteristics.

In *Dawkins v Department of the Environment* [1993] IRLR 284, the Court of Appeal held that Rastafarians are not a racial group because, *inter alia*, their 60 years' existence does not meet Lord Fraser's requirement of a 'long shared history'.

Since 2003 a remedy has been available for those discriminated against on grounds of religion (see now EqA 2010, s 10 (**8.2.7**)).

The application of the concept of 'ethnic origins' means that discrimination on the grounds of caste may, in certain circumstances, fall within the concept of race discrimination (*Chandhok v Tirkey* [2015] IRLR 195 (EAT)).

Whether an individual's racial group is defined by reference to ethnic or national origins may be significant. In *Boyce v British Airways plc* (1997) 581 IRLB 7, the EAT held that the Scottish and English do not have different 'ethnic origins'. A claim based on 'nationality' would not succeed as Scotland, in spite of having devolved powers, is not a nation state. However, a claim based on national origins may succeed (*BBC Scotland v Souster* [2001] IRLR 150 (CS); *British Airways plc v Boyce* [2001] IRLR 157 (CS)). Care, therefore, needs to be taken in drafting the ET1 form to ensure that the claim is founded on the relevant basis.

8.2.7   Religion and belief

Protection for those discriminated against because of their religion or belief was introduced in 2003. EqA 2010, s 10, defines the protection as extending to those having a religious or philosophical belief and also covering those lacking such a belief. Sects or denominations are included, as are beliefs which are not orthodox. In *R (Williamson) v Secretary of State for Employment* [2005] 2 AC 246, at [22], Lord Nicholls explained, in the context of ECHR, art 9: 'religious belief is intensely personal and can easily vary from one individual to another. Each individual is at liberty to hold his own religious beliefs, however irrational or inconsistent they may seem.'

Guidance is provided in *Grainger v Nicholson* [2010] IRLR 4, where the case law on ECHR, art 9 was expressly identified as helpful. Burton J proposed at [24]:

(i)   The belief must be genuinely held.

(ii) It must be a belief and not ... an opinion or viewpoint based on the present state of information available.

(iii) It must be a belief as to a weighty and substantial aspect of human life and behaviour.

(iv) It must attain a certain level of cogency, seriousness, cohesion and importance.

(v)   It must be worthy of respect in a democratic society, be not incompatible with human dignity and not conflict with the fundamental rights of others.

The final criterion denies protection to those whose beliefs are, for example, fascist or racist in nature. This, however, may fail to meet the requirements of European Convention on Human Rights (ECHR), art 11 according to the European Court of Human Rights (ECtHR) judgment in *Redfearn v United Kingdom* [2013] IRLR 51, where the court held: 'Article 11 is applicable not only to persons or associations whose views are favourably received ... but also those whose views offend, shock or disturb.'

Provided the belief meets these standards, there is no preference given to religious as opposed to philosophical beliefs. Thus, in *GMBU v Henderson* [2015] IRLR 451, the EAT held that belief in 'left-wing democratic socialism' was protected.

The impact of ECHR, art 9 has also played a significant part in developing the jurisprudence of this protected characteristic. The ECtHR decision in *Eweida v United Kingdom* [2013] IRLR 231 lays down a number of principles. The decision addressed four related claims. Eweida worked for British Airways in contact with customers. She wished to display a cross, against the employer's uniform policy, and refused to desist

(handwritten margin note: Conflicts)

or to accept alternative employment where she was not in contact with customers. Chaplin was a nurse who also wished to display a cross. The employer's reason for preventing this was based on health and safety grounds and an alternative job was also offered. Ladele was a registrar of births and deaths who objected to conducting civil partnership ceremonies on religious grounds. This conflicted with the employer's code of conduct and equality policy. McFarlane was a relationship counselor for Relate who objected to working with same-sex couples. This, similarly, conflicted with Relate's Equal Opportunities Policy. The ECtHR joined the four cases as they all raised claims that art 9 rights (alone or in conjunction with art 14) were breached. The issues before the court included:

(a) Whether behaviour which was motivated or inspired by religion or belief, but which was not an act of practice of a religion in a generally recognised form, fell within the protection of art 9.

(b) Whether the employers' responses were proportionate in the circumstances.

The first question was answered in the affirmative, a departure from the ruling of the English courts in *Eweida* and *Chaplin*. The court held that Eweida's desire to display a cross was protected. They concluded: 'this is a fundamental right: because a healthy democratic society needs to tolerate and sustain pluralism and diversity; but also because of the value to an individual who has made religion a central tenet of his or her life to be able to communicate that belief to others.' The employer's response was not proportionate as her discreet cross cannot have detracted from the employer's professional image. The court also noted that the employer has subsequently changed their dress code to permit such displays.

(handwritten margin note: All permitted / protected)

Chaplin's desire to display a cross was also protected, but in the circumstances the reasons for preventing it were proportionate, addressing as they did issues of clinical safety.

Ladele's objection to performing civil partnerships was motivated by her religious beliefs and thus protected. However, the court recognised a wide margin of appreciation in member states' striking a balance between conflicting ECHR rights and took the view that the employer (a public authority) had not exceeded that margin.

The court came to a similar view in respect of McFarlane. It is worth noting that the detailed circumstances of each case led to detailed arguments which should be read in order to understand what factors are relevant to the balancing act required by the concept of proportionality.

The Equality and Human Rights Commission has produced guidance on the implications of this decision (<http://www.equalityhumanrights.com/advice-and-guidance/guidance-for-employers/religion-or-belief-new-guidance-february-2013/>).

Article 9(2) limits protection to manifest belief to what is proportionate. EqA 2010, s 10, however, provides no justification for direct discrimination. In *Wasteney v East London NHS Foundation Trust* [2016] IRLR 388, the claimant was disciplined for attempting to convert a junior employee. The EAT held that the discipline was not for manifesting her religion but for the inappropriate manner in which she treated a junior colleague.

The issues relating to clothes that express religious belief have been addressed by the CJEU in two cases, *Achbita v G4S Secure Solutions NV* [2017] IRLR 466 and *Bougnaoui v Micropole SA* [2017] IRLR 447. Both related to dismissals flowing from the wearing of an Islamic headscarf. In *Achbita* the motive was a policy of religious neutrality that could equally affect the wearing of symbols of other religions; in *Bougnaoui* the motive was responding to a customer who objected to the headscarf. The CJEU found that the neutral motive in *Achbita* was not directly but was indirectly discriminatory, and was capable of objective justification if strictly necessary to achieve the goal of neutrality. The motive in *Bougnaoui* was not capable of being a genuine occupational requirement. It is worth noting that *dicta* in *Achbita* suggest that where the employee is in an outward facing role, a prohibition may be easier to justify, and *dicta* in *Bougnaoui* to suggest that where the dress objected to does not cover the face it will be hard for an employer to justify it (at [130]).

Religious motivation may produce a decision on non-religious grounds. The Supreme Court addressed this in *R (E) v Governing Body of JFS* [2010] IRLR 136. A boy was denied access to a school which only admitted those regarded as Jewish by Orthodox standards. He was not recognised as Jewish because his mother was neither born Jewish nor was her conversion in an Orthodox synagogue. The question before the Supreme Court was whether this constituted direct discrimination on grounds of ethnicity (and was thus clearly unlawful) or the application of a religious criterion which was indirectly discriminatory (and was thus capable of objective justification). A majority of the nine-judge court decided on the basis of the grounds for the decision (which were the boy's ethnicity) not the motive for the distinction applied (which was religious).

8.2.8   Sex

The earlier legislation distinguished between discrimination in the terms of the contract of employment, which was covered by the Equal Pay Act 1970 (EqPA 1970), and other discrimination, which was covered by SDA 1975. This distinction is preserved in EqA 2010. Section 11 unsurprisingly defines persons with the protected characteristic of sex as men and women. Part 5, Chapter 3 (ss 64–80) is headed 'Equality of terms' and addresses gender discrimination in the terms of the contract of employment. That is addressed in **Chapter 10**.

8.2.9   Sexual orientation

Protection was introduced in 2003 and is now provided in EqA 2010, s 12. It extends to those discriminated against because of their orientation to persons of the same, the opposite or either sex.

8.3   Direct discrimination

Direct discrimination is defined by EqA 2010, s 13(1).

A person (A) discriminates against another (B) if, because of a protected characteristic, A treats B less favourably than A treats or would treat others.

8.3.1   Treats less favourably

This requires a comparison. It is insufficient for the claimant to show that he or she has been treated unfavourably. The House of Lords has pointed out in *Zafar v Glasgow City Council* [1998] IRLR 36, a claim under RRA 1976, that in order for an inference of discrimination to be drawn there must be a comparison with the treatment of others not of the claimant's race. Mere unreasonable treatment of an employee who happens to belong to an ethnic minority is insufficient. However, the comparison may be with a hypothetical comparator.

Section 23 provides that when making comparisons there should be no material difference between the circumstances relating to each. Where no such real comparator exists it will be a matter of drawing inferences from the treatment of others in whose cases there may be material differences in order to decide how a hypothetical comparator with no material differences would have been treated. For further consideration of the process of drawing inferences, see **8.8.2.3**.

If less favourable treatment is established there is generally no basis for the employer to attempt to justify the action. It is unlawful. However, s 13(2) provides that where the protected characteristic is age there is a justification defence 'if A can show A's treatment of B to be a proportionate means of achieving a legitimate aim'.

The legislation clarifies certain issues. Thus, s 13(5) provides that where the protected characteristic is race, less favourable treatment includes segregation. Although there is no reference to segregation on grounds of sex the CA has held that segregation of the sexes in an Islamic school was direct discrimination (*HM Inspector of Education v Interim Executive Board of Al-Hijrah School* [2017] EWCA Civ 1426). The proper analysis is to consider whether the policy caused detriment to individuals, not to compare each sex as a group. Gloster LJ (dissenting) held that the policy imposed a particular detriment on female pupils. Section 13(6)(a) provides that where the protected characteristic is sex, less favourable treatment because of breast-feeding is included. In addition, protection is given to employers who provide lawful assistance to pregnant women and the disabled. Section 13(3) prevents a non-disabled person from claiming discrimination because of the more favourable treatment of disabled persons. Section 13(6)(b) prevents a man from claiming sex discrimination because of special treatment afforded to a woman in connection with pregnancy or childbirth. Although the Act says that 'no account' is to be taken of such treatment, the EAT has held that to receive this protection it should be proportionate. In *Eversheds Legal Services Ltd v De Belin* [2011] IRLR 448, the claimant was one of two employees being considered for redundancy. The other was a woman on maternity leave. She was given a notional 100 per cent score on one criterion which could not be measured in her absence. This resulted in her receiving an overall score higher than that of the claimant, who succeeded in his discrimination claim.

Examples of cases which have helped to explain what is meant by less favourable treatment arise from the earlier legislation. These often turn on an analysis of the meaning of 'detriment', the applicable concept in the SDA 1975 and the RRA 1976.

In *Schmidt v Austicks Bookshops Ltd* [1978] ICR 85 (EAT), a rule prohibiting women from wearing trousers did not amount to a detriment as men were also subject to restriction (although different) on what they could wear. It was emphasised that employers were entitled to a large degree of control in the appearance of their staff, particularly where they were in contact with the public. In *Smith v Safeway* [1996] IRLR 456, the Court of Appeal extended this to hair length and tattoos as well as clothing, in spite of an argument that such a provision intruded into the claimant's daily life. The standards applying to men and women should, however, be comparable even if different. Nevertheless, in *Burrett v West Birmingham Health Authority* [1994] IRLR 7, where a nurse was disciplined for refusing to wear a cap which served no practical purpose and which male nurses were not required to wear, there was held to be no less favourable treatment.

In *Jeremiah v Ministry of Defence* [1976] IRLR 436, the Court of Appeal held that requiring a man to work in a dirty environment when women were not so required constituted a detriment to him. The employer's objection that they made an extra payment for working in the 'obnoxious' conditions was no defence. No employer can buy the right to discriminate.

In the area of race, the EAT held, in *BL Cars Ltd v Brown* [1983] ICR 143, that issuing instructions to make special checks on black employees was sufficient to constitute a 'detriment' even before those instructions had been implemented.

In *De Souza v Automobile Association* [1986] ICR 514, the Court of Appeal held that a racial insult by itself was not actionable as in itself it did not constitute sufficient detriment. It would need to be sufficient to damage the circumstances in which the employee worked in order for it to do so. The test of whether it would do this or not was whether a reasonable worker might take the view that he had been disadvantaged in his working circumstances. An example of a case where a single remark was sufficient to constitute detriment is *In situ Cleaning Co Ltd v Heads* [1995] IRLR 4. Here a sexual remark in the presence of others caused rage, humiliation and genuine embarrassment. This was sufficient to constitute a detriment. EqA 2010, s 26, provides for a specific claim of harassment (see **8.5**).

8.3.2 Because of a protected characteristic

It is not necessary for the less favourable treatment to be exclusively because of the protected characteristic. It is sufficient for it to be a factor. In *Igen v Wong* [2005] IRLR 258, the Court of Appeal held that the respondent would only avoid liability if 'the treatment was in no sense whatsoever' on the protected ground. However, they then introduced a *de minimis* concept by adding: 'We find it hard to believe that the principle of equal treatment would be breached by the merely trivial.' This leaves some uncertainty. Where a protected characteristic has been an insignificant, but real, element in a less favourable decision it may be best resolved by the tribunal finding discrimination but reducing compensation by the likelihood that the action would have been taken anyway (*Chagger v Abbey National* [2010] IRLR 47 (CA)).

8.3.2.1 Motive

The wording of the Act brings a degree of objectivity to the test. There has been considerable judicial debate as to the role of motive (conscious or subconscious) in decisions which have a discriminatory effect. In the House of Lords judgment in *Nagarajan v London Regional Transport* [2000] 1 AC 501, it was held that the claimant was not required to show a motive consciously connected with the protected characteristic. Although this was a victimisation case (see **8.6**), Lord Steyn indicated that a similar approach should be adopted to direct discrimination cases. If motive is not what is intended by 'because of' what is? The dominant analysis has been the 'but for' test. In *James v Eastleigh Borough Council* [1990] 2 AC 751, entry to public swimming pools was available free to persons of pensionable age. Mr J and his wife were both 61 but only he had to pay. Even though the council's motive was to assist pensioners, not to discriminate on grounds of sex, the House of Lords applied the 'but for' test and found in Mr James's favour. Proposing a benign motive was more recently rejected by the Supreme Court in *R (E) v Governing Body of JFS* [2009] UKSC 15. Here, being an Orthodox Jew was an entry requirement for a school and this was held to be a racial characteristic (under RRA 1976). The school argued that its motivation was religious, not racial, but a majority of 5–4 rejected this defence.

While it appears established that a 'benign motive' defence is not available, motive may still be relevant. In *Shamoon v Chief Constable of the RUC* [2003] UKHL 11, their

Lordships appeared to consider the subjective view of the alleged discriminator. They did not mention the 'but for' test, nor *James v Eastleigh* in their opinions. In *R (E) v Governing Body of JFS* [2009] UKSC 15 a distinction was drawn between 'obvious' cases, where no enquiry into motive was necessary, and others where it might be appropriate. Lady Hale gave the example of an employer deciding between job applicants on the criterion of 'merit'. Here it was necessary to assess the motive of the defendant, recognising that bias on a protected ground might be conscious or subconscious.

Motive may be relevant in a different way. Where a manager dismisses an employee on the basis of a discriminatorily motivated independent report, the employer will not be liable, according to the Court of Appeal in *CLFIS (UK) Ltd v Reynolds* [2015] IRLR 562. Liability would arise where the discriminatory report came from an employee or another person for whom the employer had responsibility.

8.3.2.2 The 'bastard' defence

Some respondents have sought to defend a claim of less favourable treatment by claiming that a hypothetical comparator without the protected characteristic would have been treated equally unfairly. The scope of this defence has been limited by the decision in *Eagle Place Services Ltd v Rudd* [2010] IRLR 486, where the EAT held:

> It is simply not open to the respondent to say that it has not discriminated against the claimant because it would have behaved equally unreasonably in dismissing the comparator. It is unreasonable to suppose that it in fact would have dismissed the comparator for what amounts to an irrational reason.

8.3.2.3 Associative and perceived discrimination

Problems have arisen where a person has suffered discrimination because they are associated with a person who has a protected characteristic or because they were perceived to have a protected characteristic, but in fact, did not.

In *EBR Attridge Law LLP v Coleman (No 2)* [2010] IRLR 10, the EAT, applying the ECJ decision in the same case (*Coleman v Attridge Law* [2008] IRLR 722) held that it was possible to read the DDA 1995 in such a way that discrimination against a person because they cared for a disabled person was prohibited. The use of 'because of' in EqA 2010, s 13, is designed to prohibit such associative discrimination in respect of all the protected characteristics.

In *English v Thomas Sanderson* [2009] IRLR 206, the claimant suffered homophobic abuse because he had gone to a boarding school and then lived in Brighton, even though his harassers knew that he was not gay. This was held to fall within the language of the earlier regulations 'on grounds of sexual orientation' and will equally fall within the wording of s 13.

The concept of associative discrimination had enabled the courts to establish that a company may bring a discrimination claim. In *EAD Solicitors v Abrams* [2015] IRLR 978 the claimant provided his work through a company for tax reasons. The company was able to bring an age discrimination claim when he was asked to retire at the age of 62.

The EHRC Equality Act Code of Practice on Employment gives useful examples of associative and perceived discrimination (<http://www.equalityhumanrights.com/sites/default/files/employercode.pdf>).

> A manager treats a worker (who is heterosexual) less favourably because she has been seen out with a person who is gay. This could be direct sexual orientation discrimination against the worker because of her association with this person [para 3.19].

An employer rejects a job application form from a white woman whom he wrongly thinks is black, because the applicant has an African-sounding name. This would constitute direct race discrimination based on the employer's mistaken perception [para 3.21].

8.3.3   Occupational requirements

EqA 2010, Sch 9, provides a defence to allegations of direct discrimination where the discriminatory treatment arises from an occupational requirement. Paragraph 1(1) provides:

> *(1) A person (A) does not contravene [a direct discrimination provision] by applying in relation to work a requirement to have a particular protected characteristic, if A shows that, having regard to the nature or context of the work—*
>
>> *(a) it is an occupational requirement,*
>>
>> *(b) the application of the requirement is a proportionate means of achieving a legitimate aim, and*
>>
>> *(c) the person to whom A applies the requirement does not meet it (or A has reasonable grounds for not being satisfied that the person meets it).*

This represents a change from the earlier legislation which had introduced the concept of 'Genuine Occupational Qualification' (GOQ) and had identified a non-expandable list of GOQs for each protected characteristic. The old GOQs still probably represent the most likely situations in which this defence will be raised although the new wording enables courts to recognise new situations as well. Examples will be grouped under the relevant protected characteristics.

8.3.3.1   Sex, pregnancy and maternity

SDA 1975, s 7(2)(a), provided a GOQ for physiology or authenticity in dramatic entertainment. This would cover choice of actors of a specific gender or, for example, requiring a woman for a job as a wet-nurse.

Section 7(2)(b) enabled the choice of a man or woman for reasons of privacy or decency. Thus where physical contact was required (for example, in fitting clothes) or people might be in a state of undress or using sanitary facilities (for example, changing-rooms or lavatories) an employee of the appropriate gender might be chosen.

Section 7(2)(ba) allowed a GOQ where the job involved working in a private home, which could cover domestic servants or personal carers.

Section 7(2)(c) covered communal accommodation and s 7(2)(d) covered work in single-sex establishments.

Section 7(2)(e) provided a GOQ where personal services could most effectively be provided by a woman or a man.

Section 7(2)(g) allowed a GOQ where an employee was to work in a country whose laws or customs were such that the duties could not be effectively performed by a woman. This may now be questioned as a concession to discrimination and would arguably only be successful as a defence where the laws rather than the customs of that country would prevent the employment.

There was also a GOQ defence designed to enable the employment of husband and wife teams (such as the matron and bursar of a boarding school). As EqA 2010, s 13(4), limits protection to those who are married or in a civil partnership (and does not extend to those who are single) this GOQ would appear to be redundant.

8.3.3.2   Race

RRA 1976, s 5(2)(a)–(c), provided that authenticity could be a GOQ in three situations: dramatic performances or entertainment, modelling or catering. The third of these was designed to allow the employment of Indian waiters in Indian restaurants, etc., and may be hard to justify under Sch 9, para 1(1)(b).

Section 5(2)(d) applied to those employed to provide personal services. This should not be allowed to justify customer preference on racial grounds. If, however, there is a genuine reason why a person of a specific ethnicity is required this may be legitimate. The ECHR Code of Practice suggests (at 13.9) that where a health authority wishes to encourage older members of the Somali community to use health services it would be acceptable to employ a person of Somali origins as 'it involves visiting elderly people in their homes and it is necessary for the post-holder to have a good knowledge of the culture and language of the potential clients'.

8.3.3.3   Religion or belief

EqA 2010, Sch 9, para 3, largely re-enacts earlier provisions enabling a person with an ethos based on religion or belief to apply a requirement that workers have a particular religion or belief subject to the usual limitation that it be an occupational requirement and a proportionate means of achieving a legitimate aim. The extent to which this defence is available has been limited by the EAT decision in *Glasgow City Council v McNab* [2007] IRLR 476, where a teacher employed by the local education authority in a Catholic school was denied promotion because he was not a Catholic. The court held that the education authority had no business having an 'ethos based on religion' and could not, therefore, rely on this defence. Had an individual Catholic school been the employer, a different conclusion might have been reached.

8.3.3.4   Application of the occupational requirement defence

8.3.3.1–8.3.3.3 give examples of earlier provisions and some indication of the way the courts have approached them. It is notable that the new provisions extend the defence to dismissals (except in sex discrimination cases). Note also that the Directives which this is intended to implement require the occupational requirement to be 'genuine and determining' (see, for example, Directive 2000/78/EC, art 4(1)). It is arguable that this is the proper test to be applied when interpreting 'occupational requirement'.

The general terms of Sch 9, para 1, mean that new occupational requirements may be argued before the courts and tribunals. For example, in *Amnesty International v Ahmed* [2009] IRLR 884, a Sudanese job applicant was denied a job as a researcher for Sudan. The reason was that the employer feared for her safety and perceived impartiality as she came from the north of the country. This might prevent her from working effectively. However, under the legislation then in force this was only a GOQ under the SDA 1975, not the RRA 1976, and the defence failed. It might be that these circumstances would provide the employer with a defence under the new provisions.

The changes in the law have the effect of extending the defence available to the employer (for example, in terms of some dismissals and in allowing new occupational requirements to be identified). It is arguable, that, in race cases at least, this offends against the Race Directive 2000/43/EC, art 6(2), which prohibits reduction in the level of protection already afforded by Member States. Those representing claimants in race cases may consider pleading this argument.

8.3.4   Dual discrimination

Where, in the past, an individual suffered discrimination on more than one ground, it could be necessary to claim both as separate grounds, leading to difficulties where what was really complained of was the combined effect of both. EqA 2010, s 14, provides for a claim of dual discrimination, combining claims of direct discrimination in relation to two separate protected characteristics. There appears to be no provision for combining more than two protected characteristics, nor is action which is *indirectly* discriminatory as a result of its impact on two separate characteristics covered. At the time of writing s 14 is yet to be implemented.

Case law may be achieving a similar and broader result. In *Ministry of Defence v De Bique* [2010] IRLR 471, the claimant was a female single parent soldier from the Caribbean who was disciplined for attendance problems during her child's illness. She proposed to resolve this by bringing her half-sister to the UK, but this was frustrated through UK visa requirements. The disciplinary action against her was based on two provisions, criteria or practices: that of being available for duty 24/7 and that relating to immigration status. Together these were indirectly discriminatory on grounds of race and sex. Cox J provided the following guidance:

> [T]he nature of discrimination is such that it cannot always be sensibly compartmentalised into discrete categories. Whilst some complainants will raise issues relating to only one or other of the prohibited grounds, attempts to view others as raising only one form of discrimination …will result in an inadequate understanding and assessment of the complainant's true disadvantage. Discrimination is often a multi-faceted experience.

For precedents relevant to direct discrimination, see **11.7** and **11.8**.

8.4   Indirect discrimination

This limb of the statutory provisions is designed to deal with situations where discrimination is arguably unintentional. It prohibits, in effect, requirements which are made of everyone, but which have a disproportionate effect on people with a particular protected characteristic. The provisions appear in EqA 2010, s 19, and apply to all the protected characteristics except pregnancy and maternity. Section 19 provides:

(1) *A person (A) discriminates against another (B) if A applies to B a provision, criterion or practice which is discriminatory in relation to a relevant protected characteristic of B's.*

(2) *For the purposes of subsection (1), a provision, criterion or practice is discriminatory in relation to a relevant protected characteristic of B's if—*

   (a) *A applies, or would apply, it to persons with whom B does not share the characteristic,*

   (b) *it puts, or would put, persons with whom B shares the characteristic at a particular disadvantage when compared with persons with whom B does not share it,*

   (c) *it puts, or would put, B at that disadvantage,*

   (d) *A cannot show it to be a proportionate means of achieving a legitimate aim.*

8.4.1   Significant changes

This wording is designed to overcome problems with the earlier provisions. These originally required claimants to show that they had a 'requirement or condition' applied to them. This had been interpreted narrowly (see *Perera v Civil Service Commission (No 2)* [1983] ICR 428 (CA)) as something which *must be* complied with. This was often hard for claimants (who had nevertheless suffered a detriment) to show. The new definition (provision, criterion or practice (PCP)) was then introduced in respect of certain protected characteristics, which left a complicated mix depending on the protected characteristic engaged.

A second difficulty for claimants was that they had to show that they 'cannot comply' with the condition or requirement. Although this was generally interpreted 'can in practice' rather than 'can physically' (*Price v Civil Service Commission (No 2)* [1978] IRLR 3) narrower interpretations were sometimes used (*Turner v Labour Party* [1987] IRLR 101) leading to considerable uncertainty. Amended legislation imposed the lower hurdle of showing that the claimant has been put at a disadvantage, but there was a similar complicated mix of provisions.

Another change which has now been applied to all protected characteristics is the wording of the 'justifiability' defence in s 19(2)(d). Earlier versions of the legislation had used the term 'justifiable' which had led to different interpretations. The new wording, applying the concept of proportionality, requires an employer to show that not only is there a legitimate goal to be achieved by the PCP which has the indirectly discriminatory effect, but that the goal could not be achieved by less discriminatory action.

The new provisions apply the same test to all relevant protected characteristics (indicated in s 19(3)), thus remedying the complications caused by diverse provisions. These amendments mean that earlier case law establishing the meaning of 'condition or requirement' will no longer be relevant. However, other case law continues to be relevant as it indicates the ways in which this legislation may be used in practice and the shift from 'justifiable' to 'proportionate' reflects the ECJ case law in this area. (For discussion of the significance of this, see **8.4.5.1.**)

8.4.2 Applying s 19

The principle underlying indirect discrimination is exemplified in the classic case of *Price v Civil Service Commission (No 2)* [1978] IRLR 3, brought under SDA 1975. Here the requirement was that applicants for posts on the executive officer grade should be between 17½ and 28 years of age. Mrs Price was a 36-year-old woman. She argued, with statistical support, that a considerable proportion of women were not available for work between those ages as they were involved with the bearing and rearing of children. This meant that a considerably smaller proportion of women than men could comply with the requirement. This argument was accepted, thus satisfying SDA 1975, s 1(1)(b)(i). The Civil Service Commission could not justify it (it was merely convenient). This satisfied s 1(1)(b)(ii). As Mrs Price was aged 36 she could not comply with it, suffered a detriment thereby and thus satisfied s 1(1)(b)(iii). By satisfying all three parts of the statutory test, she won her indirect discrimination claim.

This case indicates how the indirect discrimination provisions may enable a claim to be brought in cases where the direct discrimination (if any) appears to be on what was then a lawful ground, in this case age.

A useful checklist considering the steps necessary to show disproportionate impact between groups is to be found in the SDA 1975 case of *Jones v Chief Adjudication Officer* [1990] IRLR 533. Mustill LJ's list is:

- identify the criterion for selection;

- identify the relevant population, comprising all those who satisfy all the other criteria for selection;
- divide the relevant population into groups representing those who satisfy the criterion and those who do not;
- predict statistically what proportion of each group should consist of women;
- ascertain what are the actual male–female balances in the two groups;
- compare the actual with the predicted balances;
- if women are found to be under-represented in the first group and over-represented in the second, it is proved that the criterion is discriminatory.

This checklist may, with appropriate adjustments, be applied to other indirect discrimination cases.

Claimants who can satisfy s 19(2)(b) in this way must, in order to satisfy s 19(2)(c), also show that the PCP puts them at a disadvantage. It is not necessary to show why (*Essop v Home Office* (*UK Border Agency*) and *Naeem v Secretary of State for Justice* [2017] IRLR 558). The Supreme Court overturns the earlier decision of the Court of Appeal, pointing out that the legislation merely requires a causal connection between the PCP and the disadvantage suffered by the claimant and the group sharing the protected characteristic. Naturally, if the claimant can demonstrate the reason why the PCP causes the disadvantage, the causal connection will be easier to prove, but it is not a legal requirement.

8.4.3 The impact of the concept of indirect discrimination

It is not only the actions of employers which have been challenged by the introduction of the concept of indirect discrimination. Legislation has also been questioned (see *R v Secretary of State for Employment, ex p Equal Opportunities Commission* [1995] AC 1, at **3.4.3.1**) as a result of the incorporation of the concept into EU law. Thus the removal of the original requirement for 16 hours' work weekly for unfair dismissal and other claims resulted from the indirectly discriminatory effect of the provision (and see the tribunal decision in *Nash v Mash/Roe Group* [1998] IRLR 168). Similarly, in *R v Secretary of State for Employment, ex p Seymour-Smith and Perez* [2000] IRLR 263, the House of Lords held that the former two-year requirement for unfair dismissal claims was indirectly discriminatory. Although the proportionate difference between men and women was not great (77.4 per cent of men and 68.9 per cent of women were able to comply in 1985, when the two-year requirement was introduced) it was persistent over a long period. Their Lordships relied on *dicta* from the ECJ in the same case ([1999] IRLR 253).

In R (*on the application of UNISON) v The Lord Chancellor* [2017] UKSC 51, Lady Hale, in considering whether the employment tribunal fees regime in force from 2013 until 26 July 2017 constituted indirect discrimination against women, drew two conclusions. Evidence that a higher proportion of Type B claimants than Type A claimants were women showed a disparate impact on women as they had a higher fee to pay. This was indirectly discriminatory and the Lord Chancellor had failed to justify it. By contrast, the argument that discrimination cases being categorised as Type B claims was indirectly discriminatory against those with a protected characteristic failed, as they were treated identically to (for example) men bringing unfair dismissal claims.

8.4.4   With whom should the claimant's group be compared?

It may be appropriate to choose a 'pool' for comparison which is not the total population. Thus, in *Price v Civil Service Commission (No 2)* [1978] IRLR 3, it was accepted that the appropriate pool for comparison would be qualified men and women as opposed to the total population of men and women.

An example of an inappropriate selection of a pool can be seen in *R v Secretary of State for Education, ex p Schaffter* [1987] IRLR 53. Here the alleged indirect discrimination was the payment of a grant to students who were single parents but had been married, but not to those who had never been married. (As SDA 1975, s 51, bars such claims the case was brought under the Equal Treatment Directive, which prohibits practices which have a disproportionate impact on one sex, and which may be directly enforced against State bodies: *Marshall v Southampton & South West Hampshire Area Health Authority (Teaching)* [1986] ECR 723.) Evidence showed that 20 per cent of single parents, regardless of sex, had never married and were thus ineligible, and that 80 per cent of single parents are women. The claimant argued that four times as many female lone parents as male lone parents were ineligible.

The Secretary of State argued that as the proportion of female lone parents who had never been married was the same as the proportion of male lone parents who had never been married, there was no adverse impact. Thus the case turned on the selection of the pool for comparison. The claimant sought a pool including all students with dependent children claiming grants. The Secretary of State sought a pool including only lone parents who had never been married.

Schiemann J accepted that to reduce the pool for comparison to a very small size, as proposed by the Secretary of State, had the effect of incorporating an act of discrimination into the definition. He concluded that the pool should be large enough to include all students with dependent children claiming grants. Using this larger pool meant indirect discrimination was clearly established.

The nature of the condition may influence what pool is appropriate. Thus, in *Greater Manchester Police Authority v Lea* [1990] IRLR 372, no one with an occupational pension would be considered for a job as a school crossing attendant. As many potential candidates would decide not to apply when they discovered the exclusionary condition (which affected more women than men) the general population was a more appropriate pool than actual applicants. The EAT also indicated that once the claimant showed a reasonable statistical argument for a disproportionate impact the employer had to present a persuasive rebuttal. It was insufficient merely to allege an inadequacy in the statistics (see further **8.8.1**).

8.4.5   A proportionate means of achieving a legitimate response

8.4.5.1   Proportionality

The new basis for a defence if the employer can show the provision, criterion or practice to be a proportionate means of achieving a legitimate aim reflects EU jurisprudence and implements an approach which has increasingly been informing judicial decisions on the old wording. Interpretation of the provisions is complicated by the fact that the adoption of 'proportionate' does not reflect the wording of the Framework Directive these provisions are designed to apply. The Directive had used the term 'appropriate and necessary'. The explanatory memorandum explained that this is because 'necessary' in the UK case law is interpreted very strictly and that 'proportionality' incorporates the concept of necessity. If this is correct it involves a reduction in the protection on grounds of race, where the stricter requirement for justification has been consistently applied.

Some guidance from the earlier case law may be helpful. Early cases placed the test close to necessity (see *Steel v Union of Post Office Workers* [1978] ICR 181, where Phillips J said that a practice could not be justifiable unless its discriminatory effect is justified by the need—not the convenience—of the business or enterprise). Subsequent decisions moved away from this strict requirement, allowing employers more scope for raising a defence. Thus, in *Panesar v Nestlé Co Ltd* the test of justification was held to be 'reasonable commercial necessity', and not 'absolute necessity'.

In *Ojutiku v Manpower Services Commission* [1982] ICR 661, the MSC denied training opportunities to people without managerial experience. Evidence showed that this discriminated against black applicants. The MSC's defence was that it was justifiable. This was accepted by the Court of Appeal. Kerr LJ said at p 670: 'I decline to put any gloss on the word "justifiable" … except that I would say that it clearly applies a lower standard than the word "necessary".' There should be 'sound and tolerable' reasons.

The Court of Appeal has provided guidance on interpretation in *Allen v GMB* [2008] IRLR 690. Here a trade union was negotiating a number of equal pay claims with a large local authority. Financial constraints meant that insistence on full compensation could cause job losses among other union members and put at risk pay protection arrangements for the (predominantly male) members whose jobs had been downgraded as part of an equalising process. The union entered an agreement which arguably failed to give the (female) equal pay claimants their full entitlement. In doing so it was held that they were indirectly discriminating against those women but were doing so in order to pursue a legitimate aim: to do a deal which was fair to all their members. However, this was not sufficient. The means used had then to be tested for proportionality. The court endorsed the tribunal's view that the means here were not proportionate.

A useful example where indirect discrimination was held to be proportionate may be seen in *Azmi v Kirklees Metropolitan Borough Council* [2007] IRLR 484, where the claimant was suspended for refusing to remove a *niqab* which covered her face apart from her eyes. Although the school's policy was potentially indirectly discriminatory it was proportionate. The employer permitted the *niqab* when she was not actively teaching and had genuine concerns about the lack of non-verbal signals required for effective communication between teacher and pupil.

Any attempt at justifying indirect discrimination must be based on evidence, not stereotypical assumptions (*Osborne Clarke Services v Purohit* [2009] IRLR 341 (EAT) and *R (Age Concern England) v Secretary of State for Business, Enterprise and Regulatory Reform* [2009] IRLR 373 (ECJ)).

The interpretation of the old concept of 'justifiable' had sought to apply the concept envisioned by the EU legislation. The case law on justifiability therefore continues to be influential in future cases as an aid to interpretation.

The leading decision is *Bilka-Kaufhaus GmbH v Weber von Hartz* (Case 170/84) [1987] ICR 110 (ECJ), which was a case brought under art 119 of the EC Treaty (now TFEU, art 157) challenging the exclusion of part-time workers from an occupational pension scheme. As it affected considerably more women than men this exclusion was held to be in breach of art 119. The court accepted that the employer would have a defence if he could show an objective justification on economic grounds. This would require the court to be satisfied that the discriminatory provisions corresponded to a real need on the part of the undertaking, were appropriate with a view to achieving the objectives pursued and were necessary to that end. It should be noted, however, that the cost of avoiding discrimination cannot in itself justify discrimination (*Steinicke v Bundesanstalt für Arbeit* [2003] IRLR 892), although recent case law (see **8.4.5.2**) has eroded this principle in respect of certain instances of discrimination.

It is important to note that the task for the tribunal in judging an employer's justification is fundamentally different from that when they judge the reasonableness of a dismissal in unfair dismissal cases. The Court of Appeal has held that there is no scope for the 'range of reasonable responses' test. Although the principle of proportionality requires the tribunal to consider the reasonable needs of the business it must make its own judgment as to whether the indirectly discriminatory action is reasonably necessary (*Hardys & Hansons plc v Lax* [2005] IRLR 668).

An employment tribunal must carefully weigh any justification against the discriminatory effect of a requirement. In *Allonby v Accrington & Rossendale College* [2001] IRLR 364 (CA), the employer dismissed the claimant on criteria which were indirectly discriminatory, but justified the decision because of financial constraints. The tribunal's failure to conduct a critical evaluation of the justification vitiated its finding that it was sufficient to operate as a defence.

The justification should not be based on the relevant protected characteristic. In *Mandla v Lee* [1983] 2 AC 548, the indirect discrimination complained of was a rule prohibiting the wearing of a turban. The claimant was a Sikh. The headmaster's justification for the rule was to prevent signs of cultural difference in order to develop harmony in his school and to prevent displays of non-Christian religions. This the court could not consider as it was not irrespective of race (defined in terms of ethnic origins), and therefore not an admissible defence.

An example of a justification which fell within the statutory requirements is *Panesar v Nestlé Co Ltd* [1980] ICR 144. Here, a 'no beards' rule was as impossible for the claimant, a Sikh, to comply with as was the 'no turban' rule in *Mandla v Lee*. However, the employer succeeded with his defence as the justification relied upon was based on hygiene requirements, and as such was 'irrespective of the colour, race, nationality or ethnic or national origins of the person to whom it is applied'.

8.4.5.2   Legitimate aim

There is no formal identification of what might be a legitimate aim in the Act. The Code of Practice gives some guidance:

The aim of the provision, criterion or practice should be legal, should not be discriminatory in itself, and must represent a real, objective consideration. The health, welfare and safety of individuals may qualify as legitimate aims provided that risks are clearly specified and supported by evidence [para 4.28].

It also indicates possible limits on the concept.

Although reasonable business needs and economic efficiency may be legitimate aims, an employer solely aiming to reduce costs cannot expect to satisfy the test. For example, the employer cannot simply argue that to discriminate is cheaper than avoiding discrimination [para 4.29]. This principle has been confirmed by the Grand Chamber of the CJEU in *Schmitzer v Bundesministerin für Inneres* [2015] IRLR 331.

While it remains the case that cost alone cannot justify discrimination, it may be a factor. In *Woodcock v Cumbria Primary Health Care Trust* [2012] IRLR 491, the claimant was prematurely dismissed for redundancy in order to avoid his qualifying for early retirement, thus saving the employer a considerable sum. The Court of Appeal held that this was justified in the unusual circumstances of the case. These circumstances included the fact that W was clearly redundant and this was the primary motive for his dismissal, the 'windfall' that he would receive if the full consultation procedure were conducted was considerable and the consultation could not have avoided the conclusion that he was redundant. The court endorsed the 'cost plus' approach established in *Cross v British Airways* [2005] IRLR 423. They did not endorse the *obiter dictum* of Underhill P in the EAT suggesting that cost alone could, in appropriate circumstances, be a sufficient justification.

A question remains as to the correctness of this decision, which seems inconsistent with the Supreme Court decision in *Seldon v Clarkson Wright and Jakes* [2012] IRLR 590 (see **8.2.1**). Moreover, a limit on the applicability of the Woodcock 'cost plus' approach has been introduced by the Supreme Court decision in *O'Brien v Ministry of Justice* [2013] IRLR 315. This concerned the pensions of part-time judges but is significant here for their Lordships' rejection of the 'cost plus' justification (although *Woodcock* was not expressly overruled). Baroness Hale, referring to the decision of the Court of Justice of the European Union (CJEU) in this case, says: 'the fundamental principles of equal treatment cannot depend on how much money happens to be available.' Thus *Woodcock* may best be understood as turning on its unusual facts.

The sufficiency of a justification will depend on the arguments presented to the tribunal and not be restricted to those in the mind of the decision-maker. However, *O'Brien* indicates that a justification will be easier to establish if it can be shown that it was in the mind of the decision-maker at the time, and not an ex post facto justification: 'it is difficult ... to justify the proportionality of the means chosen to carry out their aims if they did not conduct the exercise of examining the alternatives or gather the necessary evidence to inform the choice at that time.'

In fact it is not possible to assess proportionality without considering the legitimacy of the aim of the provision, criterion or practice. Guidance on applying the proportionality test has been provided by the Court of Appeal in *R (Elias) v Secretary of State for Defence* [2006] IRLR 934. Mummery LJ (at [165]) points out the three stages required:

First, is the objective sufficiently important to justify limiting a fundamental right? Secondly, is the measure rationally connected to the objective? Thirdly, are the means chosen no more than is necessary to accomplish the objective?

This provides a practical set of tests around which to plan submissions.

For precedents relevant to indirect discrimination, see **11.9**.

8.5 Harassment

Harassment has been recognised as a particularly unpleasant form of direct discrimination since the mid-1980s (see *Porcelli v Strathclyde Regional Council* [1986] ICR 564 (CS)). However, to bring a claim under the concept of direct discrimination required the use of a comparator, which meant that many claims failed (see, for example, *Pearce v Governing Body of Mayfield Secondary School/Macdonald v A-G for Scotland* [2003] ICR 937 (HL), where a claim resulting from disgraceful sexual harassment failed because comparators of the other gender would have been treated as badly).

EqA 2010, s 26, now provides for it to be a separate head of discrimination and is worded to avoid the difficulties under the earlier legislation:

(1) *A person (A) harasses another (B) if—*

   (a) *A engages in unwanted conduct related to a relevant protected characteristic, and*

   (b) *the conduct has the purpose or effect of—*

      (i) *violating B's dignity, or*

      (ii) *creating an intimidating, hostile, degrading, humiliating or offensive environment for B.*

(2) *A also harasses B if—*

   (a) *A engages in unwanted conduct of a sexual nature, and*

   (b) *the conduct has the purpose or effect referred to in subsection (1)(b).*

(3) *A also harasses B if—*

   (a) *A or another person engages in unwanted conduct of a sexual nature or that is related to gender reassignment or sex,*

   (b) *the conduct has the purpose or effect referred to in subsection (1)(b), and*

   (c) *because of B's rejection of or submission to the conduct, A treats B less favourably than A would treat B if B had not rejected or submitted to the conduct.*

The effect of these provisions is to make three types of behaviour unlawful:

- Harassment related to a protected characteristic;
- Sexual harassment; and
- Less favourable treatment based on a person's rejection of or submission to unwanted sexual conduct.

Each will be addressed in turn.

8.5.1 Harassment related to a protected characteristic

The use of 'related to' is designed to ensure that it is not necessary for the victim to have the relevant characteristic. Thus, a white man who objects to racist comments might find that they create an offensive environment for him. Equally, it is no obstacle to a claim that the harasser shares the protected characteristic with the victim. Furthermore, perceived harassment is covered, as where a harasser perceives the victim to be a member of a particular religion, and as in *English v Thomas Sanderson Blinds* [2008] EWCA 1421, where a straight man suffered homophobic harassment even though the harassers knew that he was not gay. 'Third party harassment' is also covered, where an employee is harassed because of another person's characteristic (see *Saini v All Saints Haque Centre* [2009] IRLR 74 (EAT), where the employee was harassed because of the religion of another worker).

Unwanted conduct is a matter of fact for the tribunal. The Code of Practice gives examples:

Unwanted conduct covers a wide range of behaviour, including spoken or written words or abuse, imagery, graffiti, physical gestures, facial expressions, mimicry, jokes, pranks, acts affecting a person's surroundings or other physical behaviour. (7.7)

The Code also gives an indication of what is meant by 'unwanted':

The word 'unwanted' means essentially the same as 'unwelcome' or 'uninvited'. 'Unwanted' does not mean that express objection must be made to the conduct before it is deemed to be unwanted. A serious one-off incident can also amount to harassment. (7.8)

In deciding whether s 26(1)(b) applies s 26(4) must be considered.

In deciding whether conduct has the effect referred to in subsection (1)(b), each of the following must be taken into account—

    (a) the perception of B;

    (b) the other circumstances of the case;

    (c) whether it is reasonable for the conduct to have that effect.

This introduces a <u>subjective element</u> in that it is the <u>victim's perception</u> which is key, not that of the harasser. However, the <u>victim's perception must be 'reasonable'</u>, thus introducing an objective element. This is not a simple test to apply and the approach of the courts has varied. A useful example is *Richmond Pharmacology v Dhaliwal* [2009] IRLR 336 (EAT). The claimant was a British woman of Indian origin. She resigned from her job seeking to give less notice than normal. Her manager, feeling that her work was deteriorating, warned her to maintain her standards and said: 'We will probably bump into each other in future, unless you are married off in India.' On a complaint of racial harassment (under RRA 1976) it was recognised that there was no intent to cause offence, but that the comment did evoke the stereotype of forced marriage and that the claimant was 'very upset'. The EAT upheld the tribunal's finding of harassment although regarding it as a 'borderline' case and observing that the compensation (£1,000) reflected that fact.

The EAT also recognised the tension arising where A engages in well-meant conduct which is regarded as unwelcome by the recipient, B. Underhill P addresses this directly, attempting to establish the respective roles of objective and subjective analysis:

The proscribed consequences are, of their nature, concerned with the feelings of the putative victim: that is, the victim must have felt, or perceived, her dignity to have been violated or an adverse environment to have been created. That can, if you like, be described as introducing a 'subjective' element; but overall the criterion is objective because what the tribunal is required to consider is whether, if the claimant has experienced those feelings or perceptions, it was reasonable for her to do so. Thus if, for example, the tribunal believes that the claimant was unreasonably prone to take offence, then, even if she did genuinely feel her dignity to have been violated, there will have been no harassment within the meaning of the section. Whether it was reasonable for a claimant to have felt her dignity to have been violated is quintessentially a matter for the factual assessment of the tribunal. ... One question that may be material is whether it should reasonably have been apparent whether the conduct was, or was not, intended to cause offence (or, more precisely, to produce the proscribed consequences): the same remark may have a very different weight if it was evidently innocently intended than if it was evidently intended to hurt [at [15]].

The EAT also indicated that case law under the previous legislation was 'unlikely to be helpful'.

These judgments do not mean that the motivation of the alleged harasser will never be relevant. According to Floyd LJ in *Lindsay v London School of Economics* [2014] IRLR 218, it may be relevant as part of the context which will help to explain whether simple words can amount to harassment.

Although the Code does not provide any definition of the concepts in s 26(1)(b) it gives a number of examples which provide useful analogies (see Code 7.6–11).

8.5.2   Sexual harassment

The terminology 'conduct of a sexual nature' focuses on the nature of the conduct rather than the gender of the victim. The Code assists with:

Key for Ukn 1

Conduct 'of a sexual nature' can cover verbal, non-verbal or physical conduct including unwelcome sexual advances, touching, forms of sexual assault, sexual jokes, displaying pornographic photographs or drawings or sending emails with material of a sexual nature. (7.13)

The concept of 'unwanted' should be treated as in EqA 2010, s 26(1) and (4). However, in cases of sexual harassment a defence that the conduct was welcome has not been uncommon. Guidance has been provided by the EAT in *Munchkins Restaurant v Karmazyn* [2010] All ER (D) 76 (Jun). Here, waitresses responded to sexual conduct from a director of the restaurant in a variety of ways. If they complained he would get angry. If they said that his behaviour upset them it appeared to encourage him. So they initiated conversations about his love life and described this as the way in which they found him easier to handle. The EAT recognised that this type of response was one which may well be a defensive technique for a victim in such circumstances ([23]) and refused the perpetrator's appeal.

8.5.3   Less favourable treatment because of rejection of or submission to unwanted sexual conduct

This provision is designed to cover the situation where a victim of unwanted sexual conduct who rejects it suffers treatment which is damaging but which does not constitute harassment. This might include a denial of overtime opportunities or a promotion. While this sort of treatment may be most commonly imposed on those who reject unwanted sexual conduct, the legislation also protects those who succumb to it.

8.5.4   Extent of employers' liability

The Act extends employers' liability beyond normal concepts of vicarious liability to cover the actions of employees outside the course of their employment. This recognises the validity of the approach in *Tower Boot Co Ltd v Jones* [1997] IRLR 168, where the Court of Appeal overruled the view of the EAT that common law principles of vicarious liability must be applied. This was a serious case of racial harassment where the victim was branded on the arm with a screwdriver, beaten and verbally abused. The EAT had accepted the argument that the harassers were not acting in the course of their employment and that the employer was thus not liable. In rejecting this view the Court of Appeal (*per* Waite LJ) observed that otherwise: 'the more heinous the act of discrimination, the less likely it would be that the employer would be liable'.

Employers may also be liable for the actions of third parties. EqA 2010, s 40(2), covers situations where a third party harasses a victim in the course of his employment on at least two occasions, the victim has complained to his employer and the employer has failed to take reasonably practicable steps to prevent repetition. This addressed the situation recognised in *Burton v De Vere Hotels* [1996] IRLR 596. Here, the EAT extended liability to the acts of non-employees, finding the employer liable for the foreseeable racist abuse of two waitresses by the comedian Bernard Manning. Liability was based on the failure to protect them from this harassment. EqPA 2010, s 40(2)–(4), has been repealed by the Enterprise and Regulatory Reform Act 2013, s 65, with effect from 1 October 2013. As a result, an employer will only be liable for third-party harassment if the failure to address it was on the grounds of the claimant's protected characteristic (*MacDonald v Advocate General for Scotland and Pearce v Mayfield School* [2003] IRLR 512 (HL)).

Finally, it is worth noting that, in addition to vicarious liability claims against the employer, liability may be established against an individual manager who has encouraged a campaign of harassment (*Gilbank v Miles* [2006] IRLR 538).

8.5.5   Protection from Harassment Act

The Protection from Harassment Act 1997 (PHA 1997) provides civil remedies and criminal penalties for conduct (including speech) which causes or may cause distress. This must involve at least two occasions and covers action at work. There is no need to establish that it is related to a protected characteristic. The civil remedy is an action in tort.

In *Council of the City of Sunderland v Conn* [2008] IRLR 324, the Court of Appeal suggested that the test of the gravity of the conduct was whether it would justify criminal sanctions. The court has now held in *Veakins v Kier Islington Ltd* [2010] IRLR 132, that although the conduct should be such as to 'sustain criminal liability' it was not necessary to establish that it would lead to criminal prosecution and that 'the primary focus is on whether the conduct is oppressive and unreasonable'.

The PHA 1997 provides a remedy in circumstances where no link with the statutory grounds for unlawful discrimination exists. In *Majrowski v Guy's and St Thomas's NHS Trust* [2006] IRLR 695, the House of Lords ruled that employers could be vicariously liable for their employees' acts of harassment, provided that there is a sufficiently close connection with employment. This will apply to partnerships as well as employers who are individuals or corporations (*Iqbal v Dean Manson Solicitors* [2011] IRLR 428). Note that an employer facing a harassment claim under the discrimination legislation who has taken all reasonable steps has a defence, but that such a defence is not available for a claim under the PHA 1997.

Combined action may be brought where appropriate, bringing together a claim for personal injury and one under the PHA 1997. In *Green v DB Services (UK) Ltd* [2006] IRLR 764 the employee making such a claim was awarded £852,000 for psychiatric injury caused by her employer failing to protect her from a campaign of bullying and harassment.

Employers must take care when seeking to negotiate settlement in proceedings. Letters warning of the consequences of claims being successful may be seen as threatening. The perspective to be adopted is that of the claimant, not the employer according to the House of Lords in *St Helens Metropolitan Borough Council v Derbyshire* [2007] IRLR 540. In *Iqbal v Dean Manson Solicitors* [2011] IRLR 428 (CA), three letters between solicitors were held to be capable of constituting a 'course of conduct amounting to harassment'. It was not necessary for each letter individually to amount to harassment. Such a course of conduct may involve incidents far apart in time. In *Marinello v City of Edinburgh Council* [2011] IRLR 669, the claimant was threatened in the street some 17 months after a series of bullying incidents which had led to his absence through depression. The Court of Session held that this was capable of forming part of a course of conduct in spite of the passage of time.

The EAT has indicated (*Richmond Pharmacology v Dhaliwal* [2009] IRLR 336) that the case law developed under the PHA 1997 is unlikely to be helpful in addressing EqA 2010 cases.

8.6   Victimisation

This is a separate head of discrimination designed to protect those who plan or attempt to make use of the discrimination legislation. EqA 2010, s 27(1), provides:

A person (A) victimises another person (B) if A subjects B to a detriment because—

    (a) B does a protected act, or

    (b) A believes that B has done, or may do, a protected act.

Protected acts are listed in subs (2):

    (a) bringing proceedings under this Act;

    (b) giving evidence or information in connection with proceedings under this Act;

    (c) doing any other thing for the purpose or in connection with this Act;

    (d) making an allegation (whether or not express) that A or another person has contravened this Act.

Malicious behaviour is not protected (see s 27(3)).

The most significant change represented by these provisions is that the victim is no longer required to show 'less favourable treatment' (which had required a comparator) but simply needs to show that he or she has suffered a detriment.

Whether a detriment has been suffered might be seen from the subjective view of the victim or in some more objective way. The House of Lords has considered this on three occasions: in *Chief Constable of West Yorkshire v Khan* [2001] ICR 1065 and in *Shamoon v Chief Constable of the Royal Ulster Constabulary* [2003] ICR, suggesting that various degrees of subjectivity were permissible; and subsequently in *St Helens BC v Derbyshire* [2007] ICR 841 arguing for an objective test. If this latter view were followed it would be hard for a victim who reasonably believed that he had suffered a detriment to succeed without evidence that there had been some actual loss. This outcome may be hard to justify given that the remedies available extend to compensation for injury to feelings without the need to prove actual loss.

Injury to feelings

The detriment must be clearly linked to the claimant's seeking to make use of the legislation. The alleged discriminator's subjective understanding of what the claimant was doing is key to this analysis. In *Woods v Pasab Ltd t/a Jhoots Pharmacy* [2013] IRLR 305 the claimant was dismissed for complaining that the employer company was 'a little Sikh club that only look[ed] after Sikhs'. The reason for dismissal was that this was seen as a racist comment. The tribunal, while accepting this as a fact, viewed the comment as a complaint of race discrimination. The Court of Appeal has held, following *Khan* that this is impermissible. It is the actual motivation of the alleged discriminator which must be considered and here the reason for the dismissal was the employer's perception that the comment was racist.

In *Cornelius v University College Swansea* [1987] IRLR 141, Mrs Cornelius was denied access to a grievance procedure because she had made a complaint under SDA 1975 which was pending. The Court of Appeal held that the fact that the employer would have treated anyone the same way if, for instance, they had been making an unfair dismissal claim, meant that she could not complain of victimisation.

Victimisation must clearly be by reason of one of the acts protected by s 27. However, there has been uncertainty as to what this means: whether it must be *consciously* motivated by race, etc. This has been resolved by the decision of the House of Lords in *Nagarajan v London Regional Transport* [1999] IRLR 572. Here the employment tribunal had found that the interviewers were 'consciously or subconsciously' influenced by the claimant's having earlier brought discrimination proceedings against the employer. The EAT and Court of Appeal had rejected the idea of subconscious motivation. The House of Lords, however, noting that it is <u>unnecessary</u> in <u>direct discrimination cases</u> to distinguish between <u>conscious</u> and <u>unconscious motivation</u> and that nothing in the Act suggests that the test for victimisation should be any different, restored the tribunal's finding. Lord Steyn identified the common sense task for the tribunal: <u>to decide whether the respondent treated the claimant less favourably because of his knowledge of a protected act.</u> No further inquiry into motive is necessary.

The prohibition against victimisation extends beyond the termination of the employment contract. In *Coote v Granada Hospitality* [1998] IRLR 656 (ECJ), a former employee victimised for bringing a claim against the employer for the latter's refusal to provide a reference was entitled to a remedy. EqA 2010 expressly provides for discrimination arising from relationships which have ended (s 108). However, s 108(7) excludes this protection in cases of victimisation. In *Jessemey v Rowstock Ltd* [2014] IRLR 368 (CA), it was held unanimously that although a strict interpretation of s 108(7) excluded victimisation, this would mean that the UK was in breach of its obligations under the Directive. Underhill LJ criticized this as a drafting error and held that post-employment victimisation should be regarded as unlawful.

For relevant precedents, see **11.7**.

8.7 Disability discrimination

As well as being a protected characteristic so that the provisions addressed above apply to disability, the particular nature of the issues arising in disability cases has led to the adoption of further provisions which apply only to this protected characteristic. These are in part designed to recognise that the issue in disability cases is not simply the *fact* of disability, but the impact of the *consequences* of disability.

8.7.1 Discrimination arising from disability

EqA 2010, s 15, provides:

> 1. *A person (A) discriminates against a disabled person (B) if—*
>
>   (a) *A treats B unfavourably because of something arising in consequence of B's disability, and*
>
>   (b) *A cannot show that the treatment is a proportionate means of achieving a legitimate aim.*

The wording of this provision avoids the need for a comparison to be drawn, easing the task for the claimant, but introduces a justification defence for employers.

8.7.1.1 Treats unfavourably

This wording is designed to avoid a problem which had arisen with the previous equivalent legislation, which had required a comparison with a non-disabled comparator. In *Clark v Novacold* [1999] ICR 951, a disabled employee was absent for several months. The Court of Appeal rejected the employer's defence that they would equally have dismissed a non-disabled person absent for the same period. Subsequently, in *Lewisham LBC v Malcolm* [2008] IRLR 700, the House of Lords rejected this approach. The case concerned a schizophrenic council tenant who, as a result of his disability, sub-let in breach of his tenancy. The *Novacold* comparison would have allowed him to be compared with a non-schizophrenic tenant who had not sub-let. However their Lordships held that the proper comparator was a non-schizophrenic tenant who had sub-let. This had the effect of making this cause of action redundant.

Under s 15 the claimant needs to show unfavourable treatment. The employer will have a defence if he can show that he did not know, and could not reasonably have been expected to know, that the claimant had the disability (s 15(2)). Case law will doubtless develop this concept, but the Code of Practice on Employment gives some guidance with this example:

A disabled man who has depression has been at a particular workplace for two years. He has a good attendance and performance record. In recent weeks, however, he has become emotional and upset at work for no apparent reason. He has also been repeatedly late for work and has made some mistakes in his work. The worker is disciplined without being given any opportunity to explain that his difficulties at work arise from a disability and that recently the effects of his depression have worsened.

The sudden deterioration in the worker's time-keeping and performance and the change in his behaviour at work should have alerted the employer to the possibility that these were connected to a disability. It is likely to be reasonable to expect the employer to explore with the worker the reason for these changes and whether the difficulties are because of something arising in consequence of a disability [para 5.15].

8.7.1.2   Objective justification

As with other provisions in the Act which are subject to a justification defence, the burden is on the employer to show that the action is proportionate and must be supported by evidence, not mere generalisations. This requires an examination of how a procedure is applied as well as the procedure itself (*Buchanan v Commissioner of Police of the Metropolis* [2016] IRLR 918). In *O'Brien v Bolton St Catherine's Academy* [2017] IRLR 547 (a claim for both unfair dismissal and disability discrimination) the CA has suggested that, in the context of dismissal for long-term sickness where the claimant is disabled, a finding that the dismissal was disproportionate for the purposes of s 15 should mean also that it is unreasonable for the purposes of ERA 1996, s 98(4). Given that 'proportionality' is a more stringent test than 'reasonableness', the court's ruling should not lead to findings that a dismissal fell within the range of reasonable responses being treated as satisfying the proportionality test.

8.7.2   The duty to make adjustments

The most radical departure from general discrimination principles is seen in this provision, which requires positive discrimination in some circumstances. EqA 2010, s 21, imposes a duty on employers to make reasonable adjustments in three situations.

1. Where a provision, criterion or practice puts a disabled person at a substantial disadvantage, the employer must take reasonable steps to avoid the disadvantage.
2. Where a physical feature puts a disabled person at a substantial disadvantage, the employer must take reasonable steps to avoid the disadvantage.
3. Where, in the absence of an auxiliary aid, a disabled person would be at a substantial disadvantage, the employer must take reasonable steps to provide the auxiliary aid.

This duty applies in respect of both employees and job applicants.

It is not uncommon for claims to arise from the dismissal for poor attendance of an employee who may be disabled. The EAT has held, in *General Dynamics Information Technology Ltd v Carranza* [2015] IRLR 43, that it is better to treat this as discrimination arising out of disability (see **8.7.1**) than as a failure to make reasonable adjustments.

8.7.2.1 Substantial disadvantage

Whether a disadvantage is 'substantial' is a matter of fact for the tribunal. In *Cave v Goodwin* [2001] All ER (D) 163, the Court of Appeal held that denying a disabled employee the facility to be accompanied by a friend at a disciplinary interview was not a substantial disadvantage. In *Midlothian Council v Elliott* (2001) 15 IRLB 664, the EAT held that a disabled employee allowed to return to work part-time by using up his annual leave had been placed at a substantial disadvantage. His job had been filled while he was off work and there was insufficient reason why it could not have continued on a part-time basis.

The duty to make reasonable adjustments extends to the decision to dismiss (*Aylott v Stockton on Tees BC* [2010] IRLR 994).

The House of Lords has held that where a disability prevents an employee from continuing with her previous job the duty of reasonable adjustment arises and includes serious consideration of transferring the employee to another job (*Archibald v Fife Council* [2004] IRLR 651).

The EAT has held that employers are only required to make adjustments relating to 'job-related' matters (*Kenny v Hampshire Constabulary* [1999] IRLR 76). The duty does not, therefore, extend to finding a personal carer to assist a claimant with urinating, nor (*obiter*) to providing home to work transport for disabled claimants. What is more, the concept of associative discrimination does not apply to the duty to make reasonable adjustments (*Hainsworth v Ministry of Defence* [2014] IRLR 728 (CA)). Thus, a non-disabled employee who was based in Germany could not seek transfer to the UK where there were better facilities for her disabled daughter.

8.7.2.2 What is the nature of the comparison?

The 'like-for-like' comparison appropriate in direct discrimination cases would fail to achieve the appropriate result under this cause of action, as it would fail to recognise the element of positive discrimination within the statutory provisions. This may be seen in *Fareham College v Waters* [2009] IRLR 991 (EAT). The employee had been absent with fibromyalgia and sought a phased return to work. The employer insisted on a return to full-time work and when she refused, dismissed her. The employer sought to compare her with a non-disabled employee who had been absent for a similar period, and would equally have been dismissed. Cox J held that the correct comparison was with 'other employees ... who are not disabled and who are able forthwith to attend work and to carry out the essential tasks required of them in their post'.

Thus, in *Aylott v Stockton on Tees BC* [2010] IRLR 994, the claimant, who suffered from bipolar affective disorder and returned from an absence from work, was subject to performance monitoring and other pressures before his subsequent dismissal. The Court of Appeal accepted the tribunal's identification of a comparator with a similar sickness record but without the claimant's disability. The employer had allowed fears based on stereotypical assumptions about mental illness to affect their decision.

8.7.2.3 What is meant by 'reasonable steps'?

The employer's statutory duty is 'to take such steps as it is reasonable, in all the circumstances of the case, for him to have to take'. This will depend very much on the facts of each case, and the Code of Practice clarifies the concept with examples of factors which should be considered:

- whether taking any particular steps would be effective in preventing the substantial disadvantage;
- the practicability of the step;
- the financial and other costs of making the adjustment and the extent of any disruption caused;
- the extent of the employer's financial or other resources;
- the availability to the employer of financial or other assistance to help make an adjustment (such as advice through Access to Work); and
- the type and size of the employer. (6.28)

The House of Lords has given a broad interpretation of this concept in *Archibald v Fife Council* [2004] IRLR 651. Moreover, it should be noted that the test is an objective one. An example can be seen in *Jennings v Barts and the London NHS Trust* [2013] All ER(D) 184, where a disabled employee sought exemption from the employer's long-term absence policy. Dismissal was held not to be unreasonable given the employee's refusal to engage in the process of exploring a phased return to work.

Where the issue is applying an absence policy it is important to recognise that it is not the policy (applied to all employees) that should be tested for reasonableness, but the decision to apply it equally to the disabled claimant (*Griffiths v Secretary of State for Work and Pensions* [2016] IRLR 216 (CA)). Similarly, in recruitment decisions, requiring candidates to sit psychometric tests may be reasonable but, according to the EAT in *The Government Legal Service v Brooks* [2017] UKEAT 0302/16, failing to consider an alternative test for a candidate with Asperger's Syndrome could constitute discrimination.

There have been conflicting decisions as to whether consultation with the disabled person is required or not. *Rothwell v Pelikan Hardcopy Scotland Ltd* [2006] IRLR 24 suggests that it may be, while *Tarbuck v Sainsbury's Supermarkets Ltd* [2006] IRLR 664 held it to be unnecessary. *Spence v Intype Libra Ltd* [2007] UK EAT/617/06 has subsequently decided that *Tarbuck* should be followed.

Problems may arise where a requested adjustment conflicts with the 'rights' of another. In *First Group plc v Paulley* [2017] IRLR 258, the Supreme Court indicates that where a wheelchair user finds the dedicated wheelchair space on a bus occupied by a child in a push chair the driver should go further than simply asking the parent to vacate the space and nothing further. Their Lordships declined to say what steps should be taken as they will be dependent upon context. The editor of IRLR observes that 'there can be a hierarchy of rights to the extent that disabled status can trump other protected characteristics ...'.

8.7.2.4   What knowledge of the disability is required?

Schedule 8, para 20(1), removes the duty from persons who do not know and could not reasonably be expected to know of the claimant's disability and the likelihood of their being placed at a substantial disadvantage. According to the EAT in *Secretary of State for Work and Pensions v Alam* [2010] IRLR 283, the first question is whether the employer knew of both the employee's disability and the fact that it placed him at a substantial disadvantage. If the employer did not know both of these, the tribunal should ask whether the employer ought to have known both.

It also removes the duty, in respect of job applicants and potential applicants, where the employer did not know and could not reasonably be expected to know that an interested disabled person is or may be an applicant. This raises a practical problem as s 60 prohibits asking applicants about their health. This provision addresses the problem of applicants being screened out on grounds of disability. However, it would mean that an employer may not be alert to a disadvantage a potential applicant faces in (for example) accessing premises for an interview or taking an assessment. This is largely addressed by s 60(6)(a)–(e), which permits limited questions to be asked for purposes which might generally be regarded as being within the spirit of the legislation.

8.7.2.5 Proving breach

The employee must establish the existence of the duty by showing that a substantial disadvantage exists. The EAT has held (*Project Management Institute v Latif* [2007] IRLR 579) that the employee must also provide evidence of adjustments which should have been made, arguing that it is an excessive burden on employers to require them to prove a negative: that there was no reasonable adjustment which could have been made. However the Code of Practice on Employment provides 'there is no onus on the disabled person to suggest what adjustments should be made' (para 6.24). Those advising respondents should therefore be cautious before assuming that this judgment imposes a high hurdle for employees.

8.8 Proof in discrimination cases

Admissibility of evidence in discrimination cases follows normal principles of relevance. It is often the case that evidence of events which would be time-barred if they were themselves the basis of a claim could be probative of the significance of later events. In *HSBC Asia Holdings v Gillespie* [2011] ILRLR 209, such evidence was in fact excluded because it related to the actions of different individuals in a different department of the employer and was thus not considered relevant. The fact that it referred to events long past was not in itself a reason for exclusion.

Two particular issues of the type and standard of proof, however, require consideration. The first arises in indirect discrimination cases.

8.8.1 Statistical information

The previous legislation had required a claimant to show that 'a considerably smaller proportion' of those sharing her protected characteristic could comply with the allegedly discriminatory requirement. This had been interpreted as requiring statistical analyses which had created practical difficulties for parties and long and expensive proceedings. The new provisions require instead that the claimant show that those sharing her protected characteristic are placed at a 'particular disadvantage' (EqA 2010, s 19(2)(b)). This may be satisfied by different approaches.

It may be sufficient to recognise what is 'common knowledge'. In *London Underground Ltd v Edwards (No 2)* [1998] IRLR 364 (CA), the claimant, a single parent train driver, needed to be at home in the mornings and evenings. New rostering arrangements prevented this. There were 21 female drivers. All the others (95.2 per cent) could comply. All (100 per cent) of the 2,023 male drivers could comply. Recognising that such a small percentage difference would not lead naturally to the conclusion that a considerably smaller proportion of women could comply, the Court of Appeal nevertheless approved the tribunal's finding to this effect. They held that the tribunal was right to go beyond a mechanistic approach and right to consider the facts that nationally the ratio of single parents having care of a child is some 10:1 as between women and men, and that while 5 per cent of the 21 women were disadvantaged, not one of the 2,023 men was.

Where statistical information is available it may well help to establish (or refute the existence of) a disadvantage. This might be acquired by using the ACAS questioning approach (see **8.8.2.2**) or by using publicly available national or regional statistics. Interpreting statistics is not a simple task and needs to be done by considering the nature and context of what is being compared. Thus, in *R v Secretary of State for Employment, ex p Seymour-Smith* [1999] IRLR 263 (ECJ), the then two-year qualifying period for unfair dismissals was challenged as indirect sex discrimination as a smaller proportion of women than men could comply with it. The statistical analysis showed a small disparity of about 8.5 per cent. This, however, was consistent over a significant period and the ECJ held that a minor but persistent disparity was sufficient to establish the claim.

Statistics may display a considerable difference between groups. In *McCausland v Dungannon DC* [1993] IRLR 583 (NICA), applicants were required to be existing local government employees. It was claimed that this indirectly discriminated against Catholics. Applicants were also required to be in standard occupational classification (SOC) 1, 2 or 3. An analysis was undertaken using the entire workforce in those SOCs and identifying the number of Protestants and Catholics (50,170 and 28,159 respectively). The existing local government workforce in those SOCs comprised 1,039 Protestants and 423 Catholics. The required comparison was between the proportions of Protestants and Catholics in the province who could comply with the requirement to be a local government employee. Those proportions were 2.1 per cent and 1.5 per cent respectively. While that may appear a small difference it is the *ratio* between them which is important. The Catholic proportion is only 71 per cent of the Protestant proportion—a considerable difference.

Where statistical evidence is unavailable or inappropriate the use of experts may be helpful (Code of Practice, para 4.13).

Frequently the statistical information required will include data on the workforce of the employer. Since the Court of Appeal's decision in *West Midlands Passenger Transport Executive v Singh* [1988] IRLR 186, it has been recognised that such information is probative and therefore subject to disclosure. Tribunals, however, should not grant disclosure unless it is necessary to do so for the fair disposal of the case, particularly if to do so would involve breach of confidentiality (*Science Research Council v Nasse* [1979] IRLR 465).

8.8.2   Burden of proof

8.8.2.1   The statutory regime

EqA 2010, s 136, establishes a process of shifting of the burden of proof:

> *(2) If there are facts from which the court could decide, in the absence of any other explanation, that a person (A) contravened the provision concerned, the court must hold that the contravention occurred.*
>
> *(3) But subsection (2) does not apply if A shows that A did not contravene the provision.*

This is most easily understood in the light of the Burden of Proof Directive 97/80/EC, which it implements:

When persons ... establish ... facts from which it may be presumed that there has been direct or indirect discrimination, it shall be for the respondent to prove that there has been no breach of the principle of equal treatment.

The Code gives as an example:

A worker of Jain faith applies for promotion but is unsuccessful. Her colleague who is a Mormon successfully gets the promotion. The unsuccessful candidate obtains information using the questions procedure in the Act which shows that she was better qualified for the promotion than her Mormon colleague. The employer will have to explain to the tribunal why the Jain worker was not promoted and that religion or belief did not form any part of the decision. (para 15.32)

Subsection (2) does not expressly require the claimant to prove those facts as there may be cases where the facts are not in dispute. In *Efobi v Royal Mail Group Ltd* [2017] UKEAT 0203/16/DA it was held that there is no burden on the claimant and that the tribunal was therefore wrong to dispose of the case on the basis that the burden had not been satisfied. It is therefore wrong to talk about a 'shifting burden', and the tribunal should weigh all the evidence presented to it in deciding what are the facts. In spite of this, it will generally be in the claimant's interest to adduce clear evidence of the facts claimed. Here the ACAS questions approach may be of help (see **8.8.2.2**).

The case law on the earlier legislation should now be treated with caution as that legislation was differently worded. It does, however, provide useful guidance. In *Igen v Wong* [2005] IRLR 258 (CA), established that the claimant must prove facts which lead the tribunal to conclude that the employer (in the absence of a satisfactory explanation) has committed unlawful discrimination. Secondly, the respondent must show that the act was not unlawful. For the burden of proof to shift in this way it is necessary to show more than less favourable treatment and a difference of gender. In *University of Huddersfield v Wolff* [2004] IRLR 534, a woman was denied a promotion that a male colleague received. The EAT held that this was insufficient to shift the burden and that evidence of causation between her gender and the less favourable treatment was also required. They offered, however, no guidance on the type of evidence which will satisfy that requirement.

It is important to recognise that the task at the first stage is not for the claimant to prove on a balance of probabilities that unlawful discrimination occurred. Instead, it should be sufficient to show facts which raise an inference of discrimination (*King v Great Britain-China Centre* [1991] IRLR 513 (CA)).

The wording of s 136 implies a two-stage process. However, this should not be seen as a straitjacket. Two issues have arisen and received guidance from the appellate courts. The first is whether, at stage one, the tribunal may consider evidence from the employer designed to rebut the factual basis of the claim. This has been answered in the affirmative by the Court of Appeal decision in *Madarassy v Nomura International plc* [2007] IRLR 246. Mummery LJ's judgment gives useful guidance on the method which tribunals and representatives should adopt. The second issue is whether the first stage may be dispensed with. *Brown v London Borough of Croydon* [2007] IRLR 259 establishes that it may. The reason is that by moving directly to the second stage the tribunal does not impose any disadvantage on the claimant. In effect, this is an acceptance of the factual basis for the claim which places the claimant in the situation they would be in after a successful stage one argument.

Further Court of Appeal guidance applies to the proper approach once the existence of a prima facie case is accepted and the second stage reached. In *EB v BA* [2006] IRLR 471, the tribunal, in such a situation said: 'All the explanations were inherently plausible, and we are not satisfied that they were discredited by the applicant.' This disclosed an incorrect approach. As Hooper LJ explains it:

> If an employer takes the stance adopted by the respondent, namely 'You prove it'—then claimants, particularly those with limited or no means, who challenge large corporations in cases of this kind would be at a great disadvantage. Such an approach may well render the reverse burden of proof provision of little or no use to a claimant.

This approach appears consistent with the new analysis in *Efobi*.

8.8.2.2   Discrimination questionnaires and other procedural factors

It is generally inherently difficult for the complainant to prove the reason for the decision. For instance, in cases of refusal of promotion the decision will be based on a managerial view of the employee's performance, records of which will be in management hands. Even with the adjustment to the burden of proof the claimant must still prove facts from which the tribunal could conclude in the absence of an adequate explanation that the respondent has acted in an unlawful manner. Moreover, according to the EAT in *Carrington v Helix Lighting Ltd* [1990] ICR 125, disclosure is limited to documents already in existence. Thus the employer cannot be required by disclosure to produce information on the ethnic composition of his workforce if he does not already have such information. Instead the complainant should use the ACAS questions approach. The guidance may be accessed at: <http://www.acas.org.uk/media/pdf/m/p/Asking-and-responding-to-questions-of-discrimination-in-the-workplace.pdf>.

This approach guides the claimant in putting questions to the employer. It may include questions designed to assist in gathering the information necessary to decide whether the case is worth pursuing and to prove the claimant's claim. If the employer fails to reply, or replies in a manner which the tribunal considers is evasive or equivocal, the tribunal may draw whatever inferences it thinks fit. This can include an inference that there has been unlawful discrimination.

The tribunal should be cautious about accepting a lack of transparency in the employer's arrangements. In *Barton v Investec Henderson Crosthwaite Securities Ltd* [2003] IRLR 332, the respondent's bonus scheme was designed to prevent employees comparing their bonuses. The respondent was also evasive in responding to the questionnaire. The tribunal had accepted the obscure bonus scheme as a necessary evil. The EAT rejected this approach, pointing out that once less favourable treatment is established the employer must demonstrate a non-discriminatory reason. The tribunal should have drawn an inference of discrimination from the obscurity of the scheme and the evasiveness of the questionnaire replies.

Barton provided guidance which has been adopted by the Court of Appeal in *Igen v Wong* [2005] IRLR 258. This confirms that once the claimant has established a prima facie case the respondent must prove, on the balance of probabilities, that the less favourable treatment was not on prohibited grounds. Moreover, where the respondent's explanation is inadequate it is *necessary* for the tribunal to find in favour of the claimant. Further valuable guidance in respect of what the claimant must show to establish a prima facie case is available in *Dresdner Kleinwort Wasserstein Ltd v Adebayo* [2005] IRLR 514.

Inadequacies in the response to a questionnaire should not lead a tribunal to infer discrimination unless there is a clear link between the inadequacy and the discrimination complained of. As the EAT said in *D'Silva v NATFHE* [2008] IRLR 412, it is not a tick-box exercise.

Further assistance may be available because failure to comply with the Race Relations Code of Practice on record-keeping (para 1.37) may also give rise to an adverse inference, or assist the tribunal to conclude that a prima facie case of discrimination has been made out.

8.8.2.3   Preparing evidence in discrimination cases

The problems faced by claimants had been recognised by the courts before the introduction of the new provisions on burden of proof. Indeed, academic opinion has queried whether the new legislation will make a significant difference. One difference may well be that the new legislation has made mandatory an approach which was merely discretionary before.

In the light of these observations, the existing case law still provides useful guidance on how to prepare the evidence in direct discrimination cases.

The authoritative view is best represented by the guidelines laid down in *King v Great Britain-China Centre* [1992] ICR 516 (CA):

(1) It is for the applicant who complains of racial discrimination to make out his or her case. Thus if the applicant does not prove the case on the balance of probabilities he or she will fail. (2) It is important to bear in mind that it is unusual to find direct evidence of racial discrimination. Few employers will be prepared to admit to such discrimination even to themselves. In some cases the discrimination will not be ill-intentioned but merely based on an assumption that 'he or she would not have fitted in'. (3) The outcome of the case will therefore usually depend on what inferences it is proper to draw from the primary facts found by the tribunal. These inferences can include, in appropriate cases, any inferences that it is just and equitable to draw in accordance with s 65(2)(b) of the Act of 1976 from an evasive or equivocal reply to a questionnaire. (4) Though there will be some cases where, for example, the non-selection of the applicant for a post or for promotion is clearly not on racial grounds, a finding of discrimination and a finding of a difference in race will often point to the possibility of racial discrimination. In such circumstances, the tribunal will look to the employer for an explanation. If no explanation is then put forward or if the tribunal considers the explanation to be inadequate or unsatisfactory it will be legitimate for the tribunal to infer that the discrimination was on racial grounds. This is not a matter of law but ... 'almost common sense'. (5) It is unnecessary and unhelpful to introduce the concept of a shifting evidential burden of proof. At the conclusion of all the evidence the tribunal should make findings as to the primary facts and draw such inferences as they consider proper from those facts. They should then reach a conclusion on the balance of probabilities, bearing in mind both the difficulties which face a person who complains of unlawful discrimination and the fact that it is for the complainant to prove his or her case. (*per* Neill LJ pp 528–9)

This does not mean to say that inferences which *may* be drawn from inadequate explanations by an employer must *automatically* be drawn (*Leicester University Students' Union v Mahomed* [1995] ICR 270). The tribunal must consider the test proposed by Neill LJ in the third part of his guideline judgment.

Moreover, it is important to remember that there must be clear evidence on which the inference of discrimination is based. The fact that the claimant is a member of an ethnic minority and has suffered a detriment is insufficient. The House of Lords has pointed out (*Zafar v Glasgow City Council* [1998] IRLR 36) that in order for an inference of discrimination to be drawn there must be a comparison with the treatment of others not of the claimant's race. Mere unreasonable treatment of an employee who happens to belong to an ethnic minority is insufficient (see **8.3.1**).

In hearing such a claim, however, the tribunal must conduct a full factual enquiry on the evidence before it instead of simply preferring the evidence of one witness as opposed to that of another. It is not sufficient for a tribunal to conclude that the employer's witnesses are honest. Where conflict remains they must follow the evidence through to a reasoned conclusion (*Anya v University of Oxford* [2001] IRLR 377 (CA)).

8.9 Remedies

8.9.1 Employment tribunal jurisdiction

The employment tribunal has jurisdiction to deal with these claims (EqA 2010, s 120). Its jurisdiction extends to claims by employees and applicants (ss 39–40), contract workers (including agency workers and temps) (s 41), police officers (s 42), partners (ss 44–45), barristers in respect of pupillage and tenancy (s 47) and the holders of personal offices (s 49) and public offices (ss 50–51). Section 108 also permits claims by ex-employees, where 'the discrimination arises out of and is closely connected to a relationship which used to exist between them'.

It is worth noting that while illegality in the contract of employment may prevent a tribunal from hearing an unfair dismissal claim this is not so in respect of a discrimination claim. In *Hall v Woolston Hall Leisure Ltd* [2000] IRLR 578, the Court of Appeal held that as the existence of a contract was not a prerequisite for a discrimination claim (as it is for an unfair dismissal claim), the illegality did not prevent the tribunal accepting jurisdiction and awarding compensation.

8.9.1.1 Time limit

The time limit period is the same as for most other areas of tribunal jurisdiction: three months (EqA 2010, s 123). However, a number of points need to be remembered. The first is that the three-month period runs from the date of the alleged discriminatory act. Discriminatory behaviour often continues over a period of time. Where this is the case the period does not begin to run until the final instance of discrimination (s 123(3)). The date of its commencement is, for these purposes, irrelevant. Where the claim is for a reasonable adjustment the original omission does not necessarily trigger the start of the time period, nor is it a continuing omission, in effect avoiding the time limit. In *Matuszowicz v Kingston upon Hull City Council* [2009] IRLR 288, the Court of Appeal ruled that the time period either starts when a person does an act inconsistent with a reasonable adjustment or when a reasonable employer *would have complied* with the reasonable adjustment.

The second point is that the Act permits extension of the period where the employment tribunal considers it 'just and equitable' (s 123(1)(b)). This is a broader test than that in unfair dismissal cases (which is 'reasonably practicable', see **4.2**), and the decisions in unfair dismissal cases, which have generally been restrictive, should not be followed in discrimination cases. Thus in *Chohan v Derby Law Centre* [2004] IRLR 685, the EAT indicated that where the claimant had been given incorrect legal advice it is proper to permit a late claim. In *Department of Constitutional Affairs v Jones* [2008] IRLR 128, the claimant was dismissed after developing clinical depression. Initially reluctant to recognise that his illness constituted a disability, he delayed bringing a claim for disability discrimination. The court held that the tribunal was not in error in extending the time period under the 'just and equitable' test.

A further complication arises from the long period it has sometimes taken for the precise significance of EU provisions to be established. Suppose that an ECJ judgment interprets long-existing legislation in such a way that a claimant realises she has a claim based on actions which took place several years ago. Should the fact that EU law was not fully understood at the time of the actions justify her in bringing her claim within three months of the clarifying judgment? In *Biggs v Somerset County Council* [1996] IRLR 209, it was held that it does not. The need to ensure legal certainty overrides any argument that it would be unjust to deny her a claim.

Biggs, however, was an unfair dismissal case, even though the confusion had arisen from the interpretation of the SDA 1975, and the 'reasonably practicable' test was the one there applied. The broader test in the discrimination legislation may justify a more relaxed approach to allowing a claim to proceed after the expiry of the time limit. In *British Coal v Keeble* [1997] IRLR 336, the EAT approved such a decision in an SDA case. The *Biggs* approach should not, therefore, apply to discrimination claims.

8.9.2 Procedure

In general the procedure for bringing and defending discrimination cases before the employment tribunal is the same as that for unfair dismissal and other cases. Thus, the Early Conciliation procedure applies, a preliminary hearing may be requested to test the merits of claim or defence, the ACAS duty to promote settlements wherever possible applies and the EAT has the same jurisdiction to hear appeals on a point of law provided they are made within 42 days of the tribunal sending the reasons for its decision to the parties.

Some points of distinction should be mentioned. The tribunal itself will be drawn from a panel which has the experience necessary to deal effectively with discrimination cases. In addition to the normal interlocutory procedures available, the claimant may use the ACAS questions approach, the results of which may enable the tribunal to draw appropriate inferences. This is discussed further at **8.8.2.2**.

8.9.3 Employment tribunal remedies

The remedies available (EqA 2010, s 124) are:

(a) A declaration as to the rights of the parties.

(b) Compensation. Where more than one person or organisation is responsible for discriminatory behaviour it is possible to bring a claim against multiple defendants. In the past tribunals have sometimes apportioned the damages between individuals (*Armitage v Johnson* [1997] IRLR 162), but the Court of Appeal warns against this in *London Borough of Hackney v Sivanandan* [2013] IRLR 408. The basic approach should be that liability is joint and several, thus enabling any of the joint defendants to be fully liable for the compensation awarded.

(c) An appropriate recommendation (for action to remedy the discrimination). If this is not complied with the tribunal has the power to award compensation as at (b), or to increase the amount of compensation awarded.

Furthermore, employment tribunals have jurisdiction to award damages for the statutory tort of unlawful discrimination (*Sheriff v Klyne Tugs (Lowestoft) Ltd* [1999] IRLR 481). Where, therefore, physical or psychiatric injury has been caused, a claim should be made to the tribunal at the same time as the discrimination complaint. Where a claim for psychiatric injury is combined with a claim for injury to feelings, care must be taken to ensure that there is no double recovery (*HM Prison Service v Salmon* [2001] IRLR 425 (EAT)). It is, however, perfectly proper to incorporate psychiatric injury within the concept of injury to feelings.

Advice and assistance in bringing employment tribunal cases may be available from the Equality and Human Rights Commission, although its budget means that in practice it can only provide substantial support for test cases which are likely to have significant impact. Moreover, the High Court has suggested (*R v London Borough of Hammersmith & Fulham, ex p NALGO* [1991] IRLR 249) that judicial review will be available where an authority proposes to embark upon an employment policy in contravention of either the SDA 1975 or RRA 1976. This presumably applies to other employers whose decisions are susceptible to judicial review.

8.9.4   Assessment of quantum

Compensation for unlawful discrimination is treated differently from the compensatory award in unfair dismissal cases. As well as claiming actual loss, circumstances may justify claims for injury to feelings, aggravated damages and exemplary damages.

The former statutory limit to discrimination compensation was removed by the Sex Discrimination and Equal Pay (Remedies) Regulations (SI 1993/2798) in the case of sex discrimination claims and the Race Relations (Remedies) Act 1994 in the case of race discrimination claims, following the ECJ ruling in *Marshall v Southampton & South West Hampshire Health Authority (Teaching) (No 2)* [1993] IRLR 425. Interest may also be awarded, this provision also applying to EqA 2010, Pt 5, Chapter 3 (equality of terms) claims. Claimants face the usual requirement to mitigate any loss flowing from the discriminatory action. The EAT's decision in *Ministry of Defence v Cannock* [1994] IRLR 509 provided guidance that limited the early tendency to allow somewhat speculative assessments of future loss. Guidance on dealing with the likelihood of future loss can be found in *Ministry of Defence v Wheeler* [1998] IRLR 23 (CA). The removal of the artificial limit on compensation initially had an effect on the level of individual elements of the total compensation. Thus, in *Armitage, Marsden and HM Prison Service v Johnson* [1997] IRLR 162, the EAT upheld an award for injury to feelings of £21,000 for a black prisoner who suffered a campaign of humiliation and ostracism. A further £7,500 aggravated damages were awarded. Smith J suggested the following guidelines on compensation in race discrimination claims:

(a) Awards for injury to feelings are compensatory. They should be just to both parties. They should compensate fully without punishing the tortfeasor. Feelings of indignation at the tortfeasor's conduct should not be allowed to inflate the award.

(b) Awards should not be too low as that would diminish respect for the policy of the anti-discrimination legislation. Society has condemned discrimination and awards must ensure that it is seen to be wrong. On the other hand, awards should be restrained, as excessive awards could be seen as the way to untaxed riches.

(c) Awards should bear some broad general similarity to the range of awards in personal injury cases. We do not think this should be done by reference to any particular type of personal injury award, rather to the whole range of such awards.

(d) In exercising their discretion in assessing such a sum, tribunals should remind themselves of the value in everyday life of the sum they have in mind. This may be done by reference to purchasing power or by reference to earnings.

(e) Finally, tribunals should bear in mind the need for public respect for the level of awards made.

An example which shows how the compensatory principle links with other elements of an award is *HM Land Registry v McGlue* [2013] UKEAT/0435/11/RN. The claimant was denied access to a voluntary severance payment because she was on a career break at the time. This was held to be unjustified indirect sex discrimination and she was awarded £12,000 for injury to feelings, £5,000 aggravated damages and £71,710.95 as the severance payment to which she would have been entitled. The EAT refused to interfere with the award for injury to feelings; rejected, on the facts, the aggravated damages; and approved the full award of the compensatory element even though the claimant remained in employment. This was on the basis of her evidence that she could have obtained another job without difficulty if she had been permitted to leave while accepting the severance payment.

8.9.4.1   Injury to feelings

These principles have particularly exercised the courts in cases where compensation for injury to feelings has been claimed. Caution against derisory awards (*Alexander v Home Office* [1988] ICR 685) has been matched with the need to keep awards in line with compensation in other fields. Some resolution to the debate has been provided by the Court of Appeal in *Vento v Chief Constable of West Yorkshire Police* [2003] IRLR 102. The court identified three bands, each with a corresponding range of compensation:

- The most serious cases will normally involve a long campaign of discriminatory harassment and will justify awards of between £15,000 and £25,000.
- Other serious cases will justify awards between £5,000 and £15,000.
- Less serious cases will justify awards between £500 and £5,000.

Guidance on applying these bands can be seen in *Kemeh v MoD* [2014] IRLR 377, where the CA held that a one-off statement, however offensive, did not justify a middle band award.

The EAT has ruled that these awards need to be raised to reflect inflation since 2003. As from 11 September 2017 the bands should be:

- Lower band (less serious cases): £800–£8,400
- Middle band: £8,400–£25,200
- Upper band (the most serious cases): £25,200–£42,000
- Exceptional cases: over £42,000.

These bands are to be reviewed in March 2018 and annually thereafter.

They are of considerable assistance in a field where awards varied considerably. They remain, however, limited guidance. The Court of Appeal also recommended reference to the Judicial Studies Board's guidelines for compensation for post-traumatic stress. It may also be helpful to see how the court applied these principles to the *Vento* case. Mrs Vento was harassed and abused over a number of years. This resulted in her suffering some personal injury and losing her job. The tribunal had awarded her £50,000 for injury to feelings and £15,000 for aggravated damages. The Court of Appeal, applying these guidelines, reduced this to £18,000 for injury to feelings and £5,000 for aggravated damages.

In *Simmons v Castle* [2012] EWCA 1288, the Court of Appeal held that there should be a 10 per cent uplift in general damages in tort cases. There has been conflicting case-law as to whether this should apply to employment tribunal awards. This has been resolved by the Court of Appeal decision in *De Souza v Vinci Construction (UK) Ltd* [2017] EWCA Civ 879. The 10 per cent uplift is to be applied to awards both for psychiatric injury and for injury to feelings. This is in order to ensure correspondence between cases in the County Courts and the employment tribunals, as required by EA 2010, s 124(6). It should be clear that awards under these heads are never made without evidence that the injury claimed has actually occurred. Tribunals will not simply assume injury to feelings because discrimination has been proven. Moreover, the identification of a sum should not be a mechanical process. An effort should be made to assess the effect of the discrimination in terms of its seriousness and the actual effect on the victim. *Dicta* in the EAT decision in *Orlando v Didcot Power Station Sports and Social Club* [1996] IRLR 262 suggest that an employer's admission of fault may reduce the impact of the discrimination on the victim and thus the level of the award for injury to feelings.

Injury to feelings must flow from the discriminatory behaviour (*Skyrail Oceanic v Coleman* [1980] IRLR 226 (CA)), but this does not mean that the claimant needs to have knowledge of the discriminatory motive. In *Taylor v XLN Telecom Ltd* [2010] IRLR 499, a black employee who had complained of race discrimination through his employer's grievance procedure was subsequently dismissed. At the time he did not realise that the dismissal was an act of victimisation following his grievance, but was able to establish injury to feelings. The EAT held that he could recover for injury to feelings as it was 'still an injury attributable to the discriminatory conduct'.

It is worth noting that in extreme cases the victim of discrimination may suffer psychiatric illness. Where this is established a majority of the Court of Appeal has held (*Essa v Laing Ltd* [2004] IRLR 213) that the discriminator's liability is strict and a claim that the psychiatric illness was not foreseeable will provide no defence.

Where personal injury is suffered, compensation may be claimed from the tribunal in the same way as in normal civil proceedings (*Sheriff v Klyne Tugs (Lowestoft) Ltd* [1999] ICR 1170). Medical evidence will be required to support such a claim which may include compensation for pain, suffering and loss of amenity.

8.9.4.2 Future loss

Discriminatory action, particularly where it results in dismissal or resignation, may have long-term consequences. The Court of Appeal, in *Wardle v Crédit Agricole* [2011] IRLR 604, provides guidance as to the principles on which this inherently speculative calculation should be made. The claimant had been passed over for promotion by the appointment of a French national, a decision held to be unlawful discrimination on the grounds of nationality. His subsequent dismissal was held to be unlawful victimisation. He accepted a lower paid job in mitigation of his loss, but, at the time of the hearing, had not obtained an equivalent job. The tribunal made a finding of fact that there was a 70 per cent chance that within three years the claimant would have gained a job on a similar pay level to that from which he was dismissed. On that basis they awarded him future loss until normal retirement age and then reduced that by 70 per cent. Elias LJ held that this was wrong. Instead, the tribunal should make its best estimate of when the claimant would be likely to return to his previous salary, and award the full loss of earnings until that date. To identify the date, the tribunal should conclude when the claimant's prospects of obtaining an equivalent job were 50 per cent.

The causes of future loss may be a complex mix of the actions of the original discriminator and the actions or omissions of those to whom the person discriminated against subsequently applies for employment. This may particularly apply where the discriminator provides an adverse reference or one which refers to the discrimination proceedings. In *Bullimore v Pothecary Witham Weld Solicitors (No 2)* [2011] IRLR 18, the EAT held that the fact that subsequent prospective employers were themselves committing acts of victimisation did not break the chain of causation, and the original employer, in victimising the claimant by providing an adverse reference, was liable for the full consequences.

A similar analysis informs *Chagger v Abbey National plc* [2010] IRLR 47. Here a senior employee was able to show 111 rejections after a discriminatory dismissal. This was sufficient evidence of the long-term effect of the discrimination for the claimant to recover £1,325,322 for future loss.

8.9.4.3   Aggravated and exemplary damages

In *Armitage, Marsden and HM Prison Service v Johnson* [1997] IRLR 162, the EAT, recognising unlawful discrimination as a statutory tort, confirmed the availability of an award for aggravated damages. This would be appropriate, for example, where the tort was sufficiently intentional as to enable the claimant to rely upon malice or the respondent's manner of committing the tort or other conduct had aggravated the injury to feelings.

Aggravated damages are compensatory in nature (*Commissioner of Police of the Metropolis v Shaw* [2012] IRLR 291) and should only be awarded where the distress caused is exacerbated by being done in a particularly upsetting way, especially spitefully motivated or by subsequent aggravating conduct. Guidance can be found in *HM Land Registry v McGlue* [2013] EqLR 701 (EAT).

The long-standing view that exemplary damages are not available in discrimination cases (*Deane v London Borough of Ealing* [1993] IRLR 209 (EAT)) was overturned by the House of Lords in *Kuddus v Chief Constable of Leicester Constabulary* [2001] 3 All ER 193. Their Lordships held that the power to award exemplary damages was not limited to causes of action recognised at the time of the decision in *Rookes v Barnard* [1964] AC 1129. In order to claim exemplary damages the claimant must establish that the discriminatory conduct was: (a) oppressive, arbitrary or unconstitutional action by servants of the Government; or (b) calculated by the discriminator to make a profit for himself which may exceed compensatory damages to the claimant.

Care must be taken to avoid double recovery or overlap between awards. In *Ministry of Defence v Fletcher* the tribunal had awarded £30,000 for injury to feelings, £20,000 aggravated damages and £50,000 exemplary damages in circumstances where a lesbian soldier had suffered sexual harassment and extensive victimisation. The EAT reduced the award of aggravated damages to £8,000 and rejected the award of exemplary damages, which should 'be reserved for the most serious abuses of governmental power'.

8.9.5   Remedies through the Equality and Human Rights Commission (EHRC)

The Equality and Human Rights Commission (EHRC) took over the work of the Equal Opportunities Commission, the Commission for Racial Equality and the Disability Rights Commission in 2007. Among its various responsibilities the EHRC has the power to conduct formal investigations. These are usually at the instigation of an individual or group suffering from some discriminatory action. This approach suffers from the fact that no one (apart from the Secretary of State) may require the EHRC to conduct an investigation. Thus this remedy is not analogous to a right to bring an employment tribunal claim. This problem is exacerbated by the under-funding of the EHRC and its consequent inability to conduct all the investigations which may seem meritorious to it.

However, there are major advantages to this approach. One problem for many suffering from discrimination which stops short of dismissal (the majority of cases) is the fear that they will suffer victimisation. The protection against victimisation in EqA 2010 (see **8.6**) may often be insufficient to allay a victim's fears. This may be particularly true where discriminatory behaviour affects a group of people as opposed to a particular individual. There may, for example, be a 'glass ceiling' within an organisation, resulting in no women or members of visible minorities being promoted above a particular grade. No individual may wish to stick his or her neck out, but may avoid this risk by making a complaint to the EHRC.

Another situation where this route is of particular value is where an employer has a practice which is indirectly discriminatory in effect, but which has not, at this time, affected any individual. Such a situation may not meet the requirement that the claimant be placed at a disadvantage and thus no tribunal claim would be possible. The raising of a complaint with the EHRC may avoid the need to wait for an individual to have actually suffered from the indirectly discriminatory practice. The ECJ confirms that discriminatory advertisements may be the basis of a successful claim before any individual can be shown to have suffered (*Centrum voor gelijkheid van kansen en voor racismebestrijding v Firma Feryn NV* [2008] IRLR 732).

8.9.5.1   Procedure

Should the EHRC decide to undertake a formal investigation it must first draw up its terms of reference and state the persons believed to be doing or to have done unlawful acts. Those acts must be specified. It may require the person subject to the investigation to provide specific written information or to attend for oral examination and produce such documents as may be required which are in that person's possession or control, subject to the rules of evidence governing the production of documents in the High Court. Where a failure to comply occurs, or is reasonably believed to be likely, an order may be obtained from the County Court.

The person subject to the investigation must be given an opportunity to make oral and/or written representations and may be represented by counsel, by a solicitor or other suitable person.

8.9.5.2   The consequences of a formal investigation

Following a formal investigation the EHRC may:

- recommend future action;
- recommend a change in the law;
- deliver the report to the Secretary of State (when the investigation was requested by the Secretary of State), who shall publish it;
- publish the report or make it available for inspection;
- serve a notice on the person investigated that the EHRC is minded to serve a non-discrimination notice (NDN).

8.9.5.3 Non-discrimination notice

An NDN is a notice that identifies the actions or practice which constitute discriminatory behaviour and requires the person served to commit no further such actions. It must be accompanied by a statement of the findings of fact on which it is based. It may also require the person served to provide the EHRC with further information and specify the time and manner in which that information must be provided (not more than five years from the date of the notice).

A 'minded' notice is designed to give the person served an opportunity to make representations, either orally or in writing, within 28 days (although there is no right to cross-examine witnesses). It must specify the grounds on which the NDN is contemplated. The EHRC must consider any representations made before deciding whether to issue the NDN.

8.9.5.4 Appeals against non-discrimination notices

There is a right of appeal to an employment tribunal against an NDN within six weeks of it being served. The notice of appeal should specify each finding of fact that is challenged, each allegation of fact which it is intended to prove and any other grounds on which it is alleged that the requirements contained in the NDN are unreasonable. Any or all of the findings of fact on which the requirements contained in the notice are based may be challenged.

The tribunal must quash any requirement in an NDN which it considers unreasonable because it is based on an incorrect finding of fact or for any other reason. It may direct that a requirement be substituted for the quashed requirement.

8.9.5.5 Further investigation and enforcement

The EHRC has the power to conduct a further investigation within five years of the NDN becoming final, to ensure that its requirements are complied with.

Where such an investigation discloses that the person investigated continues to discriminate or to operate an indirectly discriminatory practice, the EHRC may apply to a County Court for an injunction.

For further details of these procedures, see the *Remedies Manual*.

8.10 Part-time workers and fixed-term employees

This section addresses protection given to two classes of worker which is not generally perceived as falling within the concept of discrimination. It is presented here because the concept applied (prohibiting 'less favourable treatment') is analogous to that in direct discrimination cases under EqA 2010.

8.10.1 Part-time workers

The PTW Regs 2000 provide part-time workers (a broader concept than employees) with the right to equal treatment to full-timers, subject to a justification defence (reg 5(2)(b)). Rights are subject to the pro rata principle so that where (for example) full-timers receive a £100 Christmas bonus, part-timers working two days a week should receive £40. Higher overtime rates are only available when the part-timer has completed a full-timer's normal working week.

A part-timer seeking to make a claim under the Regulations must find a comparator on the same type of contract. When considering the validity of such a comparator, tribunals should focus on the similarities, not the differences (*Matthews v Kent & Medway Towns Fire Authority* [2006] IRLR 367 (HL)).

Directive 97/81 limits the right to situations where workers face less favourable treatment 'solely because they work part-time'. There are conflicting decisions as to what this means. In *McMenemy v Capita Business Services Ltd* [2007] IRLR 400, the Court of Session held that a part-time worker who suffers less favourable treatment for a number of reasons, only one of which is that he is a part-time worker, will not have a remedy. However, the EAT has held in *Sharma v Manchester City Council* [2008] IRLR 336 that the reference to 'solely' in the Directive merely prevented claims when the less favourable treatment was partly for an independent reason. It does not prevent claims where only one category of part-time worker is less favourably treated.

Less favourable treatment on grounds of being a part-timer may be justified. Any such justification should be objective. The guidance note gives the example of a different hourly rate being justified by different levels of performance measured by a fair and consistent appraisal scheme.

8.10.2 Fixed-term employees

The FTE Regs 2002 extend similar provisions to fixed-term employees. In *Allen v National Australia Group Europe Ltd* [2004] IRLR 847, the EAT held that a contractual provision for earlier notice in a contract with a fixed termination date does not prevent that contract from falling within the Regulations.

More specifically, reg 8 provides that an employee who has had two or more fixed-term contracts over a period of four years without breaking continuity will become a permanent employee unless the employer can objectively justify continuing to use fixed-term contracts. Guidance on what might justify such a decision can be found in *de Diego Porras v Ministerio de Defensa* [2016] IRLR 964 (CJEU).

8.11 Discrimination flowchart

Figure 8.1 provides a general outline only and should not be relied upon without reference to the appropriate text (references in brackets) to practitioner works and the primary sources. In this diagram, following the approach of the EqA 2010, 'A' refers to the respondent and 'B' to the claimant.

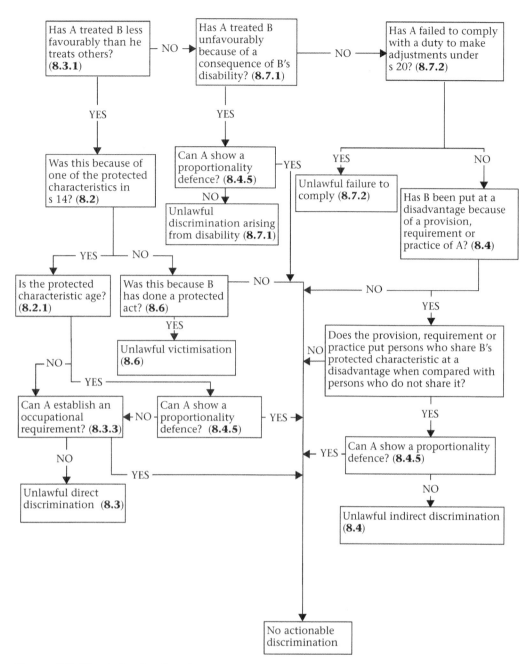

Figure 8.1 Discrimination flowchart

9 | Family-friendly provisions

While provisions have been in force for many years to provide specific rights to pregnant employees (maternity leave and maternity pay), subsequent legislation has both simplified those rights and expanded provision to add concepts such as parental, shared parental, paternity and adoption leave. The main provisions are to be found in the Employment Rights Act 1996 (ERA 1996), ss 71–85, as amended by the Children and Families Act 2014, which both simplifies and extends the provisions. Most of these provisions are enabling only, and have been implemented in detail by a series of Regulations.

9.1 Antenatal provisions

9.1.1 Paid time off for antenatal care

ERA 1996, ss 55–57, entitles a pregnant employee under medical supervision not to be unreasonably refused paid time off to keep appointments.

9.1.2 Unpaid time off for antenatal appointments

Prospective fathers and prospective surrogate parents have the right to take unpaid time off to accompany the expectant mother to antenatal appointments on two occasions of up to 6½ hours at each time.

9.2 Maternity leave and the right to return to work

These provisions provide 26 weeks' maternity leave to all women and an extended period for those with longer service. In return there are strict procedural requirements with which a pregnant employee must comply. In this section, references to regulations are to the Maternity and Parental Leave Regulations 1999 (SI 1999/3312) as amended.

9.2.1 Ordinary maternity leave (OML)

This is a period of 26 weeks starting on a date:

- chosen by the pregnant employee, provided it is after the 11th week before the expected week of childbirth (EWC) (reg 6(1)(a)), *or,* arising automatically:
  - after the fourth week before the EWC, the first date on which she is absent from work wholly or partly because of her pregnancy (reg 6(1)(b)); *or*
  - the day after that on which the child is born (reg 6(2)).

9.2.2   Additional maternity leave (AML)

This is a period of 26 weeks which starts the day after the end of OML. This, when combined with OML, provides for a full year's leave.

9.2.3   Compulsory maternity leave

All women are prohibited from working for a period of two weeks after the birth of the child (ERA 1996, s 72(1) and reg 8).

9.2.4   Eligibility requirements

If an employee discovers she is pregnant she must determine the EWC and thus establish the date 15 weeks before the EWC. If she has less than 26 weeks' continuous service before that date (EWC–15) she is entitled to OML. If she has 26 weeks' continuous service 15 weeks before the EWC she is also entitled to AML and statutory maternity pay.

   She must provide her employer with notice of a number of facts and dates if she is to exercise her rights.

Information	When provided
The fact of pregnancy	End of 15th week before EWC
EWC (by medical certificate)	End of 15th week before EWC
OML start date (in writing if required)	End of 15th week before EWC
Change of start date	28 days before earlier of old or new start date

Where the OML period starts automatically (see **9.2.1**) she must inform her employer of the circumstances as soon as reasonably practicable.

   In return, within 28 days of receiving notice from the employee of the EWC the employer must state the expected date of return.

   If the pregnant employee fails to comply with these notice requirements she loses her rights to OML and AML, unless it was not reasonably practicable to comply.

9.2.5   Shared parental leave

Amendments in CFA 2014 enable a mother to curtail her period of ordinary or additional maternity leave in order to allow her partner to take shared parental leave under ERA 1996 s 75E. For this to happen, both partners must satisfy the relevant eligibility requirements (see **9.2.4**). The parents may choose to take their shared parental leave concurrently and/or in more than one block of at least one week in length.

9.2.6   The right to return to work

The nature of this right depends on whether the woman is returning from OML or AML.

9.2.6.1   Return from OML

ERA 1996, s 71(4)(c) applies. The employee is entitled to return to the 'same job'. Therefore the nature of the work, the employee's capacity and her place of work must all be the same. If that job is being made redundant she must be offered any suitable alternative employment (MPL Regs 1999, reg 10). The terms and conditions must not be substantially less favourable. In practice this places her at the head of the queue if more are being made redundant than there are jobs available.

In situations other than redundancy the employer may not argue that it is not reasonably practicable to allow her to return to her job.

9.2.6.2 Return from AML

Regulation 18 of the MPL Regs 1999 applies.

The employee is equally entitled to return to the 'same job'. Similar provisions arise where the job is being made redundant.

However, if it is not reasonably practicable to allow her to return to the same job she must be offered a job which is 'both suitable for her and appropriate for her to do in the circumstances'. The terms should not be less favourable than those which would have applied in the old job.

9.2.6.3 Procedural requirements

The employer is obliged to give notice of the expected return date (ERD) (within 28 days of receiving notification of the EWC). If the employer has failed to give this notice the employee is entitled to return early if she wishes.

Where the employer has given proper notice the employee must give 28 days' notice of her intention to return. If she fails to do so the employer may defer her return until the earlier of the end of maternity leave or the end of the 28-day notice period.

A refusal to allow a woman to return to work in these circumstances is treated as a dismissal (ERA 1996, s 96(1)).

If a woman is unable to return on the ERD because of illness, the normal contractual provisions apply.

9.2.7 Contractual status during maternity leave

The contract of employment continues in existence during all types of maternity leave. However, obligations inconsistent with leave do not, for obvious reasons, apply (ERA 1996, s 71(4)(b), (OML) and ERA 1996, s 73(4)(b) (AML)). According to the MPL Regs 1999, reg 17(b) a woman on AML remains bound by duties of good faith and contractual provisions relating to notice periods, confidentiality, acceptance of gifts and competition.

Likewise, the employer's obligation to pay wages or salary other than statutory maternity pay (see **9.7**) is suspended. However, EqA 2010, s. 73, inserts a maternity equality clause which ensures that should she have received an increase in pay had she continued to work, any payments she is entitled to will be taken into account in assessing any such increase.

Being on maternity leave cannot be counted against the right to four weeks' annual holiday under the Working Time Directive, implemented in the UK by SI 1998/1833 (*Maria Gomez v Continental Industrias del Caucho* [2004] IRLR 407 (ECJ)).

9.2.8 Relationship with unfair dismissal and discrimination provisions

9.2.8.1 Pregnancy dismissals

According to ERA 1996, s 99, dismissal connected with pregnancy or giving birth is automatically unfair, entitling the employee to bring an unfair dismissal claim without any qualifying period of continuous employment and, should the reason be established, making the ERA 1996, s 98(4) analysis unnecessary. This provision covers women made redundant during the maternity period and not offered suitable alternative employment if available. In *Riezniece v Zemkopibas Ministria* [2013] Case C-7/12, the CJEU has held that those absent on parental leave must be treated in exactly the same way for redundancy selection purposes as employees still at work.

9.2.8.2   Discrimination on grounds of sex

Although the legislation makes the express provisions above it is important to remember that EqA 2010, s 18, will apply where a pregnant woman has suffered a detriment. No comparator is required, the legislation providing that it is discrimination for the woman to be treated 'unfavourably'. The protection extends from the start of the pregnancy and continues until her return to work or the end of either the OML or (if she is entitled to it) the AML period. This is known as the 'protected period'. Certainly, dismissal for a pregnancy-related reason will constitute direct discrimination. Moreover, any failure to provide a woman's entitlement to maternity leave or pay may constitute indirect discrimination. It will generally be appropriate to include a sex discrimination claim in these circumstances as there is no artificial cap to the compensation which may be ordered and in appropriate circumstances there may be a claim for injury to feelings, not available in an unfair dismissal claim.

A woman who is on maternity leave is not entitled to claim her normal pay during that period (EqA 2010, s 76(1A), however, she may be entitled to maternity pay (see **9.6**).

Should a woman suffer from a pregnancy-related illness any dismissal during the maternity leave period will constitute direct discrimination on grounds of sex. After the leave period (extended by up to four weeks if necessary) has concluded, this protection ends. However, an employer who provides in the contract of employment that employees will be dismissed after a specific period of absence may only begin the calculation when the maternity leave period has ended (*Brown v Rentokil* [1998] IRLR 445 (ECJ)).

Employers are required to undertake a risk assessment where work could involve risk to a pregnant woman (Management of Health and Safety at Work Regs 1999 (SI 1999/32242), reg 16). If the assessment discloses such a risk the employer should seek alternative work and if no safe work is available, the woman should be suspended. A failure to conduct the assessment will constitute unlawful sex discrimination (*Hardman v Mallon t/a Orchard Lodge Nursing Home* [2002] IRLR 516).

9.3   Adoption leave

Provisions may be found in the PAL Regs 2002. In this section, references to regulations are to these Regulations.

9.3.1   Comparison with maternity leave

These provisions mirror maternity leave. Being matched with an adoptive child is analogous to discovering you are pregnant; the date of placement is analogous to the date of birth. The periods of OML and AML are the same as with maternity leave. There are similar provisions as to the right to return (regs 23, 25 and 26), the continuation of terms and conditions of employment during adoption leave (regs 19 and 21A) and the ability of one partner to curtail his/her leave in order to permit the other to take 'shared parental leave: adoption' (ERA 2006, s 75G).

Some differences, however, need to be noted. There is no longer a requirement for a period of continuous service for OAL (reg 15). As a consequence, anyone who has taken OAL is entitled to additional adoption leave (AAL) unless the placement ends prematurely (reg 20).

9.3.2   Notice requirements

The employee must notify the employer within seven days of receiving notification of being matched with the child. This notice must state the date of placement and the date on which leave is to begin. The employer may require notices to be in writing and may require evidence about the adoption agency, the child and the relevant dates.

The start date may be varied on giving 28 days' notice and the employer is required to give notice of the date leave is expected to end.

The adoptive parents may choose which of them is to have adoption leave. The other will be entitled to claim paternity leave, regardless of gender.

9.4   Paternity leave

Provisions may be found in the PAL Regs 2002. In this section, references to regulations are to these Regulations.

The right is to one week's leave (or two weeks if he wishes to take them consecutively) (regs 5 and 9) to be completed within 56 days of the birth or of the first day of the EWC, whichever is later. It applies both to cases of birth and adoption (regs 4 and 8). Terms and conditions other than pay continue to apply, but the man on leave is entitled to statutory paternity pay (EA 2002, s 2; see **9.8**). Leave starts on the birth/placement of the child or a date specified by the employee in a notice to the employer (regs 7 and 11).

9.4.1   Eligibility

According to regs 4 and 8, the employee must satisfy three conditions:

* having 26 weeks' continuous service before the end of the 14th week before the EWC;
* being the father of the child or the mother's partner (including same-sex partner); and
* having responsibility for the upbringing of the child.

He must give notice of the EWC, the period he intends to take as paternity leave and the start date (regs 6 and 10). The employer may require this notice to be in writing and may also require the employee to certify that he is taking leave for a statutory purpose (to care for the child or the mother). The employee may change the start date on giving 28 days' notice and must give notice of the birth as soon as reasonably practicable.

9.5   Parental leave

The Maternity and Parental Leave Regulations 1999 (SI 1999/3312) as amended provide that those with responsibility for children may take up to 18 weeks' unpaid leave in respect of each child under the age of 18. One year's continuous employment is required for eligibility. Three weeks' notice must be given and the employer may postpone the period of leave for good reason. Leave may only be taken in blocks of one or more weeks (reg 14 and *Rodway v South Central Trains Ltd* [2005] IRLR 583 (CA)). This entitlement arises whether or not parents have taken advantage of the flexibility provided for by shared parental leave (see **9.2.5**).

9.6   Statutory maternity pay

This does not provide for payment throughout a period of maternity or adoption leave, but only for the first 39 weeks. There are two levels. The higher level is paid at the rate of 90 per cent of average weekly earnings. The lower level is currently (2017–18) £140.98 per week and is increased each April in line with inflation. Where the contract provides for higher payments these will apply.

9.6.1   Eligibility

Entitlement is acquired by 26 weeks' continuous employment immediately preceding the 14th week before the EWC. Should an employer attempt to avoid this liability by terminating the woman's contract before the qualifying week, she will be deemed to have been employed until that date (Statutory Maternity Pay (General) Regulations 1986 (SI 1986/1960) as amended, reg 4).

9.6.2   Payments

The higher rate is payable for six weeks; the lower rate for the following 33 weeks provided the woman continues to be absent on maternity leave. Payment starts when the woman stops working provided this is no more than 11 weeks before the EWC.

9.6.3   Shared parental pay

Where shared parental leave is taken the partner curtailing her right to leave will lose her right to maternity pay from that date, but her partner taking shared parental leave will be entitled to shared parental pay for the remaining period of leave (CFA 2014, ss 119, 120).

9.7   Statutory adoption pay

EA 2002, s 4, provides for 26 weeks' pay during adoption leave. Pay will be at the lesser of £140.98 per week or 90 per cent of normal weekly earnings. The same eligibility requirements as for adoption leave apply.

9.8   Statutory paternity pay

EA 2002, s 2, provides for pay of £140.98 per week or 90 per cent of normal weekly earnings (whichever is less) during paternity leave. The same eligibility requirements as for paternity leave apply.

9.9   Maternity allowance

This is paid to women who are not entitled to statutory maternity pay (for example, because they do not have 26 weeks' continuous service). Eligibility is gained by having paid 13 standard rate National Insurance contributions within the 66 weeks before the baby is expected. The allowance is paid by the Department for Work and Pensions (DWP) for up to 39 weeks.

9.10   Surrogate parents

Where a couple uses a surrogacy arrangement in order to become parents, different provisions apply. The woman who gives birth to the child is regarded in law as the mother unless a parental order is made under the Human Fertilisation and Embryology Act 2008, s 54. This has the effect of transferring parental rights and responsibilities to the applicants. Although the Pregnant Workers Directive 92/85 does not require the provision of maternity leave to such parents (*CD v ST* [2014] IRLR 551, CJEU), Regulation 2014/3096 in effect extends adoption leave and pay to them.

9.11   Time off to care for a dependant

ERA 1996, s 57A, provides that an employee is entitled to be permitted by his employer to take a reasonable amount of unpaid time off during working hours in order to take necessary action to assist a dependant. The definition of dependant varies with the nature of the assistance required.

This is designed to enable brief periods of 'necessary' time off to deal with 'unexpected disruption or termination of arrangements for the care of a dependant' rather than to take on the care of a dependant. 'Unexpected', however, does not mean 'sudden'. In *Royal Bank of Scotland v Harrison* [2009] IRLR 28, where the claimant had two weeks' notice of a disruption to her childcare arrangements, the Employment Appeal Tribunal (EAT) held that the greater the period of notice, the more difficult it would be to establish necessity.

The employee must give notice as soon as reasonably possible as to the reason for absence. An employer is prohibited from causing any detriment to an employee making proper use of these provisions.

A remedy may be sought from an employment tribunal which may award such compensation as appears to it to be just and equitable.

Some guidance on applying this provision is available in *Qua v John, Ford, Morrison, Solicitors* [2003] IRLR 184.

9.12   Flexible working

These provisions have been introduced into the ERA 1996, s 80F. Significant extensions were introduced by CFA 2014, Pt 9, implemented in the Flexible Working Regulations 2014 (SI 2014/1398).

9.12.1   The nature of the right

This differs from most employment protection rights as it merely entitles the employee to ask for a change in conditions of employment. The employer must consider the request in a reasonable manner, but is not obliged to agree to the changes requested.

9.12.2   Eligibility

To be eligible an employee must have 26 weeks' continuous service on the date the application is made. Earlier requirements that the employee be a carer have been repealed.

9.12.3   The application

This is regulated by ERA 1996, s 80F.
   The variation the employee may request must be either:

- place of work; or
- hours of work (either the total number or when they are worked).

The request must be made formally (forms are available on the Department for Business, Energy and Industrial Strategy (BEIS) website), in writing and dated. It must:

- contain a statement that it is an application under the statute;
- certify that the employee has the necessary relationship with the child;
- specify the change in terms of employment required;
- specify the date on which the change should take effect;
- specify the date of any previous applications;
- specify the effect the change will have on the employer's business and how this might be dealt with.

Requests may be made only once in any year.

9.12.4   The employer's response

This is regulated by ERA 1996, s 80G.
   The employer may only refuse the request on one of the following grounds:

- burden of additional costs;
- detrimental effect on ability to meet customer demand;
- inability to reorganise work among existing staff;
- inability to recruit additional staff;
- detrimental impact on quality;

- detrimental impact on performance;
- insufficient work during periods employee proposes to work;
- planned structural changes.

It is, however, not necessary for the employer to prove any of these points, but merely that he considers that one or more applies and that he has come to this conclusion on 'correct facts' (ERA 1996, s 80H(1)(b)). In *Commotion Ltd v Rutty* [2006] IRLR 171, it was held that these provisions mean that the tribunal may not consider the reasonableness of the employer's decision, but may check that the evidence supports the factual basis for the decision. In this case the evidence did not support the employer's assertion that the claimant shifting to a three-day week would have a detrimental effect on performance.

9.12.5   Procedural requirements

The employer must deal with the application in a reasonable manner and notify the employee of the answer within three months or such longer period agreed between the employer and the employee.

   If the employer agrees to the change he must give notice of the date on which it is to take effect.

   There are no required procedures for dealing with flexibility requests. However, ACAS *Code of Practice 5: Handling in a Reasonable Manner Requests to Work Flexibly* gives useful guidance (<http://www.acas.org.uk/media/pdf/f/e/Code-of-Practice-on-handling-in-a-reasonable-manner-requests-to-work-flexibly.pdf>).

9.13   Remedies

9.13.1   General remedies

Claims in respect of an employer's failure to provide for any of the rights identified in this chapter may be brought in the employment tribunals.

9.13.2   Remedies in respect of flexible working

A claim may be brought to an employment tribunal alleging a failure to deal with a request reasonably or rejection taken on 'incorrect facts'. The normal limitation period of three months applies. The tribunal may award up to eight weeks' pay or order reconsideration of the request.

   Any dismissal for asserting these rights is automatically unfair and falls within the provisions of ERA 1996, s 104.

9.14   Parental rights flowchart

Figure 9.1 provides a general outline only and should not be relied upon without reference to the appropriate text (references in brackets), to practitioner works and the primary sources.

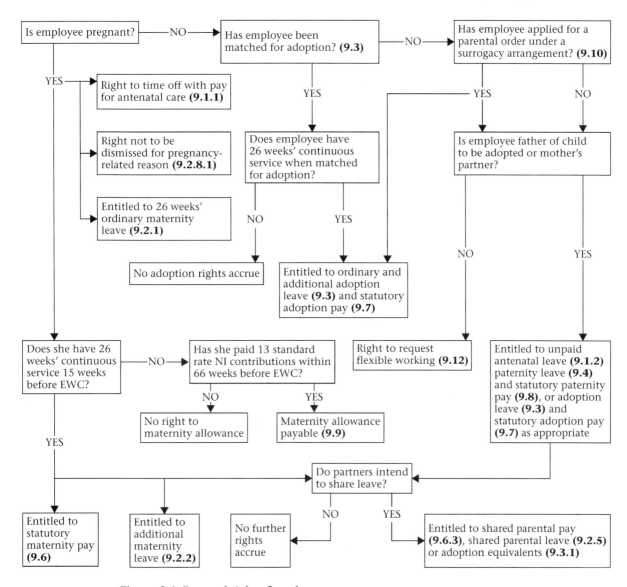

Figure 9.1 Parental rights flowchart

10

Equal terms

10.1 Introduction

Equal pay is the subject of a significant proportion of employment tribunal applications, and has become one of the major areas where the importance of EU provisions has been felt. The legislation was designed to remedy the general tendency for women's pay to be less than that of men, even when their work was similar or of equivalent value. In this it has been only partially successful.

Historically, the major source of law here is the Equal Pay Act 1970 (EPA 1970). This has been amended, and its interpretation has been influenced by EU provisions, especially art 141 (ex 119) of the EC Treaty (now TFEU, art 157), the Equal Pay Directive 75/117 and the Equal Treatment Directive 76/207. The significance of Community legislation has meant that the relevant case law includes a number of important decisions of the Court of Justice of the European Union (CJEU). The provisions of the EPA 1970 have now been re-enacted, although in different terms, in the Equality Act 2010 (EqA 2010), Pt 5, Chapter 3 (ss 64–80). This chapter will explain the development of the legislation in order to make sense of the key case law, and then turn to its current incarnation.

The EPA 1970 came into force in 1975, thus giving employers a five-year period during which to take the necessary steps to conform with the law. It was perceived as operating beside the Sex Discrimination Act 1975 (SDA 1975). Indeed, Phillips J, while President of the Employment Appeal Tribunal (EAT), in *Macarthys Ltd v Smith* [1978] IRLR 10 said, at p 504:

it is desirable that the Sex Discrimination Act 1975 and the Equal Pay Act 1970 should be construed and applied in harmony, as together in effect they constitute a single code.

While SDA 1975 included discrimination on grounds of sex which falls outside the contract of employment itself, EPA 1970 was concerned with discriminatory provisions of a contract of employment or for services. Thus it was not restricted to matters of pay, and could be used, by applicants of either sex, to challenge unequal terms of any sort. Most cases have, however, been brought by women, and this chapter necessarily reflects this fact.

EPA 1970 also applied to a wider group of workers than, for example, the unfair dismissal legislation. Section 1(6)(a) provides:

'employed' means employed under a contract of service or of apprenticeship or a contract personally to execute any work or labour ...

Thus the provisions are not restricted to employees.

The historic distinction between the EPA 1970 (applying to discrimination in contractual terms) and the SDA 1975 (applying to other discrimination) is maintained by

EqA 2010, s 70. It is best understood by remembering that discrimination is a claim in tort whereas a claim for equal terms is one for breach of contract.

10.2   Method of operation

10.2.1   The sex equality clause

EqA 2010, ss 64–80, operates by importing a 'sex equality clause' into all contracts of employment (s 66). Section 67 extends the same principle to pension schemes. Although it is thus concerned with contractual matters, the normal remedy is a complaint to an employment tribunal rather than to a court. It is concerned with inequality between the sexes, and does not provide for claiming fair differentials.

The sex equality clause operates in different ways depending on the circumstances. Where men enjoy a provision which is denied to women (for example, a contractual right to overtime) the sex equality clause operates by importing that provision into the women's contract of employment. Where contracts of both men and women cover a particular matter (for example, the number of weeks of paid sick leave permissible) and the women's term is less favourable than that of the men, the sex equality clause operates by modifying the women's term so as to make it equally favourable.

10.2.2   The comparator

An applicant must find a comparator of the other sex in the same employment in order to found a claim. It is insufficient to convince the tribunal that a hypothetical man, if he were employed, would be granted more favourable terms. EPA 1970 had restricted comparators to those employed contemporaneously. However, an applicant was able to use her immediate predecessor as a comparator if making a claim under art 141 (now TFEU, art 157) as opposed to EPA 1970 (*Macarthys Ltd v Smith* [1980] IRLR 209). Article 157 does not, however, permit use of a hypothetical comparator (*Coloroll Pension Trustees Ltd v Russell* [1994] ECR I–4389). EqA 2010 now removes the domestic restriction on non-contemporaneous comparators (s 64(2)).

Moreover, where a sex equality clause 'has no effect' (for example, in the absence of a comparator) s 71 permits a woman to bring a sex discrimination claim under s 13 provided that the discriminatory pay arose from direct sex discrimination. This effectively permits a hypothetical comparator (see **8.3.1**) and constitutes an exception from the distinction between former SDA 1975 and EPA 1970 cases (see **10.1**).

10.2.2.1   Same employment

The concept of 'same employment' limits which employees may be used as comparators. According to s 79(3) and (4) it covers men employed by the claimant's employer or any associated employer at the same establishment or one where common terms operate. Where one employer is a subsidiary of another they will be associated employers, as they will where both are subsidiaries of a third. For the male comparator to form the basis of a claim, however, he must work in the same establishment (albeit for a different, but associated employer), or in another establishment in Great Britain where all that class of employees work under common terms and conditions. Where the associated employers have established their terms and conditions of employment independently there will be no basis for male employees to be used as comparators. The Act thus provides no basis for establishing comparisons outside existing bargaining units. The House of Lords has given useful guidance on the meaning of 'common terms and conditions'. In *British Coal Corporation v Smith* [1996] IRLR 404, female canteen workers and cleaners at 47 different establishments sought to compare themselves with surface mineworkers at 14 different establishments. The applicants worked under common terms. The mineworkers worked subject to a national agreement, but there were locally negotiated variations in respect of bonuses. Their Lordships held that the proper test of 'common terms and conditions' under EPA 1970, s 1(6) (the predecessor of EqA 2010, s 79(3)–(4)) was a broad one. They took the view that the legislators had not intended to exclude a woman's claim where there were minor differences, but had wished to ensure that the groups of workers compared were working under sufficiently similar conditions for a fair comparison to be made. It is not, therefore, necessary for terms to be identical. This is likely to be of significance wherever collective bargaining operates nationally (most significantly in the public sector) even though local variations may exist.

The broad terms of art 157 mean that it may provide a remedy in situations where the more detailed drafting of s 79 would appear to deny one. In *Scullard v Knowles and Southern Regional Council for Education and Training* [1996] IRLR 344, SRCET had established 12 further education units. Mrs Scullard managed one of these, and sought to compare herself with men doing the same job in the other 11 units, all of whom received higher pay. The tribunal had held that as these units were not companies, they were not 'associated employers' as defined in the Act. The EAT, however, held that art 119 (now TFEU, art 157) was not confined to undertakings of any particular form, and that it prevailed over EPA 1970, s 1(6). The tribunal should therefore apply the test (established by the ECJ in *Defrenne v SABENA (No 2)* [1976] ECR 455); whether the work was carried out in the same establishment or service. This approach was confirmed in *South Ayrshire Council v Morton* [2001] IRLR 29.

Note also the effect of *Enderby v Frenchay Health Authority* (Case C-127/92) [1993] IRLR 591, where the ECJ contemplated comparisons across different collective bargaining units in the context of art 119 (now TFEU, art 157) claims (see **10.3.5**). A number of successful claims have been made (for example) by Scottish teachers working for different authorities as their terms and conditions are subject to a common statutory scheme (see *South Ayrshire Council v Morton* [2002] IRLR 256 (CS)). In *Allonby v Accrington and Rossendale College* [2001] IRLR 364, the Court of Appeal indicated that within the public sector, where people work for different employers but under very similar terms and conditions, there may be considerable scope to use comparators in other employment. The limits to this are indicated by the ECJ in *Lawrence v Regent Office Care Ltd* [2002] IRLR 822. Here female caterers had been employed by a county council but then transferred to a private company under less favourable terms. They were unable to use male caterers still working with their original employer as comparators as there was no one body responsible for the pay of both groups.

The principle which informs the ECJ jurisprudence here is the concept of a 'single source' for the contractual terms which are being compared. In *North Cumbria Acute Hospitals NHS Trust v Potter* [2009] IRLR 176, the EAT held that the claimant must either show that she and her comparator work within the s 1(6) criteria (same employment, associated employers or under common terms and conditions) or that their contractual terms stem from a common source (such as a specific collective agreement). It is not necessary for her to show both.

Difficulties have arisen in respect of comparisons drawn by women making claims under the 'work of equal value' principle (see **10.2.3.3**) doing very different jobs in different places from men who are nevertheless employed by the same employer. This may typically arise in a local authority, where (for example) predominantly female jobs such as that of classroom assistant may be compared with predominantly male jobs such as that of road cleaner. Not only is the work different (although it may be of equal value); one cannot imagine the work of each category being undertaken in the other's place of work. In *North v Dumfries and Galloway Council* [2013] UKSC 45, the Supreme Court held that it is not necessary to hypothesise as to the terms the men might work under were they to move to the same place of work. To do so would undermine the *British Coal* principle. It would defeat the object of the legislation: 'to secure equality of treatment, not only for the same work, but also for work rated as equivalent or assessed by the experts to be of equal value.' The Supreme Court also confirmed that where the terms of the two groups had a common source an equal value comparison should be available in order to ensure consistency with TFEU, art 157 and the ECJ decision in *Defrenne v SABENA (No 2)* [1976] ECR 455.

In equality of terms cases based on indirect discrimination the claimant will need to identify a comparator group, as in EqA 2010, s 19 cases (see **8.4**). In *Cheshire & Wirral Partnership NHS Trust v Abbott* [2006] IRLR 546, the Court of Appeal provides guidance, indicating that the group should be as large as possible, provided it shares the relevant characteristics and does work of equal value.

There is one situation in which the Court of Appeal has indicated that no comparator is required. This is where the pay discrimination arises because a woman is pregnant or on maternity leave (*Alabaster v Barclays Bank (No 2)* [2005] IRLR 576). This is now enacted in EqA 2010, ss 72–76.

10.2.3 The work

It is rare for there to be a male comparator doing identical work for higher pay. Most contracts of employment are complex and the diversity of jobs within any one employment may be considerable. There are bound, therefore, to be differences between jobs in the majority of cases. Where these differences are trivial they should not prevent an equal pay claim, but where they are of significance they may do. This raises two problems:

- How can the link between the two be established?
- Where the differences are not significant, how can the law make a fair comparison between workers doing different jobs?

The Act's approach is not to require the jobs compared to be identical. EqA 2010, s 65, identifies the relationship between the work of the woman and her male comparator necessary for an equality clause to operate. In its original version the Act adopted a very limited approach, restricting that relationship to 'like work', or 'work rated as equivalent' (through a job evaluation study). 'Work of equal value' was added in 1983.

10.2.3.1 Like work

EqA 2010, s 65(1)(a), introduces this concept, which is defined by s 65(2) as work of the same or a broadly similar nature, where any differences between the things a woman does and the things her male comparator does are not of practical importance. Section 65(3) provides further explanation. This wording in its earlier incarnation as EPA 1970, s 1(4), has been important in establishing the tribunals' approach.

In *Dugdale v Kraft Foods Ltd* [1977] ICR 48, the work was of a 'broadly similar nature', except for the men's obligatory night-work. The tribunal had thought this to be of practical importance. The EAT, however, held that this did not come within s 1(4) as it is not 'the things she does and the things they do' but the time at which they do it. Therefore this difference was not sufficient to prevent it from being like work.

This approach was consistent with the recognition that to make the concept of like work effective it should be interpreted broadly. In *Shields v E. Coomes (Holdings) Ltd* [1978] ICR 1159 (CA), a woman working in a betting shop received 62 pence per hour while her male counterparts received £1.06. The employer's justification was the contractual requirement that men deal with troublemakers. As there was no evidence that the men had in fact had to deal with such problems, the applicant established her case. The principle is that tribunals should consider the actual frequency of any differences in the work done rather than a difference in contractual obligations. It is worth noting that this decision was made under art 119 of the EC Treaty (now TFEU, art 157), rather than EPA 1970.

Is the time at which the work is done significant?

It is common practice in industry for workers to be paid a premium for working unsocial or long hours (through shift allowances or higher overtime rates). *Dugdale v Kraft Foods Ltd* [1977] ICR 48 established that working at different times did not prevent the work from being 'like work' within the s 1(4) definition. Differences in working hours should not therefore be a justification for different basic rates of pay. This does not prevent an employer from paying a higher rate to those working at night or on Sundays, or from making a payment to workers undertaking an obligation to work at such times. However, any such extra pay should be no greater than necessary to reflect the unsociable nature of the time at which the work was done (*National Coal Board v Sherwin* [1978] ICR 700).

Does the undertaking of responsibility make a job dissimilar?

A contractual obligation to supervise others' work, or to undertake similar responsibilities, provided it is actually performed, is sufficient to prevent two jobs from being 'like work' (*Waddington v Leicester Council for Voluntary Service* [1977] ICR 266).

Working without supervision may entail enough responsibility to make a job sufficiently different from one where the work is supervised. In *Thomas v National Coal Board* [1987] ICR 757 (EAT), working alone permanently at night with no supervision could prevent the work from being 'like' even though the work was otherwise similar. Note that the significant difference here was the extra responsibility undertaken, not the time at which the work was carried out.

10.2.3.2   Work rated as equivalent

Where a job evaluation study has been carried out, this is the appropriate test (EqA 2010, s 65(1)(b)). Section 65(4) provides as follows:

A's work is rated as equivalent to B's work if a job evaluation study –

> *(a)   Gives an equal value to A's job and B's job in terms of the demands made on a worker, or*

> *(b)   Would give an equal value to A's job and B's job in those terms were the evaluation not made on a sex-specific system.*

This wording differs from that in EPA 1970, s 1(5), and seeks to codify the case law interpretations since then. These cases, therefore, remain useful. It was established early (*Eaton Ltd v Nuttall* [1977] ICR 272) that only job analyses which are impartial and thorough in their analysis meet these requirements. What is more, the parties to the performance of the job evaluation study must have accepted its validity (*Arnold v Beecham Group Ltd* [1982] ICR 744), thus preventing one party from imposing a disputed analysis.

Where a job evaluation study is itself discriminatory it can be challenged. In *Rummler v Dato-Druck GmbH* (Case 237/85) [1987] ICR 774, the study gave considerable weight to 'physical effort'. The ECJ, hearing the application under art 1(2) of the Equal Treatment Directive (76/207), held that, although it was not discriminatory in itself to give weight to characteristics more commonly found among men, it must also consider characteristics for which female employees may score highly if it is not to be discriminatory overall. The court decided that a system based on the criterion of muscular effort is only discriminatory if it excludes from consideration the activation of small groups of muscles which typifies manual dexterity. Thus an evaluation which gave weight to lifting heavy weights, yet ignored manual dexterity in evaluating different jobs could be discriminatory and fail to comply with EPA 1970, s 1(5).

The woman does not need to have been given a points score identical to that of her comparator by the job evaluation study provided it places her in the same grade. In *Springboard Sunderland Trust v Robson* [1992] IRLR 261, where the study awarded points under a number of headings, R was given 410 points while her comparator received 428. The method used for converting these into grades, however, slotted both these scores into the same grade. It was held that this conversion into grades formed part of the study and that therefore the two jobs had been evaluated as equal. This approach had the twin merits of being more practical, and recognising that job evaluation was not a precise science.

10.2.3.3 Work of equal value

This concept appears in EqA 2010, s 65(1)(c). It is defined in s 65(6):

A's work is of equal value to B's work if it is—

    (a)   *neither like B's work nor rated as equivalent to B's work, but*

    (b)   *nevertheless equal to B's work in terms of the demands made on A by reference to factors such as effort, skill and decision-making.*

Section 131 provides a special procedure for these cases. Where a woman claims her work to be of equal value to her comparator's in terms of demands made on her (for instance under such headings as effort, skill and decision) the employment tribunal, unless it is sure that there is no case, may commission a report from a member of the panel of independent experts appointed by ACAS. Both parties are entitled to make representations and to challenge the report before the tribunal.

Employment Tribunals (Rules of Procedure) Regulations 2004 (SI 2004/1861), Sch 6, provides detailed rules for the conduct of hearings addressing experts' reports. This involves a stage 1 hearing at which the tribunal decides whether to commission an expert report and a stage 2 hearing at which the report is considered and disputed facts resolved. Finally, there is a stage 3 hearing (which will be stage 2 if no report was commissioned) at which the question of equal value is resolved.

Some major cases have settled questions about the interpretation of these equal value provisions. These all refer to the provisions of the EPA 1970.

May the provisions be used when there is a man working on identical conditions to the woman?

In *Pickstone v Freemans plc* [1989] AC 66, five women warehouse operatives were paid the same as a male warehouse operative, but less than a male warehouse checker. They argued that their work was of equal value to that of the checker. Section 1(2)(c) allowed an equal value claim 'where a woman is employed on work which, not being work in relation to which paragraph (a) or (b) above applies, is … of equal value to that of a man in the same employment'. The employer's objection that para (c) only applied where there was no man doing 'like work' was upheld by the tribunal and the EAT. The Court of Appeal, whilst agreeing with this analysis, nevertheless held that a claim existed under art 119 (now TFEU, art 157), which takes precedence over conflicting UK legislation. The House of Lords, however, pointed out that the Regulations which introduced s 1(2)(c) were designed to implement EEC Directive 75/117 and should be interpreted in this light. To achieve this, the section should be read as only prohibiting an equal value claim where paras (a) or (b) apply to the man with whom she was claiming equality. This interpretation prevents employers from avoiding the provisions of the Act by employing a 'token male'.

May a woman claim equal pay where she receives other benefits which the employer claims compensate for her low pay?

In *Hayward v Cammell Laird Shipbuilders Ltd* [1988] AC 894, Hayward, employed on work of equal value to male employees, had lower pay, but better sickness benefits and meal breaks. The Court of Appeal had denied her claim by looking at the whole employment package. On appeal, the House of Lords pointed out that s 1 provides that where any term of the woman's contract is less favourable than a term of a similar kind under the man's contract it shall be so modified as not to be less favourable. Each term had to be considered separately. She could therefore demand equal pay even though she received these extra benefits. The House of Lords recognised that this interpretation could enable leap-frogging claims. Hayward's male comparators could presumably now demand her sickness benefits. If, however, such differences are justified regardless of sex there is a defence under s 1(3) (see **10.3**).

This decision was distinguished by the Court of Appeal in *Degnan v Redcar and Cleveland Borough Council* [2005] IRLR 615. The court held that the different terms of compared contracts of employment (in this case, attendance allowances, an hourly rate and fixed bonuses) should be aggregated together with the basic hourly rate of pay and dealt with as an overall pay package. This analysis achieved the policy objective of avoiding the selection of different elements of different comparators' contracts to achieve an advantage. It appeared, therefore, that financial provisions of the contract may be aggregated while other terms may not.

Degnan itself has subsequently been distinguished as turning on its own facts, by the Court of Appeal in *St Helens & Knowsley Hospital NHS Trust v Brownbill* [2011] IRLR 815, where, even though the female claimants earned more than their male comparators, basic salary and payments for unsocial hours were best seen as separate terms. Maurice Kay LJ points out that 'the men's terms in *Degnan* had features of artificiality and historical anomaly which tended to disguise the reality'. He agrees with Cox J in the EAT who had confirmed the analysis in *Hayward* and pointed out the limitations of the equal terms provisions. They are 'not a fair wages statute, it is impermissible for the tribunal to select the terms as to pay to be compared, for the purposes of achieving a broadly equitable outcome'. The revisions in EqA 2010 do not make any change to this limited function of the equal terms provisions.

What is the function of the independent evaluation?

The expert's report is evidence before the tribunal and although significant is not conclusive. The decision remains one of fact for the tribunal (*Tennants Textile Colours Ltd v Todd* [1989] IRLR 3).

Can the evaluation of the independent expert be challenged?

An employer must bring any objections as to the facts on which the report is to be based as a part of a challenge to the admissibility of the expert's report. It applies to new evidence only (*Tennants Textile Colours Ltd v Todd* [1989] IRLR 3 (NICA)) allowing either party to question the expert's findings of fact as to their accuracy or as to the weight to be given to them. The court also confirmed that the expert's report has no special status as evidence and the tribunal may disagree with its findings without going so far as to find it perverse. The final decision is in the hands of the tribunal and there may be cases where parties are justified in commissioning their own reports where they consider there are grounds for challenging that of the expert appointed from the ACAS panel. Moreover, it was held in *Dibro Ltd v Hore* [1990] ICR 370, that an appropriate job evaluation, commissioned even as late as between the expert's report and the reconvening of the tribunal to consider the report, could act as a complete defence to an equal value claim, provided it referred to conditions at the time the proceedings were initiated.

Anyone pursuing such a course should note that, although the normal written answers procedure is available, there are no powers to compel an applicant to be interviewed by such a privately commissioned expert (*Lloyds Bank plc v Fox* [1989] ICR 80).

The ACAS questions approach may be used in equality of terms cases (see **10.2.4**).

Employer's own evaluations

Under s 65(6)(a) an equal value complaint cannot proceed if jobs have been assessed as of unequal value. However, in *Bromley v H. & J. Quick Ltd* [1988] ICR 623, a 'whole job' evaluation had been carried out, finding jobs unequal. The Court of Appeal said this was not enough. An equal value complaint may only be stopped by an analytical job evaluation which was shown not to be tainted by sex discrimination itself. This is consistent with the approach in *Eaton Ltd v Nuttall* [1977] ICR 272, where the inadequacy of the job evaluation enabled the applicant to make a s 1(2)(a) (now s 65(1)(a)) 'like work' claim.

10.2.3.4   Direct application of EU provisions

The limitations of the EPA 1970 were reduced by the direct applicability of certain EU provisions. There are two significant ways in which this may be done. The first concerns the Treaty on the Functioning of the European Union itself, the second concerns Directives. For a fuller discussion of these concepts, see **3.4.1–3.4.2.1**.

Treaty on the Functioning of the European Union

TFEU, art 157 (formerly art 119, later art 141, EC Treaty), may be directly applied (see *Barber v Guardian Royal Exchange Assurance Group* (Case C-262/88) [1991] 1 QB 344), and in being applied may develop domestic law. Thus in *Kowalska v Freie und Hansestadt Hamburg* (Case C-33/89) [1990] IRLR 447, a collective agreement which indirectly discriminated against women by treating full-timers more favourably than part-timers was held to contravene art 119 (now TFEU, art 157) unless the employer could show it to be objectively justifiable. This went beyond the EPA 1970 which only controlled the contract of employment itself. Of particular significance was the remedy provided by the ECJ. Unlike the UK approach, which would have been to render the objectionable provision void and leave the parties to negotiate a new one, the ECJ's approach was to provide the part-timers with benefits *proportionate* to their hours of work. Time limits for art 157 claims will generally be the same as in the domestic implementing legislation. However, they will not start to run until such time as it becomes reasonably clear to an applicant that the art 157 claim exists (*Rankin v BCC* [1993] IRLR 69).

Directives

EC Directives are not directly applicable as such, as they impose an obligation on Member States to act where they do not already make appropriate provision. Member States which fail to take appropriate steps may be challenged in the ECJ. The significance of this was extended by *Marshall v Southampton & South West Hampshire Area Health Authority (Teaching)* [1986] ECR 723 (for discussion see **3.4.2.1**). This case was brought before the SDA 1986, which prohibits compulsory sex-based differentials in retirement ages, was enacted. Such differentials were already contrary to the Equal Treatment Directive (76/207). Although the UK was in breach, individuals could not enforce the Directive against their employers. However, the health authority was held to be a part of the State. Since it would be wrong for the State to be protected by its failure to comply with the Directive, the ECJ applied the Directive directly, and the employee succeeded in a claim for breach of the Directive. Thus public sector employees will generally be able to enforce EU Directives against their employers where not implemented by national legislation, but those in the private sector will not. The dividing line between the sectors has been the subject of judicial consideration since *Marshall* (*Foster, Griffin, Doughty* and *NUT* also discussed at **3.4.2.1**).

Article 157 or Directive?

The question of whether a right is conferred by art 157 or a Directive may therefore be crucial for private sector employees. In *McKechnie v UBM Building Supplies (Southern) Ltd* [1991] IRLR 283, the applicant initially failed in her claim for statutory and *ex gratia* redundancy payments which were denied to her at the age of 61 as she was a woman (the Employment Act 1989 has since removed this discriminatory statutory provision). The tribunal had concluded that this fell within the Equal Treatment Directive covering discrimination in working conditions, which was not directly applicable as she was employed in the private sector. The EAT held, however, that, in the light of the ECJ decision in *Barber v Guardian Royal Exchange Assurance Group* (Case C-262/88) [1991] 1 QB 344, benefits payable in connection with redundancy fell within the definition of 'pay', and thus within the scope of art 119 (now TFEU, art 157). Thus Mrs McKechnie could pursue her claim directly.

Note that there is a strong argument to the effect that the Equal Pay Directive (75/117) has direct effect against all employers as the ECJ has said it does no more than 'facilitate the practical application of the principle of equal pay outlined in Article 119 [now TFEU, art 157]' (*Jenkins v Kingsgate (Clothing Productions) Ltd (No 2)* [1981] ICR 715). This argument was strengthened by the adoption in the Amsterdam Treaty 1997 of measures to extend sex equality principles beyond equality in pay.

The House of Lords decision in *Webb v EMO Air Cargo (UK) Ltd* [1993] IRLR 27 (see **3.4.3.2**), recognises that domestic legislation must be interpreted in line with relevant EU provisions, including Directives, but not if to do so would distort or add new measures to the domestic provisions. The distinction between Treaty and Directive provisions thus remains significant.

10.2.4 Proof in equal pay cases

The formal burden of proof is on the applicant, who will encounter difficulties in establishing the reasons for discriminatory contractual provisions as with the other anti-discrimination legislation. ACAS offers guidance as to how questions might be asked (see http://www.acas.org.uk/media/pdf/m/p/Asking-and-responding-to-questions-of-discrimination-in-the-workplace.pdf). A failure to reply or an evasive reply will enable the tribunal to draw appropriate inferences, as will be familiar from the discrimination legislation (see **8.8.2.2**).

10.3   Defences to an equal pay claim

As Part 5, Chapter 3, is designed only to prevent inequality in contracts of employment arising from sex differences it provides a defence for employers who have genuine non-sex-related reasons for pay or other differences. This is known as the 'material factor defence' and is provided for by EqA 2010, s 69:

(1) *The sex equality clause in A's terms has no effect in relation to a difference between A's terms and B's terms if the responsible person shows that the difference is because of a material factor reliance on which—*

   (a) *does not involve treating A less favourably because of A's sex than the responsible person treats B, and*

   (b) *if the factor is within subsection (2), is a proportionate means of achieving a legitimate aim.*

(2) *A factor is within this subsection if A shows that, as a result of the factor, A and persons of the same sex doing work equal to A's are put at a particular disadvantage when compared with persons of the opposite sex doing work equal to A's.*

(3) *For the purposes of subsection (1), the long-term objective of reducing inequality between men's and women's terms of work is always to be regarded as a legitimate aim.*

The object is to permit pay differences for genuine reasons which are not sex-related. These provisions are differently worded from the equivalent provisions in EPA 1970, s 1(3), but are designed to achieve the same goals and resolve some of the difficulties considered in the case law.

The burden of establishing such a defence rests on the employer on a balance of probabilities as in ordinary civil cases (see *Financial Times Ltd v Byrne (No 2)* [1992] IRLR 163). If the employer can establish that there is no sex discrimination underlying the pay differential, he has a good defence (*Glasgow City Council v Marshall* [2000] IRLR 272 (HL)). If, however, there is evidence of sex discrimination the employer will have to justify the difference in pay objectively (*Jenkins v Kingsgate (Clothing Productions) Ltd (No 2)* [1981] ICR 715; *Bilka Kaufhaus GmbH v Weber von Hartz* (Case C-170/84) [1987] ICR 110). This test, as with that for the justification of indirect discrimination (EqA 2010, s 19(2)(d)), requires the employer to show something approaching a need for the unequal provision and that the provision is appropriate and reasonably necessary in order to meet that need. It clearly prevents a mere matter of convenience from justifying a departure from equal terms in a woman's contract, as was accepted by the House of Lords in *Rainey v Greater Glasgow Health Board* (see **10.3.4**).

The jurisprudence on legitimate aim and proportionality (see **8.4.5**) is clearly relevant to the genuine material factor defence and recent case law has emphasised the need for employers to provide clear evidence of genuine justification.

The concept of material factor is best illustrated with some examples.

10.3.1   Grading schemes allowing for differences in skill, capacity or experience

In *National Vulcan Engineering Insurance Group Ltd v Wade* [1979] QB 132, clerks were doing identical jobs but on different grades depending on how well they worked. There was evidence that women as well as men could get on to higher grades. The Court of Appeal held that this was a defence for the employer. It is worth noting that the logic of cases like *Rummler v Dato-Druck GmbH* (Case C-237/85) [1987] ICR 774, is that an inquiry should be allowed into whether the criteria for allocating grades may introduce sex bias.

Many employees work on incremental scales, where a pay rise to reflect the value of experience is received annually until the top of the scale is reached. This, however, often discriminates against women, who tend to have shorter periods of continuous service. In *Cadman v Health & Safety Executive* [2006] IRLR 969, the ECJ has indicated that such scales do not need to be justified by the employer. However, where a claimant raises 'serious doubts' as to whether the length of service criterion is justified, the burden passes to the employer to provide evidence that the criterion is fully justified. Thus, in *Wilson v Health and Safety Executive* [2009] IRLR 282, it was alleged that inspectors became fully proficient after five years, thus challenging a 10-year incremental scale. The EAT remitted the case to the tribunal to decide whether the claimant's evidence had raised such a 'serious doubt'.

Bonus schemes are another method of reflecting employees' performance. However, where they are available in male-dominated, but not in female-dominated jobs they may lead to unequal pay. The EAT, in *Hartlepool Borough Council v Dolphin* [2009] IRLR 168, has held that such schemes will only provide a material factor defence if genuine. Thus, if they are designed to reward productivity they will only be genuine if they continue to achieve productivity improvements. A failure to monitor the effectiveness of a bonus scheme will indicate that it is not genuine.

10.3.2   Red-circling

This is the name given to the practice whereby an individual, while being moved to a lower-status job, retains existing pay levels. It is often used as an alternative to redundancy. The courts have accepted this provided it is for a genuine *personal* reason, and is open to men and women alike. This test becomes clear from two cases considered together by the EAT.

In *Charles Early & Marriott (Witney) Ltd v Smith* [1978] QB 11, a warehouseman had been demoted to ticket-writer, but his pay was protected. Women ticket-writers were held to be unable to claim equal pay with him because his pay was personal to him and not based on discriminatory grounds. By contrast, in *Snoxell v Vauxhall Motors Ltd* [1978] QB 11, male inspectors had been paid more than female inspectors. In order to comply with EPA 1970 the employer regraded the men, bringing their wages down in line with the women. Existing male inspectors, however, were allowed to retain their original pay, new ones being given the lower rate. When women inspectors claimed equal pay the employer raised a s 1(3) (now s 69) defence. The EAT held that this example of 'red-circling' was clearly based on past discriminatory practice and was therefore no defence. Thus it is not sufficient for such defences merely to be raised. They must be tested to ensure that they do not conceal sex discrimination.

What is more, a red-circling scheme which is justified when introduced must remain under review. The respondent must 'show that the mooted factor retains the essential attributes of genuineness and materiality' (*Fearnon v Smurfit Corrugated Cases (Lurgan) Ltd* [2009] IRLR 132 (NICA)).

Red-circling following a TUPE transfer may also constitute a material factor. What is more, in *Skills Development Scotland v Buchanan* [2011] UKEAT 0042/10/2505, it was held that, provided the original pay gap was not gender-related, there is no need to take steps (such as freezing the transferred employees' pay until the others have caught up) to equalise the situation.

10.3.3   Pay protection schemes

When an employer discovers gender-based pay inequality through a job evaluation scheme it often provides for the downgrading of jobs conventionally done by men or, where resources are scarce, a reduction in the pay of some workers in order to achieve equality for all. Pay protection schemes are designed to cushion the impact of this and thus have similarities to red-circling (see **10.3.2**). This is likely to result in (some) men continuing to be paid more than women. Might this provide a material factor defence?

In principle it appears that it might. According to the Court of Appeal in *Redcar & Cleveland Borough Council v Bainbridge Surtees* [2008] IRLR 776, such schemes may justify a continuing inequality, but 'the employer will have great difficulty in justifying the continuation of any discriminatory element'. It appears that this difficulty will be greater where the employer knew that the pay protection scheme had a continuing discriminatory effect. In the instant cases neither employer was able to rely on it as a material factor defence.

It is important to be clear what it is that needs to be justified. In *Glasgow City Council v Unison claimants* [2017] IRLR 739 a pay protection scheme protected manual workers, predominantly men, who had received bonuses. Their work had been rated as equivalent to that of women who had not received the bonuses and who were not therefore facing a pay reduction. Although it was indirectly discriminatory to continue to pay the men more, the tribunal had found it to be proportionate. On appeal both the EAT and the Inner House of the Court of Session pointed out that what needed to be justified was not the protection scheme itself, but the decision to exclude the women claimants from the benefit accorded to the manual workers. The court noted that although the employers were motivated to avoid industrial strife from failing to protect those whose pay was being reduced 'there was no evidence to suggest any such risk would have arisen from extending the payments to the claimants'.

10.3.4   Market forces

Where an employer pays a higher salary to attract into employment an individual who is already earning the higher amount, does this provide a material factor defence?

Although earlier cases (for example, *Fletcher v Clay Cross (Quarry Services) Ltd* [1978] IRLR 361) had held that market forces, being the result of past discriminatory practice, should not act as material factor defences, the House of Lords in *Rainey v Greater Glasgow Health Board* [1987] AC 224, has rejected that view where the sex difference is incidental. In 1980 it was decided to start a prosthesis fitting service in the National Health Service. Previously this had been done by private contractors. In order to recruit experienced prosthetists from those contractors the employer offered the alternative of the standard Whitley Council rate or the private sector pay and conditions. Twenty prosthetists, all of whom were male, joined the service on the private sector rates. Thereafter, newly employed prosthetists were to receive the standard Whitley Council rate. The appellant, employed later on the standard rate, and earning £7,295 p.a., claimed equal pay with one of the original group paid on the private sector rate of £10,085 p.a. The employer claimed a material factor defence.

The House of Lords held that the difference was that the appellant had entered the NHS direct, her comparator through a private contractor. The sex difference was accidental. A material difference could embrace all the significant and relevant circumstances, including economic factors or organisational efficiency. As the NHS prosthesis service could never have been set up in time without attracting such people, this was a good and objectively justified ground.

The scope of the market forces defence was restricted by the decision of the House of Lords in *Ratcliffe v North Yorks County Council* [1995] IRLR 439. In a compulsory competitive tendering situation, the employer's perceived need to cut the wages of dinner ladies to compete with private contractors did not meet the requirement of an objective justification. The wage cut was described by Lord Slynn as 'the very kind of discrimination in relation to pay which the Act sought to remove'. The case law referred to in **8.4.5.2** is also relevant to these questions.

What is more, an employer seeking to justify a differential in this way must provide evidence that the entire differential, not merely some of it, is justified (*Cumbria County Council v Dow (No 1)* [2008] IRLR 91).

10.3.4.1 Do financial factors provide a continuing defence?

Where financial constraints have operated to provide the employer with a defence to a claim against a decision to pay a woman less than the amount paid to existing male employees, they will cease to act as a defence when they themselves cease. In *Benveniste v University of Southampton* [1989] IRLR 122, Dr B accepted a lower salary than normal as the university was under severe financial constraints. This was held to be a material difference between her and her male comparators. The Court of Appeal, however, held that once the constraints disappeared the justification for the lower rate of pay also disappeared. The employer was therefore unable to rely on this defence.

10.3.5 Extent of the defence

This is not an exhaustive list of material factor defences and new ones do emerge. The courts will not, however, recognise new defences without good reason. Thus, in *Coventry City Council v Nicholls* [2009] IRLR 345, the EAT rejected an argument that trade union intransigence justified their failure to introduce pay equality.

The ECJ decision in *Enderby v Frenchay Health Authority* (Case C-127/92) [1993] IRLR 591, resolved a number of questions referred to it by the Court of Appeal. Mrs Enderby was a speech therapist who compared herself with clinical psychologists and pharmacists, whose pay exceeded hers by up to 60 per cent. Speech therapy, an almost exclusively female profession, had conditions of service negotiated in a different collective bargaining forum from the other professions, which, in their senior levels, were predominantly male. The Court of Appeal's questions were:

(a) Did art 119 (now TFEU, art 157) require the employer to justify objectively the pay differences between these professions?

(b) Was the fact that pay levels were determined by separate bargaining structures which were not in themselves tainted by sex discrimination a sufficient objective justification?

(c) If part of the pay disparity could be justified by reference to market forces, did that justify the entire disparity, or only that part of it?

The ECJ answered the first question in the affirmative, thus making it clear that there is no need for the applicant to show a 'requirement or condition' which has an indirectly discriminatory effect in art 157 cases as was then required for claims under SDA 1975, s 1(1)(b). The second question was answered in the negative, thus emphasising the ECJ's approach of concentrating on results, rather than how discriminatory consequences arise, and recognising the way in which existing arrangements may perpetuate institutional discrimination. The third question was answered by ruling that only that proportion of a pay differential which can be attributed to market forces can be justified by them. This leaves the tribunal with the unenviable task of assessing the proportion of a disparity which flows from market forces, and fails to recognise the extent (see *Fletcher* at **10.3.4**) to which market forces can perpetuate historical assumptions about women's roles.

The practical effect of *Enderby* has been limited by the House of Lords decisions in *Strathclyde Regional Council v Wallace* [1998] IRLR 146 and *Glasgow City Council v Marshall* [2000] IRLR 272 to the effect that an employer need only justify a factor leading to a pay difference if that factor is itself gender discriminatory.

10.4 Remedies in equal pay proceedings

EqA 2010, s 120, provides that an employment tribunal has jurisdiction to hear these complaints. The applicant may claim for arrears of pay or damages for failure to comply with the equality clause, and, where the dispute is about the effect of the equality clause, may seek an order declaring the rights of the parties.

Section 129(3) provides that the claimant must have been employed in the employment at issue within six months before the date of the claim. There is, however, no requirement for a minimum period of employment as there is with unfair dismissal claims (see **Chapter 6**). The six-month period is subject to extensions in certain cases, such as when the employer has concealed facts without which the applicant would not have realised a claim was possible.

The six-month criterion may act to limit recovery where a claimant with considerable continuity of employment has accepted a new contract, as claims relating to the earlier, superseded contract will be time-barred. The tribunal will need to be sure that the new contract expressly supersedes the earlier one and is not a sham. However, where this occurs within the context of 'stable employment' within s 129(3) the limitation period will begin when the stable employment relationship ends (*Slack v Cumbria County Council* [2009] IRLR 463 (CA)).

As the equality clause operates as an implied term of the contract of employment, an action for breach of it may be brought in a County Court. Section 128(1), however, empowers the court to strike out the claim and refer it to an employment tribunal if it considers that the question of the operation of the equality clause may more conveniently be disposed of by the tribunal. It may stay the proceedings to allow this to happen. In most circumstances, therefore, questions arising under Part 5, Chapter 3, will be heard by an employment tribunal. Questions about the applicability of EU Directives, or the effectiveness of UK legislation in meeting them, will be a matter for the CJEU.

The Supreme Court has held that there is nothing to prevent a claimant from bringing an equal pay claim in the ordinary courts and thus taking advantage of the normal six-year limitation period (*Birmingham City Council v Abdulla* [2013] IRLR 38). This is in spite of EqA 2010, s 128, as it could never be convenient to bring a time-barred claim in a tribunal. However, there is no basis for seeking to transfer an equal pay claim from the tribunal to the High Court on grounds, for example, of complexity (*Asda Stores Ltd v Brierley and others* [2016] IRLR 709).

EPA 1970, s 2(5), imposed a limit on quantum of any damages or compensation. Any claim for arrears of pay or any other damages was limited to a period of two years before the proceedings were instituted. The House of Lords rejected this limitation in *Preston v Wolverhampton Healthcare NHS Trust* and *Fletcher v Midland Bank plc* [2001] IRLR 237, as making reliance on EU law impossible in practice. EqA 2010, s 132(4), now provides for arrears to be payable for up to six years. In 'work rated as equivalent' cases, however, the arrears may not pre-date the timing of the job evaluation exercise (*Bainbridge v Redcar & Cleveland Borough Council* [2007] IRLR 494 (EAT)). There are special provisions when the employer deliberately concealed pertinent facts or when the applicant was under a disability.

Unlike provisions of the discrimination legislation, compensation for equal pay does not include any element for injury to feelings (*Council of the City of Newcastle upon Tyne v Allan* and *Degnan v Redcar and Cleveland Borough Council* [2005] IRLR 504). This is because damages under Part 5, Chapter 3, are contractual, not tortious.

A person succeeding in an equal pay claim is entitled to be put into the same position as her comparator. If she is more senior than her comparator and entitled to be on a higher point on the incremental scale no regard will be paid to that fact (*Evesham v North Hertfordshire Health Authority and Secretary of State for Health* [1999] IRLR 155).

Unlike compensatory awards in unfair dismissal cases there is no prescribed maximum award.

Part 5, Chapter 3, is restricted to providing a remedy for inequalities of pay or other terms in the contract of employment. There is no mechanism for establishing fair differentials. Thus, a highly qualified woman undertaking responsible duties may not complain that she earns little more than an unqualified man working to her directions. Nor may a woman object that a man whose job she regards as only slightly more demanding than hers earns twice her rate of pay. The jobs are not equal and thus fall outside the provisions of the legislation. The development of a proportionality argument (see *Enderby* earlier) does not apply to these cases, as the work is not equal.

The conduct of a case: employment tribunal precedents

11.1 Introduction

11.1.1 General observations

Employment tribunal procedure in England and Wales is governed by the Employment Tribunal (Constitution and Rules of Procedure) Regulations 2013 (SI 2013/1237) (the 'Rules') (as amended). The Employment Tribunal Rules of Procedure are contained in Schedule 1 to the Regulations. The procedure of the Employment Appeal Tribunal (EAT) is subject to the Employment Appeal Tribunal Rules 1993 (SI 1993/2854) (the 'EAT Rules') as amended by the Employment Appeal Tribunal (Amendment) Rules 2001 and 2004, which should be read in conjunction with *Practice Direction (Employment Appeal Tribunal—Procedure) 2013*. References to rules are to the Employment Tribunal Rules of Procedure 2013 unless otherwise stated. Where there are variations between the procedure applicable in England and Wales and that governing Scotland or Northern Ireland, readers will need to refer themselves to the relevant provisions.

Where there are standard forms for use in tribunal proceedings these have been reproduced in the appropriate part of the text.

11.1.2 How to use this chapter

This chapter does not deal with the substantive law or procedure but merely provides precedents which may be used for guidance. It is not a substitute for the other chapters and should be used alongside them. In particular, reference should be made to **Chapter 4** on employment tribunal procedure.

The precedents work around seven sample cases and try to deal with most of the common forms used in employment tribunals. Equal pay cases and collective claims are not covered and reference should be made to the relevant practitioners' guides in these cases (see **Chapter 2**). Many of the sample cases involve more than one cause of action and/or more than one 'defence'; they can be adapted for use in more straightforward (or more complex) claims as appropriate.

11.1.3 Guidance on 'pleadings' in employment tribunal cases

The Employment Tribunal Rules of Procedure set out requirements for documents submitted to the tribunal (such as the claim form and the response form). You are advised to check them in *Harvey on Industrial Relations and Employment Law*. However, the forms used in employment tribunals are not considered to be pleadings in the same way as Particulars of Claim on a Claim Form would be in the High or County Court. As a result, the more specific formal requirements of drafting do not apply here. This means there is more scope for individual style to be used. Please note that as a result of this, these precedents are for guidance only.

11.2 The basic forms: the claim form and response form

The claim form is referred to by practitioners as the ET1, after the form number given to it. The response form is similarly referred to as the ET3. ET2 is, in fact, the claim notification sent to the respondent once a valid claim is accepted by the employment tribunal.

The 2013 Rules introduced issue fees and hearing fees which must be paid to make a claim. These have been quashed by the Supreme Court in *R (on the Application of UNISON) v Lord Chancellor* [2017] UKSC 51. Claims will now be free of charge, and those who paid fees should be able to claim refunds.

11.2.1 The claim form: commentary

The claim form (commonly referred to as the ET1, since this is the form number given to it by the employment tribunal) is the document which starts employment tribunal proceedings and the means by which a claimant makes his or her claim. This is not the same as the Claim Form required by the Civil Procedure Rules 1998, as amended, (CPR 1998) for claims in the High or County Court.

A claim must be submitted on the prescribed form, either by hard copy or via the Internet, and must contain a minimum level of information:

- the claimant's name and address (and, if different, an address within the United Kingdom to which notices and other documents relating to the claim may be sent, if the claimant is represented);

- the names and addresses of the person or persons against whom relief is sought (the 'respondent');

- the details of the claim;

- whether or not the claimant is or was an employee of the respondent;

- whether or not the claim includes a complaint that the respondent has dismissed the claimant or has contemplated doing so (to alert the tribunal to the applicability of the statutory dismissal and disciplinary procedures).

Full details of the requirements can be found in rr 8 and 10 of the Rules. It is particularly important to ensure the claim is compliant with the Rules, since under rr 10–12 the tribunal can reject the claim. However, in the past, the omission of required details would not always result in the rejection of a claim, as shown by *Hampling v Coxlease School Ltd* [2007] IRLR 8 (see **4.1.2**), but whether this approach will continue remains to be seen.

Employment Tribunal

Claim form

You must complete all questions marked with an '*'

Official Use Only			
Tribunal office			
Case number		Date received	

1 Your details

1.1 Title
☐ Mr   ☐ Mrs   ☐ Miss   ☐ Ms

1.2* First name (or names)

1.3* Surname or family name

1.4 Date of birth   ☐☐ / ☐☐ / ☐☐☐☐   Are you? ☐ Male   ☐ Female

1.5* Address

Number or name

Street

Town/City

County

Postcode

1.6 Phone number
Where we can contact you during the day

1.7 Mobile number (if different)

1.8 How would you prefer us to contact you?
(Please tick only one box)
☐ Email   ☐ Post   ☐ Fax   Whatever your preference please note that some documents cannot be sent electronically

1.9 Email address

1.10 Fax number

2 Respondent's details (that is the employer, person or organisation against whom you are making a claim)

2.1* Give the name of your employer or the person or organisation you are claiming against (If you need to you can add more respondents at 2.4)

2.2* Address

Number or name

Street

Town/City

County

Postcode

Phone number

ET1A - Claim form (07.13)   © Crown copyright 2013

Form 11.1 Claim form

2.3   If you worked at a different address from the one you have given at 2.2 please give the full address

Address

Number or name

Street

Town/City

County

Postcode

Phone number

2.4   If there are other respondents please tick this box and put their
names and addresses here.
(If there is not enough room here for the names of all the additional
respondents then you can add any others at Section 13.)

Respondent 2

Name

Address

Number or name

Street

Town/City

County

Postcode

Phone number

Respondent 3

Name

Address

Number or name

Street

Town/City

County

Postcode

Phone number

Form 11.1 Claim form (*continued*)

3 Multiple cases

3.1 Are you aware that your claim is one of a number of claims against the same employer arising from the same, or similar, circumstances?

☐ Yes   ☐ No

If Yes, and you know the names of any other claimants, add them here. This will allow us to link your claim to other related claims.

4 Cases where the respondent was not your employer

4.1 If you were not employed by any of the respondents you have named but are making a claim for some reason connected to employment (for example, relating to a job application which you made or against a trade union, qualifying body or the like) please state the type of claim you are making here. (You will get the chance to provide details later):

Now go to Section 8

5 Employment details

If you are or were employed please give the following information, if possible.

5.1 When did your employment start?

Is your employment continuing?   ☐ Yes   ☐ No

If your employment has ended, when did it end?

If your employment has not ended, are you in a period of notice and, if so, when will that end?

5.2 Please say what job you do or did.

Form 11.1 Claim form (*continued*)

6 Earnings and benefits

6.1 How many hours on average do, or did you work each week in the job this claim is about?

[   ] hours each week

6.2 How much are, or were you paid?

Pay before tax £ [   ] ☐ Weekly ☐ Monthly

Normal take-home pay £ [   ] ☐ Weekly ☐ Monthly
(Incl. overtime, commission, bonuses etc.)

6.3 If your employment has ended, did you work (or were you paid for) a period of notice? ☐ Yes ☐ No

If Yes, how many weeks, or months' notice did you work, or were you paid for? [   ] weeks [   ] months

6.4 Were you in your employer's pension scheme? ☐ Yes ☐ No

6.5 If you received any other benefits, e.g. company car, medical insurance, etc, from your employer, please give details.

[   ]

7 If your employment with the respondent has ended, what has happened since?

7.1 Have you got another job? ☐ Yes ☐ No

If No, please **go to section 8**

7.2 Please say when you started (or will start) work. [   ]

7.3 Please say how much you are now earning (or will earn). £ [   ]

Form 11.1 Claim form (*continued*)

8 Type and details of claim

8.1*   Please indicate the type of claim you are making by ticking one or more of the boxes below.

☐ I was unfairly dismissed (including constructive dismissal)

☐ I was discriminated against on the grounds of:

☐ age   ☐ race

☐ gender reassignment   ☐ disability

☐ pregnancy or maternity   ☐ marriage or civil partnership

☐ sexual orientation   ☐ sex (including equal pay)

☐ religion or belief

☐ I am claiming a redundancy payment

☐ I am owed

☐ notice pay

☐ holiday pay

☐ arrears of pay

☐ other payments

☐ I am making another type of claim which the Employment Tribunal can deal with.
(Please state the nature of the claim. Examples are provided in the Guidance.)

Form 11.1 Claim form (*continued*)

8.2*   Please set out the background and details of your claim in the space below.

The details of your claim should include **the date(s) when the event(s) you are complaining about happened.** Please use the blank sheet at the end of the form if needed.

Form 11.1 Claim form (*continued*)

8.2*   Please set out the background and details of your claim in the space below.

The details of your claim should include **the date(s) when the event(s) you are complaining about happened.** Please use the blank sheet at the end of the form if needed.

9 **What do you want if your claim is successful?**

9.1   Please tick the relevant box(es) to say what you
        want if your claim is successful:

☐ If claiming unfair dismissal, to get your old job back and compensation (reinstatement)

☐ If claiming unfair dismissal, to get another job with the same employer or associated
   employer and compensation (re-engagement)

☐ Compensation only

☐ If claiming discrimination, a recommendation (see Guidance).

9.2   What compensation or remedy are you seeking?

If you are claiming financial compensation please give as much detail as you can about how much you are claiming and how you have calculated this sum.
(Please note any figure stated below will be viewed as helpful information but it will not restrict what you can claim and you will be permitted to revise the sum claimed
later. See the Guidance for further information about how you can calculate compensation). **If you are seeking any other remedy from the Tribunal which you have
not already identified please also state this below.**

Form 11.1 Claim form (*continued*)

10 **Information to regulators in protected disclosure cases**

10.1 If your claim consists of, or includes, a claim that you are making a protected disclosure under the Employment Rights Act 1996 (otherwise known as a 'whistleblowing' claim), please tick the box if you want a copy of this form, or information from it, to be forwarded on your behalf to a relevant regulator (known as a 'prescribed person' under the relevant legislation) by tribunal staff. (See Guidance).

☐

11 **Your representative**

If someone has agreed to represent you, please fill in the following. We will in future only contact your representative and not you.

11.1 Name of representative

11.2 Name of organisation

11.3 Address

Number or name

Street

Town/City

County

Postcode

11.4 DX number (If known)

11.5 Phone number

11.6 Mobile number (If different)

11.7 Their reference for correspondence

11.8 Email address

11.9 How would you prefer us to communicate with them? (Please tick only one box)   ☐ Email   ☐ Post   ☐ Fax

11.10 Fax number

12 **Disability**

12.1 Do you have a disability?   ☐ Yes   ☐ No

If Yes, it would help us if you could say what this disability is and tell us what assistance, if any, you will need as your claim progresses through the system, including for any hearings that maybe held at tribunal premises.

Form 11.1 Claim form (*continued*)

13 Details of additional respondents

Section 2.4 allows you to list up to three respondents. If there are any more respondents please provide their details here

Respondent 4

Name

Address

Number or name

Street

Town/City

County

Postcode

Phone number

Respondent 5

Name

Address

Number or name

Street

Town/City

County

Postcode

Phone number

14 Fee

**Please re-read the form and check you have entered all the relevant information.
Once you are satisfied, please tick this box.** ☐

For those submitting their claim by post

☐ I enclose the appropriate fee

OR

☐ I enclose an application for remission of the fee

If you fail to do so your claim form will be returned to you and you will be told it has been rejected. This means that any time limit which applies to your claim will still be running and the claim form will have to be re-submitted within that time limit.

Data Protection Act 1998.
We will send a copy of this form to the respondent and Acas. We will put the information you give us on this form onto a computer. This helps us to monitor progress and produce statistics. Information provided on this form is passed to the Department for Business, Innovation and Skills to assist research into the use and effectiveness of employment tribunals. (URN 05/874)

Page 9

Form 11.1 Claim form (*continued*)

15 **Additional information**

Please use this space to provide any important additional information about your claim which you have not been able to include so far.

Form 11.1 Claim form (*continued*)

Employment Tribunals – Multiple Claim form

Please use this form if you wish to present two or more claims which arise from the same set of facts. Use additional sheets if necessary.

The following claimants are represented by

and the information required for all the additional claimants is the same as stated in the main claim of

Title	☐ Mr ☐ Mrs ☐ Miss ☐ Ms

First name (or names)

Surname or family name

Date of birth [ ] / [ ] / [ ]

Address
Number or name
Street
Town/City
County
Postcode

Title	☐ Mr ☐ Mrs ☐ Miss ☐ Ms

First name (or names)

Surname or family name

Date of birth [ ] / [ ] / [ ]

Address
Number or name
Street
Town/City
County
Postcode

Form 11.1 Claim form (*continued*)

Title   ☐ Mr   ☐ Mrs   ☐ Miss   ☐ Ms

First name (or names)   [_____]

Surname or family name   [_____]

Date of birth   [__|__] / [__|__] / [__|__|__|__]

Address
    Number or name   [_____]
    Street   [_____]
    Town/City   [_____]
    County   [_____]
    Postcode   [__|__|__|__|__|__|__]

Title   ☐ Mr   ☐ Mrs   ☐ Miss   ☐ Ms

First name (or names)   [_____]

Surname or family name   [_____]

Date of birth   [__|__] / [__|__] / [__|__|__|__]

Address
    Number or name   [_____]
    Street   [_____]
    Town/City   [_____]
    County   [_____]
    Postcode   [__|__|__|__|__|__|__]

Form 11.1 Claim form (*continued*)

Title   ☐ Mr   ☐ Mrs   ☐ Miss   ☐ Ms

First name (or names)

Surname or family name

Date of birth   ☐☐ / ☐☐ / ☐☐☐☐

Address   Number or name

                 Street

                 Town/City

                 County

                 Postcode

Title   ☐ Mr   ☐ Mrs   ☐ Miss   ☐ Ms

First name (or names)

Surname or family name

Date of birth   ☐☐ / ☐☐ / ☐☐☐☐

Address   Number or name

                 Street

                 Town/City

                 County

                 Postcode

Form 11.1 Claim form (*continued*)

HM Courts & Tribunals Service

Diversity Monitoring Questionnaire

It is important to us that everyone who has contact with HM Courts & Tribunals Service, receives equal treatment. We need to find out whether our policies are effective and to take steps to ensure the impact of future policies can be fully assessed to try to avoid any adverse impacts on any particular groups of people. That is why we are asking you to complete the following questionnaire, which will be used to provide us with the relevant statistical information. **Your answers will be treated in strict confidence.**

Thank you in advance for your co-operation.

Claim type

Please confirm the type of claim that you are bringing to the employment tribunal. This will help us in analysing the other information provided in this form.

- (a) ☐ Unfair dismissal or constructive dismissal
- (b) ☐ Discrimination
- (c) ☐ Redundancy payment
- (d) ☐ Other payments you are owed
- (e) ☐ Other complaints

Sex

What is your sex?

- (a) ☐ Female
- (b) ☐ Male
- (c) ☐ Prefer not to say

Age group

Which age group are you in?

- (a) ☐ Under 25
- (b) ☐ 25-34
- (c) ☐ 35-44
- (d) ☐ 45-54
- (e) ☐ 55-64
- (f) ☐ 65 and over
- (g) ☐ Prefer not to say

Ethnicity

What is your ethnic group?

White

- (a) ☐ English / Welsh / Scottish / Northern Irish / British
- (b) ☐ Irish
- (c) ☐ Gypsy or Irish Traveller
- (d) ☐ Any other White background

Mixed / multiple ethnic groups

- (e) ☐ White and Black Caribbean
- (f) ☐ White and Black African
- (g) ☐ White and Asian
- (h) ☐ Any other Mixed / multiple ethnic background

Asian / Asian British

- (i) ☐ Indian
- (j) ☐ Pakistani
- (k) ☐ Bangladeshi
- (l) ☐ Chinese
- (m) ☐ Any other Asian background

Black / African / Caribbean / Black British

- (n) ☐ African
- (o) ☐ Caribbean
- (p) ☐ Any other Black / African / Caribbean background

Other ethnic group

- (q) ☐ Arab
- (r) ☐ Any other ethnic group

- (s) ☐ Prefer not to say

Page 14

Form 11.1 Claim form– Diversity Monitoring Questionnaire

Disability

The Equality Act 2010 defines a disabled person as 'Someone who has a physical or mental impairment and the impairment has a substantial and long-term adverse effect on his or her ability to carry out normal day-to-day activities'.

Conditions covered may include, for example, severe depression, dyslexia, epilepsy and arthritis.

Do you have any physical or mental health conditions or illnesses lasting or expected to last for 12 months or more?

(a) ☐ Yes

(b) ☐ No

(c) ☐ Prefer not to say

Marriage and Civil Partnership

Are you?

(a) ☐ Single, that is, never married and never registered in a same-sex civil partnership

(b) ☐ Married

(c) ☐ Separated, but still legally married

(d) ☐ Divorced

(e) ☐ Widowed

(f) ☐ In a registered same-sex civil partnership

(g) ☐ Separated, but still legally in a same-sex civil partnership

(h) ☐ Formerly in a same-sex civil partnership which is now legally dissolved

(I) ☐ Surviving partner from a same-sex civil partnership

(J) ☐ Prefer not to say

Religion and belief

What is your religion?

(a) ☐ No religion

(b) ☐ Christian (including Church of England, Catholic, Protestant and all other Christian denominations)

(c) ☐ Buddhist

(d) ☐ Hindu

(e) ☐ Jewish

(f) ☐ Muslim

(g) ☐ Sikh

(h) ☐ Any other religion (please describe)

[   ]

(I) ☐ Prefer not to say

Caring responsibilites

Do you have any caring responsibilities, (for example; children, elderly relatives, partners etc.)?

(a) ☐ Yes

(b) ☐ No

(c) ☐ Prefer not to say

Sexual identity

Which of the options below best describes how you think of yourself?

(a) ☐ Heterosexual/Straight

(b) ☐ Gay /Lesbian

(c) ☐ Bisexual

(d) ☐ Other

(e) ☐ Prefer not to say

Gender identity

Please describe your gender identity?

(a) ☐ Male (including female-to-male trans men)

(b) ☐ Female (including male-to-female trans women)

(c) ☐ Prefer not to say

Is your gender identity different to the sex you were assumed to be at birth?

(f) ☐ Yes

(g) ☐ No

(h) ☐ Prefer not to say

Pregnancy and maternity

Were you pregant when the issue you are making a claim about took place?

(a) ☐ Yes

(b) ☐ No

(c) ☐ Prefer not to say

Thank you for taking the time to complete this questionnaire.

Form 11.1 Claim form– Diversity Monitoring Questionnaire

Employment Tribunals check list and cover sheet

Please check the following:

1. Read the form to make sure the information given is correct and truthful, and that you have
    not left out any information which you feel may be relevant to you or your client.
2. Do not attach a covering letter to your form. If you have any further relevant information
    please enter it in the 'Additional Information' space provided in the form.
3. Send the completed form to the relevant office address.
4. Keep a copy of your form posted to us.

If your claim has been submitted on-line or posted in with the appropriate fee you should
receive confirmation of receipt from the office dealing with your claim within five working
days. If you have not heard from them within five days, please contact that office directly. If
the deadline for submitting the claim is closer than five days you should check that it has been
received before the time limit expires. Claims which include an application for a full or partial
remission of the fee may take a little longer to deal with.

You have opted to print and post your form. We would like to remind you that forms submitted on-line are processed much faster than ones posted to us.
If you want to submit on-line please go back to the form and click the submit button, otherwise follow the check list before you post the completed form to the
relevant office address.

A list of our office's contact details can be found at the hearing centre page of our website at – www.justice.gov.uk/tribunals/employment/venues ; if you are
still unsure about which office to contact please call our national enquiry line on 0845 7959775 (Mon – Fri, 9am – 5pm) or Minicom 0845 757 3772; they can also
provide general procedural information about the employment tribunals.

Form 11.1 Claim form (*continued*)

It is good practice for the claimant to ensure that the claim form sets out the claim with sufficient detail and particularity that the respondent knows the case to be met and the nature of the complaint being made can be clearly identified.

11.2.2 The claim form: Form ET1

Until it was quashed as a result of *R (on the Application of UNISON) v Lord Chancellor* [2017] UKSC 51, the 2013 Rules had introduced a fees regime in the employment tribunals. It required a claimant to submit a 'Fees and Remissions' form and the relevant fee (unless remission is being applied for). There were two levels of fee, depending on the type of claim being made. Group claimants had higher levels of fees. There were three levels of remission, which depend on the means of the claimant. Fees may be recovered by a claimant if a costs order is made under rr 75–82. Claims and hearings will now attract no charges from the Employment Tribunal Service.

As stated at **11.2.1**, Form ET1 may be submitted by hard copy to the Employment Tribunal Central Office or via the Internet. The Internet version of the form has the same sections, but has a different appearance to the paper copy of the form. This chapter will reproduce paper copies of ET1 and ET3 in their current versions, but you may not be required to use this particular version, see **11.2** for details. You will see that the items marked with * are the mandatory matters which must be stated. Guidance notes have been provided, which you will find in document T420 on the Ministry of Justice Form Finder website (<http://hmctsformfinder.justice.gov.uk/courtfinder/forms/t420-eng.pdf>).

In relation to each section of the Form ET1:

1 'Your details': the claimant's details
The required details on this part of the form are the claimant's name and address. The address must be stated regardless of whether the claimant has a representative. However, if the claimant is represented, tribunal correspondence (including orders and notices) will be sent to the representative. The claimant is responsible for supplying the correct details and should inform the tribunal and the respondent of any change of address. If an email address is specified, the tribunal's expectation will be that it is checked daily for possible tribunal correspondence.

Although not mandatory, the claimant's date of birth ought to be stated, since it is relevant to calculate the basic award or redundancy payment, should one be found to be due.

Under r 9, it is possible for more than one claimant to make his or her claim on the same Form ET1 where the relief sought arises from the same facts. It is possible to submit separate claim forms where necessary. The tribunal may, upon receipt, consolidate the claims. If tactically advantageous, the claimant or respondent can oppose the consolidation provided they have sound reasons for so doing.

2 'Respondent's details': the employer's details
Usually the claim will be brought against the employer. However, in some cases (such as discrimination cases) the respondent may be an individual (such as a harasser). The claimant should give sufficient detail to ensure that the tribunal can identify and communicate with the appropriate respondent. The claimant may name more than one

respondent on the ET1, and should the claimant be unsure of the correct identity of the respondent, all possible respondents should be identified with the reasons for so doing in the details of the complaint (see point 8). It is particularly in cases involving any transfer of employment relations under the Transfer of Undertakings (Protection of Employment) Regulations 2006 that more than one respondent is named; the employer before and the employer after the transfer, to ensure that remedy is obtainable from someone. A mistake as to the identity of the correct respondent should not be fatal as an application to amend the identity of the respondent can be made at a later date, although care should be taken to ensure correctness at the outset.

3   'Multiple cases'

This part of the form allows the employment tribunal to identify other claims which arise out of the same (or similar) circumstances against the same employer which ought to be consolidated.

4   'Cases where the respondent was not your employer'

The employment tribunal has jurisdiction to deal with claims against trade unions, individuals in discrimination/harassment claims, and claims in relation to Industry Training Board assessments. Claims relating to job applications can be made in limited circumstances. Hence this part of the form assists the tribunal in identifying such issues in the claimant's claim.

5   'Employment details'

At 5.1 the claimant is asked to set out the date of starting employment, whether the employment is continuing, when employment has ended or will end and the relevant dates. The dates should be stated accurately since they may bring up questions as to the tribunal's jurisdiction to hear the complaint (for example, issues of continuity of employment or time limits) and in addition will be used for any calculations of basic award or redundancy payment, should one be found to be due.

The claimant's start date should be the date of commencement of continuous employment, even if under different terms and conditions, a different contract or with a previous employer (in the case of transfers or where the same business has changed its name).

The date of termination will be the date on which notice expired, or if no notice was given or the claimant was paid in lieu of notice, the actual date the claimant left his or her employment. Regard should be had to the relevant statutory provisions applicable to a particular complaint where the start or leaving date of employment might be in issue (such as Employment Rights Act 1996 (ERA 1996), Pt XIV Chapter 1 and s 97 which are often relevant to unfair dismissal). Box 5.2 is where the job title should be stated.

6   'Earnings and benefits'

The requested factual detail should be set out. It is not part of the required information, but will assist the tribunal on quantum, whether any notice pay is due and other matters. The wage of the relevant current or former employment may be stated as either a weekly, monthly or annual figure. If possible, a weekly figure should be stated as this is the figure which the tribunal will use to calculate the basic award or redundancy payment. The pay before tax is obviously the gross figure before any deductions and the take-home figure is the net amount, after deductions of tax and National Insurance. The claimant will not be held to a mistaken weekly wage rate if an error is made, although proof by means of wage slips may be useful. Where the wage varies from week to week, it is useful to give the average amount for the last 12 calendar weeks. The hours worked will be of particular relevance should claims under the Working Time Directive or in relation to 'whistleblowing' or health and safety be made.

7 'If your employment with the respondent has ended, what has happened since?'
The employment tribunal, when considering the level of damages, particularly in unfair dismissal cases, will be concerned with the issues of mitigation of loss and the recovery of welfare benefits by the State. The details requested here, namely, whether the claimant has found new employment, when and what is the level of wages, are relevant to these issues.

8 'Type and details of claim'
Box 8.1 is where the general type of the claim should be indicated.

Box 8.2 is where the general factual details of the claim should be given. Where the details of the claim are brief, then the details may be set out (in handwriting or type) in the box provided. However, where the details are lengthier, it would be advisable to insert 'see attached details of complaint' in the relevant box. The full details should then be set out in another document with the clear title 'details of complaint'. There will be examples set out in the precedents in this chapter.

9 'What do you want if your claim is successful?'
Here is where the claimant is asked which remedy is sought which will depend on the type of claim being made. If indicated (and this section is optional) it assists the tribunal and the respondent in understanding the claimant's objective in the proceedings. It could assist in any conciliation or negotiation. However, the claimant will not be bound by the answer given here, and should the claimant be successful on liability, when the issue of remedy arises, the tribunal will address this matter with the claimant.

10 'Information to regulators in protected disclosure cases'
Where a claimant is making a 'whistleblowing' claim after having made a protected disclosure, should the claimant give consent by ticking the box in this section of the form, the employment tribunal will copy the form to the relevant regulatory body. The purpose of this is to give the regulatory body the main details of the public interest issue raised by the claimant during his/her employment for further investigation. The respondent is informed where this takes place.

11 'Your representative'
The details of the claimant's representative should be given here, and the tribunal will send all correspondence and notices to the representative not the claimant. Please note that if an email address is supplied, it will be the tribunal's expectation that the representative will check it daily. The respondent should only communicate with

the representative and not the claimant directly. As a result the claimant should ensure, should he or she change his or her representative, that the tribunal and respondent are informed as soon as possible.

12 'Disability'

As part of its obligations as a public service under disability legislation, the employment tribunal must ensure disabled people have equal access to justice. Therefore, if a claimant has a disability indicated in this section, the tribunal will, where possible, provide assistance.

13 'Details of additional respondents'

This is self-explanatory.

14 'Fee'

At time of writing, the Employment Tribunal Service has not reissued form ET1 as a result of the quashing of the fees regime (following *R (on the Application of UNISON) v Lord Chancellor* [2017] UKSC 51). Until it does, this part of the form does not need to be completed by the claimant. This part of the form served as an opportunity for the claimant or his/her representatives to review the form and confirm the details given are correct. An indication had been required that either the relevant fee has been included or an application for remission has been made. The Fees and Remissions Form was also required.

15 'Additional information'

Since no covering letter to the ET1 is permitted, any further information should be set out here. Care must be taken that information relevant to the other sections is not stated here, since it may detract from the clarity of the claimant's case.

11.2.3 Guidance on general factual details

The tribunal members hearing the case at trial and at any preliminary hearing will read the ET1 first when informing themselves of the issues in the case. The large boxes for the claimant's complaints to be set out are the claimant's opportunity to state the nature of his or her case. The details should therefore be set out to the claimant's advantage both tactically and practically.

It is not necessary to set out the law in the ET1. Therefore, cases relied upon need not be stated. However, although statutory provisions are not required, it may sometimes be helpful to use references to sections of the legislation where it clarifies the nature of the claim made.

It will be necessary to weigh up the competing interests of setting out all the details in full and the need to keep avenues open. For example, since the respondent must prove the reason for dismissal in an unfair dismissal case, the claimant need not state the reason for dismissal. It may be tactically advantageous to leave the respondent to prove this matter to the tribunal. However, regard should be given to the principle that the respondent should be able to see the case the respondent has to meet. If the respondent cannot ascertain what the claimant's case is or it is not stated with sufficient particulars, the respondent may be able to require the claimant to provide further particulars before making its response on the response form (see **11.2.4**).

Generally, where the claimant has the burden of proof of a matter or issue, it will be advisable to set out detailed particulars. One example is in a constructive dismissal case, where the claimant must prove that the respondent has acted in fundamental breach of contract. Here, the facts which show the respondent's breach of, for example, the implied term of mutual trust and confidence should be set out fully.

Further, it may be advisable to set out details of multiple incidents. This is tactically advantageous in cases of discrimination where the complaint is of harassment which is ongoing, or in a constructive dismissal case where the final act complained of is the 'last straw' prompting the claimant's resignation. All of the incidents complained of should be set out in outline. It is not necessary to set out every detail, since that can be done in the witness statement before trial, but outline detail will ensure the relevance of the previous incidents is clear and the claimant cannot be accused of raising them at the hearing for the first time.

Counsel, if asked to draft this information, may choose to do so in a similar vein to when drafting pleadings. Use of 'the claimant', 'the respondent' and the language of pleadings is acceptable throughout and the use of clearly numbered sequential paragraphs is to be encouraged. However, the signature of counsel (as commonly set out in formal pleadings) is not necessary because employment tribunal forms are not considered formal pleadings.

11.2.4   The response form: commentary

The response form (commonly referred to by its tribunal form number ET3) is the respondent's 'defence' to the claim made to the tribunal. Just as in civil proceedings where the Claim Form and Defence are among the first papers read by the judge, the claim form and response form are the papers to which the tribunal will turn first in dealing with a hearing. The ET3 is therefore the respondent's opportunity to set out its case and identify which are the disputed and undisputed issues.

The paper copy of the current form is reproduced for your reference in this chapter. As with the claim form reproduced at **11.2**, you will see that the items marked with * are the mandatory matters which must be stated.

When a claimant starts a claim, should it be accepted by the tribunal under the rules, the claim form and a blank response form are sent to the respondent. The names of the parties, the case number and the date by which the completed ET3 should be received by the tribunal are filled in on the front sheet by the tribunal staff.

The date by which the ET3 should be returned is particularly important and should be diarised by the legal representative, who are strongly advised not to miss this date, because of the powers of the employment tribunals to grant 'default' judgment and to prevent defaulting parties from participating in proceedings.

Since the tribunal staff will have allocated the case number after receiving the ET1, the parties should use the case number in all correspondence after the number has been issued.

The response must be on the prescribed Form ET3 and must include:

- the respondent's full name and address (if different, an address within the United Kingdom to which notices and other documents relating to the claim can be sent, such as to their representatives);
- whether or not the respondent intends to resist any part of the claim (and if in part, the respondent must be specific).

Under r 16(1) the response must be presented to the employment tribunal office within 28 days of the date on which the respondent was sent a copy of the claim by the tribunal. This is supported by *Bone v Fabcon Projects Ltd* [2006] IRLR 908 where the date of receipt was rejected as the trigger date. If necessary, an application to extend this time limit may be made; you should refer to r 20 for the grounds and circumstances required. Please note that any application must be made within the 28-day time limit. As stated, given the tribunals' powers to give a form of 'default judgment' under r 21(2) and prevent or restrict the defaulting party from participating in the proceedings (under r 21(3)), the time limit for the ET3 is highly important.

Please note that, as with the claim form, the tribunal has powers not to accept the response form. You are referred to r 17, which sets out the tribunal's powers for acceptance.

11.2.5   Can the respondent respond yet? Further particulars of the ET1 and tactical considerations

If the respondent believes that it is unable to answer the case set out by the claimant in the claim form because insufficient details have been given, the proper course of action is to write to the claimant (or his or her representatives) asking for further particulars of the claim form and also to write to the tribunal enclosing details of the request made and making an application for the extension of the 28-day time limit. If the request is not satisfactorily answered on a voluntary basis, a further letter to the tribunal making an application that the claimant be ordered to respond should be made under r 31. However, the respondent should be aware that there is a danger that the tribunal may take a different view on the sufficiency of detail provided by the claimant and refuse the order (which would oblige the respondent to respond to the claim form as it is or risk default judgment).

A method of proceeding with less risk would be to make the request for further particulars of the claimant, and for the respondent to return the response form. The response form should state in section 5 that insufficient details of the claimant's case have been given to enable the respondent to give details of the grounds for resistance but that further particulars have been sought and fuller details of the respondent's case will be given once these are received. This form of 'holding ET3' may often be preferable to seeking to extend the time limit and protects the respondent from the consequences of not submitting a response form.

11.2.6   The response form: Form ET3

Employment Tribunal

Response form

Case number	

You must complete all questions marked with an '*'

1 Claimant's name

1.1   Claimant's name

2 Respondent's details

2.1* Name of individual,
company or organisation

2.2   Name of contact

2.3* Address

Number or name

Street

Town/City

County

Postcode

DX number (If known)

2.4   Phone number
Where we can contact you during the day

Mobile number (If different)

2.5   How would you prefer us to contact you?
(Please tick only one box)

☐ Email   ☐ Post   ☐ Fax   Whatever your preference please note that some documents cannot be sent electronically

2.6   Email address

Fax number

2.7   How many people does this
organisation employ in Great Britain?

2.8   Does this organisation have more than
one site in Great Britain?   ☐ Yes   ☐ No

2.9   If Yes, how many people are employed at
the place where the claimant worked?

Form 11.2 Form ET3

3 Employment details

3.1 Are the dates of employment given by the claimant correct?   ☐ Yes   ☐ No

If Yes, please **go to question 3.2**

If No, please give the dates and say why you disagree with the dates given by the claimant

When their employment started

When their employment ended or will end

I disagree with the dates for the following reasons

3.2 Is their employment continuing?   ☐ Yes   ☐ No

3.3 Is the claimant's description of their job or job title correct?   ☐ Yes   ☐ No

If Yes, please **go to Section 4**

If No, please give the details you believe to be correct

4 Earnings and benefits

4.1 Are the claimant's hours of work correct?   ☐ Yes   ☐ No

If No, please enter the details you believe to be correct.   hours each week

4.2 Are the earnings details given by the claimant correct?   ☐ Yes   ☐ No

If Yes, please **go to question 4.3**

If No, please give the details you believe to be correct below

Pay before tax   £   ☐ Weekly   ☐ Monthly
(Incl. overtime, commission, bonuses etc.)

Normal take-home pay   £   ☐ Weekly   ☐ Monthly
(Incl. overtime, commission, bonuses etc.)

Form 11.2 Form ET3 (*continued*)

4.3 Is the information given by the claimant correct about being paid for, or working a period of notice?   ☐ Yes   ☐ No

If Yes, please **go to question 4.4**

If No, please give the details you believe to be correct below. If you gave them no notice or didn't pay them instead of letting them work their notice, please explain what happened and why.

4.4 Are the details about pension and other benefits e.g. company car, medical insurance, etc. given by the claimant correct?   ☐ Yes   ☐ No

If Yes, please **go to Section 5**

If No, please give the details you believe to be correct.

5 Response

5.1* Do you defend the claim?   ☐ Yes   ☐ No

If No, please **go to Section 6**

If Yes, please set out the facts which you rely on to defend the claim.
(See Guidance - If needed, please use the blank sheet at the end of this form.)

Page 3

Form 11.2 Form ET3 (*continued*)

6 Employer's Contract Claim

6.1   Only available in limited circumstances where the claimant has made a contract claim. (See Guidance)

6.2   If you wish to make an Employer's Contract Claim in response to the claimant's claim, please tick this box and complete question 6.3   ☐

6.3   Please set out the background and details of your claim below, which should include all important dates
(see Guidance for more information on what details should be included)

Form 11.2 Form ET3 (*continued*)

7 Your representative

If someone has agreed to represent you, please fill in the following. We will in future only contact your representative and not you.

7.1 Name of representative

7.2 Name of organisation

7.3 Address

Number or name

Street

Town/City

County

Postcode

7.4 **DX number** (If known)

7.5 Phone number

7.6 Mobile phone

7.7 Their reference for correspondence

7.8 How would you prefer us to communicate with them? (Please tick only one box)   ☐ Email   ☐ Post   ☐ Fax

7.9 Email address

7.10 Fax number

8 Disability

8.1 Do you have a disability?   ☐ Yes   ☐ No

If Yes, it would help us if you could say what this disability is and tell us what assistance, if any, you will need as your claim progresses through the system, including for any hearings that maybe held at tribunal premises.

Please re-read the form and check you have entered all the relevant information. Once you are satisfied, please tick this box. ☐

Data Protection Act 1998.

We will send a copy of this form to the claimant and Acas. We will put the information you give us on this form onto a computer. This helps us to monitor progress and produce statistics. Information provided on this form is passed to the Department for Business, Innovation and Skills to assist research into the use and effectiveness of employment tribunals. (URN 05/874)

Page 5

Form 11.2 Form ET3 (continued)

Employment Tribunals check list and cover sheet

Please check the following:

1. Read the form to make sure the information given is correct and truthful, and that you have not left out any information which you feel may be relevant to you or your client.
2. Do not attach a covering letter to your form. If you have any further relevant information please enter it in the 'Additional Information' space provided in the form.
3. Send the completed form to the relevant office address.
4. Keep a copy of your form posted to us.

Once your response has been received, you should receive confirmation from the office dealing with your claim within five working days. If you have not heard from them within five days, please contact that office directly. If the deadline for submitting the response is closer than five days you should check that it has been received before the time limit expires.

You have opted to print and post your form. We would like to remind you that forms submitted on-line are processed much faster than ones posted to us. If you want to submit on-line please go back to the form and click the submit button, otherwise follow the check list before you post the completed form to the relevant office address.

A list of our office's contact details can be found at the hearing centre page of our website at – www.justice.gov.uk/tribunals/employment/venues ; if you are still unsure about which office to contact please call our national enquiry line on 0845 7959775 (Mon – Fri, 9am – 5pm) or Minicom 0845 757 3772; they can also provide general procedural information about the employment tribunals.

Continuation sheet

URN 09/1442 0713

Form 11.2 Form ET3 (*continued*)

1 The claimant's name

This is self-explanatory.

2 'Respondent's details'

The name and address of the respondent are required by the Rules, which must be stated regardless of whether the respondent has a representative. If the respondent is represented, tribunal correspondence (including orders and notices) will be sent to the representative.

3 'Employment details'

This part of the form gives the respondent the opportunity to correct any mistakes in the details given by the claimant as to dates of commencement of employment, termination of employment and job title. Care should be taken with ensuring correct details for the pay and dates are given as they are used by the tribunal for the calculation of compensation should it be ordered (although evidence can be considered and the ET3 should not be considered final).

4 'Earnings and benefits'

This part of the form allows the respondent to set out the working hours and earnings of the claimant if the ET1 is disputed. In addition, the respondent may confirm if the pension and benefit details given by the claimant about the relevant employment are correct, and whether the notice period has been paid in lieu or worked out.

5 'Response'

If the claim is to be disputed, 'yes' at 5.1 should be ticked, and the box at 5.1 is the place for the respondent's detailed response to the allegations made by the claimant, regardless of the type of claim it is. The details should be presented with care and precision since it is the part of the ET3 to which the tribunal will pay particular attention at the hearing. The purpose of this part of the response form is to set out the respondent's case in answer to the matters in the claim form and to allow easy identification of what matters are in issue or not in issue.

As with the ET1, it is not necessary to set out the law in the ET3. Therefore, cases relied upon need not be stated. However, although statutory provisions are not required, it may sometimes be helpful to use references to sections of the legislation where it makes the nature of the respondent's defence clear.

For any issue (such as the reason for dismissal) where the respondent has the burden of proof, the respondent or its representative should ensure that the case set out here is accurate and can be consistently presented at the tribunal hearing.

Although the respondent will need to set out 'sufficient' detail, tactical considerations will apply. In a case of unfair dismissal where the reason relied upon is conduct and the claimant has a history of warnings and disciplinary matters, detail should be provided to show the overall conduct of the claimant and to ensure the claimant is aware of the matters to be put before the tribunal in advance. However, in other matters, giving certain factual details will not be of assistance. If we take the example of an unfair dismissal case involving redundancy where the claimant seeks only to challenge fairness of the selection procedure, the claimant's capability will not be relevant unless the respondent's selection criteria included capability.

The respondent's representatives are sometimes reluctant to set out factual detail, preferring instead to give vague allegations such as 'the claimant had been given a number of warnings'. This approach is often inappropriate. Where information is relevant and may later form the subject of a request for further particulars or written answers, it will assist to provide the details from the outset to avoid any accusation that the respondent has raised issues for the first time at the final hearing. If necessary, the details should be given on the facts relied upon, such as names of relevant staff, dates of incidents, the nature of conversations and so on.

It is important to consider if there are any alternative grounds which may be raised in the respondent's favour. If dismissal is not admitted (as is frequently the case in constructive dismissal cases), and the tribunal finds for the claimant, the tribunal moves on to consider if the 'dismissal' was fair. As a result, the respondent must put forward alternative grounds contesting that such a dismissal was fair. Respondents should not rely upon the need to make an amendment to the ET3 at a later date, since any application may be refused if requiring further evidence to be adduced or an adjournment of the hearing.

If the respondent does not contest liability, but the remedy sought is, the respondent should make clear the reasons for such a challenge. If the only contested issue is the sum of money due and payable (rather than the claimant's entitlement to such payment) then the respondent's method of calculation and the facts relied upon to support such a calculation should be set out.

Counsel, if asked to draft this information, may choose to do so in a similar vein to when drafting pleadings. Use of 'the claimant', 'the respondent' and the language of pleadings is acceptable throughout and the use of clearly numbered sequential paragraphs is to be encouraged. However, the signature of counsel as commonly set out in formal pleadings is not necessary because employment tribunal forms are not considered formal pleadings.

Other issues that can may arise can include:

Incorrect identification of the respondent

If the body named as respondent by the claimant is mistakenly identified, or, at least, the respondent intends to argue that this is the case, the point should be raised in the response form. Provided that it is consistent with the rest of the respondent's case, the response ought to state that the respondent contends the claimant was never employed by them, and should set out the full reasons why the respondent named is the incorrect party to the proceedings. If the identification of the correct respondent requires resolution of some preliminary legal or factual point (one typical example is where there is the transfer of an undertaking), the respondent may wish to make an application that the matter be dealt with at a preliminary hearing under r 53. Further guidance on preliminary hearings can be found at rr 54–56.

Jurisdictional points

If a jurisdictional point is apparent to a respondent upon receiving the claim form, the best course is to raise this as a preliminary point in section 5 of the response form before going on to set out the details of the grounds on which the claim is resisted. This arises where the claim form is presented out of time or the claimant fails to meet the qualifying requirements (such as two years' continuing service) for the type of claim submitted. It is also important to ensure that the facts supporting the jurisdictional point are set out in the other sections of the ET3 (for example, the start and end dates required by section 3 are relevant to both the time limit and continuity of employment). If appropriate, the respondent may wish to apply that the jurisdictional point be dealt with at a preliminary hearing under r 53.

Notwithstanding any question of jurisdiction, a respondent should also look ahead to consider what might happen if the tribunal finds that it does have jurisdiction to hear the complaint. The substantive defence to the claim should be put forward 'without prejudice' to the respondent's contention that the tribunal has no jurisdiction to hear the complaint. In other words, multiple arguments should be set out in the alternative (for example: that the tribunal has no jurisdiction because the claim is out of time and, further or alternatively, the dismissal was fair in all the circumstances).

6 'Employer's Contract Claim'

Where an employee claimant makes a claim for breach of contract, the employer is able to make a 'counterclaim' for breach of contract should the employee have acted in breach. This is permitted as a result of Employment Tribunals Extension of Jurisdiction (England and Wales) Order 1994 (SI 1994/1623). A fee will apply to such a claim.

The claim has to be set out with relevant dates and facts, in much the same way as a claimant's ET1 statement, in box 6.3.

7 'Your representative': the respondent's representative

Please see the guidance given on the corresponding section of the claim form at **11.2.2** point 11.

8 'Disability'

Please see the guidance given on the corresponding section of the claim form at **11.2.2**, point 12.

11.3 Mr Red's case: (1) written reasons for dismissal; (2) breach of contract

11.3.1 Overview of Mr Red's case

Mr Red has been summarily dismissed from his employment before qualifying for the statutory right to complain of unfair dismissal. He wishes, however, to recover damages for his contractual notice period and to find out the real reason for his dismissal and accordingly submits a claim form to the tribunal setting out these complaints.

Mr Red's former employer asserts that the real reason for the dismissal was gross misconduct, that is, behaviour of a kind such as to amount to a repudiation of the contract by Mr Red and therefore justifying the summary termination of his employment. The employer contests that the reasons given were sufficient and that in any event, Mr Red does not have sufficient continuity of service to make any claim in this regard.

After receiving the ET3, Mr Red seeks to obtain further particulars of the employer's case and written answers to his questions. He also requests discovery of certain documents.

11.3.2 Mr Red's claim form ET1

Boxes 1 to 7 and 9 to 15 should have the relevant factual details inserted.

The substance of Mr Red's complaint should be set out in box 8.

Box 8: 'Type and details of claim'

  (1) *The claimant was employed by the respondent as a sales assistant from 1 June 2016, pursuant to a contract of employment service, the terms and conditions of which were contained in a written contract dated 13 July 2016.*

(2) *The claimant's contract of employment contained the following, amongst other, terms and conditions:*

   (a) *that the claimant would be paid by the respondent at the rate of £1,500 net per month (as set out in clause 6);*

   (b) *that the claimant's employment could be terminated by the respondent on giving 3 months' notice in writing (as set out in clause 10);*

(3) *In breach of contract, without giving the notice required under clause 10, on 25 May 2018, Mr Sifter, the shop manager of the respondent told the claimant that his employment was to be terminated with immediate effect. That termination was confirmed in writing by letter of the same date.*

(4) *Following the claimant's dismissal on 25 May 2018 as set out in Box 8 above, the claimant was given no reason/s for his dismissal and on 29 May 2018 wrote to the respondent requesting that he be provided with a written statement of the reason/s for his dismissal.*

(5) *On 1 June 2018, the respondent wrote to the claimant, purportedly responding to his request, stating that the reason/s for his dismissal was gross misconduct. The particulars of the reasons given in this statement are inadequate and/or untrue as the claimant had been told on 25 May 2018 he had done nothing wrong.*

(6) *By reason of that breach the claimant has suffered loss and damage.*

PARTICULARS

Loss of £1,500 per month
For period 25 May 2018 to 25 August 2018 (3 months) 3 × £1,500 = £4,500.00

(7) *The claimant claims damages for breach of contract, and:*

   (a) *a declaration as to the true reason/s for his dismissal;*

   (b) *an award of a sum equal to two weeks' pay for the failure to provide written reasons for dismissal.*

11.3.3   Mr Red's claim form ET1: commentary

Here, the ET1 has been completed by filling out the details in the relevant boxes. As stated at **11.2.2**, it would have been possible to put the details in separate documents and insert 'see attached details of complaint' in the relevant boxes. Given the relative brevity of the details, they have been treated as if inserted into the boxes.

Since Mr Red cannot claim unfair dismissal, the claim for wrongful dismissal must be clear. Hence the claim is labelled clearly as 'breach of contract' and the remedy is stated as 'damages for breach of contract'.

The notice period needs to be set out, and its foundation in the contract of employment, since if it is not stated, the tribunal will only consider the minimum statutory notice entitlement. Hence the contract of employment is pleaded in detail: the document is identified by its date and the relevant terms are set out in full.

The member of the respondent organisation who carried out the dismissal should be identified by name and position, to ensure the respondents know which personnel are involved in the claim.

The amount owed should be stated on the claim form along with the method of calculation. Setting out the 'working out' assists the tribunal and the respondent to appreciate the claimant's assertions (and perhaps facilitate settlement of the claim).

It is a requirement that where a claim is being made for a declaration of the true reason for dismissal and an award of two weeks' wages for the failure to provide written reasons, that the claimant has made a request for the reasons. Hence the date of any letter making such request must be included.

If no response had been sent to the claimant stating reasons for the dismissal, this precedent ET1 might be amended to read at box 8:

(4) *Following the claimant's dismissal on 25 May 2018 as set out above, the claimant was given no reason/s for his dismissal and on 29 May 2018 wrote to the respondent requesting that he be provided with a written statement of the reason/s for his dismissal. No response has been received to that letter.*

(5) *In the circumstances the respondent has unreasonably failed to provide a written statement of the reason/s for the claimant's dismissal within 14 days of his request or at all.*

11.3.4   The respondent's response to Mr Red's claim (Form ET3)

It will be assumed that all of the boxes other than box 5 have the appropriate information.

Box 5

(1) *It is admitted that the claimant was employed by the respondent from 1 June 2016 pursuant to a contract of service, the terms of which were evidenced by a contract of employment dated 13 July 2016.*

(2) *The terms set out at box 8 paragraph 2 of the claimant's claim form are admitted save that they must be read subject to other express or implied terms of the contract, as follows:*

(a) *that the claimant would obey all reasonable instructions given to him by the respondent, to give business efficacy to the contract;*

(b) *that the claimant would serve the respondent faithfully and would not act in such a way as to undermine the mutual trust and confidence existing between himself and his employer, to be implied as a matter of law;*

(c) *that the respondent would be entitled to terminate the contract summarily in the event of the claimant having committed an act of gross misconduct (clause 11);*

(d) *that the respondent would be entitled, without giving notice, to treat the contract as having come to an end in the event of the claimant having acted in repudiatory breach of the same, to be implied as a matter of law.*

(3) *On 25 May 2018, the claimant refused to obey a reasonable instruction given by the duty manager Miss Benn, and was rude to her in front of a number of other employees and members of the public.*

(4) *This amounted to gross misconduct and/or to a repudiatory breach of the contract entitling the respondent to terminate the claimant's employment without notice which the respondent duly did on 25 May 2018.*

(5) *In the circumstances it is denied that the respondent has acted in breach of the contract.*

(6) *It is accepted that the respondent did reply to the claimant's letter of 29 May 2018. The respondent's letter dated 1 June 2018 stated the claimant was dismissed for gross misconduct. It is contended that in the circumstances such notification was sufficient. It is the respondent's case, in any event, that the claimant knew the reason for his dismissal.*

(7) Further, and in any event, the claimant has insufficient continuity of service to make a claim in respect of a failure to provide a written statement of the reason(s) for his dismissal under s 92, Employment Rights Act 1996.

11.3.5 The respondent's response to Mr Red's claim: commentary

Terms may be implied into a contract of employment by a matter of law (either through recognition in case law or by statutory intervention) or to give business efficacy to the contract or through custom and practice (see **5.2.4**). If an implied term is to be asserted, its authority should be made clear. If however, a written term is relied upon, it should be clearly identified by reference to the appropriate document (contract of employment, statement of written terms and conditions, staff handbook, etc.).

In any case of misconduct leading to dismissal, it is advisable to give particulars of the misconduct relied upon. This is particularly important where it is alleged that the claimant has acted in gross misconduct. Caution has been employed here by not expressly stating what the claimant's 'rude' conduct to Miss Benn has been, since the respondent's representatives would not at this stage have had the opportunity to take Miss Benn's statement to define the claimant's conduct with certainty. However, should such information be known, it can be tactically advantageous to provide fuller details (particularly when a represented claimant may use the mechanism of a request for further particulars as set out at **11.3.6**).

11.3.6 Request for further particulars of the response form

This request should be set out in a clearly dated letter.

Dear [name],

Re: [Mr Red v Respondent, Case number xxxx 2018]

The respondent is requested to supply the following further particulars of its Response Form within 21 days of the date of this request. If these further particulars are not supplied on a voluntary basis within this time, the claimant will apply for an order from the Tribunal that these be provided under r 31 and r 32 of the Employment Tribunals Rules of Procedure 2013.

Under box 5 paragraph 3

OF: 'On 25 May 2018 the claimant refused to obey a reasonable instruction given by the duty manager Miss Benn, and was rude to her in front of a number of other employees and members of the public.'

REQUESTS:

Please give full particulars of:

1. *the instruction said to have been made;*

2. *the time and occasion when it is said to have been made;*

3. *all facts and matters relied upon to support the allegation that the claimant refused to obey that instruction;*

4. *all facts and matters relied upon to support the allegation that the claimant was rude;*

5. *the identities of the employees alleged to have been present, indicating precisely where, in relation to the claimant and the duty manager, they are said to have been.*

6. *the exact number and identities of the members of the public alleged to have been present, indicating precisely where, in relation to the claimant and the duty manager, they are said to have been.*

Under box 5 paragraph 6

OF: '...*the claimant knew the reason for his dismissal.*'

REQUEST:

   7. *State now all facts and matters relied upon in support of the allegation that the claimant knew the reason for his dismissal.*

Under box 5 paragraph 7

OF: '*Further, and in any event, the claimant has insufficient continuity of service to make a claim in respect of a failure to provide a written statement of the reason(s) for his dismissal under s 92, Employment Rights Act 1996.*'

REQUEST:

   8. *Please state now all facts and matters relied upon in support of the allegation that the claimant has insufficient continuity of service.*

   Signed:

11.3.7   Request for further particulars of the response form: commentary

The case should be identified by setting out the names of the parties and the case number, even when writing to a party to the proceedings, since it may be necessary to send copies of the correspondence to the tribunal.

The requests made here seek to clarify the vague assertions made by the respondent. There is little detail set out, which when raised at the full hearing may take the claimant by surprise. The claimant may have factual issues in response. Therefore, request 1 seeks to clarify the 'reasonable instruction' alleged (what exactly was it? was it reasonable?); request 2 asks the time and occasion it is alleged to have been made (was the claimant in the workplace at the precise time? was Miss Benn in the vicinity at the precise time?); requests 3 and 4 ensure that the reasons why the respondent alleges the claimant refused to obey that instruction and was rude are known by the claimant; and requests 5 and 6 seek specific identities of the employees and members of the public so that their correctness can be checked by the claimant and potential witnesses identified.

Time limits for requests

Here, the request allows for a voluntary response to be sent within 21 days of the date of the letter. The time limit need not be 21 days in all cases. Since respondents frequently fail to give a response voluntarily, there may be a need to apply for an order. As a result, the hearing date or any directions in the case must be considered. There must be enough time allowed for the purposes of writing a letter requesting an order to the tribunal, waiting for the order to be granted and then sent to the respondent and finally for the respondent to comply. Where time is scarce, then less time for voluntary compliance should be left.

It is useful where the time limit is set out (in the form of 'within *X* days of this request'), that the last day for response is set out as a calendar date. This removes any doubt, and can assist in showing the tribunal the default of the receiving party should application for an order become necessary.

Obtaining an order

Explicit reference has been made here to rr 31 and 32 of the Employment Tribunals Rules of Procedure 2013, which give the tribunal the power to order 'information' to be given. An alternative method of expressing this might be: '*Please supply these further particulars within X days (by X date), failing which the claimant will apply to the Employment Tribunal for the appropriate orders compelling you to do so.'*

Should no response to this letter be received, the representatives of the claimant should, the day after the final day for compliance, send a letter to the tribunal (attaching a copy of this request) setting out the reason/s why the further particulars are required and asking for an order to be granted. A precedent letter of this type can be found in Lewis's *Employment Law: An Adviser's Handbook* (11th edn, 2015, Legal Action Group) and Cunningham and Reed's *Employment Tribunal Claims tactics and precedents* (4th edn, 2013, Legal Action Group).

11.3.8 Further particulars of the response form pursuant to the claimant's request

Dear [name],

Re: [Mr Red v Respondent, Case number xxxx 2018]

Pursuant to the claimant's request, the respondent provides the following further particulars of the notice of appearance:

Under box 5 paragraph 3

OF: 'On 25 May 2018 the claimant refused to obey a reasonable instruction given by the duty manager Miss Benn, and was rude to her in front of a number of other employees and members of the public.'

Please give full particulars of:

REQUEST:

1. the instruction said to have been made;

ANSWER:

1. The claimant was asked to open another till since there were customers waiting to be served.

REQUEST:

2. the time and occasion when it is said to have been made;

ANSWER:

2. The instruction was made at 12:05 on the shop floor on 25 May 2018.

REQUEST:

3. all facts and matters relied upon to support the allegation that the claimant refused to obey that instruction;

ANSWER:

3. The claimant said 'no f *** ing way, I'm not working on the f *** ing till today!'.

REQUEST:

4. all facts and matters relied upon to support the allegation that the claimant was rude;

ANSWER:

4. The claimant is referred to the answer at 3 above.

REQUEST:

5. the identities of the employees alleged to have been present, indicating precisely where, in relation to the claimant and the duty manager, they are said to have been.

ANSWER:

5. Mr Bean was on the shop floor patrolling the shop and Mr Spud was working on another till.

REQUEST:

6. the exact number and identities of the members of the public alleged to have been present, indicating precisely where, in relation to the claimant and the duty manager, they are said to have been.

ANSWER:

6. The exact number of members of the public and their identities are unknown. However, it is the respondent's case that there was a queue of customers waiting to be served who were at the tills.

Under box 5 paragraph 6

OF: '…the claimant knew the reason for his dismissal.'

REQUEST:

7. State now all facts and matters relied upon in support of the allegation that the claimant knew the reason for his dismissal.

ANSWER:

7. The claimant was told verbally by Mr Sifter on 25 May 2018 of the reason for his dismissal, being his gross misconduct of refusing to obey a reasonable instruction and rudeness to the duty manager. He did not at that time deny that he had behaved as set out above. The reason for dismissal was confirmed in the letter dated 1 June 2018 to the claimant.

Under box 5 paragraph 7

OF: 'Further, and in any event, the claimant has insufficient continuity of service to make a claim in respect of a failure to provide a written statement of the reason(s) for his dismissal under s 92, Employment Rights Act 1996.'

REQUEST:

8. Please state now all facts and matters relied upon in support of the allegation that the claimant has insufficient continuity of service.

ANSWER:

8. The claimant commenced employment on 1 June 2016, his employment terminated with immediate effect on 25 May 2018. The respondent was entitled contractually to terminate his employment without notice due to his gross misconduct as set out above.

Signed:

11.3.9 Further particulars of the response form pursuant to the claimant's request: commentary

The representatives of the respondents would have obtained full instructions before setting out this response. In this instance, the response has been voluntary, however, tactically the respondent may choose not to respond voluntarily and wait until the claimant obtains an order.

Here, the factual details are generally helpful to the respondent and therefore have been set out in detail wherever possible. It is permissible where exact details are not known to set out what is within the knowledge of the respondent's personnel.

11.3.10 Request for written answers and respondent's response

Requests for written answers are not used in practice as frequently as requests for further particulars or requests for discovery. Therefore this type of request will not be covered in as much detail as those procedural tools in this chapter. The reader is referred to the guidance at **11.3.7** on time limits for requests and obtaining an order, as the guidance is equally applicable here.

The request should be set out in a clearly dated letter.

The request for written answers

Dear [name],

Re: [Mr Red v Respondent, Case number xxxx 2018]

The respondent is requested to supply the following written answers within 21 days of the date of this request [set out calendar date deadline for response]. If these answers are not supplied on a voluntary basis within this time, the claimant will apply for an order from the tribunal that these be provided under r 31 and r 32 of the Employment Tribunals Rules of Procedure 2013, as amended.

QUESTIONS:

(1) In relation to box 5 paragraph 6 of the Response Form, is it not the case that not only did the letter of 1 June 2018 not give 'detailed' reasons for the claimant's dismissal but it did not in fact given any reasons for that dismissal?

(2) Is it not also right that upon telling the claimant that he was being dismissed summarily, Mr Sifter expressly stated to him: 'You did nothing wrong'?

(3) Is it not further the case that the claimant's dismissal took place only 1 week prior to his having completed 2 years continuous employment with the respondent and thereby obtaining statutory rights?

Signed:

Written answers provided by the respondent

Dear [name],

Re: [Mr Red v Respondent, Case number xxxx 2018]

Pursuant to the [claimant's request/tribunal's order of [date]], the respondent provides the following written answers:

[set out questions in full as set out above]

ANSWERS

1. In answer to the first question, …

2. In answer to the second question, …etc.

[provide answers as relevant]

Signed:

11.3.11   Letter requesting disclosure of documentary evidence

The request should be set out in a clearly dated letter.

Dear [name],

Re: [Mr Red v Respondent, Case number xxxx 2018]

We act for Mr Red, the claimant in this matter.

Having now had the opportunity to consider the Response Form submitted by the respondent, we ask that the following documents be disclosed within 21 days of this letter [set out calendar date deadline for response], by sending copies of them to this office:

1. The contract of employment of the claimant.

2. The respondent's disciplinary and grievance procedure.

3. The respondent's staff handbook.

4. All documents (including notes, memos, minutes or any other document) related to the process leading to the decision to dismiss Mr Red.

5. The claimant's letter to the respondent dated 29 May 2018.

6. The letter to the claimant dated 1 June 2018.

7. A copy of the claimant's personal/personnel file.

If the respondent does not disclose these documents within the time requested on a voluntary basis, we will apply to the tribunal for an order under r 31 and r 32 of the Employment Tribunals Rules of Procedure 2013, as amended.

Signed:

11.3.12   Letter requesting discovery of documentary evidence: commentary

The reader is referred to the guidance at **11.3.7** on time limits for requests and obtaining an order, as the guidance is equally applicable here.

When obtaining discovery, it is useful to give consideration to the types of document which employers create in the course of their business in relation to the employment of workers. The contract of employment or ERA 1996, s 1, statement of terms and conditions may not state all the relevant contractual terms or relevant matters such as disciplinary or grievance procedure. As a result, the representative should initially enquire with the client as to which pieces of documentary evidence should be requested. It may well be that collective agreements between the employers and trade unions have varied the contract of employment or that the relevant procedures are contained in separate documents or a 'handbook'. Therefore the scope for enquiries may be wider than initially expected.

It is advisable to set out a wide definition of the word 'document', which may include notes, minutes, memoranda, contemporaneous notes, subsequent typed notes (since they may not be identical to the original handwritten note), reports, telephone call notes (sometimes called 'attendance notes') and emails.

It is possible to make the request for disclosure as set out at **11.3.11**, with copies being sent to the representative's offices. However, it is also possible to make the request for disclosure *by list* or *by providing the same for inspection at [address]*. If required the letter should be amended accordingly.

11.4   Ms Orange's case: unfair dismissal/redundancy payment

11.4.1   Overview of Ms Orange's case

Ms Orange believes that she has been dismissed by reason of redundancy but has not received a statutory redundancy payment. She also believes that she has been unfairly dismissed and has presented a complaint to the tribunal seeking her full redundancy entitlement and compensation for unfair dismissal.

Ms Orange's employer accepts that a redundancy situation existed but contends that suitable alternative employment was offered to her which she unreasonably refused and therefore disputes her claim for a redundancy payment. In the alternative, the employer argues that she would only be entitled to a lesser sum as a statutory redundancy payment than that claimed. Furthermore, the employer contends that the dismissal was fair in all the circumstances of the case.

Ultimately, the parties settle the claim under a compromise/settlement agreement.

11.4.2   Ms Orange's claim form ET1

It will be assumed that all of the boxes except for box 8 have the relevant factual details inserted.

The substance of Ms Orange's complaint should be set out in box 8 and there should be ticks to indicate claims of unfair dismissal and a redundancy payment (which are obviously in the alternative).

Box 8

(1) *The claimant was employed as a catering team operative by the respondent, at its premises at Fast Food Heaven, 22 Old Essex Road, London, from 6 February 2012, until her dismissal on 25 August 2017. The respondent is a large company in business as a take away food chain and employs some 1,000 people.*

(2) *The claimant's employment was at all times subject to the redundancy procedure set out in the respondent's Staff Handbook.*

(3) *On 12 July 2017, the respondent told the claimant by letter dated 12 July 2017 that she was to be dismissed with effect from 25 August 2017 by reason of redundancy.*

(4) *The claimant sought to appeal the decision to dismiss her by letter dated 14 July 2017. However, at a meeting on 25 July 2017, and letter of the same date, she was informed her appeal had been unsuccessful.*

(5) *The claimant considers her dismissal to have been unfair.*

(6) *In particular, the claimant will rely on the fact that:*

   (a) *the respondent acted in breach of the staff redundancy procedure and/or unfairly:*

      (i) *in restricting the pool for selection to catering team operatives when it should have included all catering and till operatives; and/or*

      (ii) *in failing to consult as to the criteria and/or the operation of the selection procedure utilised; and/or*

   (b) *the respondent failed to warn the claimant of the possibility that she might be dismissed by reason of redundancy and/or to consult with her about the same;*

(7) *It is the claimant's primary case that she was unfairly dismissed for the reasons set out above. However, she would contend that further or alternatively she is due a redundancy payment.*

(8) *No statutory redundancy payment was paid to the claimant, and this remains due to her.*

PARTICULARS

Continuous employment from 6 February   *5 complete years*

2012 to 29 August 2017

The claimant's age at termination of employment *33*

Gross weekly wage £400   *5 × £400 = £2,000.00*

11.4.3   Ms Orange's claim form ET1: commentary

Since Ms Orange's claim is of unfair dismissal primarily and for a redundancy payment in the alternative, the legal issues relating to unfair dismissal must be kept in mind. For example, in dealing with the reasonableness test in ERA 1996, s 98(4), the tribunal has regard to the size and administrative resources available to the respondent. Therefore, particularly if the respondent is large and well resourced, it is tactically advantageous for the claimant to state it and request the tribunal to apply a higher standard as a result.

It may well be that any redundancy procedure is set out in another document (collective agreements, a separate policy document, the contract of employment), in which case the relevant document must be identified.

When setting out details of the dismissal, the claim form should indicate whether the dismissal was summary or with notice. If the dismissal was summary or if full notice was not given, the claimant may wish to include a contractual claim for damages in her application, or claim for 'wrongful dismissal'. This would be included in the text set out in box 8.

When challenging the decision to dismiss, it is advisable if possible, to try to indicate the particular grounds relied on for claiming that the dismissal was unfair. In this example (as with most redundancy cases) there are a number of grounds. If the nature of the challenge is that there was no redundancy situation, then the wording of the statutory definition at ERA 1996, s 139 should be used: *the claimant's position was not redundant as there was no diminution in the respondent's need for employees to carry out the kind of work s/he was employed to do at that workplace.*

Here, the selection and methods used by the respondent are being challenged. Where selection is the issue, it is tactically useful to set out in the claim form the pool chosen by the employer and then set out the correct pool. In the instance of a 'last in, first out' policy this can be done with reference to the date of commencement or years of service. Please note that some further arguments which may be raised include: *failing to provide the claimant with the opportunity to appeal against the decision that she should be dismissed; the respondent failed to consider or to provide alternative employment opportunities for the claimant and/or to training so that she might be re-deployed within the respondent company.*

In relation to the claim for a redundancy payment, the claimant's entitlement should be set out (calculations are particularly helpful) and the attempts to obtain payment.

11.4.4 The respondent's response form to Ms Orange's claim

It will be assumed that all of the boxes other than box 5 will be filled in with the appropriate information.

Box 5

> *(1) It is admitted that the respondent is a large company in business as a take away food chain and employs some 1,000 people. It is further admitted that the claimant was employed as a catering team operative by the respondent, from 6 February 2012 to 25 August 2017 at its premises at Fast Food Heaven, 22 Old Essex Road, London.*

> *(2) The respondent accepts that on 12 July 2017 it dismissed the claimant by reason of redundancy from her position as catering team operative with effect from 25 August 2017.*

> *(3) Prior to the ending of the claimant's employment, however, on 12 July 2017, the respondent offered her, by letter dated 12 July 2017, suitable alternative employment as a catering team operative at its premises at Fast Food Heaven at 353 Silverhawk Road, London. Save as to the place of work, the terms and conditions of employment offered to the claimant were the same as those she had enjoyed before and, in all the circumstances, the employment was a suitable alternative for her. Further it was made clear to the claimant in the same letter that the alternative employment offered was subject to a 4-week trial period.*

> *(4) On 12 July 2017, on being made this offer the claimant unreasonably refused the alternative employment.*

(5) *The claimant wrote a letter dated 14 July 2017 seeking to complain about her redundancy. The respondent wrote a letter dated 25 July 2017 dealing with her complaints. Unfortunately, owing to the lack of business as set out below, it was not possible to allow the claimant to continue working as a catering team operative at the Old Essex Road branch.*

(6) *In the circumstances the claimant was not entitled to a redundancy payment and cannot claim such an entitlement before the employment tribunal.*

(7) *Further, the respondent denies that the claimant's dismissal was unfair, in particular:*

(a) *The respondent suffered a decline in sales at its Old Essex Road branch and did not require as many catering team operatives. The respondent needed to reduce the number of catering team operatives by three. This did not affect the respondent's need for till operatives.*

(b) *Two catering team operatives were made redundant and were informed of the decision by letters dated 12 July 2017. It was only the claimant who was offered alternative employment in recognition of her length of service. The claimant was therefore not selected unfairly.*

(c) *There was no requirement for consultation as in the circumstances such consultation would have been futile. The redundancies were necessary in order to prevent the overall closure of the Old Essex Road branch.*

11.4.5   The respondent's response form to Ms Orange's claim: commentary

There are two legal tests a respondent must meet when resisting a claim for unfair dismissal for redundancy. The first is to ensure that the statutory definition of redundancy in ERA 1996, s 139, is applicable to the claimant's situation. Hence this draft sets out the business circumstances leading to the redundancy situation. The second is to show that the dismissal was fair in all the circumstances (the ERA 1996, s 98(4) 'reasonableness' test). Here it is useful to give particulars of the matters relied upon as demonstrating the fairness of the dismissal, answering, so far as possible, the case put in the claimant's claim form. Consultation, notification, selection and alternative employment may all be issues arising here. The ground, that consultation would be futile, can be argued by a respondent as a result of *Mugford v Midland Bank* [1997] IRLR 208. If there has been any form of consultation and notification, it is preferable to set out the steps taken and only rely on this argument as an alternative should the tribunal find the consultation process lacking. Where there has been no consultation, it may be the only means of avoiding liability.

If the claimant had claimed an incorrect figure for the redundancy payment, then the respondent may have added the paragraph: '*In the alternative, if, contrary to the respondent's case, the claimant is found to be entitled to a statutory redundancy payment, it is contended that the amount due would be in the sum of £[amount].*'

11.4.6   Compromise/settlement agreement/contract

AN AGREEMENT to refrain from instituting or continuing with proceedings before an employment tribunal made pursuant to the provisions of s 203(2) of the Employment Rights Act 1996. This [agreement/contract] is made between:

Ms Orange ......('the employee')

of 28A Old Essex Road, London ...... and

Fast Food Heaven .... ('the employer')

of 22 Old Essex Road, London ......

1. *The employer will pay to the employee the sum of £3,000 and will provide her with a reference, in the form attached to this agreement and no other, within 14 days of the date of this agreement and the employee agrees to accept this sum and this reference in full and final settlement of all contractual claims outstanding at and/or arising out of the termination of her employment by the employer on 25 August 2017.*

2. *The employer will further pay to the employee the sum of £3,000, in consideration of which the employee will refrain from continuing her complaint against the employer before the employment tribunal under Case No. [specify] in respect of her allegation that on 25 August 2017 the employer:*

   dismissed her unfairly; and
   failed to pay her a statutory redundancy payment.

3. *The employee accepts the payment made by the employer in full and final settlement of all other claims which she has or may have against the employer arising out of her employment or the termination thereof, being claims in respect of which an employment tribunal has no jurisdiction, with the exception of pension rights and claims for personal injury.*

4. *The employee acknowledges that, before signing this Agreement, she received independent legal advice from Marshall Hall, a solicitor currently in possession of a practising certificate from the Law Society, as to the terms and effect of this Agreement and in particular its effect on her ability to pursue her rights before an employment tribunal.*

5. *The conditions regulating compromise agreements under the Employment Rights Act 1996 are satisfied in relation to this Agreement.*

Signed: **Satsuma Orange**...*(employee) 3 October 2017*

Signed: **Town Burger on behalf of Fast Food Heaven**...*(employer) 3 October 2017*

Statement by adviser to employee

I, Marshall Hall of Door, Hall & Co of 17 Old Essex Road, London, confirm that I am a solicitor currently in possession of a practising certificate from the Law Society and that I have advised the employee as to the terms of this agreement, in particular as to its effect in relation to rights to continue claims in the employment tribunal.

Signed: **Marshall Hall**

Dated: 3 October 2017

11.4.7   Compromise agreement/contract: commentary

This form of settlement is appropriate where the settlement has been reached without the assistance of ACAS, through negotiation by legal representatives.

Since this type of settlement is authorised by statute, it must comply with the relevant requirements. Here, the most significant requirement is that the employee has received legal advice. Here the requirement is met by the countersignature of the employee's legal representative. However, this is not always necessary, provided that paras 4 and 5 are present. The employee having received legal advice is necessary since in signing the agreement, the employee gives up the right to pursue and/or bring claims in the employment tribunal.

Please note that such a compromise agreement can be used before any tribunal proceedings are started. In practice, they are used by some employers at the time of making an employee redundant to ensure that the employee accepts the sum offered and is prevented from making a tribunal claim. If such an agreement is being drafted, para 2 should be amended with the words *'in consideration of which the employee will refrain from instituting a complaint against the employer before an employment tribunal'*.

The claimant's adviser must be a 'relevant independent adviser' for the purposes of ERA 1996, s 203(3)(c), therefore the example here of a solicitor adviser is acceptable. Other permissible advisers would be a barrister, solicitor of the Supreme Court, currently in possession of a practising certificate from the Law Society or advocate.

Making settlement attractive

The precedent used here does not employ all of the features often used to make settlement attractive to the parties. Respondents commonly have an objective of avoiding adverse publicity arising from employment tribunal litigation. Therefore, one method of ensuring this is avoided is by settling the proceedings with a 'confidentiality clause'. This could be worded thus: *'The claimant [and the respondent] undertake not to make the nature of this compromise agreement or the subject matter of the proceedings be known to anyone other than as required by law or their legal advisers and immediate family members.'*

Claimants, on the other hand, fear that their tribunal proceedings will poison the opinion of their former employer against them and result in difficulties in finding employment due to adverse references. This can be remedied by inserting a clause obliging the respondent to use the wording of a reference the content of which is agreed between the parties ('an agreed reference'). A specimen clause has been included here at para 1. However, this form of words is fairly unspecific and of the type proposed by the respondent's representatives. A claimant may be concerned about pro forma or telephone references not being covered. The method of drafting the clause might be: *'The employer agrees to supply references requested by prospective employers of the employee in the form attached to this compromise agreement. Any requests made by pro forma means or by telephone shall be responded to in the spirit of the agreed reference attached in the schedule hereto.'*

11.5 Mr Yellow's case: constructive unfair dismissal

11.5.1 Overview of Mr Yellow's case

Mr Yellow left his employment as he believed that his employer was trying to require him to do more than his contract of employment provided and was thereby seeking unilaterally to introduce new terms and conditions of employment. He claims that this was a fundamental breach of his contract of employment, that he was dismissed (constructively) and that the dismissal was unfair in all the circumstances of the case. Mr Yellow left his employment immediately, so he has an additional claim for notice pay (breach of contract).

Mr Yellow's former employer puts the case against him in a number of alternatives: first the employer denies that Mr Yellow was dismissed. In the alternative, however, the employer claims that any dismissal was either by reason of the claimant's conduct in refusing to comply with a reasonable instruction or for some other substantial reason, namely a need to introduce new terms and conditions due to pressing business reasons. In either event, the employer claims that any dismissal found was fair in all the circumstances of the case.

Ultimately, the case is settled at the door of the tribunal and the terms are recorded in an agreement between the parties. Two forms of the agreement have been included to illustrate alternative methods of recording such a court door settlement.

11.5.2 Mr Yellow's claim form ET1

It will be assumed that all of the boxes except for box 8 have the relevant factual details inserted.

Box 8

(1) *The claimant was employed as a finance worker by the respondent from 9 July 2012 until 11 August 2017. The respondent is a medium-sized company in business as supplier of telecommunications and employs some 100 people.*

(2) *It was an implied term of the claimant's employment, implied as a matter of law, and/ or to give business efficacy to the contract of employment, that the respondent would not act so as to damage the relationship of mutual trust and confidence between it and the claimant as its employee.*

(3) *On 10 August 2017 the respondent purported to introduce, by letter dated 10 August 2017 a unilateral variation to the claimant's contract of employment, namely that the claimant's working hours would be extended from 35 hours per week to 45 hours per week and that the claimant would have added responsibility of checking purchase orders.*

(4) *The same amounted to a fundamental breach of the claimant's contract of employment, as to the implied term that the respondent would not act so as to damage the relationship of mutual trust and confidence between it and the claimant as its employee.*

(5) *By reason of this breach and in response to the same, on 11 August 2017, the claimant informed his manager Mr Driver of the respondent by letter, that he was treating the breach as terminating his contract of employment with immediate effect. The claimant did in fact leave his employment on 11 August 2017. The above circumstances entitled him to terminate the contract without notice to the respondent.*

(6) *In the circumstances, the claimant considers that he was constructively dismissed.*

(7) *The claimant also believes that his dismissal was unfair. In particular, the claimant will rely on the fact that:*

(a) *the respondent's unilateral decision to change his terms and conditions of employment was unreasonable in all the circumstances of the case, in particular:*

(i) *the degree of change proposed was not necessitated by the needs of the business; and/or*

(ii) *it was unreasonable to expect the claimant to accept the proposed changes; and/or*

(b) *the respondent failed to give any or any adequate warning of the proposed changes; and/or*

(c) *the respondent failed to negotiate and/or consult with the claimant's trade union about the changes proposed, the timing of their introduction and/or their effect; and/or*

(d) *the respondent failed to consider alternatives to the proposed changes and/or to consult with the claimant's trade union about the same.*

(8) *Following the claimant's dismissal on 11 August 2017 as set out above, the claimant was given no reason/s for his dismissal and on 14 August 2017 wrote to the respondent requesting that he be provided with a written statement of the reason/s for his dismissal. No response has been received to that letter.*

(9) *In the circumstances the respondent has unreasonably failed to provide a written state-ment of the reason/s for the claimant's dismissal within 14 days of his request or at all.*

11.5.3   Mr Yellow's claim form: commentary

Whether or not there is any express term which the claimant considers has been breached, it is always prudent in constructive dismissal cases to rely upon breach of an accepted implied term. It gives the employment tribunal the alternative of finding fun-damental breach of the implied term if there is insufficient material to support breach of the express term.

If breach of an express term is being asserted, then the following form of words may be used: *The claimant's employment was at all times subject to the terms set out in the Contract of Employment/Statement of Terms and Conditions sent to him by the respon-dent dated [date] [and/or identify relevant documents or other evidence relied on as forming the basis of the contractual entitlement the claimant contends was breached]. In particular: [set out the particular terms relevant to the issues in the case].* Do remember that in some circumstances, rights or entitlements set out in collective agreements, job descrip-tions and staff handbooks become incorporated into the contract of employment. Alternatively, it can be argued that there is an implied term that the employer will act in accordance with the rights and entitlements set out in such documents.

Just because the claimant may be able to establish that he was (constructively) dismissed does not mean to say that the dismissal was unfair. If possible, one should indicate the particular grounds relied on for claiming that the dismissal was unfair. For further details on how the tribunal deals with constructive unfair dismissal claims, see **Chapter 6**.

When setting out details of the dismissal, the claim form should indicate whether the dismissal was summary or with notice. If the dismissal was summary or if full notice was not given, the claimant may wish to include a contractual claim for damages in her application, or claim for 'wrongful dismissal'. This would follow a similar form to Mr Red's claim as set out at **11.3.2**.

11.5.4   The respondent's response form to Mr Yellow's claim form

It is assumed that all of the boxes other than box 5 will be filled in with the appropri-ate information.

Box 5

(1) *It is accepted that the respondent is a medium-sized company in business as a supplier of telecommunications, employing some 100 people. It is accepted that the claimant was employed by the respondent as a finance worker from 9 July 2012 until 11 August 2017.*

(2) *The respondent also accepts that the claimant's contract of employment contained an implied term, implied as a matter of law, and/or to give business efficacy to the contract of employment, that the respondent would not act so as to damage the relationship of mutual trust and confidence between it and the claimant as its employee.*

(3) *It is accepted that, as part of the contract of employment, there was an implied obligation upon the respondent not to act so as to damage the relationship of trust and confidence between it and its employees. This was, however, an obligation also imposed upon the claimant in his dealings with the respondent.*

(4) *It is further contended by the respondent that the claimant's employment was also sub-ject to the implied obligation that he would obey all reasonable instructions given to him by the respondent during the course of his employment.*

(5) *Contrary to the claimant's assertions, the respondent never sought to vary the claimant's contract of employment by any form of permanent extension of the claimant's working hours from 35 hours per week to 45 hours per week or a permanent added responsibility of checking purchase orders. In fact the respondent merely requested the claimant to check purchase orders during a period of three weeks whilst his colleague was on annual leave (such a duty having been his colleague's responsibility), this being a lawful and reasonable instruction.*

(6) *In the circumstances, the respondent denies that there has been any breach of any terms of the claimant's contract of employment.*

(7) *In fact, on 11 August 2017, the claimant voluntarily resigned from his employment by letter. He was not dismissed.*

(8) *In the alternative (and contrary to the respondent's main case as set out above), if the claimant is found to have been dismissed, the respondent will say that this was by reason of his failure to obey a reasonable instruction given by his employer and was a fair reason. The claimant committed an act of gross misconduct.*

(9) *Furthermore, any dismissal of the claimant for that reason was fair in all the circumstances of the case, in particular on 11 August 2017 the claimant had a conversation with Mr Driver where he was assured that the changes were temporary and would end upon his colleague's return from leave. He refused to obey the reasonable instruction, and on 11 August 2017 the claimant went to Mr Driver's office and in front of a number of colleagues shouted 'Mr Driver? More like a f***ing slave driver! You should be strung up for treating your workers like cattle. You are the lowest life form I have ever come across and you deserve to die!'. It is submitted that such conduct constituted gross misconduct.*

11.5.5   The respondent's response form to Mr Yellow's claim: commentary

The respondent in constructive dismissal cases has two main legal issues to rely upon to escape liability. Since the claimant must prove dismissal and must show it is within the strict definition in ERA 1996, s 95, the respondent can deny there has been a dismissal, and assert that the claimant resigned voluntarily. This provides the claimant with a difficult legal requirement to fulfil. The respondent's second main argument is that in the event the tribunal finds the claimant was dismissed (which of course, they deny), the dismissal was fair. Please see **Chapter 6** for more details on the tribunal's approach to constructive unfair dismissal cases. Here, the respondent relies on the claimant's conduct on 11 August 2017 to demonstrate fairness. The allegation of gross misconduct is particularly attractive, since it would justify summary dismissal.

To show that there has been no dismissal, the respondent can rely on a number of matters, depending on the facts of the case.

The first set of arguments relate to terms and breach. The respondent may want to deny that express terms asserted by the claimant in fact exist, which would be done by pleading: *It is, however, denied that the claimant's contract of employment included the express term that [state term]. [Give relevant particulars to support denial, e.g.: This was in fact never agreed to by the respondent and therefore never became part of the contract of employment.]* Further, there may be factual issues which support a denial of breach by the employer. Here, the term which obliges the claimant to follow a reasonable instruction and the temporary nature of the extra duties allow the respondent to argue that there was no breach. Finally, and perhaps with the most risk attached to it, the respondent may argue if there is a breach, then it was not fundamental.

The respondent may also argue that the resignation is not 'connected' to any breach, or that there has been delay by the claimant. These could be pleaded thus (provided they are supported by the facts): *'The claimant accepted the variation of the terms and conditions of employment, working under these new conditions from their introduction on 10 August 2017 to his resignation on 2 October 2017. It is further submitted that the claimant's resignation is not connected with the variation of his terms and conditions owing to the passage of time as set out above.'* A further approach may be to give details of how resignation was effected, that is, whether by letter or orally, stating the gist of the words used to demonstrate the fact of resignation rather than dismissal.

11.5.6 Settlements: (a) settlement appendixed to tribunal order and (b) *Tomlin* order (consent order)

SCHEDULE APPENDIXED TO TRIBUNAL ORDER

IN THE [LOCATION] EMPLOYMENT TRIBUNAL   *Case No.*

BETWEEN:

MELLOW YELLOW   *Claimant*

-and-

NET TELECOMS LTD   *Respondent*

DECISION

1. *Settlement having been agreed between the parties in accordance with the terms set out in the Schedule hereto, by consent, this claim is withdrawn upon compliance with the terms of the settlement on or before [insert date after the date provided for compliance by the respondent; usually some 14 days after the date of compliance, thereby allowing time for a cheque to clear].*

2. *Liberty to apply on or before [insert date as above] and if no application is made by this date, this claim on withdrawal by the claimant.*

SCHEDULE

[set out terms of agreement] or

1. *Settlement having been agreed between the parties in accordance with the terms endorsed [on Counsels' briefs/in the sealed envelope annexed to this decision/insert as appropriate by reference to document which will not form part of the public record], by consent, this claim is withdrawn upon compliance by the respondent with the terms of the settlement on or before [date as above].*

2. *Liberty to apply on or before [date as above] and if no application is made by this date, this claim is dismissed on withdrawal by the claimant.*

'*TOMLIN*' OR CONSENT ORDER

IN THE [LOCATION] EMPLOYMENT TRIBUNAL   *Case No.*

BETWEEN:

MELLOW YELLOW   *Claimant*

-and-

NET TELECOMS LTD   *Respondent*

ORDER

The parties having agreed to the terms set out in the attached schedule

IT IS ORDERED BY CONSENT:

1. *That, this claim is withdrawn upon compliance with the terms of the settlement on or before [insert date after the date provided for compliance by the respondent; usually some 14 days after the date of compliance, thereby allowing time for a cheque to clear].*

2. *Liberty to apply on or before [date as above] and if no application is made by this date, this claim is dismissed on withdrawal by the claimant.*

SCHEDULE

AGREEMENT

The parties have agreed as follows:

[set out terms of agreement] or

1. *Settlement having been agreed between the parties in accordance with the terms endorsed [on Counsels' briefs/in the sealed envelope annexed to this decision/insert as appropriate by reference to document which will not form part of the public record], by consent, this claim is withdrawn upon compliance by the respondent with the terms of the settlement on or before [date as above].*

2. *Liberty to apply on or before [date as above] and if no application is made by this date, this claim is dismissed on withdrawal by the claimant.*

Signed for claimant	*Date*
Signed for respondent	*Date*

11.5.7 Commentary on settlements

There is little practical difference in these settlements in their effect. Both are acceptable in practice.

The precedent for the settlement appended to the tribunal order is a document to which the decision of the employment tribunal will make reference when stating the reasons for the case having been stayed pending compliance with the terms of that agreement. It means that the settlement is the tribunal's decision.

The precedent for the *Tomlin* order is an order made by consent ('consent order'). Although it means that the settlement is not the tribunal's decision, it will still be endorsed by the tribunal who will 'rubber stamp' it. Neither party's rights are compromised by the use of this format as opposed to the settlement appended to the tribunal order.

The reader is referred to the guidance at **11.4.7** on making settlement attractive.

11.6 Mr Green's case: unfair dismissal/transfer of an undertaking

11.6.1 Overview of Mr Green's case

Mr Green believes that he was dismissed by reason of a transfer of the undertaking (or part) in which he was employed and that the dismissal was thereby rendered unfair by reason of the Transfer of Undertakings (Protection of Employment) Regulations 2006 and/or the Acquired Rights Directive. He has therefore brought a claim for unfair dismissal against the company which he considers to be the transferee (the first respondent). In case the tribunal finds that there was not a relevant transfer, Mr Green has also claimed, in the alternative, against his former employer (the second respondent). In such cases, it is always tactically advantageous to the claimant to bring the claim against both organisations. Given the complexity of the law relating to TUPE, the claimant is unlikely to be criticised for being uncertain as to who the correct respondent should be! There may be a need to review later whom to pursue the claim against, given the tribunal's powers to make costs orders.

The first respondent denies that there was a relevant transfer for the purposes of domestic or European law and/or that Mr Green was employed in the relevant part of the business transferred in any event. In the alternative the first respondent relies upon the dismissal having been for an economic, technical or organisational reason and as being fair in all the circumstances of the case.

The second respondent (Mr Green's former employer) supports Mr Green's contention that there was a relevant transfer so that any liability has passed to the transferee (the first respondent). In the alternative, the second respondent argues that the dismissal was for some other substantial reason, namely a business reorganisation and was fair in all the circumstances.

Ultimately, the decision goes against the first respondent and an application for a review of that decision is made on a number of grounds.

11.6.2 Mr Green's claim form ET1

It will be assumed that all of the boxes except for box 8 should have the relevant factual details inserted.

The substance of Mr Green's claim should be set out in box 8. Of course both respondents should be identified in box 2.

Box 8

(1) *From 13 May 2013, the claimant was employed by the second respondent, Trumpton Refuse Services (the transferor) as a refuse collector. The second respondent was a company in business as a refuse disposal service contractor at premises at the Refuse Depot, Trumpton. At all material times the claimant was employed in refuse collection services.*

(2) *On or about 4 August 2017, the undertaking in which the claimant was employed was transferred from the second respondent to the first respondent. The first respondent, Trumpton DSO, is a company which is controlled by Trumpton Borough Council, a large organisation engaged in the operations of a local authority and as such is a state authority, in respect of which the provisions of the Acquired Rights Directive 2001/23/EEC have direct effect.*

(3) *The same amounted to a relevant transfer for the purposes of the Transfer of Undertakings (Protection of Employment) Regulations 2006 and/or the Acquired Rights Directive 2001/23/EEC.*

(4) *On the 7 August 2017, the claimant was informed by Miss Curtly, the Executive Director of the First respondent that he was dismissed with effect from 18 September 2017. Prior to this the claimant had not been warned or consulted as to the possibility of his employment being terminated nor were any alternatives apparently considered. The claimant was not given any opportunity to appeal.*

(5) *In the circumstances, the claimant believes that he was unfairly dismissed by reason of the transfer.*

(6) *In the alternative, the claimant believes his dismissal to have been unfair in any event:*

(a) the respondent failed to give any or any adequate warning of the proposed dismissal; and/or

(b) the respondent failed to negotiate and/or consult with the claimant about the proposed dismissal; and/or

(c) the respondent failed to consider alternatives to the proposed dismissal and/or to consult with the claimant about the same; and/or

(d) the dismissal cannot be justified by one of the potentially fair reasons for dismissal; and/or

(e) the claimant's dismissal was as a result of the transfer and was not for an economic technical or organisational reason.

11.6.3   Mr Green's claim form: commentary

This ET1 contains a description of the relationship between the claimant and each of the respondents. This is to ensure that it is apparent why each of the respondents is being pursued. It may well be that the dismissal, being so closely linked in time to the transfer, could have been the decision of either respondent. Since the tribunal has new powers on accepting claims (which allow a claim to be rejected in certain circumstances), it is important for the reasons for pursuing both parties to be clear. Further, it can prevent either of the respondents from trying to apply for a pre-hearing review with the aim of being removed as a party to the proceedings (on the ground that they are not the correct respondent).

If the dismissal is found to be connected with the transfer, it is automatically unfair, which is why paras 5 and 6(f) are pleaded as such. However, to maximise Mr Green's chances of success, the alternative allegations are presented in para 6 to rely on the principles of 'ordinary' unfair dismissal.

When setting out details of the dismissal, the claim form should indicate whether the dismissal was summary or with notice. If the dismissal was summary or if full notice was not given, the claimant may wish to include a contractual claim for damages in the application, or claim for 'wrongful dismissal'. This would be set out in a similar form to Mr Red's claim as set out **11.3.2**. However, here, Mr Green has worked out his notice.

11.6.4   The first respondent's response form ET3

Boxes 1–4 must be filled in with the appropriate information, the majority of which is not disputed.

Since there is a conflict on the dates (the first respondent does not want the claimant to rely on the transfer and that he has insufficient continuity of employment), box 3.1 should be ticked 'no' and at 3.2 the claimant's dates should be corrected to state a start date of 4 or 7 August 2017 and end date of 18 September 2017.

The respondent's case in full should be set out in box 5.2, and box 5.1 should be ticked to show the respondent's intention to dispute the claim.

Box 5

(1) It is admitted that the first respondent, Trumpton DSO, is a company which is controlled by Trumpton Borough Council. Trumpton DSO is a medium-sized company in business as a refuse disposal contractor, employing some 75 people.

(2) It is denied that there was a transfer of an undertaking, or part, from the second respondent to the first respondent on 4 August 2017 or at all. The first respondent relies upon

the nature of its operations in reliance on this assertion, namely that the first respondent operates as a modern, non-labour intensive, mechanised refuse disposal contractor. All work is conducted using the plant and equipment purchased by the first respondent (not obtained from the second respondent) and that there has been no transfer of tangible assets to the first respondent.

(3) It is asserted that the claimant has less than two years' continuous service with the first respondent.

(4) If, contrary to the first respondent's primary case, it is found that there was a relevant transfer of part of the undertaking of the second respondent, it is denied that the claimant was employed in that part of the undertaking transferred to the first respondent.

(5) In the further alternative, if, contrary to the first respondent's primary case, it is found that the claimant's employment did in fact transfer to the first respondent, it is contended that the claimant was dismissed from that employment for some other substantial reason, namely an economic, technical or organisational reason, namely the new efficient mechanised methods of refuse collection employed by the first respondents, and, the dismissal being fair in all the circumstances of the case. In particular the first respondent will rely on:

(a) The first respondent uses more modern methods of collection than the second respondent. Namely, the clients of the refuse services have been given new style 'wheelie' bins as opposed to dustbins and the modern collecting vehicles with a hoist designed to lift and tip out the contents of the 'wheelie' bins. These methods require fewer refuse collectors on each round;

(b) The organisational structure of the first respondent meant that there was no requirement for the claimant to carry out the work he had previously undertaken for the second respondent;

(c) On various dates between 4 August 2017 and 4 September 2017 the first respondent consulted with the claimant's trade union on the modernised refuse collection service, the trade union having accepted modernisation as 'the way forward';

(d) The first respondent further considered whether there were any alternative duties or positions or other alternatives to dismissing the claimant but to no avail, since none of the refuse collection rounds required more personnel.

11.6.5   The first respondent's response form: commentary

The first respondent in such a case will usually deny that there was a relevant transfer for the purposes of domestic or European law and/or that Mr Green was employed in the relevant part of the business transferred in any event. This argument, if successful, ensures all liability is with the second respondent. It means that in practice the two respondents have conflicting cases on whether there was a transfer. However, to ensure that if the tribunal decides that the transfer did occur, then it is advisable to argue in the alternative that the dismissal was for an economic, technical or organisational reason (which is potentially fair in TUPE cases) and as being fair in all the circumstances of the case.

The argument that the first respondent was unable to offer alternative duties or positions or other alternatives to dismissing the claimant due to none of the refuse collection rounds requiring more personnel could be a weak argument, since the claimant may be able to show that there was another worker (Mr X) whom he could have replaced on the rounds and that Mr X should have been dismissed ('bumping'), but that will depend on the facts which the claimant can prove. It is tactically more sound to ensure that as many viable arguable points are raised in the ET3 to ensure the respondent has its options open.

If the respondent wishes to argue that there is no application of the Acquired Rights Directive in this case, this may be drafted thus: *Further, the first respondent does not recognise any legal relevance of the Acquired Rights Directive 2001/23 EEC to the claimant's stated case but to the extent that it might be relevant, it is expressly denied that the first respondent is an emanation of the State in respect of which the provisions of that Directive would have direct effect.*

11.6.6 The second respondent's response form ET3

It will be assumed that all of the boxes except for box 5 have been filled in with the appropriate information.

In contrast to the first respondent, the second respondent will not need to contest the claimant's dates of employment.

The respondent's case in full should be set out in box 5.

Box 5

(1) It is admitted that the second respondent is a medium-sized company in business as refuse disposal service contractor, employing some 75 people. It is further admitted that the second respondent employed the claimant as a refuse collector from 13 May 2013 to 18 September 2017.

(2) The second respondent further accepts that on 4 August 2017 there was a transfer of part of the undertaking of the second respondent to the first respondent. At all material times prior to this transfer, the claimant was employed in that part of the second respondent's business that did so transfer, namely refuse collection services.

(3) In the circumstances, all employees of the second respondent employed in the part of its undertaking which transferred to the first respondent became employees of the first respondent with effect from 4 August 2017 and all rights and liabilities relating to their contracts of employment likewise so transferred to the first respondent.

(4) For the reasons stated above, it is denied that the claimant was dismissed by the second respondent: his employment merely transferred to the first respondent. Any dismissal was carried out by the first respondent.

(5) In the alternative, if, contrary to the second respondent's primary case, there is found to have been no relevant transfer of the claimant's employment, the second respondent contends that the claimant was dismissed for some other substantial reason, namely that the second respondent lost the contract for the supply of refuse collection services for Trumpton and as a result was unable to continue to employ the claimant. The loss of the contract was beyond the control of the second respondent and as a result of the decision by Trumpton Borough Council to bring the service under its own control. The second respondent now only operates small scale specialised operations in skilled refuse collections for large businesses around the outskirts of Trumpton. The claimant is not trained or experienced in skilled specialist waste disposal.

11.6.7 The second respondent's response form: commentary

The second respondent in this case is arguing there has been a transfer, in order to ensure that liability falls upon the first respondent. The second respondent's case on this point is legally and factually a strong one. There is no real need for more detail to be set out in this precedent as a result. In a more borderline case, it would be necessary to look at issues such as how many staff were transferred, whether the activity is labour intensive, transfer of tangible assets and suggest that these give rise to a transfer.

In the event of the tribunal concluding there was no transfer, the second respondent must argue that the dismissal was fair and here relies upon some other substantial reason. It is unlikely this argument will be tested, but the grounds for resisting the claim should be set out to reserve the second's respondent's position.

11.6.8 Application for a reconsideration of judgment

To:

The Secretary of the Tribunals

[address of Employment Tribunal]

Dear Sir/Madam,

Re: Mr Green v Trumpton DSO & Trumpton Refuse Services [case number YYY 2017]

With reference to the decision by the employment tribunal sitting at [location] on [date] that the first respondent unfairly dismissed the claimant, Mr Green following the transfer of his employment under the Transfer of Undertakings (Protection of Employment) Regulations 2006.

The first respondent applies for a review of that decision under rule 70 of the Employment Tribunal Rules of Procedure 2013, as amended, on the grounds that:

The decision was made in the absence of the second respondent, who was unable to attend the hearing, having received no notification of the hearing, when it would have wished to contest issues relating to liability and compensation. This matter was not discovered until the second respondent's representatives made an enquiry with the tribunal relating to the lack of contact from the tribunal on [date] only to discover the hearing had taken place. The second respondent's representatives will be able to give evidence at a review hearing that notice of the hearing date was not received by them.

It would be in the interests of justice for this matter to be reviewed and we would request that this be dealt with as soon as possible.

11.6.9 Application for reconsideration of judgment: commentary

The 2013 Rules (as amended) have some scope for a party to apply for a reconsideration of judgment where it is in the interests of justice. From the case law it would appear that the tribunal will look at the credibility of the explanation and the respondent's ability to prove the circumstances claimed. Therefore, in the case of compelling circumstances, full details ought to be given in a manner such as:

The decision was made in the absence of the respondent, whose managing director, Mr Diddley, was due to attend the hearing but was unable to attend since he suffered a sudden accident on the hearing date. He attended at Trumpton Hospital Accident and Emergency Unit and was found to have suffered a broken leg as a result of falling down some stairs. The respondent would have wished to contest issues relating to liability and compensation.

As here, where it is claimed that the respondent had no knowledge of the proceedings or of the hearing date, the respondent may have a more difficult task. The 2013 Rules (as amended) follow the approach of the Civil Procedure Rules 1998. Hence it is likely that the presumption of service is difficult to rebut and therefore, the party seeking the review must seek to prove the lack of notice of the hearing or the proceedings.

Other possible arguments may include:

- New evidence has become available to the second respondent since the conclusion of the hearing the existence of which it could not reasonably have known or foreseen before the hearing, namely [give details of the evidence, for example, document reference/identity of witness and substance of evidence] which would have a material bearing on the question of [identify question considered by the tribunal to which the evidence would relate], namely [indicate how reliance is placed on that evidence].

- The interests of justice require such a review as [set out grounds, for example, the tribunal's decision on compensation was made without giving the second respondent the opportunity to adduce evidence and address the tribunal on the question whether it was just and equitable for a full award to be made to the claimant in the light of facts discovered after his dismissal relating to (give details, indicating the evidence the second respondent wished to adduce and the points upon which it would have sought to have addressed the tribunal)].

If the error is merely a clerical one, the power to correct a small error under r 69 of the 2013 Rules (as amended) can be used at any time. This is a different power from the power to reconsider a judgment. If the application was merely to correct a clerical error, the appropriate method of drafting the application could read thus:

The respondent applies for the correction of an error under r 69 of the Employment Tribunal Rules of Procedure 2013 (as amended). The decision was wrongly made as a result of an error on the part of the staff of the tribunal, in that the decision orders the second respondent to pay compensation in the sum of £11,000.00, when the tribunal's calculation at paragraph 20 of the decision demonstrates that this should be £1,000.00.

11.7 Mr Blue's case: unlawful race discrimination: direct discrimination (claims of harassment and victimisation)

11.7.1 Overview of Mr Blue's case

IMPORTANT NOTE: **To ensure that no offence is caused to any particular racial or ethnic group by the subject matter of these precedents, Mr Blue is from the fictitious Blueland and is ethnically Bluish. This is not in any way intended to detract from the precedents themselves or to trivialise the seriousness of any form of unlawful discrimination.**

Mr Blue remains in his employment while he brings this complaint of race discrimination against his employer. He complains of having suffered harassment at the hands of another employee and alleges that his employer is vicariously liable for this treatment. He has not brought a claim against the other employee, although he is entitled to do so. Mr Blue also claims that, after raising a complaint with his employer about this harassment, he was then victimised, another form of unlawful direct discrimination for the purposes of the Equality Act 2010 (EqA 2010).

Mr Blue's employer generally denies all the allegations made but also contends that it is not vicariously liable for the acts of harassment and that, in any event, it took all reasonable steps to avoid such discrimination. It also denies any causative link between any complaint about this (itself denied) and the less favourable treatment meted out to him.

Ultimately, Mr Blue is unsuccessful before the employment tribunal and he enters a notice of appeal against that decision.

Mr Blue's employer resists the appeal and cross-appeals one point of the tribunal's decision.

11.7.2   Mr Blue's claim form

It will be assumed that all of the boxes except for box 8 have the relevant factual details inserted.

Box 8

(1) The claimant is of Bluish origins, having been born and brought up in Blueland, employed by the respondent as a shoe heel worker at the respondent's shoe factory. The claimant's employment commenced on 9 January 2017. The respondent is a medium-sized company in business as manufacturer of shoes and footwear, employing some 150 employees.

(2) From 9 January 2017 to 9 June 2017, whilst carrying out his duties, the claimant began to suffer racial abuse and harassment from Mr Biggott, an eyelet puncher, an employee of the respondent. In particular, the claimant complains of the following incidents:

(a) On 11 January 2017, Mr Biggott shouted 'Look at the new guy—he's a useless Bluish idiot. How can we give such useless workers a job instead of our own!' This occurred during Mr Biggott's shift and on the factory floor.

(b) On 18 January 2017, Mr Biggott struck the claimant's arm and said 'This is what you useless Bluish lot need to put you right—a good punching!' This occurred during Mr Biggott's shift and on the factory floor.

(c) On 20 February 2017, Mr Biggott told other workers that Mr Blue was untrustworthy because he was Bluish. This occurred during Mr Biggott's shift and on the factory floor.

(d) On 2 March 2017 and 6 March 2017 Mr Biggott repeated the behaviour complained of in (c) above. This occurred during Mr Biggott's shift and on the factory floor.

(e) On 10 April 2017, Mr Biggott took Mr Blue's tools and put them in a bucket filled with bleach, stating it was necessary in case other workers were 'infected with Blue germs'. This occurred during Mr Biggott's shift and on the factory floor.

(f) On 28 April 2017, Mr Biggott put up a banner on the factory floor stating: 'We hate Blueland and all of its people. Go home now!'.

(g) On 8 May 2017, Mr Biggott took a bradawl and stabbed the claimant. This occurred during Mr Biggott's shift and on the factory floor.

(3) The claimant believes that the same amounted to direct discrimination against him on the ground of his race, in contravention of the Equality Act 2010. On 10 April 2017 the claimant made a verbal complaint to the factory floor manager, Ms Flakey. The claimant's complaint was not investigated adequately or at all.

(4) On 11 May 2017 the claimant complained about this racial discrimination in writing to Mr Boss, the Personnel Manager of the respondents. He then submitted a written statement of grievance to Mr Boss on the same day. His written grievance constituted a 'protected act' within the meaning of the Equality Act 2010.

(5) In response to his complaint, on 12 May 2017 the claimant was told by Mr Boss, Personnel Manager, that he was to be moved from working on the factory floor to a prefabricated portakabin where he was to work alone.

(6) *Further, the respondent took no action to investigate, or handle the claimant's grievance adequately or at all. To date the claimant has received no response to his grievance.*

(7) *The claimant believes that the same amounted to less favourable treatment meted out to him because he had complained that an act had been committed against him in contravention of the Equality Act 2010.*

(8) *By reason of these acts of discrimination the claimant has suffered injury to feelings and loss and damage.*

<u>Particulars of Injury to Feelings</u>

The claimant has lost his dignity in the workplace and has been subjected to demeaning treatment. The lack of intervention by the respondent has increased the claimant's distress. The claimant being sent to work by himself in a portakabin caused him to feel ridiculed and isolated. On 8 May 2017 as stated above, the claimant suffered physical injury.

<u>Particulars of Loss and Damage</u>

The claimant was not awarded a Summer Bonus of £500 for the respondent's increased productivity.
The claimant has suffered injury to feelings.

(9) *The claimant therefore claims:*

  (a) *a declaration that the respondent has discriminated against him on the ground of his race; and*

  (b) *a declaration that the respondent has discriminated against him by way of victimisation; and*

  (c) *a recommendation that the respondent returns the claimant to his post as a shoe heel worker on the factory floor;*

  (d) *compensation (including hurt to feelings);*

  (e) *interest.*

11.7.3   Mr Blue's claim form: commentary

The principal noticeable feature of this claim form is the level of factual detail set out. Each incident is dated with personnel identified by name and the incident described in outline. This is important in cases where ongoing discrimination is alleged. Vague hints that discrimination has occurred 'on numerous occasions' will result in either a pre-hearing review being sought by the respondents or a request for further particulars. Please see the guidance at **11.2.3**.

When giving details of the incidents themselves, it is important to demonstrate how it is alleged that the harassment took place in the course of employment. This is to anticipate the respondent's defence available under the EqA 2010. This is the reason that it is repeated for each allegation that the incidents occurred during the harasser's shift on the factory floor. Alternatively, it may be useful to introduce each incident by explaining what the claimant and harasser were doing at the time: *'whilst the claimant was [state task being performed by the claimant], or [name of harasser], whilst instructing the claimant in his task.'*

A victimisation claim can only succeed if the detrimental treatment is because the claimant committed a 'protected' act. Therefore it is useful to identify which act is the necessary protected act.

Discrimination: the need to be specific

It is important to note that when a claimant makes a claim of unlawful discrimination, the type of discrimination should be indicated. This means not only that the claimant must specify whether the discrimination is on racial, sexual, disability or other grounds, but also whether the claim is for direct discrimination, indirect discrimination or both. The Court of Appeal in *Ali v Office of National Statistics* [2005] IRLR 201 ruled that a claim where the claimant stated he had been *'discriminated against on racial grounds'* could not be said to include claims for both indirect and direct discrimination, after the claimant's claim for direct discrimination failed and he sought to argue there was indirect discrimination. As a result, the claim form should set out the exact nature of the claimant's claim/s.

11.7.4   The respondent's response form to Mr Blue's claim

Boxes 1–4 must be filled in with the appropriate information, which is unlikely to be disputed.

Box 5

(1) It is admitted that the respondent is a medium-sized company in business as shoe and footwear manufacturer, employing some 150 people. It is further admitted that the claimant has been employed as a shoe heel worker by the respondent from 9 January 2017 at its premises at Big Shoe Factory, Factory Lane, Brocktown. No admission is made as to the claimant's ethnic origin.

(2) No admission is made as to the events described by the claimant at box 8 of the claim form. Nor does the respondent accept that the same would amount to direct race discrimination such as to contravene the provisions of the Equality Act 2010.

(3) In any event, if Mr Biggott did commit the acts as alleged by the claimant, which is denied, the respondent contends that these fell outside the course of Mr Biggott's employment as an eyelet puncher for the purposes of the 2010 Act and that the respondent is therefore not vicariously liable.

(4) In the alternative, if, contrary to its primary case, the respondent is found to be vicariously liable for the alleged acts of Mr Biggott, the respondent will further contend that it took all such steps as were reasonably practicable to prevent Mr Biggott as its employee from carrying out those acts or from doing in the course of her employment acts of that description. In particular the respondent will rely on its communication of its Equal Opportunities Policy to all staff by means of copies being distributed in the Staff Handbook.

(5) It is denied that the claimant complained to the respondent about the alleged acts, whether on 10 April 2017 or 11 May 2017 as alleged in the claim form or at all. In fact, the respondent did not know of the claimant's complaints until receipt of the claim form in these proceedings.

(6) The respondent accepts that on 12 May 2017, Mr Boss told the claimant that he was to work in the new portakabin annex to the factory but it is denied that the same occurred in response to any complaint by the claimant or that the same constituted less favourable treatment. The respondent's business has had surplus orders and to cope with demand is in the process of moving a number of factory workers to the new annex. In particular other shoe heel workers are being recruited, all of whom will work in the annex.

(7) In the alternative, if, contrary to the respondent's primary case, it is found to have subjected the claimant to less favourable treatment, the respondent contends that it would

have done so to any employee in the claimant's position, namely a shoe heel worker and that treatment was unrelated to the claimant's race.

(8) No admission is made as to the loss or damage as alleged or at all.

(9) In the circumstances, the claimant's claims under the Equality Act 2010 are denied.

11.7.5   The respondent's response form to Mr Blue's claim: commentary

In such a discrimination claim, there are two legal defences open to the respondent. The first is that the actions of the harasser were not 'in the course of employment' (which is subject to a wide 'common sense' definition as a result of *Jones v Tower Boot Co Ltd* [1997] IRLR 168). The second is described by practitioners as the 'employer's defence', namely that the employer took all reasonable steps to prevent discrimination in the workplace. To demonstrate this defence it is useful to refer to any documented policy or guidelines given to staff (such as an Equal Opportunities Policy). If training on diversity is given, it will assist the employer to set out the detail. If steps were taken following a complaint such as disciplining of a perpetrator or training to other staff, this will assist a respondent.

The failure to admit Mr Blue's ethnic origin or the events described would not be acceptable in ordinary civil proceedings. However, since employment tribunal forms are not considered to be 'pleadings' as such, the strict rules of drafting (where the only acceptable answers when responding to a claim are to admit, deny or put to proof) do not apply. As a result, such general denials are possible, although it is likely that an astute claimant's representative will request further particulars of the response form.

11.7.6   Mr Blue's notice of appeal to the Employment Appeal Tribunal

EAT/

IN THE EMPLOYMENT APPEAL TRIBUNAL

BETWEEN:

DEEP BLUE   *Appellant*

-and-

KITTEN HEEL SHOE CO. LTD   *Respondent*

NOTICE OF APPEAL

TO:

The Registrar,

Employment Appeal Tribunal, Audit House, 58 Victoria Embankment, London EC4Y 0DS

1. *The appellant is Mr Deep Blue of 76 Factory Gardens, Brocktown.*

2. *Any communication relating to this appeal may be sent to the appellant at Brocktown Law Centre, 28 Brockton High Street, Brocktown.*

3. *The appellant appeals from the decision of the employment tribunal sitting at [location of tribunal] on [date/s of hearing] that the appellant's complaint of race discrimination be dismissed.*

4. *The only party to the proceedings before the employment tribunal other than the appellant was Kitten Heel Shoe Co Ltd, Big Shoe Factory, Factory Lane, Brocktown.*

5. *A copy of the employment tribunal's decision and of the extended reasons for that decision is attached to this notice.*

6. *The grounds upon which this appeal are brought are that:*

    (1) *In concluding that Mr Biggott was not acting in the course of employment in paragraph 12 of the decision the tribunal acted perversely in that there was no evidence to support such a conclusion. It was clear from the evidence before the tribunal that each incident occurred in the workplace during Mr Biggott's shifts at work.*

    (2) *The tribunal's conclusion that the appellant's ethnic origin of Bluish is not a racial group within the meaning of the Equality Act 2010 was perverse in the light of Mandla v Lee [1983] IRLR 209.*

THE ORDER SOUGHT

That the decision of the Employment Tribunal is overturned and this matter be remitted to a freshly constituted Tribunal for re-hearing.

11.7.7   Mr Blue's notice of appeal to the Employment Appeal Tribunal: commentary

This is a short-form notice of appeal. The grounds of appeal are set out succinctly and precisely. There is no need to set out full legal arguments at this stage. It is, however, useful to give paragraph references to the aspects of the decision challenged and any case law relied upon. This will assist in demonstrating the strength of the appellant's case at an early stage.

Alternative grounds of appeal may be: '*The tribunal failed to give any reasons for its finding that [give details]*' or '*The tribunal erred in law in construing [relevant statutory provision] as meaning [give details] when the correct approach is [set out correct construction]*'.

Since the order sought must be set out, it is useful to consider what outcome the client would like. It is possible (as in this precedent) to ask for the decision to be overturned and sent to a new employment tribunal panel. However, other possibilities are for the other to be overturned AND '*a decision substituted in its place to the effect that …*', OR '*this matter be remitted to the same tribunal for re-hearing*'.

11.7.8   Respondent's answer to notice of appeal and cross-appeal

EAT/

IN THE EMPLOYMENT APPEAL TRIBUNAL

BETWEEN:

DEEP BLUE   *Appellant*

-and-

KITTEN HEEL SHOE CO. LTD   *Respondent*

RESPONDENT'S ANSWER

1. *The respondent is Kitten Heel Shoe Co Ltd, Big Shoe Factory, Factory Lane, Brocktown. Any communication relating to this appeal may be sent to the respondent at [name, address and telephone number of representative or identify other address etc for service].*

2. *The respondent intends to resist the appeal of Mr Deep Blue of 76 Factory Gardens, Brocktown. The grounds upon which the respondent will rely are:*

3. *The tribunal's finding that the respondent was not liable for discrimination or victimisation was supported by the evidence that the respondent had an equal opportunities policy given to all staff in their staff handbook (hence the respondent was not vicariously liable for the acts of Mr Biggott even if the tribunal had found they were committed in the course of employment) and that in October 2017 Mr Biggott (the alleged harasser) was dismissed for gross misconduct.*

11.7.9 Respondent's answer to notice of appeal and cross-appeal: commentary

Here, the respondent is submitting an answer to the notice of appeal only. There is no cross-appeal. Should the respondent wish to cross-appeal, the heading in tramlines at the top of the document should read: *'RESPONDENT'S ANSWER AND CROSS-APPEAL'*. Then each section should have a heading: *'ANSWER'* and *'CROSS-APPEAL'* in much the same way as a Defence and Counterclaim would be split into *DEFENCE* and *COUNTER-CLAIM* (see the *Drafting Manual* for details). It would then be necessary, after the heading *'CROSS APPEAL'* to add in paragraphs along the lines of:

4. *The respondent cross-appeals from [refer to part of tribunal decision appealed from].*

5. *The respondent's grounds of appeal are that:*

[set out grounds of cross-appeal]

If seeking to rely on a tribunal decision which is supported by a lack of reasoning, a respondent may assert: *'In relation to the tribunal's conclusion that [give details], even if the tribunal did not set out its full reasons for reaching this conclusion, these are implicit from [give details by reference to decision] and/or are unnecessary given the tribunal's finding that [give details].'*

11.8   Ms Indigo's case: (1) written reasons for dismissal; (2) (automatically) unfair dismissal by reason of pregnancy; and (3) unlawful sex discrimination

11.8.1 Overview of Ms Indigo's case

Ms Indigo was dismissed from her employment without a reason being given. She believes that the reason was in fact her pregnancy and so complains to the tribunal not only of the failure to give written reasons for her dismissal but also that she has been (automatically) unfairly dismissed and/or discriminated against on the ground of her sex.

Ms Indigo's former employer relies primarily on the fact that her claim has been brought out of time and that the tribunal accordingly has no jurisdiction to hear it. In the alternative, the employer denies that the reason for the dismissal was Ms Indigo's pregnancy and instead contends that the cause of the dismissal was her persistent lateness and failure to notify her manager of absences (conduct). It is alleged that adequate written reasons have been given.

11.8.2 Ms Indigo's claim form

It is assumed that all of the boxes except for box 8 have the relevant factual details inserted.

Box 8

(1) The claimant was employed as an IT support worker by the respondent from 4 October 2010 until her dismissal on 2 June 2017. The respondent is a medium-sized company in business as a computer software consultancy and employs some 60 people.

(2) On 1 June 2017, the claimant informed Miss Happ, the Support Services Manager of the respondent that she was pregnant and that she expected to give birth to her child in the week commencing 18 September 2017. At the same time, the claimant also informed the respondent that she intended to return to work after having her child but would take a period of maternity leave which she intended to commence on 21 September 2017.

(3) Subsequently, on 2 June 2017, the claimant was told by Miss Happ that the respondent could no longer employ her and that she would be dismissed with immediate effect.

(4) No reason was given for the claimant's dismissal and a replacement was recruited into her position after the termination of her employment. On 9 June 2017 the claimant wrote to the respondent requesting a written statement of the reason/s for her dismissal.

(5) The respondent has unreasonably failed to provide a written statement of the reason/s for the claimant's dismissal within 14 days of her request or at all.

(6) In the circumstances, the claimant believes that she was unfairly dismissed by reason of/for a reason connected with her pregnancy.

(7) In the alternative, the claimant believes her dismissal to have been unfair in any event. Further or alternatively, the claimant's dismissal has been in breach of contract.

(8) The claimant claims compensation for unfair dismissal, and/or wrongful dismissal.

(9) The claimant further believes that she has been discriminated against on the ground of her sex.

(10) By reason of this discrimination the claimant has suffered injury to feelings and loss and damage.

PARTICULARS OF INJURY TO FEELINGS

The claimant has been subjected to the loss of dignity in the workplace as a result of her dismissal. Her value as a worker has been demeaned by her employer's conduct. The claimant has suffered distress as a result of her treatment.

PARTICULARS OF LOSS AND DAMAGE

The claimant has suffered loss of wages from the date of her dismissal.
The claimant has lost rights incidental to her employment as a result of its termination (including her right to paid maternity leave and additional maternity leave, rights to accrue annual leave, continuity of employment, and rights relating to her ability to take time off for the care of dependents).
The claimant has suffered injury to feelings.

(11) Further and/or alternatively the claimant claims:

(a) compensation for unfair dismissal, or

(b) a declaration that she has been discriminated against; and

(c) compensation for sex discrimination, including compensation for injury to feelings; and

(d) interest; and/or

(e) a declaration as to the reason/s for her dismissal;

(f) an award of a sum equal to two weeks' pay in respect of the respondent's failure to supply a written statement of the reason/s for dismissal.

11.8.3   Ms Indigo's claim form: commentary

Here, the reason for dismissal according to the claimant is linked to her pregnancy. Therefore the most obvious form of claim would be unfair dismissal since dismissal due to pregnancy is a recognised automatically unfair reason for dismissal. However, it is also tactically advantageous to consider pursuing a claim in sex discrimination, both financially and procedurally. The financial advantage is theoretically unlimited damages, although in practice the ability to claim injury to feelings is of more benefit. Injury to feelings is not recoverable for unfair dismissal claims. The procedural advantage is the ability to use the questionnaire procedure for obtaining information as provided for by EqA 2010, and the tribunal's power to draw inferences from a failure to respond or responses that are found to be evasive and/or untrue.

Since many employers are aware that they are dismissing for an unacceptable reason (and are therefore unlikely to admit this in writing), another possible claim is that the respondent has unreasonably failed to provide written reasons for the dismissal or failed to provide the real reasons for dismissal. The claimant can claim both two weeks' wages and a declaration of the reason for dismissal.

From the respondent's response form, it can be seen that it is the respondent's case that Ms Indigo appealed the decision to dismiss her, having written a letter of appeal and that she attended an appeal hearing. These matters are not set out in this claim form. If it is correct that the claimant did appeal, the claim form should set out the details, but emphasising factual issues favourable to the claimant. These may be issues such as a lack of fairness (for example, not being given the opportunity to explain herself, being given insufficient time to prepare, not being given relevant information, the appeal being heard by someone involved in the decision to dismiss). In this case, the claimant may not have given clear instructions to her representative.

When setting out details of the dismissal, the claim form should indicate whether the dismissal was summary or with notice. If the dismissal was summary or if full notice was not given, the claimant may wish to include a contractual claim for damages in her application, or claim for 'wrongful dismissal'. This would be set out in box 8 and would follow a similar form to Mr Red's claim as set out at **11.3.2**.

11.8.4   The respondent's response form

It will be assumed that all of the boxes except for box 5 have been filled in with the appropriate information.

Box 5

(1)   The claimant was employed by the respondent from 4 October 2010 to 2 June 2017, when she was dismissed summarily. The claimant's claim form was submitted to the tribunal on 4 September 2017. This was outside the statutory time limit for the presentation of complaints of this nature. In the circumstances the respondent contends that the tribunal has no jurisdiction to hear the claimant's claims.

(2)   The respondent accepts that it is a medium-sized company in business as a software consultancy and employing some 60 people.

(3)   If, contrary to the respondent's primary case as set out above, the tribunal is held to have jurisdiction to hear the claimant's complaint of unfair dismissal, the respondent in any event resists the complaint for the reasons that follow.

(4)   The claimant was dismissed by reason of conduct, i.e., her persistent lateness and failure to notify her manager of absences and the dismissal was fair in all the circumstances.

(5) *The claimant, during her employment, had received a verbal warning in January 2015 for the unauthorised purchase of stationery and a written warning in February 2016 for use of abusive language to a customer.*

(6) *It is known by the respondent's employees that the hours of work are 9am to 5pm. The claimant was aware of the required hours for work.*

(7) *On numerous occasions in late April and early May 2017 the claimant was late for work with no explanation.*

(8) *On 15 May 2017, the claimant did not attend work until 1 pm, without any explanation and without having booked a half day of annual leave (which would have been required to authorise such an absence).*

(9) *On 16 May 2017, the claimant was invited to a disciplinary meeting on 22 May 2017 with Miss Happ, the Support Services Manager to discuss her lateness and unauthorised absence. The claimant duly attended on that date, and having offered no explanation for her actions was given a final written warning in accordance with the respondent's disciplinary procedure. The claimant was warned that as a result of a final written warning, any further misconduct would result in summary dismissal.*

(10) *On 2 June 2017, the claimant arrived at work at 2.30 pm without any previous contact or authorisation from the respondent.*

(11) *The respondent accepts that on 2 June 2017, the claimant was told verbally by Miss Happ that she was to be dismissed with immediate effect due to her unauthorised absence/lateness whilst on a final written warning. This was confirmed in writing by letter to the claimant of the same date. The claimant's summary dismissal means she is not entitled to be dismissed with notice.*

(12) *The respondent's decision to dismiss the claimant was taken by Miss Happ, an experienced manager, taking into account the claimant's length of service, the previous warnings given to the claimant, the previous latenesses which were overlooked, and the time and opportunity given for improvement and balancing these against the needs of the respondent's business, namely to provide good quality software technical support to customers in a competitive market.*

(13) *Further the claimant was given the opportunity to appeal against the decision that she should be dismissed and did in fact take up that. The claimant was represented at this appeal hearing and did not at any time offer an explanation or apology for her conduct.*

(14) *The respondent believes that its decision to dismiss the claimant by reason of her persistent misconduct was reasonable in all the circumstances of the case.*

(15) *It is expressly denied that the claimant was dismissed by reason of pregnancy and/or was discriminated against on the ground of her sex. It is further denied that the respondent knew of the claimant's pregnancy at the date of her dismissal in any event.*

(16) *In the circumstances it is further denied that the respondent has failed to give written reasons for the claimant's dismissal.*

11.8.5 The respondent's response form to Ms Indigo's claim: commentary

In order to avoid liability, not only must the respondent here deny that the reason for Ms Indigo's dismissal is connected to her pregnancy, but must assert that the dismissal was for one of the potentially fair reasons and was reasonable in all the circumstances. It has been necessary to set out a number of background facts in order to make the respondent's case clear. The decision to dismiss might appear to be unreasonable by itself without the required working hours and the claimant's previous warnings being set out. It is tactically advantageous to state these matters at the beginning rather than wait for the disclosure stage. It may well be that these issues may persuade the claimant to accept settlement of lower financial value in recognition of the weaknesses in her case before significant costs in the preparation of the case are incurred by the respondent.

The decision-making approach of the respondent is set out in detail at para 12 to attempt to show the strength of the respondent's case in showing the decision to dismiss came within a band of reasonable responses.

11.9   Ms Violet's case: indirect sex discrimination: job claimant

11.9.1   Overview of Ms Violet's case

Ms Violet brings her complaint to the employment tribunal as a job claimant against a potential employer. She complains that she was asked questions about her childcare arrangements during the interview and that the reason given for her not getting the position, her inability to meet the criterion of weekend working, was indirectly discriminatory. In order to obtain information to bolster the strength of her case she has made requests for information under rr 31 and 32 of the Employment Tribunal Rules of Procedure 2013 (as amended).

In its response form, the company denies that there is any factual basis for the complaint of direct sex discrimination but accepts that the criterion of weekend working was imposed and may be indirectly discriminatory against women. The response form relies, however, on the company's business needs as justifying this requirement.

11.9.2   Ms Violet's claim form ET1

It will be assumed that all of the boxes except for box 8 have the relevant factual details inserted.

Box 8

(1) *The claimant is a woman and applied for a position with the respondent company as a kitchen design adviser, being interviewed for this post on 4 September 2017.*

(2) *During the course of the interview, which was conducted by two male managers of the respondent, Mr Dodge and Mr Sly, the claimant was asked about her childcare arrangements.*

(3) *At the conclusion of the interview the claimant was informed that she would not be offered the position as it was a requirement of the vacancy that the post holder was able to work weekends; a requirement the claimant had admitted to not being able to fulfil due to her childcare responsibilities. The claimant has since discovered that the position was given to a man.*

(4) *In the circumstances, the claimant considers that the respondent has discriminated against her on the ground of her sex.*

(5) *By asking the claimant as to her childcare responsibilities the respondent was directly discriminating against her and was demonstrating a stereotyped view of gender roles. The claimant does not believe any male candidate interviewed by the respondent to have been asked the same or similar questions. Further or alternatively, had any male candidate been asked such a question, it would not have affected the decision to recruit him.*

(6) *Further/in the alternative, the respondent applied to her a provision, criterion or practice, i.e., to work weekends, with which a smaller proportion of women than men could comply because of the childcare responsibilities of women, with which the claimant could not comply and which was to the claimant's detriment.*

(7) *Further/in the alternative, the respondent applied to her a provision, criterion or practice, i.e., that the claimant currently had inadequate childcare to be able to take the post of kitchen design adviser, with which a smaller proportion of women than men could comply with which the claimant could not comply and which was to the claimant's detriment.*

(8) *By reason of the respondent's discrimination as described above, the claimant has suffered loss.*

PARTICULARS OF LOSS

Loss of wages as a kitchen design adviser from projected date of commencement of 11 September 2017 at the rate of £310 net per week. Distress and hurt to feelings caused by being a victim of sex discrimination.

(9) *The claimant therefore claims:*

    (a) *a declaration that the respondent has discriminated against her on the ground of her sex; and*

    (b) *a recommendation that the respondent should not in future ask job applicants about their family status or childcare arrangements and adopts an equal opportunities policy;*

    (c) *compensation, including compensation for injury to feelings;*

    (d) *interest.*

11.9.3   Ms Violet's claim form: commentary

Please see the guidance at **11.7.3** on Discrimination: the need to be specific.

Here, Ms Violet is claiming for both direct and indirect sex discrimination in order to maximise her chances of success. For the legal basis of her claims, please see *Blackstone's Employment Law Practice 2017* (or later) or **Chapter 8**.

11.9.4   The respondent's response form to Ms Violet's claim

It will be assumed that all of the boxes apart from box 5 have been filled in with the appropriate information.

Box 5

(1) *The respondent is a company in the business of supplying high end fitted kitchens and accepts that the claimant was a female candidate for a vacant position as kitchen design advisor with the respondent. The respondent further accepts and contends that the claimant was one of 6 women and 3 men interviewed for this post on 4 September 2017.*

(2) *While it is accepted that the claimant was interviewed by two male managers, Messrs Dodge and Sly, it is denied that either man asked the claimant questions as to childcare arrangements. In fact, the claimant herself raised this subject when informed during the course of the interview that the position would require weekend working.*

(3) *It is further denied that the claimant was asked questions of a different nature to those asked of other candidates, whether male or female. In fact, the questions asked were of a standard form, it was only the responses that differed.*

(4) It is accepted that the claimant was not offered the position due to her inability to meet the criterion of weekend working. It is further accepted that the position was ultimately offered to a male candidate.

(5) The respondent also accepts that the criterion of weekend working may be one with which a lower proportion of women can comply than men.

(6) The criterion is, however, justifiable irrespective of the sex of the person to whom it was applied on the basis that the requirements of the business are such that the premises must be staffed at the weekend (which is the respondent's most important trading time) and to employ the claimant from Monday to Friday and another worker for the weekend working was impracticable. As a result, there was no other reasonable or practicable non-discriminatory method by which the respondent could achieve this object.

11.9.5   The respondent's response form to Ms Violet's claim: commentary

To escape liability for indirect discrimination, there are a number of avenues for challenge, depending on the facts of the case. The requirement or condition may not actually exist. There may not be a significant proportion of one sex which cannot comply with it (in other words, both men and women can meet it). However, childcare responsibilities falling generally upon women and women's relative difficulty in evening and weekend working are already recognised by the tribunals as falling within requirements or conditions that fewer women can comply with. As a result, these arguments have not been used in this precedent. Even where such arguments may be raised, the approach employed in this precedent of arguing the requirement is 'justified' should be used in the alternative. The requirement can be justified by reference to the requirements of the business, the nature of the job or the impracticability of removing the requirement. If it can be argued that there was no reasonable or non-discriminatory method of achieving the respondent's objectives, this is helpful. However, the current case law on indirect sex discrimination should be checked before embarking on such arguments.

11.9.6   Request for information by claimant

This request should be set out in a clearly dated letter:

Dear [name]

Re:

The respondent is requested to supply the following information relating to the claimant's case within 21 days of this request, namely by 5pm on [date]. If this information is not supplied on a voluntary basis within this time, the claimant will apply for an order from the tribunal that this information be provided under rules 31 and 32 of the Employment Tribunals Rules of Procedure 2013, as amended.

(1) Please state the number of men and the number of women employed by you.

(2) Please state the number of managers employed by you, showing how many are men and how many are women, identifying the positions held and the dates of appointment.

(3) In respect of the vacancy for the position of kitchen design advisor, please state:

   (a) how many men and how many women applied for that post (i) in response to the advertisement to which I replied, and (ii) at any other time;

   (b) how many men and how many women were interviewed by you (i) in the same round of interviews as me (ii) at any other time;

    (c) *the selection criteria used in relation to the appointment (i) at the stage of selection for interview and (ii) at the interview stage (iii) the names and job titles of those people involved in the short-listing process, and (iv) the names and job titles of those people involved in the final selection process;*

    (d) *whether any other candidate was asked about their childcare arrangements? If so (i) when (ii) by whom (iii) identify the candidate'/s' gender (iv) state whether that candidate was appointed to the position of kitchen design advisor or not;*

    (e) *In relation to your recruitment procedure, please state: (i) your normal recruitment procedure (ii) the recruitment procedure utilised for the above post and (iii) if the recruitment procedure for the above post differed from the usual procedure please describe how and why;*

    (f) *the sex, marital status, qualifications and experience of the candidate appointed.*

(4) *Please state what steps, if any, you have taken to eliminate discrimination on the grounds of sex and marriage and to promote equality of opportunity in employment. If you have taken steps which are recorded in a written Equal Opportunities Policy or other document, please say so and supply a copy of the same.*

11.9.7   Request for information: commentary

Please refer to **11.3.7** for more general remarks on such requests.

These questions are designed to obtain the information Ms Violet needs to prove her claim. Ms Violet must show facts which suggest unlawful discrimination (the respondent must then, to avoid liability, provide a satisfactory explanation). She needs to be able to show that her treatment in her interview was different from that of male candidates for the same job (to succeed in her direct discrimination claim). In relation to her indirect discrimination claim she does not need to ask about how many men or women were able to work weekends, since Ms Violet can ask the tribunal to apply its own knowledge to the situation and argue that it is generally accepted in society that fewer women than men can comply with a requirement of weekend work. General queries about the number of women and men workers and their status within the respondent company can help paint a background picture of a respondent. If there are few women or few women in senior or lucrative posts, it can help suggest that there is discrimination.

INDEX